The Practice of Cultural Studies

The Practice of Cultural Studies

Richard Johnson, Deborah Chambers,
Parvati Raghuram and Estella Tincknell

First published 2004

SAGE Publications Ltd
1 Oliver's Yard
55 City Road
London EC1Y 1SP

SAGE Publications Inc.
2455 Teller Road
Thousand Oaks, California 91320

SAGE Publications India Pvt Ltd
B-42, Panchsheel Enclave
Post Box 4109
New Delhi 110 017

British Library Cataloguing in Publication data

A catalogue record for this book is available from the British Library

ISBN 0 7619 6099 6
ISBN 0 7619 6100 3 (pbk)

Library of Congress Control Number available

Typeset by M Rules
Printed and bound in Great Britain by TJ International, Padstow, Cornwall

Acknowledgements

We would like to thank our publisher at Sage, Julia Hall, for her patience during the long gestation of this book. At the Nottingham Trent University we would particularly like to thank Olwyn Ince for her careful attention in formatting the book and completing the bibliography; and Nichola Hudson for her bibliographic assistance in the early stages. Our thanks also go to successive groups of students on the Postgraduate Research Practice course, whose lively critical discussions of ideas that were being 'tried out' was invaluable. Finally, we would like to thank our faculty for granting sabbaticals that enabled us to work on this book. The Centre for Contemporary Cultural Studies at Birmingham University provided the intellectual space for the development of some of the ideas expressed here. We note the unwarranted closure of its successor, The Department of Sociology and Cultural Studies, with great sadness.

Contents

Acknowledgements v

Introduction 1

Part I Groundings

Introduction 7

1 Cultural studies and the study of culture: disciplines and dialogues 9

Asking the cultural question – seven different agendas 10
Historical contexts of the culture agenda 14
Cultural studies and social movements 14
Dominant misrepresentations and popular agency 15
Finding a philosophy? Cultural studies, feminist philosophy and hermeneutics 16
Relations to other academic disciplines 19
Explaining transdisciplinarity: a story in four acts 20
Implications of transdisciplinarity for method 22
Transdisciplinary strategies 24
Conclusion 24

2 Multiplying methods: from pluralism to combination 26

Methodological pluralism or a Method? 26
Objects and strategies of cultural research 27
Cultural circuits: cultural studies meets hermeneutics 37
Conclusion: combined and multiple methods? 42

3 Method and the researching self 44

'Inside culture': cultural research as a cultural circuit 44
Objectivism, self and other 46
From 'standpoint' to 'positionalities' 48
Making claims to truth: conventions and truthfulness 50
Is truth only a convention then? 51
'Reflexivity' versus the confessional 52
Realizing reflexivity: social, spatial, temporal and cultural aspects 53
Dialogue and difference 57
Accountability and responsibilities 59
Conclusion: the logic of combination 60

4 The research process: moments and strategies 62

Choosing and Developing a topic 63
Starting 64
Managing time 65
Working with others: supervisors and peers 66
Reviewing the literature, mapping the field 68
Developing research proposals 71
General models of researching 73
Starting from a source not data? 74
Sources and questions 74
Research, analysis and textuality 75
Contextualization and creating a distance 77
Writing as a moment – functions and forms 78
Diversity in the writing process: planning and writing 80
Writing and the autobiographical voice 81
Writing ethics and politics: authorial power and its deployment 82
Conclusion 84

Part II Settings

Introduction 85

5 Theory in the practice of research 87

Theory, fear and loathing 87
Theory as opposed to practice 89
Theory and practice as praxis 90
Theory and the empirical 93
Reading for theory as a method 97
The argument so far 98
Theory as abstraction 98
Levels of abstraction 99
Kinds of abstraction: strengths and limits 100
Conclusion: theorizing as a practice 102

6 Make space! Spatial dimensions in cultural research 104

Bringing place and space into focus 105
Complicated spatialities 107
Theoretical tools for researching spatiality 108
Spatiality as a metaphor for power 110
Virtual spaces, technologized places 112
Complex places 113
Bringing it all together again: transdisciplinary integrations 117
Conclusion: the return of abstraction 118

7 Time please! Historical perspectives 119

Thinking about time 120
Writing cultural histories part I: radical popular histories 123
Writing cultural histories part II: history's cultural turn 124
The argument so far: history and cultural studies - convergence and tension 126
Public representations of the past and popular memory 127
Thinking historically: historicizing theory 129
Historicizing the present 130
Conclusion 134

8 Culture, power and economy 135

Cultural studies 'versus' political economy: failures of dialogue 136
Baselines: separating power and culture 137
Ideology analysis 139
Representation and the limits of ideology critique 140
Power and culture: expanding the agenda 142
Where does power lie? The popular and the dominant 143
Starting elsewhere: economies as culturally embedded 145
Economies as representation and discourse 146
Cultural and economic circuits: overlap, interdependence, identity? 148
The question of consumption 149
Cultural conditions of economic systems 150
Changing determinations: the economy as culture 151
Conclusion 152

Part III Readings

Readings and meetings 153
Reading as method, method as reading 153
Plan of part III 154

9 Reading popular narratives: from structure to context 157

Structural readings: textual strategies 158
Structural readings: contextualizing strategies 162
Beyond structuralism: poststructuralist approaches 167
Combining methods 168
Conclusion 00

10 Reading texts of or for dominance 170

Reading texts of dominance: a possible reading path 171
Why (not) texts? The value of a textual approach to an analysis of anti-terrorism 173
How much text? 176
Which texts? Dialogue and dominance 178

Opening the text, starting the dialogue 179
Elaborating a (theoretically informed) reading 182
Moral absolutes, the 'other' and unconscious processes 183
Making a reading convincing 184
Conclusion 185

11 Reading fictions, reading histories 187

Fiction and/or history? 187
Cultural materialism: rereading literature 189
'New historicism' and historical discourse 193
Staging and silencing: explicit and implicit meanings 194
Elementary, my dear Foucault 197
Beyond a (national) boundary: post-colonial encounters 198
Conclusion 199

Part IV Meetings

Introduction 201

12 Researching others: from autobiography to ethnography 205

The auto/ethno continuum as a process 206
The auto/ethno continuum as a range of methods 208
The indispensability of meetings in cultural research 209
Pathways in ethnographic and auto/biographical research: two checklists 216
Checklist 1: Interviews 217
Checklist 2: Memory work 220
Conclusion and some limits of the auto/ethno continuum 222

13 Representing the other: interpretation and cultural readings 225

Analysis as dialogue 225
Multiple readings, multiple theories 226
Reading for actors' meanings 227
Reading for cultural structures and processes 229
Working the other way: individualizing conventional forms 230
Making yourself in and against the school 231
Reading for structure and context 233
The four dialogues of analysis: a checklist 234
Representing the other: dialogic implications 237
Representing across power: particular strategies 239
Conclusion 241

14 Remaking methods: from audience research to studying subjectives 243

'Indiscipline' and combination 243
Studying media audiences: promises unfulfilled? 245
Researching subjectivities: reflexive selves, discursive subjects 255
Conclusion: remaking methods 266

In conclusion 268

References 270
Index 290

Introduction

Aims of the book

This is a book about the practice of researching culture. It offers, as our title suggests, a clarification and elaboration of the methodological basis for 'cultural studies', which we understand to be a particular approach within the study of culture. It reflects both on the range of methods used in cultural research and their integrity or possibilities for combination. It asks what the implications for method are of being inside your object of study, of seeking to produce knowledge about cultural processes. It addresses in detail and in sequence all the main clusters of methods that are used in cultural studies, often grouped in terms of 'reading texts' on the one side and 'talking to people' on the other. While we start from this division in Part III – Readings – and Part IV – Meetings – we seek to break it down.

Although we are very concerned to be practical (see under the heading Research practice – an approach to method below) this book is not a guide or handbook in the usual sense; nor is it another introduction to cultural studies as a whole. Our chapters are typically rather argumentative and the book itself is an extended argument. This is because we are trying to clarify questions of approach in a field where they have often remained quite implicit. We often begin a chapter by arguing for a broad orientation towards research as a process, then illustrate this argument with reference to particular points of practice. We do not, in any chapter, try to cover in detail all the practical choices involved in a particular method, nor cover all the work in a particular subfield of cultural research. On the other hand, in almost every chapter we discuss some aspects of research as a daily practice and certain chapters are primarily of this kind (see especially Chapters 4 and 10). We think that this book is quite rich in advice of many different kinds, but it is always governed by the advice to think for yourself.

Writers and readers

We have tried to construct an authorial voice – a 'we' – who not only speaks from inside cultural studies but also clarifies and develops ideas by drawing on other traditions and seeks out and learns from those critical margins that cultural studies has itself produced. We seek a conversation with the *many* voices that speak of culture today, especially the geographic, historical, literary, political-economic, psychological and sociological. This arises, in part, from conversations across our own disciplinary affiliations, which embrace not only cultural studies but also literary studies, history, geography, women's studies, sociology and social theory, development studies, media studies, film studies and studies of migration and ethnic minorities.

Similarly, in terms of readership, this is not intended as a book for cultural studies students and teachers only. It is also for readers who are interested in a tendency to the cultural in their own discipline or who want to pursue a cultural topic in a dissertation or a thesis. For these readers we seek to introduce cultural studies (see especially Chapter 1), as well as to clarify its approaches. Throughout the book, particular chapters engage in particular cross-disciplinary dialogues (see under the heading Plan of the book below).

We envisage our 'typical' readers as being students-as-researchers, together with their teachers and research supervisors. The student-as-researcher has been hugely creative in cultural studies and at the centre of a version of educational practice that underpins our own approach to method. For this is a book about research that has grown out of teaching, particularly out of teaching about method.[1] We are writing it, in many ways, for the students we teach – students in their last year of their first degree, MA students and those setting out on MPhil/PhD programmes. Most importantly, we address the experience of working on a research project, a dissertation or a thesis, offering support as well as intellectual challenges.

Research practice – an approach to method

The book takes – or develops – a particular approach to method. Much methodology – the discourse on method – seems to us to be dull and overly elaborate without quite touching the point of practice, which is the activity itself. Our dissatisfaction is expressed in our preference for the term 'research practice', which seems more aligned to the general character of cultural studies than the usual 'method', 'methods' or 'methodology' – terms often used with indiscriminate interchangeability. Practice emphasizes the activity itself – the doing, the process, the production. It foregrounds the shifting, changing nature of any enquiry, its ongoing and dialogic character, as well as the struggle to pose questions and listen for answers, to re-pose them, adjust method to question, see the method itself exert a pressure, stay open to others, as people, 'sources' or texts. The term 'research practice' includes activities often left out of method – choosing your topic, for instance, and writing in the full sense of a critical process, although this is acquiring more attention.

'Practice' also foregrounds the politics and ethics of research, including issues around power, responsibility and identity construction. Researching is itself a cultural activity, often pursed within the power relations of the academy and in an educational setting. However, it is also a practice of engaging with a wider world and bearing witness to events, issues and memories. It is both a 'studentship' and a very grown-up activity indeed. Stressing practice foregrounds our agency as researchers, the differences we can make to a situation, both in what we do when we are researching (our relationship with those who are being researched, for instance) and the more distant effects of our work, such as the publications we produce.

Most importantly, the word 'practice' highlights the researcher's own aims and questions. Throughout this book we argue for the dependence of method on the questions that are asked and the nature of the dialogue that follows. Like Hans-Georg Gadamer – whose classic book on 'understanding' in the humanities actually opposes 'method' to 'truth' in its title – we have more faith in the process of 'questioning and enquiring' than in any procedural guarantee (Gadamer, 1989).

Method as 'a special form of procedure' (*The Concise Oxford English Dictionary*, 8th edition) can dominate and determine an enquiry, as though intellectual work is just a way of showing we can do it, in a prescribed way. The emergence of specialists on method – 'methodologists' – reinforces this pressure. Indeed, 'methodology' is sometimes taught as a stock repertoire, to be taken off the shelf and practised in the weaker you've-got-to-learn-it sense and can readily collapse into 'methods', as tools or techniques. The larger and more unified sense of 'Method' as a whole philosophy or approach can be lost as a result.

Research practice, by contrast, implies that we must develop our own approach and methods suited to our specific aims and questions. We do not do this in isolation, of course, but in relation to debates about Method and the methods others have used. Often, we find ourselves using techniques and familiar arguments, but tailored or tuned in subtly different ways. Small adjustments may be just what are needed to accommodate the logic of a specific enquiry process.

Method in cultural studies

Cultural studies has always had distinctive ways of working, but it has lacked a developed methodological discourse and debate. It has been commoner to map theoretical frameworks than explore methods of research (Hall, 1980a; Storey, 1996). More recently, method has been one stake in a renewed polemic about cultural studies, with some practitioners regretting 'the still rather indeterminate status of cultural studies in terms of academic legitimacy' (McGuigan, 1997: 1). Although there are now several books on method in cultural studies (Alasuutari, 1995; Barker, 2000; Brunsdon, 2000; Couldry, 2000; du Gay et al., 1997; McGuigan, 1997; Seale, 1998; Willis, 2000) and many sympathetic texts in adjacent disciplines and feminist/women's studies, there is nothing like the elaborated discourse on method that exists in the social sciences. Cultural studies has been more like the humanities, where method is carried in practical skills, ways of reading, for instance, that remain unacknowledged – except perhaps as theory. Yet, by remaining implicit, methods of cultural study can function as a form of intellectual privilege or cultural capital, making the difference between being inside and outside a cultural studies club. Critical self-awareness about cultural studies as a practice is, therefore, part of the struggle to keep it open, democratic and capable of development. At the same time, it is no part of our purpose to impose a burdensome methodological apparatus. It is a tight space we are trying to occupy and extend – one between tyrannical implicitness on the one hand and a disciplinary, regulative, you-can't-do-it-another-way codification on the other.

Issues of 'Britishness'

Cultural studies in its narrower sense has developed mainly within the anglophone academy, while the profile of 'the cultural sciences' in other national and regional intellectual formations has often been very different. England, for example, is almost unique in the virtual absence of folklore studies or 'ethnology' within its academy. There is, therefore, a real danger not only of a disciplinary closure around cultural studies but also a spatial/national one that would lead to a failure to grasp the globalization as well as the transdisciplinarity of the study of culture today. When, for example, we interrogated our own relationships to Britishness, we were struck by the diversity among us: we had very different stories to tell of national, regional and transnational histories and personal identifications. One of the struggles in writing this book has therefore been to try to bring our intellectual points of reference into line with the diversity of our lives and the lives of our friends, families, children and wider kin, and our networks and places of significance. We do not claim complete success in this: the dialogues that we need to have may sometimes have to follow this book rather than fully inform it.

Plan of the book

The book is divided into four parts, each with several chapters and a part introduction. Together, and in the relationships we weave across them, the parts make up an accumulative argument both about method in a larger philosophical sense and methods as working practices; they offer a version of what might be distinctive about cultural studies as a developed practice and situate this within a larger, transdisciplinary arena of the study of culture.

In Part I, Groundings, we address starting points and key definitions. In Chapter 1 we define cultural studies and its relation to the wider transdisciplinary field of the study of culture. In Chapter 2 we explore its methodological diversity, arguing against methodological pluralism and for the conscious *combination* of methods. Chapter 3 centres on 'the researching self' and dialogue with others, seeking a method for cultural studies in a more unified sense. In Chapter 4, we detail the practical implications of this broad approach by considering each of the key practices in the actual process of research, from choosing a topic to writing a presentation.

In Part II, Settings, we look at some of the key contexts of research activity and cultural processes more generally. Research into culture is shaped by certain basic conditions – that human beings think and reflect, live in time and space and are involved in social relationships of power. How, then, can we handle these different dimensions in cultural research? Chapter 5 tackles the vexed question of theory – defined here as relatively abstract thinking. Chapter 6 draws on debates in and around cultural geography to explore the spatial settings, contents and determinations of research, especially the relationship of the global to the local in today's expanded/compressed world. It is here also that we consider most fully the anglocentricity of the traditions with which we are aligned. Chapter 7 revisits a broken dialogue between cultural studies and historical disciplines, but addresses the more general questions of how to historicize even contemporary happenings and handle the vital dimension of memory, which enters into all cultural research. Chapter 8 considers some of the issues of the social setting and power relationships by returning to debates between cultural studies and political economy. It also explores different ways in which to avoid the conceptual separation of the cultural and the economic.

Parts III, Readings, and IV, Meetings, deal with the two main clusters of methods in cultural studies – those that are based on the reading of texts and those based on social exchange with people, as embodied cultural practitioners. There is a certain reality about the text/persons distinction and it is strongly reinforced by disciplinary divisions. Yet, as the early chapters of the book argue, the best work in cultural studies has often transgressed this distinction, especially where a fascination with texts, styles, conventions and meaning has been allied to preoccupations with social power, group identity and everyday cultural creativity.

The chapters in Part III are particularly concerned, therefore, with the extension of narrowly text-based approaches (Chapter 9), the problem of relating cultural and other forms of power in textual analysis (Chapter 10) and issues of text and historical context (Chapter 11). Similarly, the first two chapters in Part IV revisit cultural ethnography through the lens of combined methods, arguing for the association of autobiography and ethnography as methods of enquiry (Chapter 12) and for multiple readings of ethnographic texts (Chapter 13).

In Chapter 14, the theme of combined methods is brought to a kind of conclusion by considering two key moments of methodological integration: the study of the audience or consumer as a cultural practitioner and of identity and subjectivity. It is here also that we chiefly address the relationships between cultural studies and psychology, including cultural studies' elective affinities with certain types of psychoanalysis.

Finally, we offer what we hope is a conclusion without closure. In the spirit of the book, we look forwards to further dialogue rather than simply backwards to what we have already said. We hope that our readers will share in that dialogue with us.

Note

1 Especially formative recently has been our teaching of method and other topics on a current MA programme entitled Globalization, Identity and Technology, a former MA in International Cultural Studies and a current research practice programme for beginning PhD students in the Faculty of Humanities at The Nottingham Trent University.

Part I
GROUNDINGS

Introduction

We have called the first part of this book Groundings because it lays out the basics of our approach to method and is the foundation on which the rest is built. Though we can say this in retrospect, we did not start out with a ready-made theory that we could apply to the rest of the book. Rather, Part I was an exploration, a challenge and a struggle involving successive rewriting of the whole book.

We felt that it was important, first, to answer the question still sometimes asked – 'What *is* cultural studies?' This is especially important for those readers who have not already had an introduction to the subject. In Chapter 1, we answer this question in two main ways. First, by identifying cultural studies, comparatively, as a specific tradition of research and education. Second, by placing it, as a generative presence, within a wider cross-disciplinary academic field of the study of culture.

Chapters 2 and 3 deal with the central tension in views of cultural studies as method. On the one hand, it is often seen as having many methods and being eclectic or pluralist. On the other hand it often seems methodologically distinctive – that is, with a method of its own. In Chapter 2, therefore, we explore the range of methods used in cultural studies, but we argue that they are typically combined. We use a strong notion of 'combination' that becomes a key theme of the book as a whole. This is that methods that are truly combined are also transformed in relation to each other. We explore the logic of combination in terms of the different (but related) objects that different methods recognize or construct.

In Chapter 3, we seek the basis of combined methods in a general methodological outlook or method in the larger sense. Here we draw – more extensively than in Chapter 2 – on two philosophical traditions: the tradition of humanistic philosophy known as hermeneutics and feminist debates about knowledge and 'standpoint'. We end this chapter by showing how the expanded themes of reflexivity, dialogue and accountability, as well as the nature of cultural processes themselves, provide the basis for combining methods and theories.

Chapter 4 approaches the same themes but in a different way, via the detailed practices of research. In a way, this is our own first detailed testing of our general approach to method, though, of course, much real testing happened before this in the theory and practice of our own teaching. We asked, 'What are the implications of our general principles for the advice we give to student researchers on all the main processes of researching, from defining a topic to writing for presentation?' This is thus the most practical of all the chapters in this book, though there are similar passages in most later chapters.

One alternative way in which to read Part I of the book – especially for those unfamiliar with cultural studies in the narrower sense – would be to read Chapter 4 (which stands relatively independently) before Chapters 2 and 3 (which are quite complex in parts), but after the introduction to cultural studies in Chapter 1. This would mean starting with the practical applications, then unearthing their principles – a not uncommon method in cultural studies and a powerful one.

1 Cultural studies and the study of culture: disciplines and dialogues

Asking the cultural question – seven different agenda 10
Historical contexts of the culture agenda 14
Cultural studies and social movements 14
Dominant misrepresentations and popular agency 15
Finding a philosophy? Cultural studies, feminist philosophy and hermeneutics 16
Relations to other academic disciplines 19
Explaining transdisciplinarity: a story in four acts 20
Implications of transdisciplinarity for method 22
Transdisciplinary strategies 24
Conclusion 24

When teaching students across the humanities, practical arts and social sciences, and from many different countries, we are still sometimes asked, 'What is cultural studies?' In this chapter we respond afresh to this question by introducing cultural studies as a particular approach within a wider field of the study of culture.

We have organized the chapter around two further questions, trying to offer something new for older readers too. Our first question concerns the reasons for an interest in culture in the first place: why does it become an object of critical study? In answering this question we approach cultural studies as one selective tradition that defines what is interesting about culture in a particular way. We take the idea of a selective tradition from Raymond Williams, who mainly uses it to criticize the 'deliberately selective and connecting process which offers a historical and cultural ratification of a contemporary order' (1977: 116). We use it here, however, as a means of critiquing our own tradition building and, therefore, for critical self-reflection and renewal. We view the cultural studies tradition alongside other approaches to the study of culture, other selective traditions, the complicated and contested history of which we can only evoke. This may be enough, however, to identify what has been distinctive about the cultural studies approach and set the scene for dialogues with others.

The second organizing question has to do with the relation with academic disciplines and disciplinarity more generally. If our research questions come from a larger, often political, concern with the cultural, our approaches and methods are drawn, initially at least, from adjacent disciplines. This is a familiar issue, but today it has some new features. What is cultural studies today when every discipline has made the cultural turn? What are the implications for our intellectual strategies of this transdisciplinarity of the study of culture?

Asking the cultural question – seven different agenda

Despite the fact that we may all make such claims occasionally, objects of research are not really interesting in themselves. The intensity of our engagement, which such phrases express, comes, rather, from a relationship between ourselves and the topics we choose – or that choose us. The idea of 'the question' or 'the research agenda' are useful ways of describing the bridge between researcher and researched implied by any enquiry (this is an idea to which we will return in Chapter 3).

Culture and power

In a narrowly defined version of cultural studies, the typical questions have been about the production or organization of meaning as a site of power. Cultural processes are important and interesting because they are a medium within which powerful social relationships are played out and possibilities for social betterment are opened up or closed down. A typical way of posing power questions has been in terms of identity – especially where identity is seen as a problematic issue and individual and collective identities are understood as being always created under social pressures (for recent debates on identity, see Brah and Coombes, 2000; Hall and du Gay, 1996).

The cultural question can be asked differently. Implicit in the culture-as-power issue and the questions that arise from it is the idea that everyone participates, however unequally, in the cultural process of making meanings and fixing and shifting identities. Yet, the best-known definition of the cultural – and perhaps still the dominant one in everyday use – tends to narrow the cultural field down to specialized, often elite, high cultural practices and products that are distinguished from common culture and 'owned' by experts or privileged groups.

Culture as 'value'

In this approach, it is the aesthetic or moral value of literature, music or art that is supposed to make them worth studying, not primarily their complicity in powerful inclusions and exclusions. This way of thinking about culture held sway in traditional humanities disciplines until quite recently and continues to be powerfully defended outside the academy. Indeed, conservative academicians still fight for it, often against the canon-breaking claims of cultural and other interdisciplinary approaches (Bloom, 1987). There remains a widespread incredulity, surfacing in attacks on media studies especially, that anyone could spend academic time – and therefore take seriously – studying pop star celebrities, television quiz shows or romantic fiction. It is important to note that, though we may be critical of excluding the popular in this way, researchers in the culture-as-power tradition have their own problems with issues of value.

Culture as policy

Culture is also conceptualized narrowly, though in a different way, when the question is about cultural policy. This discourse of cultural policy is selective in two ways.

First, it tends to address only the policies of large-scale institutions, especially those of governments. In the versions that have grown out of cultural studies, by debt and critique, the study of cultural policy is structured around a particular reading of Foucault. The key focus is on 'governmentality' or, in Tony Bennett's words, 'the governmental programs through which particular fields of conduct are organized and regulated' (1998: 84; see also the series introduction in the same volume: ii–iv). 'Governmentality' is wider than 'government', as the stress on conduct implies. Yet, in practice, policy studies tend to return us to the needs of formal institutions, not least as a result of the funding of research.

Second, the discourse on cultural policy tends, in practice, to treat culture as limited to these particular fields of conduct. Although these fields transgress the older high/low divisions, they are limited to practices in which formal institutions have an interest – typically, sport, art and museums and heritage. To promote a primarily policy-orientation within cultural studies can therefore recapitulate some older reductions. As Raymond Williams argued, such usages involve a class or hierarchical appropriation of culture in its more general and positive root meanings, as cultivation, education or individual and social improvement (1983: 87–93). In the case of policy studies, they also reproduce the old identifications of cultural agency with state – or quasi-state – institutions or cultural elites and forms of official action. This can imply that some of the characteristic addressees of cultural studies – radical professionals, artistic practitioners, students, academics and social movements or indeed, ordinary citizens – do not have cultural policies or strategies for living of their own.

Culture as cohesion

The policy agenda has often been associated with another, potentially more inclusive, agenda – culture as a source of social cohesion and belonging. In this framework, consensus, community or core values are opposed to individualistic or anomic states – typically the social disorder or fragmentation sometimes held to characterize modernity. A classic statement of this framework can be found in Emile Durkheim's Suicide, itself a response to what Stephen Lukes calls 'the theme of social dissolution' widespread among nineteenth-century French intellectuals. (Durkheim, 1952; Lukes, 1973)

Within this agenda, the pressure is to conceive of cultures as shared, homogeneous and tightly bound. This may still be the case even where such unities are viewed as constructed or imagined (for example, Anderson, 1991; Gellner, 1983). Such conceptualizations do not rule out difference and power, but they are assigned to the relations *between* whole cultures, not *within* them. Cultures, in their internal relations, according to this account, are (or should be) conflict-free zones. Difference within these zones thus become signs of social pathology.

This type of cultural agenda is politically alive today despite extensive intellectual critiques. It is especially associated with the racialization of politics and national identity in Western European states and neo-conservative movements. Stressing the essential unity of the (white) nation goes along with identifying the (black, immigrant, asylum seeker or *ausländer*) other as the source of social disorder. Thus, the racialization of street crime as mugging was a key theme in one of the first studies of Thatcherism as a law and order politics in the late 1970s (Hall et al, 1978), while later analysis argued that a particular cultural theory – a new racism or ethnic absolutism – was central to New Right politics more generally. (Gilroy, 1987; A.M. Smith, 1994).

Another example of conservative cultural theory today can be seen in post-Cold War international relations, where cultural difference may be understood as the clash of civilizations when whole value systems collide. In liberal multicultural discourse, too, diversity is sometimes grasped as the peaceful coexistence of whole, discretely bounded cultures, not as the living out of power-laden differences or basis for border crossing and cultural syncreticism (Donald and Rattansi, 1992).

Historically, however, this combination of racism and conservative cultural theory is neither so new, nor so exclusively right wing. There is a long history in Europe of the construction of national identities as a result of the idea of a people, or *volk*, with some essential characteristics. This essence has often been racialized and assigned typical cultural expressions. Such a combination was a powerful feature of Nazi philosophy and underpinned its racist and genocidal practice, but, as recent studies in the Netherlands have shown, these *volkisch* versions of 'the people' and national identity were a standard feature of European academic work on history and popular culture – and in the human sciences more generally – both before and after World War II, as well as informing popular politics. They also underpinned many different kinds of political stance, including, for instance, an anti-Nazi patriotism (Eickhoff, Henkes and van Vree, 2000).

It is important to understand the continuity of racialized thinking within academic disciplines in Europe for two main reasons. First, as racism was so often associated with essentialist thinking – the reduction of cultures or societies to a central core or feature – the growth of systematically anti-essentialist thinking in cultural and social theory, especially from the 1970s, acquires a new significance (see Chapter 3).

Second, it is important to recognize that cultural studies, as a tradition, has not been exempt from this version of cultural conservatism. Because of its association with Englishness, it has often worn, in Paul Gilroy's phrase, 'an ethnic garb' (1992: 187). It has also been complicit in the tendency to conflate culture, nation and 'race' – that is, whiteness – a tendency made manifest by the struggle to get black British cultural traditions, themselves hybrid 'Atlantic' formations, fully recognized within cultural research. Moreover, Gilroy, among many other anti-essentialist writers, observes that other collectivities – including class cultures, but also communities or political identities such as 'women', 'gay' and, indeed 'black' – have been conceptualized according to a similar essentialist model. (1992, 1993b).

As we will argue in Chapter 2, one of the key theoretical movements within cultural studies has involved the critique of the model of cultures as pure, bounded, whole or entire. Indeed, cultural studies has been forced to question 'culture' itself, its own key category.

Culture as standardization

A different question about culture has focused attention on standardization or convergence. Uniformities can arise from mass culture – the capitalist commercialization or commodification of forms of popular culture – or globalization or bureaucratic or instrumental rationality, work discipline or other forms of social control.

Standardization or regulation are often seen as accompaniments of modernity and have been a pervasive preoccupation of sociological theory from Max Weber onwards. Such concern has a Marxist variant in the cultural and aesthetic critique of mass culture among some Frankfurt School theorists (Held, 1980; Horkheimer and Adorno, 1972). Indeed, some versions of globalization theory and studies of international communication paint this picture large on a worldwide scale, while, in many ways, standardization remains the cultural thesis of sociological theory. This form of abstract and generalizing social description tends to centre on a single dynamic of change – the risk society, McDonaldization, Disneyfication and some versions of globalization (for example, Beck, 1992; Ritzer, 1993).

Though diversity is often an implied and preferred critical value here, this form of cultural study rarely grasps cultural differences or investigates particular ways of living. Again, there are points of exchange (and contestation) between this common sociological agenda and cultural studies, especially in the conceptualization of ideology or hegemony (Hall, 1988; Larrain, 1983; Thomas, 1999; Thomson, 1984). Does cultural power function by securing cultural sameness or working on and through the differences? This question will concern us again in Chapter 7 when we address the analysis of dominance.

Culture as language or understanding

Not all agenda of interest in the cultural are so obviously political, though they all have political connections. Neither classical structuralism nor contemporary hermeneutics, which offer important resources for cultural studies, can be understood (or understand themselves) in such directly political ways. Structuralism has asked how meaning is constructed by means of the conventions and codes of languages in the broadest sense, signs, myths or symbols. Hermeneutics has asked how understanding the other is possible, whether the other is a text or a different language or an alien culture or a different point in time. Though it contains, as we shall see, a view of the whole circuit of culture, it has focused on reading or interpetation (Gadamer, 1989, and see Chapter 2 below).

Historical contexts of the culture agenda

In the quest for culture, we can also see evidence of larger historical processes at work that have contributed to its increased visibility and significance. The rise of the cultural agenda seems to be related to five such processes, each of which feeds cultural questioning in different ways.

- The development of *capitalist modernity*, in which more and more aspects of social life are commodified, becoming objects of capitalist production and exchange. This has raised issues about standardization and the loss of cultural value.
- The construction of *nations* and national popular movements. Citizens are addressed as sharing a cultural heritage. By also placing citizens hierarchically within the nation (as exemplary or marginal, for example) nationalism feeds an interest in cultural difference within and between nations.
- The *cross-cultural* encounters of peoples in processes of colonization, decolonization and the later forms of globalization, including tourism, international communications and the migration of people on a worldwide scale. These have been as important as ethnicized nationbuilding, adding whole dimensions of difference and relationship.
- The growth of *specialized forms of cultural production*, which create a relatively separated cultural sphere, in some ways abstracted from the ordinary daily production of meanings, often as culture industries. This occurred first in the separation of print production and the spread of literacy, but later in film-based and electronic media.
- The enormous, contemporary *elaboration of these media on a global scale* associated with neo-liberal deregulation and large-scale and monopolistic capitalist corporations.

Cultural studies and social movements

It is within this larger context, then, that we must view the particular relationship between the culture-as-power agenda and social movements, a relationship that has been very generative for cultural studies. The movements arose out of the contradictions of modernity, especially those between its promises of progress and the actuality of continuing, if not deepening, inequalities. They also arose in a context where issues of representation, especially in the public media, assumed a new political significance.

Those at odds with these processes, including socialists (especially of the various flavours of New Left), student radicals, feminist critics, black activists, anti-colonial intellectuals, sexual dissidents and anti-capitalist and environmental campaigners, have had to struggle to understand what holds the conventional or mainstream forms of life and belief in place or directs the main tendencies of change. The movements they formed have often themselves been conditioned by older forms of politics of identity, especially the politics of the nation as a racial concept. Even today, national differences and contexts remain as important politically as the need to match the dominant global processes and institutions. Sometimes, movements have sought to represent an alternative nation, as the British Communist party attempted to do in the period from the 1930s to the late 1950s (Schwarz, 1982); sometimes, they have treated an emergent social identity as though it were a new kind of nation – 'black' or 'queer', for instance (for an account and critique of the 'queer nation', see Hennesey, 1995); sometimes, they have tried to overcome national divisions by insisting on internationalism. These issues have been discussed with a particular urgency during the last two decades within contemporary feminism, both in relation to differences of North and South and in the context of the European Union.

It is important to stress, however, that, within these movements, especially perhaps within socialism, the *political* question has often been separated from the *cultural* question. The emergence of the culture-as-power agenda has been a story within the story of critical political theory. For long periods, inequalities have appeared so systemic and entrenched that they have seemed to produce and reproduce themselves almost automatically, as a result of economic necessities and other forms of coercion, propaganda or, at most, a conscious ideological manipulation. What is specific to *cultural* domination has not always been explored. We can best understand cultural studies, perhaps, as part of a movement to assert the importance of the cultural in critical political theory and action. Indeed, it is partly because of rival connections with the political that debates between some kinds of political economy and cultural studies have been long, bitter and continuous.

Dominant misrepresentations and popular agency

Cultural questions came to be more central within political movements from the 1960s onwards as the complex relationship between power and representation began to be recognized. There were, however, always two related sides to this questioning. The first stemmed from experiences of being misrepresented and misrecognized – as a woman, gay man, black person – in public media or commercial forms, such as advertising, or political versions of the nation or academic knowledge. This common experience often quite directly fuelled a kind of cultural study that interrogated dominant representations and hegemonic cultural formations. The critique of the dominant, however, has had a second side: the aim to secure the representation of marginalized or subordinated groups, spaces or themes in various ways.

This latter objective has often involved the cultural elaboration of some emergent political identity. One of the most striking instances of this is the extended, many-voiced struggle for black self-representation in the United States and UK – a struggle that cannot be understood outside the larger histories of slavery, empire and racism (see for example, Gilroy, 1993a; Hall, 1996a, 1996b; Mercer, 1994). Pride in blackness or in the resilience of black women and men or black cultural creativity are forms of the (politicized) popular that make sense in societies that continue to operate binaries of black and white to the invariable advantage of whiteness and racialize, or make pure or absolute, cultural differences. We can read many forms of black representation, such as the work of black American women novelists, as constructions or reconstructions – 're-memorying' is Toni Morrison's term – of complex identities under sustained historical pressures (1987: 215). Similar, intersecting histories are present in the politics of representation of women's movements, sexual minorities and sexual dissidents – and, most recently, a politics of disability. These kinds of representation have taken many forms, often expressive rather than aligned to academic practice or cultural studies, and include the rewriting of history.

As we will argue at more length in Chapter 6, the criticism of cultural studies as 'populist' (McGuigan, 1992) can miss the connection between these two sides: the assertion of popular culture and the questioning of dominant structures. Respect for the disabled, for instance, can only be given full weight if taken-for-granted assumptions about ablebodiedness and all bodily norms are questioned. The politics of disability has indeed been accompanied (though not in any simple causal relation) by the growth of critical intellectual work around the body, including the exploration of body modification in relation to technologies of different kinds.

Concern for the relation between culture and power has, we therefore want to argue, reconfigured critical political theory itself in a sort of 'politics of truth' (Barrett, 1991). Conceptualizations of knowledge, culture and politics have all been subject to revision and cultural studies has been part of that process as well as helping to frame the questions that needed to be asked. These have included the following. Why is the status quo – or the dominant trajectory of change – so hard to shift or reverse? How is its naturalness and givenness secured? What new ways of thinking or feeling would help bring about some change? What is the role of the way we think about knowledge itself in a different, alternative process of change?

Finding a philosophy? Cultural studies, feminist philosophy and hermeneutics

In writing about cultural studies so far in this chapter we have ourselves used a particular method. We have stressed the importance of the *question* in research. We have illustrated the importance of reflecting on the *history* of research agenda, *traditions* of enquiry and the larger historical conditions and possibilities. We have tried to pinpoint what is particular about cultural studies as an approach and emphasize that it is only one possible view of the cultural. We have indicated some of the social experiences and points of view from which this agenda arises.

If we relate these features to more philosophical debates about theories of knowledge (epistemology), and theories of method (methodology) we can see that cultural studies aligns strongly with an anti-objectivist view of knowledge. The object of knowledge is not something that we find as an object, separate from ourselves. Our participation in our subject of research is, on the contrary, inevitable. The particularity or even the partisanship of a research agenda is not, therefore, a disqualification for pursuing it. The primary methodological task is not to correct for bias in our research procedures. Rather, what Donna Haraway calls 'partiality' is inevitable, for all approaches are partial, in the double meaning of the term – limited by a particular time, space and social horizon and also motivated, more or less consciously, by desire, interest and power. Moreover, partiality is not only inevitable – a necessary human condition of knowledge production – it is also, potentially, a resource or asset, provided it is made explicit and debated and reflected on. As Haraway puts it in a beautifully condensed epigram: 'the only way to find a larger vision is to be somewhere in particular' (1991b: 196).

An early and full formulation of this philosophical position is to be found in Hans-Georg Gadamer's revision of the hermeneutic tradition – that strand in (mainly) German philosophy preoccupied with understanding (*verstehen*). Gadamer's major text *Truth and Method*, counterposes truth with rigid ideas of method and argues that orthodox notions of objectivity in science are insufficient. It explores the claims of situated understanding and interpretation – claims associated especially with the humanities. Gadamer's stress is on time, history and tradition rather than power, difference and social position, but many of his themes, developed before 1960 when *Truth and Method* was first published in German, anticipate later debates in the 1970s and 1980s, especially those in feminist philosophy:

> A person who believes he is free of prejudices, relying on the objectivity of his procedures and denying that he is himself conditioned by historical circumstances, experiences the power of the prejudices that unconsciously dominate him as vis a tergo [a force behind his back]. A person who does not admit that he is dominated by prejudices will fail to see what manifests itself by their light. It is like the relation between I and Thou. A person who reflects himself out of the mutuality of such a relation changes this relationship and destroys its moral bond . . . In seeking to understand tradition historical consciousness must not rely on the critical method with which it approaches its sources, as if this preserved it from mixing in its own judgements and prejudices. It must, in fact, think within its own historicity. (1989: 360–61)

So, methodological questioning begins before entry into the field or the choice of an object of research. It begins with a self-consciousness about who we are and why we ask the questions that we do and what our prior relationships might be to our objects of study. It begins, for instance, with us, the writers of this book, asking ourselves why culture is so important to us and our work. It begins with you, the reader of our book, asking similar questions about your agenda. In Gadamer's terms (which he takes from Heidegger), understanding begins with our 'fore-meanings'. These, however, are starting points only. They are modified in the process of understanding. In this next passage, Gadamer has in mind 'the other' as a text from another place and time:

> A person trying to understand something will not resign himself from the start to relying on his own accidental fore-meanings, ignoring as consistently and stubbornly as possible the actual meaning of the text until the latter becomes so persistently audible that it breaks through what the interpreter imagines it to be. Rather, a person trying to understand a text is prepared for it to tell him something. That is why a hermeneutically trained consciousness must be, from the start, sensitive to the text's alterity. (1989: 269)

Understanding, therefore, is based in a dialogue with an 'other'. In attending to the otherness of his source, however, Gadamer avoids leaving behind a sense of his own position and his subjectivity as an interpreter. Understanding and self-understanding go together:

> But this kind of sensitivity involves neither 'neutrality' with respect to content nor the extinction of one's self, but the foregrounding and appropriation of one's own fore-meanings and prejudices. The important thing is to be aware of one's own bias, so that the text can present itself in all its otherness and thus assert its own truth against one's own fore-meanings. (1989: 269)

Consciousness of our own partiality is an essential part of the dialogue with the other. It is this that constitutes the process of research.

This is an illuminating argument to bring to cultural studies, clarifying a standpoint more often assumed than analysed. When expressed in practice, it has more often been an educational rather than an epistemological commitment. From its moments of inception in adult education, schooling and the academy, students in cultural studies were encouraged to understand their own lives and those of friends, family, movement or community. The stress on project, dissertation or thesis work – relatively self-directed modes of study – was also a feature of most educational programmes. Of course, it was recognized that education involves, by definition, an advance on such starting points, some reworking of prejudice and, at best, this occurred on the part of the student and also on the part of the teacher, who also learns (see Johnson, 1997a, 1999). A willingness to value the subjective involvements of researchers in their topics converges with a type of progressive pedagogy in which existing questions and knowledge are a resource. Once acknowledged, such commitments themselves become objects of (self-)scrutiny. They are risked in the logic of an enquiry. Every project, therefore, is, more or less explicitly, a working out of experience and value in the world, the search for a personal point of view and a contribution, however modest, to wider ethics and politics.

We will return from time to time in this book to the insights of Gadamer and Paul Ricoeur, who extends and supplements them so creatively (Ricoeur, 1991). It is worth noting, at this stage, however, that hermeneutic philosophy cannot replace cultural studies, however much it may supplement it, for there is a marked neglect of issues of power and difference within the philosophy of interpretation that shows up, for example, in a certain gentlemanly assurance about the possibility of understanding. Cultural studies shares more with feminist philosophy and women's studies in its recognition of the place of power and difference in all cultural processes, including those of research. Of course, we have to share this ground, given the nature of our respective agendas. The fuller implications of our living inside our objects of study, politically as well as personally, will be opened out in Chapter 3.

Relationships with other academic disciplines

So far in this chapter we have discussed the constitution of cultural studies as a selective tradition in relation to social movements, other cultural agendas and larger historical contexts. We turn now to our second organizing question: the relation with academic disciplines.

Academic disciplines are constituted, in part, around distinctive ways of working. This element is sometimes made explicit in educational curricula, with the theory and methods core or the preoccupation with research training in social science disciplines, for instance. In many disciplines, thesis or dissertation work has meant, among other things, demonstrating a competence in these methods. In other disciplines, especially in the humanities, a methodological core is less explicit, appearing, for example, in cross-disciplinary polemics. We are thinking of the commitment to close reading and attentiveness to language in literary studies or the focus on sources and evidence in history.

An obvious question about cultural studies is whether or not it has already – or should have – a methodological core of this kind. This is a running question in this book. We are concerned in this chapter, however, with a slightly different question: what are the relations between cultural studies and other disciplines? We have two main purposes here. We want to argue that we have reached a particular stage in these relations and advocate a broad strategy to deal with this.

Cultural studies now exists within a wider field – that of the study of culture. This takes many forms, more or less framed by specific disciplines. What is cultural studies, we might ask, when everyone has taken a cultural turn and added culture to their agenda? Indeed, what is the role of a cultural studies when we have:

- a developed sociology of culture (for example, *Theory, Culture and Society*, the journal and the book series)
- English studies and critical text work (spilling well outside a traditional literary canon)
- a cultural geography (for example, Jackson, 1989; Skelton and Valentine, 1998)
- an anthropology that recognizes the problem of representation (for example, Clifford and Marcus, 1986; Marcus, 1992)
- a marked shift from a social to a cultural history (for example, the shifts in emphasis in the radical historical forum *Historical Workshop Journa*l over the last ten years)
- a strong interest among historians and others in memory, heritage and the past in the present more generally (for example, Nora, 1997; Samuel, 1994)

- a psychology that is interested in the cultural forms of self-representation – in discourses and narratives, for instance (for example, Billig, 1997)
- a take-up of cultural theory within political science (for example, Laclau and Mouffe, 1985; A.M. Smith, 1994)
- a growing interest in the international relations of culture (for example, Chan, 2001)

To any necessarily incomplete list such as this, we would have to add some multidisciplinary clusters. These engage with parts of the same cultural topic, often in similar ways, and may well be thoroughly embedded in our teaching and research practice. In the British academic context, the list might include communication studies, film studies, gay and lesbian studies, media studies, women's and gender studies and studies of particular countries or areas. For the United States especially, ethnically defined interdisciplinary studies are also important, such as Afro-American and Hispanic studies.

Explaining transdisciplinarity: a story in four acts

One way in which we can understand this situation is by means of an account of the effects of the cultural studies intervention. Initially, in the first act of this drama, cultural studies took a stance that was, in part at least, outside or even against the existing disciplinary map. The concern with culture, power and difference exceeded the brief of any academic discipline. It even crossed the boundary between humanities disciplines, with their intense gaze on questions of language and meaning, and the social sciences, with their preoccupation with social process and society.

In the second act of our story, cultural studies assembled a set of approaches drawn, necessarily, from other, older disciplines. Interestingly, these borrowings often went back to an earlier disciplinary politics within the movements, especially within the New Left, where history, sociology, English and an early form of media studies made rival claims for relevance. Cultural studies in the academy borrowed in particular from English (or, more broadly, literary studies), sociology (especially from social theory and ethnographic fieldwork) and history (especially a concern with historical contextualization and the movement of larger-scale cultural formations). It also neglected others, especially geography, anthropology, psychology and folklore. We will look more closely at most of these interrelationships in later chapters. Sometimes these disciplinary borrowings have been held separate, in combinations we can call multidisciplinary. This was typical of programmes in media and communication studies, though some cultural studies programmes also preserved disciplinary strands. Elsewhere, in the Centre for Contemporary Cultural Studies (CCCS) at Birmingham University, for example, there was an aspiration to construct a new *interdisciplinary* area. As a consequence, many research texts in cultural studies, including theses and dissertations, are indeed hard to allocate to a particular academic discipline and may thus be misjudged on disciplinary grounds.

The third act in our story sees the transformations wrought by cultural studies on the disciplines so engaged, which take on cultural questions in their own ways and their own agenda. The longest histories of dialogue are with English (especially), sociology and, despite interruptions, history. It was in the wake of cultural studies, for instance, that a process of rereading and rewriting English was set in train (Batsleer et al., 1985). Other recent histories have been less dialogic, though provocation at the absences in cultural studies seems to have played a part in, for example, the development of a more cultural psychology (Billig, 1997; Walkerdine, 1997).

So, to use the term 'transdisciplinarity' is to describe a situation in which cultural studies is not alone in pursuing an extended cultural agenda (compare the use in Kellner, 1997) and recognize that it is no longer in a pioneering situation. Rather, there are many different, productive intellectual spaces for serious work on cultural questions. In the fourth act of the story, then, cultural studies practitioners become net learners in new cross-disciplinary exchanges, not, as may have been the case before, net teachers, listening closely – with due scepticism perhaps – to adjacent approaches. Are they suspiciously familiar? Are they excitingly innovative? Do they extend the work by challenging it? Are they just very different, driven by concerns that are at best analogous, at worst systematically hostile? These complicated, often competitive relations, offer temptations to retrenchment and opportunities for renewal.

Of course, our story, so far, given our earlier attention to wider contexts, is deliberately self-centred and has an ironic twist. The intellectual and political movements of the last 30 years, often absorbed as theory, have cut right across the disciplinary map – in the reception of Foucauldian or other kinds of poststructuralist theory, for instance. Moreover, theoretical traditions are absorbed differently according to disciplinary agenda and timing. The current reception of Antonio Gramsci's writings on hegemony by students of the discipline of international relations, for instance, brings a different Gramsci to view – more international, more concerned with political economy – than the one produced by the reading of the *Prison Notebooks* from within cultural studies in the 1970s (for example, compare Hall, Lumley and McLennan, 1978, and Hall, 1988, with Cox and Sinclair, 1996). Yet, the histories that shaped the culture-and-power agenda influenced most disciplines. Feminism and women's studies, for example, have created cross-disciplinary dialogues of their own (often held separate from the 'malestream'), while human geography, social theory and political economy have moved towards the new cultural agenda arising from globalization.

Transdisciplinarity is also a real condition in our everyday academic life. All four of us work in a faculty of humanities that includes social scientists, many of whom are collaborators on other projects. As individuals, we address cultural questions from different angles and sometimes only secondarily. Around us, most areas of the Faculty's work have taken on a cultural agenda in some sense. Many colleagues, including ourselves, have rather hybrid multihyphenated academic identities. Our own are complicated enough – sociology-media-cultural studies, development studies-geography-gender and ethnic studies, cultural studies-historical studies; cultural studies-English studies-gender studies and so on. Even when identifying with cultural studies, we keep a foothold somewhere else. We work with social theorists, human geographers, cultural historians, postcolonial critics, queer theorists, feminist autobiographers, cross-cultural international relations scholars. It is hard to say where cultural studies begins or ends in the melée. With our cultural studies hats on, we are often surprised to hear the subject invoked for impossibly strange or depressingly familiar topics. With other hats on, cultural studies turns out to be very close to current best practices – in geography or sociology for instance – though often with some critical qualification. This combination of difference and familiarity is often hard to negotiate when we are designing a new MA programme or examining a PhD thesis. It is even more difficult, sometimes, for students making choices between programmes and double-guessing criteria of evaluation, including being *examined* as PhD candidates. Again, because we are all involved in supporting and advising writers of projects, dissertations and theses, these issues of intellectual identity and boundary crossing are very real. The question of when the disciplinary barriers are going to be brought down often hovers as a phantom during these exchanges. These are key reasons for trying to be explicit about method while not becoming border guards ourselves.

Our experience suggests that a degree of cross-disciplinary interest in culturality is new, but that it does not replace the older dynamics. We are definitely not in a postdisciplinary situation. Nor are older strategies – interdisciplinary combination, for instance – now redundant. Nor is cultural studies itself redundant, as a project. The new situation does, however, reposition the older strategies and forces us to develop new ones.

Implications of transdisciplinarity for method

As we have explored, cultural studies is produced in a complicated set of relations with academic disciplines and disciplinarity itself – its history has anti-disciplinary, interdisciplinary, multidisciplinary and transdisciplinary aspects. In addition, there is always a pressure to construct cultural studies as a regular academic discipline. Our analysis here may even seem overcomplicated and evasive – isn't cultural studies a discipline when all is said and done? We think it more helpful, however, to see that there are always different pulls and tendencies at work in the history of an approach, both for understanding the present and deciding on future strategies.

The story of cultural studies suggests an approach to method in which the requirements of a discipline are deliberately *not* foregrounded. It is relatively unusual, in our experience, for project, dissertation or thesis work in cultural studies to be presented (or examined) primarily as an apprenticeship to a discipline. This does not mean that the story so far will not have a presence in the work as a starting point, resource or object of criticism. Indeed, as we will argue later, one possible aspect of a cultural studies method is a hypersensitivity to the history of the approach, especially to its theories. There are, however, three main reasons for us to feel that disciplinarity is not, or should not be, the main dynamic, nor produce the main criteria of method or evaluation.

- **Space for questions from outside a discipline**
  There should be space for research questions to come from an explicitly personal or extra-curricula agenda, from movements and lives – especially those that are marginalized or disregarded. As we have seen, this has been a point of pedagogic principle among many teachers of cultural studies, including ourselves. Similarly, in this book, we do not start from a set of methods that have acquired some academic authorization as necessary to a discipline or proper to a science. Rather, we start from the inquiry itself, seeking appropriate resources from different places. As every project differs and culture exceeds the terms of any one discipline, it is likely that our methodologies will be interdisciplinary, drawing on existing syntheses or borrowing and mixing in new ways.
- **Disciplinarity as regulation**
  Second, within a larger cultural analysis, disciplinarity can be seen as one of the ways in which academic life is controlled and policed, though it may also be an (always ambiguous) defence against external pressures of a kind that ought to be resisted. To state a preference for a particular question or extra-curricula agenda of research is also to create some distance between that researcher and the academy and its institutions, including the disciplinary separations. Any challenge of this kind involves risk and may have real costs, so it is important to be as clear-sighted as possible about what the conventions are, as well as when and how they can be breached. Again, our view of cultural studies as an approach is that it should support such necessary challenges, especially when they are associated with the representation of groups and issues usually unrecognized or repressed. We should never forget the difference – which today is often substantial – between the requirements of academic self-reproduction in institutions and careers and careful, systematic and creative intellectual work that is both critical and useful. This does not mean that we should be inattentive to institutional demands and personal aspirations. On the contrary, it means being very watchful of them, while recognizing that they are not the whole story.
- **Disciplines as partial**
  Third, disciplinary approaches to the cultural are always partial in particular ways. Cultural studies is partial, too, but its form of partiality – especially the concern with cultural fields or circuits as a whole – resists some common reductions. The study of culture is often reduced in other, more disciplinary, appropriations. Sometimes it is also reduced in the approaches nearest to home. We have in mind the simplification of culture to subculture or popular culture, to media or texts. As culture becomes the site of competing disciplinary claims and imperial skirmishes, cultural studies has a role, still, in exceeding conventional definitions.

Transdisciplinary strategies

What, then, does this analysis suggest for the strategies available to us? In conditions of transdisciplinarity, there can be an apparent contradiction between two different approaches. The first is to insist on the difference or specificity of cultural studies, in terms of pedagogy, method or content, and try to define it as clearly as possible. The second strategy is to be exceptionally open to developments in the study of culture in other disciplines in order to make fresh appropriations, in order to renew our approach. The first strategy seems to compose cultural studies as a distinctive approach, as a discipline even; the second to dissolve it or at least construct very permeable boundaries.

This contradiction, like so many dualisms, may in practice be misleading. There are two main qualifications perhaps. First, these issues about openness and closedness in academic disciplines have many different aspects. Basil Bernstein's distinction between 'classification' ('the strength of the boundary between contents' – the way subjects and disciplines are separated as formal entities in a curriculum or the timetable, for instance) and 'framing' ('the strength of the boundary between what may be transmitted and what may not be transmitted, in the pedagogical relationship') is a case in point (1973: 230–1). This might suggest, for example, a current strategy for cultural studies of somewhat stronger classification, where approaches and methods are clarified and their distinctiveness upheld. This could be accompanied, however, by a consistently weak framing to allow the maximum permeability of the curriculum to questions arising from everyday life. The first asserts the distinctiveness of cultural studies within an academic context; the second preserves the open relation to new social agenda and students' existing knowledges. Our concern with method is a move towards a somewhat stronger classification, but the combination, effectively pursued, can create homes for work that cannot be done elsewhere in the academy.

A second qualification concerns the interdependence of strategies of self-definition and renewal. The term 'appropriation' implies these two sides, for appropriation is a borrowing (back) according to an agenda of your own. Perhaps cultural studies is now involved in a process of reappropriation, of borrowing back again what it previously borrowed, then lent out again! Openness to others depends on a certain confidence about where we stand. Considerations of this kind underpin the double movements of this book: the attempt to define the distinctive research practices of cultural studies and the openness to dialogue with other positions.

Conclusion

In this chapter we have sought to answer an old question – 'What is cultural studies?' – in fresh ways. We have given two sorts of answers.

First, cultural studies is a selective tradition that is interested in culture as a source of power, difference and emancipation, closely connected with social movements and cultural critique.

Second, cultural studies is a way of being in the academy, academic or not quite academic. This means prioritizing agendas from outside the academy, being critical of academic limits, but using and developing the resources we find there. In the current situation, when most or all humanities and social science disciplines have something to say about the cultural, this includes being especially attentive to the work of colleagues and students in or around other disciplines.

2 Multiplying methods: from pluralism to combination

Methodological pluralism or a Method?	**26**
Objects and strategies of cultural research	**27**
Cultural circuits: cultural studies meets hermeneutics	**37**
Conclusion: combined and multiple methods?	**42**

In this chapter, we ask why methods of cultural study are so diverse. We trace the circumstances that have led to this diversity and the sense (or non-sense) it makes. We do not take methodological diversity as a given, but, rather, propose that understanding *why* a multiplicity of methods is necessary is a part of *our* method. So, in the first part of this chapter, we explore the accumulation of methods in cultural studies in something like their historical sequence. We do not claim any kind of universality for this account, nor do we wish to give it a normative force as representing what everyone should do. We recognize that its immediate basis is a story of cultural studies in the UK, though elements may be recognizable in many different, especially anglophone, cultural contexts, but, whether it seems strange or all too familiar, we hope that our account will stimulate further dialogue. (For reflections on 'where is cultural studies' see Ang, 1998; Schwarz, 1994.)

The second part of this chapter takes a different approach to the diversity of methods. By means of the idea of a cultural circuit, it shows how all the different methods have their own legitimate objects and use as well as how they need to be combined. We are helped in this by drawing on a parallel argument about circuits and methods in the philosophy of hermeneutics.

Methodological pluralism or a Method?

Most writers on method see cultural studies as profoundly pluralistic in its approaches. It is a 'plural field of contesting perspectives' (Barker, 2000: 34) or 'insistently plural' (McGuigan, 1997: 1). For Douglas Kellner, cultural studies should be 'multi-perspectival', using the perspectives of political economy, textual methods and audience reception (1997: 102), while for Pertti Alasuutari cultural studies has a single perspective (taking culture seriously in connection with questions of power), but is eclectic in its methods: 'Cultural Studies methodology has often been described by the concept of bricolage: one is pragmatic and strategic in choosing and applying different methods and practices'(1995: 2).

Of recent writers, only Nick Couldry (2000) – and, more implicitly perhaps, Charlotte Brunsdon (2000) and Paul Willis (2000) – diverge from this methodological pluralism. Couldry argues against Lawrence Grossberg's view that cultural studies 'always and only exists in contextually specific theoretical and institutional formations' and 'has to be made up as it goes along' (Grossberg quoted in Couldry, 2000: 9) and gives priority to questions of disciplinary identity: for him, cultural studies is a discipline and it has a distinctive method.

We want to argue that methodological divergence occurs, in part, because culture has come to matter in different ways. Different methods correspond to the different modes by means of which culture impresses itself on us as an object. This relationship between methodologies and ontologies has already informed our identification in Chapter 1 of the culture-as-power approach, but it holds for differences *within* cultural studies, too. Here, different aims and objects select different research strategies, prompt borrowings from different disciplines and privilege different theoretical frameworks.

Objects and strategies of cultural research

In what follows we distinguish three main ways in which the objects of cultural studies have been defined and explore their implications for method. We start with the familiar definition of culture as a way of life of particular social groups. We trace the emergence of a new interest in cultural formations as a whole. Finally, we look at the contemporary critiques of the idea of culture itself, stemming especially from poststructuralist approaches, and consider some implications of this ongoing revision for questions of method.

Culture as the 'way of life' for groups and nations

Raymond Williams' redefinition of culture as 'ordinary' is more familiar than another feature of his work – the extraordinary range of his connected cultural projects even before 1980. He was interested in art, literature *and* everyday popular creativity, in classic novels and contemporary media. His work was deeply historical, but engaged with present possibilities and hopes for the future. His working-class loyalties were accompanied by a concern for larger cultural formations. He undertook close historical research in *The Country and the City* (1973) and debated general categories in *Marxism and Literature* (1977). He recognized *all* the meanings of culture, including the values of collective development and individual education.

In other versions of cultural research, such as in German intellectual traditions, Williams' various concerns would be assigned to different disciplines: the popular to folklore studies or *volkskunde*, for instance, and the 'high', artistic or philosophical aspects of culture to aesthetics and hermeneutics. As an interpreter of hermeneutics, Gadamer does some of the things that Williams does (Gadamer, 1989). He is an educator, studies words historically and discusses art and aesthetics. He only engages indirectly, however, with ordinary, socially situated meaning-making, when, for example, he compares artistic representation with learning by experience. Paul Ricoeur, too, takes high forms of culture, such as literary fiction and history-writing, as his examples (1984, 1985, 1988). These comparisons give clues to cultural studies' methodological dilemmas, drawing attention to the tension between the combination and the separation of objects and methods.

Culture as 'a whole way of life' (Williams, 1961) or 'a particular way of life' (Williams, 1965) or as 'a way of struggle' (Edward P. Thompson, 1961) can become a relatively separated object of study of this kind. Here, the specific practices of a particular class or social group are being examined, especially at moments of emergence or self-production. The appearance of 'new' political identities around gender or race in the emancipatory social movements of the 1960s and 1970s powerfully reinforced this cultural model, prompting much research in social history, literary studies and cultural studies and also shaping curricular developments in several subjects.

Behind these New Left revisions lay an older Marxist argument (Lukacs, 1971; Marx and Engels, 1977) that ideas and consciousness are always properties of particular social groups. Class consciousness was an aspect of working-class activism and self-realization, a process by which proletarians, who exist by working for pay, grow from individual victimhood to collective political agency, to heroes who make the world – and history – anew. This dialectical model of collective identity was both enabling and limiting. In the 1960s and 1970s, largely as a result of the influence of E. P. Thompson's *The Making of the English Working Class*, a whole school of class-based history-writing was formed, mainly in the anglophone world but also with influence in Continental Europe (Kaye and McClelland, 1990) and India (Chandavarkar, 1997). An analogous model of culture as agency underpinned studies of black people as slaves or colonized people or settlers and survivors in the metropolis (for example, Fryer, 1984; Genovese, 1974). Feminist history and women's studies deployed similar frameworks, while criticizing the gender biases and absences of left-wing social history (D. Thompson, 1976). Early work on sexual dissidents often took the same shape (Weeks, 1977).

Culture as a way of life can also be understood in national terms, so that this framework can be read as a kind of left-wing cultural nationalism. In his formative early work, Williams did not really question these nationalist associations and their ethnic exclusions. His project converged with the rewriting of Englishness in terms of neglected and subordinated traditions of radicalism, popular turbulence and democratic protest by communist and socialist historians (Schwarz, 1982). It was only in the 1980s, as part of a larger revision of this model, that the way of life definition was fully critiqued in cultural studies as a construction of identity underpinned by radicalized conceptions of the nation (Gilroy, 1987, 1993b).

Methods for studying a way of life

Studying a way of life makes particular demands on method. The methodological filter must sift out shared, communal or common elements and patterns of commonalty within the group, even where internal differences are recognized. *The Making of the English Working Class* is organized around just such a tension between the forging of a common class outlook, which is Thompson's preferred thesis, and the differences within popular forces, some of which his research revealed. Method must be sensitive also to the connections between social consciousness and social being. Culture is the subjective side of social relationships and social experiences; it is a tissue of lives lived under pressure (for key formulations, see E. P. Thompson, 1963, 1978, 1993).

The negative side of this is a strong resistance in much cultural studies work to any method that abstracts aspects of social life from the whole social process. Such resistance initially arose from criticism of the base-superstructure metaphor within orthodox Marxism, associated with Soviet communism or Stalinism's dogmatic distortions of morality and knowledge for oppressive political ends (E. P. Thompson, 1961, 1978; Williams, 1961, 1977). The methodological principle (the resistance to abstraction) has therefore long been tied up with moral and political values, especially with the belief in human agency and grounded concrete knowledge. Indeed, the resistance to abstraction extended into a suspicion of theory as a methodological principle and became an important strand in opposing Althusserianism in the late 1970s (Johnson, 1979b; Samuel, 1981; E. P. Thompson, 1978). At this moment the word 'theory' carried such a concentration of issues that it was hard to untangle them. An interest in theory could, for example, be taken as a symptom of intellectual elitism and disconnection from the 'real worlds' of activist politics, popular agency and empirical controls on speculation. We will return to both the positive and negative aspects of the resistance to abstraction in Chapters 5 and 8.

Methods that privilege the concrete and use rich or thick description can be found in many disciplines, but especially in social history, human geography and anthropological or sociological fieldwork. Some forms of literary study also take texts to represent a way of life or a structure of feeling. The cross-disciplinary continuum of methods often described today as auto/biography (Stanley, 1993) are usually concrete in these senses, too – biography, autobiography, memory work, life history and oral history. Methods adopted from all these sources are found in cultural studies with or without explicit methodological debate (for example, on autobiography, Couldry, 2000; Probyn, 1993). They are discussed in detail in our chapters on specific settings in Part II (the historical, spatial and so on) and particular clusters of method (fieldwork, reading fiction historically and so on). Here, however, we draw attention to two features of these borrowings. First, from the point of view of specialists, they often seem limited – not historical enough for the historians (C. Hall, 1992; Steedman, 1992) or with an ethnography that is particularly thin (Jenson and Pauly, 1997: 165). Second, we can note that these elements are often combined with others. An ethnographic element, for example, may be combined with auto/biography or historical contextualization or, in audience studies, with work on popular media texts.

Methodological combinations, often of an original kind, are a feature of well-known cultural studies texts. Richard Hoggart's *The Uses of Literacy* combined a kind of half-hidden autobiography and strongly literary mode of reading and writing with an intensity of observation and memory work we *could* call ethnographic. *Resistance Through Rituals* is a study of group cultures, but youth subcultures are interpreted, first, by being set within an ambitious account of post-war hegemony in the UK and, second, by being read textually using a structuralist conception of style as a bricolage, a putting together or pasting in of signs from different sources. In this sequence of studies, perhaps only Paul Willis' and, later, Christine Griffin's work is more fully ethnographic (Willis, 1977, 1978, 2000), though Willis' deep debt to Hoggart's literary methods of reading should also be noted. Even in these most concrete examples, we can see the force of Alasuutari's apt description of cultural studies itself as bricolage.

Culture as cultural formations

In a second version of the cultural, culture is not primarily the product and property of a group or class, but, rather, a level or aspect of social practice within the social formation as a whole. It is an aspect of social organization and domination and resistance. Terms such as 'cultural formation' or 'cultural hegemony' are preferred over 'cultures', because they capture the relations between ways of living and the differences *within* them. Cultural formations are complex or composite, relational rather than expressing single identities. They include free-floating elements – 'public' without being wholly 'bourgeois', 'popular' without being simply working class. Theoretically, this version of the cultural involved what Stuart Hall called 'the break into a complex Marxism', itself involving a rethinking of the base-superstructure metaphor (1980a: 25).

While early New Left theory had rejected this metaphor for a more integrated view of group and culture, the new strategy was to value the big picture but rethink the relations of aspects or levels. Especially attractive were those versions of complex Marxism that enlarged the scope for cultural analysis, either by making the ideological more autonomous from other aspects or cultural processes more effective in the whole ensemble of relationships. In the Althusserian language of the 1970s, 'the problematic of Cultural Studies thus became closely identified with the problem of the "relative autonomy" of cultural practices' (Hall, 1980a: 29).

This shift of emphasis was one of those widespread, transdisciplinary changes we noted in Chapter 1. The middle chapters of Williams' *Marxism and Literature* (1977) address the problem of how to describe large-scale cultural formations in their historical movement and in their relations of dominance, subordination and opposition. Similarly, E. P. Thompson's later histories concern eighteenth-century gentry paternalism as a form of hegemony in crisis (1993). In feminist work, the shift from studying the concrete bits of women's lives to tackling larger formations of gendered and other relations was a similar movement. 'Complex Marxism' also involved a revival of interest in theories of ideology so that the concept was stretched and tested well beyond its limits (Barrett, 1991; Centre for Contemporary Cultural Studies (CCCS), 1977; Larrain, 1983; J.B. Thompson, 1984; and see Chapter 8 below). In cultural studies, the new model was clearest empirically in *Policing the Crisis* (Hall et al., 1978) – first of the studies of the emergent New Right formation in the UK, which became known as Thatcherism.

The shift from 'cultures' to 'formations' involved a changed relation to theory. Because they theorized totalities (actually *national* formations) in complex, culture-rich ways, Althusser's Marxist structuralism and Gramsci's *Prison Notebooks* were central (Althusser, 1971; Centre for Contemporary Cultural Studies (CCCS), 1977; Gramsci, 1971). As a theorist, teacher, group worker and researcher, Stuart Hall was the major creative influence in the formation of this second version of cultural studies, but, again, larger historical currents provided the changing agenda. By the late 1970s, the new social movements were discovering the limits of their earlier strategies and meeting resistance from counter-movements of the New Right and neo-liberalism in the UK and the United States especially. Shifts in the agenda of cultural research occurred, in part, as a response to some of the most troubling dilemmas of the time.

'Mapping the field': a method for theories?

To many commentators, then and since, the most obvious methodological change of the 1970s was the heightened importance of theoretical work itself and the relative subordination of concrete studies. Although there was no simple substitution, relatively abstract thinking certainly acquired a new importance and perhaps too great a prestige. In Chapter 5 we explore the resulting dilemmas more fully. Here, however, we can note how theoretical clarification was rarely an end in itself and was usually combined with other aims.

It was most often combined with different kinds of contemporary cultural history or 'mapping'. 'Mapping the field' was a kind of laying out of theoretical frameworks or approaches around a particular topic – approaches to ideology, say, or views of art and politics (see Centre for Contemporary Cultural Studies (CCCS), 1973 for an early example). As theories themselves are cultural products, mapping was *doing* cultural studies, not merely preparing for it. Maps nearly always had an argumentative dimension and commonly explored theoretical tensions – between 'cultural materialism' and structuralism, for example (Hall, 1980a; Johnson, 1979a) – in a non-polemical, syncretizing way. At a time when polemical dismissals were common, this was important (Hall, 1980a, 1981; Johnson, 1978, 1979b, 1981; E. P. Thompson, 1978, 1981).

Mapping has limits, though. If the point of view of map and mapper are not reflected on, such overviews imply an all-seeing eye and can canonize a particular set of texts (Johnson, 1999). It could, however, take many different forms. It could draw close to a Williams-like literary history or a contemporary political history influenced by Gramscian theory. It could resemble the formalism of text-based models typical of structuralism or adopt the argumentative types of mapping of 'problematics' or 'traditions' found in Continental European philosophers such as Althusser (1969) or Gadamer (1989). We will return to allied methods in our discussions of theory (Chapter 5), historical cultural studies (Chapter 7) and text/contexts relationships (Chapter 11 especially).

Mapping differences in a field or formation depends on the willingness of analysts to make a temporary abstraction of the cultural elements that are of most interest. This abstraction enables much closer attention to be paid to the text as the vehicle of the languages, codes or discourses by means of which meaning is produced. A similar abstraction underpins the development of a text-based media and film studies that focuses on the features of particular genres. Theoretically, this move in method was reinforced by the absorption of structuralist and poststructuralist approaches from the Francophone intellectual world and was part of the more general reception of European literary and cultural theory. We will discuss the wide-ranging effects of this linguistic turn in the next section as it marks a further shift of object.

The 'local' redefined and contextualized: other combinations

An apparently contrasting and perhaps deliberately compensating development of the 1970s and 1980s was a concentration on particular cultural 'sites' or institutional spaces. This reshaped the earlier interest in local cultural worlds that were beyond or resistant to the dominant public gaze. Before the development of cultural geography (see Chapter 6), the local was specified not in spatial but social terms – the school as a place of child–adult interactions, for example, or the home as the space of 'the housewife' and her media-related practices. Groups, it was assumed, constructed their own identities within such spaces. The sequence of youth studies, for example, runs from the early subcultural studies (Hall and Jefferson, 1976; Hebdige, 1979; Willis, 1977, 1978) through feminist redefinitions (Griffin, 1985; Angela McRobbie, 1991; Angela McRobbie and Nava, 1984; Roman, Christian-Smith and Ellsworth, 1988) to a concern with masculinities and sexuality (Mac An Ghaill, 1994) and the contemporary interest in new ethnicities in the context of racism (Back, 1994; Hall, 1996a; Mercer, 1994) and global youth debates and movements (Skelton and Valentine, 1998). Much of this sequence can be seen in the work of one researcher, Phil Cohen (for example, 1972, 1993). Exchanges with sociology, some forms of anthropology and cultural geography have been intense. Today it is often impossible to say if studies of youth cultures, cultures of schooling and forms of youth-related consumer culture are researched and written by sociologists, anthropologists, educationalists, geographers or (various kinds of) cultural studies persons.

So far, we have identified two rather different definitions of culture in cultural studies. We have also seen how methods depend on objects or methodologies on ontologies. We have also noted that methods are often combined. It begins to look as though *combination* is *characteristic* of method in cultural studies. It has also been associated with *theoretical* dialogue and the combination of theories, which is one of the aims of mapping.

These syncretic moves can also be seen in media studies within this tradition. Cultural studies of the media almost always refer to social groups, textual genres and, sometimes more implicitly, broader historical contexts (see, for example, Brunsdon and Morley, 1978; Hobson, 1982; Morley, 1980). This is especially true of feminist work on women's genres, an especially generative area for the whole media and cultural studies field (see, for example, R. McRobbie, 1978; Radway, 1984; for a review, van Zoonen, 1994).

A strongly group-specific focus, 'women', remained important through the 1980s, because women and the various relations of gendered power were still persistently absent or marginalized in more universalizing debates. Charlotte Brunsdon has discussed the difficulties of doing work on 'women's genres' in the Centre for Contemporary Cultural Studies (CCCS) at Birmingham University in the mid-1970s and her study of the development of academic interest in soap opera provides many illustrations of the combinations we are identifying (Brunsdon, 2000). The book itself uses reflective autobiography and biography (interviews with key soap opera scholars) as the main method, but sets interest in soap opera within a larger history of feminist repudiation, reinvestigation and re-evaluation of conventional feminine forms. Soap opera studies allowed feminists in the academy to construct and negotiate relations with 'the housewife' or 'ordinary woman' – a figure who inevitably includes aspects of themselves. The book also traces the shift away from essentialist and exclusionary identifications of women, the feminine and the female and engages with the changing place of soap opera and feminism in the lives of new generations of younger women. The study of soaps aimed to explore and uphold female experiences and agency, but it was also the expression of a kind of feminist desire:

> These examples [of the study of soap opera] reveal a different kind of feminist engagement with the texts of femininity. It is not just a recruitist project – an investigation of the pleasures of others. There is a self – a feminist self – to be investigated too. (Brunsdon, 2000: 27)

Brunsdon's book, like the soap opera studies themselves, uses a combined methodology. We stress *combined* here – because the methods are not just used side by side, they are complementary. They include:

- an autobiographical and biographical starting point and continued self-reflection
- an engagement with texts that are significant for the self and group with whom the researcher does or does not identify
- a self-conscious 'historical' setting in place of the whole interaction
- a wish, also, to narrate retrospectively 'the story so far'
- *and* a desire to map – perhaps – the future possibilities.

These are keynotes that we will want to sound out again in Chapter 3.

The critique of 'culture'

The third set of redefinitions of the objects of cultural studies are harder to summarize and still in process. 'Postmodernism' is a possible but too easy heading. In part, an older story continues, a dialogue between two extended research programmes – the cultural materialist positions already described and the programme of structuralism and its 'posts'. As Stuart Hall has argued, structuralism amounted to 'a formative intervention which coloured and influenced everything that followed', but it was not '"a fixed orthodoxy" uncritically subscribed to' (Hall, 1980a: 29). There were tensions between the traditions, but structuralist and other theories provided new languages of complexity, just as complex Marxism was being stretched and tested by changing historical conditions.

Structuralism abstracts and privileges language and language-like cultural forms. Cultural agency, or productivity, is ascribed to the forms through which meaning is signified. Later in this tradition, in Michel Foucault's work especially, discourses and discursive formations are viewed also as the main conduits of power (see, for example, Foucault, 1980; Rabinow, 1984).

The underlying abstraction of such work derives from Saussure's original treatment of language as a structure or system of differences. Poststructuralist theories retain some elements of this but actively rethink the rigid binary schemes of classic structuralism. Language is now theorized as looser, more contingent, more associative and always in process, developing early critiques of Saussure and drawing closer to more dialogic or contextual approaches to language (see, for example, Volosinov, 1973). In poststructuralism, however, cultural forms and conventions remain central: they are the sources of meaning, power and, especially, identity and subjectivity. The question of who produces the discourses, where and how, are rarely posed and questions of human and social agency are left unresolved (compare Couldry, 2000; Probyn, 1993). Here, then, are two colliding intellectual and political histories: the struggle of structuralists with simple human-centred ideas of agency and cultural materialists' recovery of the creative self and agency from mechanical Marxism. No wonder relations have often exploded into polemic!

Structuralist thinking, however, was already a presence in the second 1970s formation of cultural studies – notably in a take-up of Barthes' semiotics of everyday life and the semiologically influenced idea of style in the subculture work (Barthes, 1971, 1972, 1977; Hebdige, 1979) and in the complex Marxism of social formations (Althusser and Balibar, 1970). In its British borrowings, structuralism gave a new importance and clarity to culture as an object. It made it harder to go back to economic determinism or reabsorb culture into everything. Moreover, it showed how power was intrinsic to cultural processes, not just reflected or reinforced in them (see especially Chapter 8). Foucault's arguments about subjectivity and the self – as always constructed in discourse – held immense promise for the development of a cultural psychology compatible with the cultural studies project (Foucault, 1979; Henriques et al., 1984).

As these ideas were being absorbed, political problems were becoming more complex. The new political movements had multiplied political agents and extended the sphere of politics – to the domestic and personal especially. At the same time, the political theories of the time tended to organize struggles into straightforward binaries – class against class, women and men, black and white, gay and straight. It was hard to get 'beyond the fragments' or, more accurately, perhaps, beyond the antagonism and competition between movements. Binary thinking about politics made it hard to see the differences within a single movement or handle relations between movements, each of which claimed priority. In the women's movement – a key locus for these debates – the new theories suggested that the movement had constituted itself as all white, First World and exclusively heterosexual, producing exclusions anew. In the same period, in the academy, class, gender and race-based theories were often placed in intense competition within radical curricula, for want of ways of thinking about them together.

Structuralism and its 'posts' provided new ways of thinking about complexity in this political sense. In particular, it provided ways in which to fundamentally criticize any theory that reduced power to one central location or dynamo. Among the casualties of the critique of essentialist ways of thinking was 'culture' itself, for it implied that ways of life always hold together, are relatively homogeneous, firmly bounded, pure and even organized around an essence or core. Even 'cultural formations', with its concessions to complexity, implies a 'complex unity'. As we noted in Chapter 1, culture in Europe was associated with a more or less explicitly racialized conception of a people, a nation, 'the folk' or '*volk*' (Eickhof, Henkes and van Vree, 2000). This form of cultural essentialism was uncovered in 1980s UK as 'the new racism' (Barker, 1981) and as a white English ethnicity haunting the culture debate (Gilroy, 1987). It has been suggested that it was only the growth of anti-essentialist theories that finally enabled this legacy to be questioned and displaced (Johnson, 2000b: 197–200, 206–7).

So, poststructuralism helped to conceptualize the multiplicity of political subjects, but also, together with psychoanalytical borrowings, deepened thinking about identity and interrelationships. In the old dialectic of social difference, antagonisms were seen as mainly external, one culture or group against another. In the new theories, social identities were seen as deeply relational and internal. The production of a self always involved the production of others, at least partly imaginary and so internal to the self (see, for example, Benjamin, 1990; Bhabha, 1994). The exercise of power was always accompanied by an emotional or psychic labour – expelling the other in fantasy, for example, as well as physically in a real world. Within the older frameworks, too, cultures tended to have relatively fixed and impermeable boundaries. In a world of border-crossing and ambivalence about nations and syncretic cultural activities or mixing and matching, such a theory became a form of oppression in itself, complicit with the policing of ethnicity or nationality (Bhabha, 1994; Brah, 1996; Butler, 1993, 1999; Hall, 1996c). The idea of culture was caught in an interplay of social and intellectual movements. It became a kind of holding term, summing up a tradition, only used perhaps 'where imprecision matters' (Johnson, 1996: 80).

Postmodern fragmentation affected the field of cultural theories, too, with no new dominant paradigm emerging. In this situation, some writers sought new general categories, or simple abstractions to indicate what was distinctive about the cultural – 'the historical forms of consciousness or subjectivity', for instance (Johnson, 1996: 80). Others rethought the cultural as a fluid process of representation and self-composition (Grossberg, 1992; Hall, 1997). Sections of the anglophone academy continued to learn from the extraordinary philosophical creativity of francophone intellectual traditions, especially from the diverse strands of French feminism, the cultural sociology of Pierre Bourdieu and, in a kind of poststructuralist mainstream, many aspects of Michel Foucault's later work. However, the challenge of difference after difference produced, everywhere, a much more fragmented or dispersed cultural model in which metaphors of 'fields' or 'fragments' or 'rhizomes' replaced the idea of a patterned cultural whole. At most, activist cultural analysis became a way of connecting fragments, linking differences – hence, the currency, in the later 1980s and early 1990s, of the key word 'articulation', with its sense of movement in more than one direction (Grossberg, 1992; Hall, 1986; Laclau and Mouffe, 1985). If terms such as 'formation' are still used (for example, 'discursive formation'), stress is laid on their internal differentiation, movement and relative lack of boundaries, rather than the patterning or 'structure' of a knowable whole.

Poststructuralist methodologies?

It is not easy to trace the effects of this shift on forms of cultural study, but two developments seem important for our themes.

First, the (re)turn to language certainly led to a reinforcement of broadly literary and linguistic methodologies in cultural studies – new forms of 'critical textwork', but with a different agenda. In earlier structuralist-influenced work, the focus was on the conventions of a particular genre or mode of cultural production (the literary, cinematographic, photographic and so on) and the ways in which these produced meaning (see Chapter 9). Poststructuralist interventions shifted interest towards the reader or 'subject' of the text, opening up questions of identity and subjectivity in new ways.

Enquiry focused on the subjective dimensions of the cultural, on discourse or performance as self-production (for example, Butler, 1999; Henriques et al., 1984). Both the main streams of postmodern theory – the Foucauldian and the psychoanalytical – centre on subjectivity in this sense, so that the question of culture is increasingly refocused through the lens of individual and collective identities (see, for example, Du Gay, Evans and Redman, 2000; Hall and Du Gay, 1996). Humanness itself is never a given – like sex-gender identity or race and even the body, the last redoubt of the reductively biological, it is always constructed or produced. Within this broad stream of anti-essentialist thinking, two political agendas stimulated both theory and research. The first – which came to be labelled 'post-colonial' – includes both the critical assessment of the cultural legacies of colonialism and Empire in the West and recognition of the cultural creativity of marginalized migrants and diasporic traditions (see, for example, Bhabha, 1994; Brah, 1996; Gilroy, 1993a, 1993b; Hall, 1996c; Said, 1978, 1990; Spivak, 1994). The second – 'queer theory' – centres on criticism of the older binaries of lesbian and gay theory and the taken-for-grantedness of the heterosexual norm (see, for example, Butler, 1993, 1999; Dollimore, 1991; Sedgwick, 1990, 1994). We will look at the strengths and limits of the (broadly literary) methodologies generated by these redefinitions in Chapter 14 especially.

Second, postmodernism has rightly been identified with a change in intellectual ambitions and styles related to the recognition of difference and process. This is seen in the retreat from the macro – indeed epic – ambitions of the 1970s, a moving away from grasping cultures as a whole, for instance. While such ambitions are alive and well in some versions of social theory, cultural analysis has since become more partial, piecemeal and rather pragmatic, often self-consciously so. At the same time, researchers have become preoccupied with their own forms of cultural work, including writing and the representation of others (see Chapter 4).

We experience both losses and liberations in these changes. Attempts at totality produce theories that are hard to break into with new voices or viewpoints. Today's stress on particularity allows for different starting points and frees up intellectual activity, so that projects are easier to begin – and finish. On the other hand, there has been a loss of dialogue and, we would argue, seriousness about intellectual work. This is reinforced by state and corporate control and the marketization of the academy, all of which encourage instrumental attitudes to writing and research. In this context, it is important to continue to make generalizations so they can be challenged and revised. This is why we value the overview as an aspect of method and why we have employed it in this chapter as a way of recognizing partiality and difference – including our own – while mapping changes and seeking links.

Cultural circuits: cultural studies meets hermeneutics

So far we have sought to understand the multiplicity of methods there are by providing a short history of political pressures and changing paradigms, viewed from a methodological angle. Because we recognize multiplicity, there is no grand finale to this chapter. As Stuart Hall has repeatedly urged, each new episode 'repositions' earlier theories without making them redundant (see, for example, 1992). At the same time, we remain dissatisfied with listing methods in an accumulating 'repertoire', as though they had no relation to each other, and had no history of entanglement.

Another way in which to understand difference and combination is to relate the diversity of methods to a more differentiated view of the cultural process. Perhaps methodological differences arise from the cultural process itself. This involves abstracting a general model that fits most cultural instances. Such an approach has been developed in a series of studies based first in Stuart Hall's reading of the Introduction to Marx's *Grundrisse* (his preparatory notebooks for *Capital*), then on an engagement with models of communication (encoding and decoding) and finally in models or 'circuits' of cultural production and consumption (du Gay et al, 1997; Hall, 1973a; Hall, 1973b; Johnson, 1996). A simplified version is shown in Figure 2.1.

All cultural products go through the moments shown in Figure 2.1, though we can start the circuit at different points. The model fits face-to-face exchanges or forms such as television programmes or useful and meaningful objects such as personal hi-fi. Importantly, everyday life is both a starting point (A) and an end

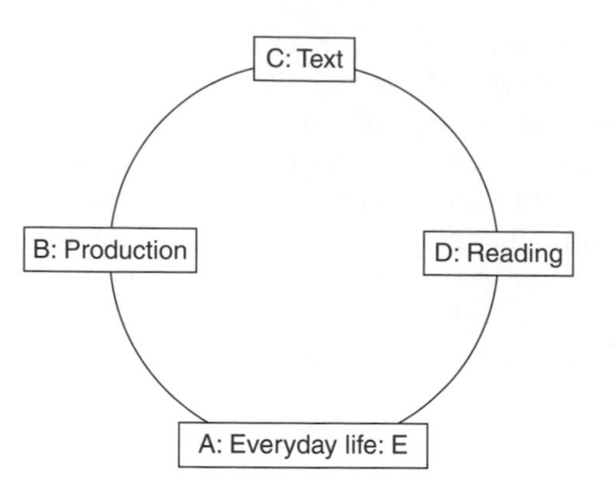

Figure 2.1 Cultural Circuit

point or result (E) of the process. In this model, specialist cultural producers (B) make representations in the forms of texts (C). These are read under definite conditions (D) and have consequences at the level of everyday life (E). There are, however, innumerable cultural circuits, the conditions of which are constantly in process, so they are, perhaps, more spirals than circuits.

This way of thinking is not restricted to cultural studies. As well as paralleling Marx's economic arguments, the circuit model resembles some basic principles of hermeneutics. As Paul Ricoeur puts it.

> It is the task of hermeneutics . . . to reconstruct the set of operations by which a work lifts itself above the opaque depths of living, acting, and suffering, to be given by an author to readers who revise it and thereby change their acting. (1984: 53)

Ricoeur continues by distinguishing hermeneutics from what he sees as the limited agenda of semiotic or structuralist analysis:

> For semiotic theory the only operative concept is that of the literary text. Hermeneutics, however, is concerned with reconstructing the entire arc of operations by which practical experience provides itself with works, authors and readers.

We might add that poststructuralism *is* interested in the reader also, but only as derived from the text, although this may be broadly defined. However, Ricoeur's 'arc' resembles the 'cultural circuit' (see Figure 2.2).

Ricoeur's 'mimesis 1' corresponds to the moment of 'everyday life' in the cultural circuit shown in Figure 2.1. He wants to argue that, before more elaborated acts of representation occur (his mimesis 2), the possibility of representation is present in the 'forms of living' themselves – that is, in the cultural practices of day-to-day activity. In *Time and Narrative*, this is illustrated by the daily experience of time. Everyday living is organized according to the passage of time and so is already narratable in the form of a story of a day, for instance. Storytelling arises from human 'acting and suffering'.

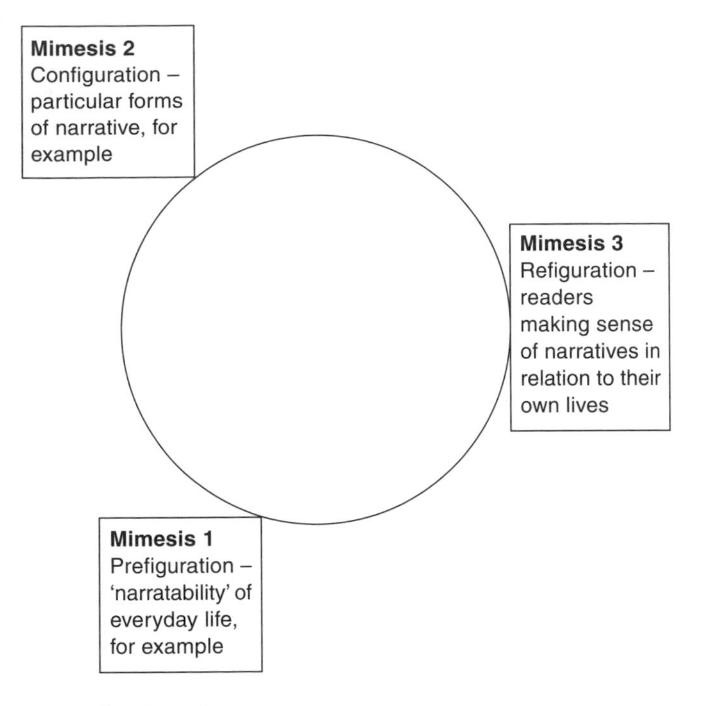

Figure 2.2 Moments in mimesis
(*Source*: Paul Ricoeur, 1984: 52–87)

Ricoeur's second moment – 'mimesis 2' or 'configuration' – resembles the moment of relatively separated cultural production and textual encoding of Figure 2.1. This involves the abstraction of meaning in a separated text and what Ricoeur calls 'schematization' in the language system according to its conventions and genres. Mimesis 2 involves, for example, *specific forms* of narrative (for example, history-writing, literary fiction) as ways of handling time. Ricoeur does not reflect, as we would, on what is lost or suppressed or unsayable in the passage from mimesis 1 to mimesis 2. Unlike Marx or Gramsci or feminist standpoint theorists, he is not concerned with representation as a form of power. For Gramsci, for instance, the distinction between 'common sense' (popular and practically embedded meanings, close to 'mimesis 1') and 'philosophy' (articulated and critical thinking, close to 'mimesis 2') is central to his account of hegemony and counter-hegemonic activity – counter-hegemony being, from this point of view, an educative work with the 'good sense' of popular common sense.

Ricoeur's 'mimesis 3' is termed 'refiguration'. Like most cultural studies writers, he foregrounds the productive work of readers: 'the reader is the operator par excellence' whose practice unifies the three moments of mimesis. Three aspects are involved here: there are traditions of storytelling that are shared between writers and readers; there is the act of reading itself, which revises what the author gives to the reader; and there is the reader's life, which is also changed.

Circuits and methods

The diversity of cultural methods can be grasped anew by means of these accounts of the cultural which are more differentiated and dynamic than those discussed so far. Like Ricoeur, we believe that cultural processes exert pressures on the ways in which they can be represented or researched, so that the diversity of methods is also produced by the forms and complexity of cultural circuits. Culture is not only represented, it is also representable, in particular ways.

The methods associated with 'the way of life' paradigm correspond to the moment when cultural forms are most embedded in the practices of daily life (at A in our own circuit in Figure 2.1 and at 1 in Ricoeur's, shown in Figure 2.2). Here, cultural production is not a separated practice; it is part of the process of ordinary living. Method configures the nature of this moment by resisting abstraction and insisting on concrete contexts, including often a certain authenticity of representation, against silences or misrecognitions in the public sphere. The representational activity of the researchers themselves, however – in the writing of ethnographies, for instance – conforms to the next moment in the circuit – that of a more specialized cultural production with all its power dimensions.

Specialized cultural production occurs on top of daily practices, selecting for power and significance. This is the standpoint of the artist, cultural organizer or politician, the media professional – and cultural researcher. They are all 'intellectuals' in Gramsci's expanded sense, because they work on and with common sense by representing it publicly. This involves a certain abstraction and 'schematization', which analysts of the local and concrete are right to suspect, but cannot themselves avoid. Representation or 'configuration' (Ricoeur) always adds, selects and transforms. At this moment (B/C or 2 in the diagrams), cultural production and the text that is its product becomes more separated and specialized. The forms of study are also more abstract, concentrating typically on cultural specialists and their products. The study of emergent hegemonic formations, of law-and-order moral panics in *Policing the Crisis*, for example, identified typical agents of hegemony (such as public media, police, the judiciary, political parties) as well as the cultural formations themselves (forms of racism and moral traditionalism, say).

Methods that describe cultural formations also depend on the abstraction involved in producing texts. This allows for an emphasis on the *language* of the text or 'the statement', as though the text says something of itself. This useful illusion is possible because the producer and the conditions of production are rendered absent. As we have seen, however, in poststructuralism, the analyst's concerns move the other way round the circuit, to the pressures that texts put on readers. The text is still central here. This kind of analysis does not start from a concrete reader as it is the reader in and of the text that fascinates the structuralist critic, not what readers bring to texts from their everyday lives.

Other forms of analysis, however, concentrate on the act and context of reading. The many forms of audience or reception study, for example, do just this (for useful discussions, see Ang, 1996; Brunsdon, 2000; Morley, 1986, 1992; and Chapter 14).

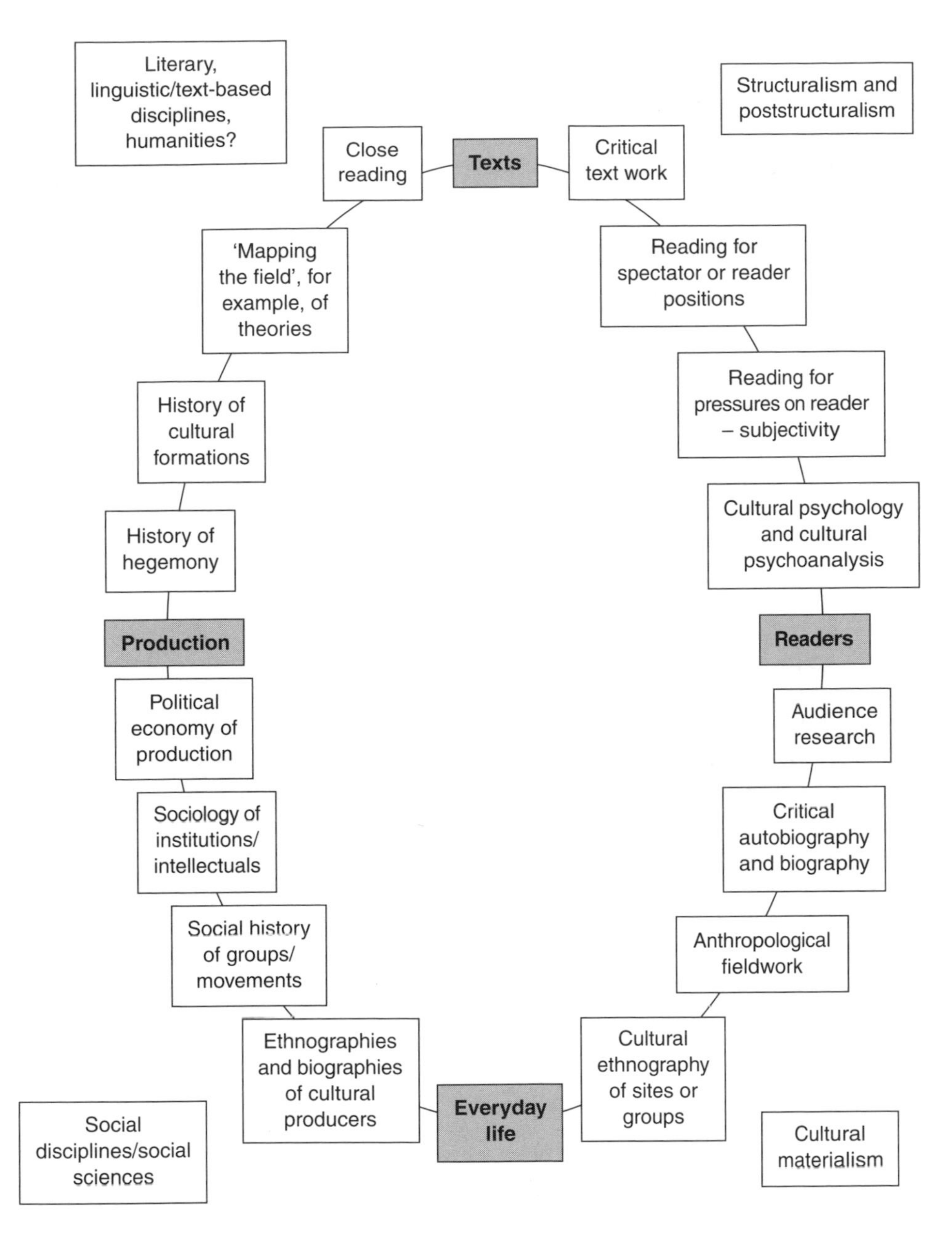

Figure 2.3 The cultural circuit and cultural methods

Audience research may link text and readership by exploring how particular kinds of texts – television soap operas, women's magazines – are consumed by particular kinds of audiences or interrogate how such audiences are produced. In cultural studies, while attention may shift away from the medium itself and towards the everyday lives of users, the text itself remains important in giving clues for lived themes – spelt out more explicitly there, perhaps, than in interviews or conversations. Thus, emergent issues in women's lives have been explored by means of new trends in readership, just as attitudes and assumptions about girls' sex education may be illuminated by exploring their use of magazines (Epstein and Johnson, 1998; Tincknell, van Loon and Hudson, 2003).

Our 'realist' thesis – that the plurality of methods is related to the complexity of the cultural process – can be illustrated in one last way: by trying to map the full range of cultural methods (not just in cultural studies) on to a version of our circuit. This is an illustrative exercise only and we won't explain all our terms, but hope most readers can position their projects and methods somewhere on Figure 2.3.

Conclusion: combined and multiple methods?

We have argued that a multiplicity of methods is necessary because no one method is intrinsically superior to the rest and each provides a more or less appropriate way of exploring some different aspect of cultural process. Our analysis also implies that all methods have limits. If stretched beyond them, they mislead. Cultural analysts rightly resist the implication that the meaning of a text to a reader can be inferred from the conditions of its first production, especially from the fact that it is a mass-produced commodity. This stretches a political economy of production beyond its competence. Similarly, textual analysis of a media form cannot yield an account of production conditions, nor should we infer the way of life of a particular group from its public representation.

Yet, we also want to insist that methods always explore a system of connections and relations and so are themselves connected. The fact that a text is also a commodity, produced under capitalist conditions, is *relevant* to the way we and others read it. Texts themselves, as well as having an abstract form, are an aspect of a larger socio-cultural practice. Is it necessary, then, for every research project to research every moment in the circuit? (This is a question that is often asked by anxious student researchers.) Must an account of a television chat show, for instance, always include research on its audience and their daily lives? This is not possible in every study and not all lines of questioning require it, but *a theoretical awareness* of other moments and methods should inform the research design and the representation of findings – always. Furthermore, methods are often most productive when their rules and conventions are transgressed or combined – when we use close textual analysis to analyse face-to-face exchanges, for instance.

We can conclude that not only do we need a multiplicity of methods but we also need dialogue and exchange between them and, therefore, between different methodologies, disciplines and paradigms. This is a general requirement, perhaps, for intellectual work in our times, but, as we have also suggested throughout this chapter, methodological combination is a key to cultural studies method more generally. Elaborating this point is a concern of Chapter 3.

3 Method and the researching self

'Inside culture': cultural research as a cultural circuit 44
Objectivism, self and other 46
From 'standpoint' to 'positionalities' 48
Making claims to truth: conventions and truthfulness 50
Is truth only a convention then? 51
'Reflexivity' versus the confessional 52
Realizing reflexivity: social, spatial, temporal and cultural aspects 53
Dialogue and difference 57
Accountability and responsibilities 59
Conclusion: the logic of combination 60

In this chapter we seek to outline an overall orientation to cultural research, a method in the broader sense. This method both locates the self firmly in the practice of research and provides a context within which each of the methods we discussed in Chapter 2 can find a place. Although such combination is commonplace in cultural studies, it is rarely discussed in methodological terms. We therefore find resources in two adjacent philosophies – hermeneutics and feminist political epistemologies, in interpretive and critical-political traditions respectively.

This chapter offers a dialogue with these two traditions. It starts from the character of cultural enquiry, theorized as a cultural process itself, moves through a discussion of the ways in which self-awareness and self-reflexivity are part of the research process and develops an outline for a method for cultural studies as we currently see it.

'Inside culture': cultural research as a cultural circuit

We agree with Nick Couldry (2000) that, as cultural researchers, we are 'inside' our object of study, fully and intimately. Cultural research is cultural through and through. All research starts out from what Hans-Georg Gadamer calls our 'prejudices' or more neutrally, our 'fore-meanings' (Gadamer, 1989: 265–71; and see Chapter 1 above). These 'fore-meanings' are both personal and come from larger historical traditions. The prejudice for discussing culture in relation to power is a case in point: it reflects both the traditions of cultural studies and our own concerns as researchers. Yet, 'fore-meanings' and 'prejudices' are rather limited ways of describing the cultural starting points of research, just as tradition – another of Gadamer's keywords – is insufficient to express all our involvements in the past, present and future (see Chapter 7). As poststructuralist theories suggest, we are actively constituted as knowing subjects by the theories and discourses we work with – which, in a sense, work us. We come to our topics with a particular biography, a path through many formations of culture and identity. As Gramsci most memorably put it, 'The starting point of critical elaboration is the consciousness of what one really is, and is "knowing thyself" as a product of the historical process to date which has deposited in you an infinity of traces, without leaving an inventory' (1971: 324).

Our 'topic', as we define and study it, is entangled in this cultural biography, but also exists as a Figure 3.1 Cultural research as a cultural circuit Figure 3.1 Cultural research as a cultural circuit cultural process outside of it. All objects of research put their own pressures on the methods of enquiry, though this may be in different ways. Beyond this, culture is a condition and a saturating medium of the enquiry itself, as well as being something that is changed by the whole transaction. When communicating discoveries to others, we also employ means of cultural representation and communication – typically of writing. Our topic thus keeps folding back on us, enveloping us again and again. We research culture by cultural means and this 'we' is itself already produced in culture and again in the writing. So, to Gadamer's proposition that a proper 'historical consciousness' must 'think within its own historicity', we can add the further suggestion to think within our own 'culturality' (Passerini, Fridenson and Niethammer, 1998). Also, because of these entanglements, we can represent cultural research as itself being a cultural circuit (see Figure 3.1).

This version of the circuit combines insights from hermeneutics and cultural studies (see Figures 2.2 and 2.3 in Chapter 2 above). Here (and more substantively in Parts III and IV), we concentrate on the central empirically-based

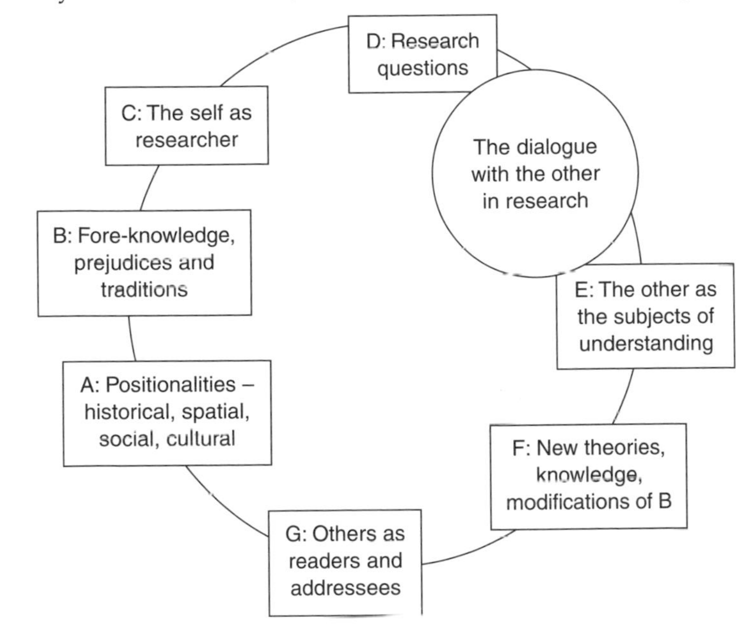

Figure 3.1 Cultural research as a cultural circuit

dialogue of researching, represented here as the circuit within the circuit. This is the dialogue between the researcher's questioning (C and D) and their sources (E) – a relationship theorized in hermeneutics as that between self and other or between an 'I' and a 'thou'. This 'otherness' may apply to a person, text, another country or historical period, but research always involves such a dialogue between the self and a thou. It is this 'alterity' that makes understanding necessary and self-questioning possible.

We have noted how hermeneutics does not tackle social difference, pitching its categories at the level of a universal human nature. The first moment in our circuit (A) is intended as a reminder that social difference and power (summarized here by the word 'positionalities' – explained later) are active right round the circuit, not only in the relations between researchers and researched, but also in those with our readers (G), who may be academic colleagues, teachers and examiners, certainly, but also, perhaps, sponsors, policymakers, community groups. Expectations and pressures around readership feed back round the circuit, influencing choice of topic, methods of research and ways of writing. The issue of who and what our research is *for* thus affects the research process from the beginning.

In this chapter, we focus on the researching self, who is always 'somewhere in particular' (Haraway, 1991: 196). Thoughtfulness about the relationships between researcher, researched and addressee (the reader of the research) has been a marked feature of cultural studies. It connects, however, with concerns that are everywhere in today's intellectual practice.

Objectivism, self and other

Until quite recently, the way in which research practice focused on the other involved creating 'it' as an 'object' for research, separated from the researching subject, whose character and positioning might not figure at all. This corresponded to the impersonality of academic writing, with its deletion of 'I' and preference for the passive mood. The removal of the researching self from the frame, and the separation of 'self' from 'other', stems from a belief in an objective world 'out there' that can be split off from the researchers' lives and values (Guba and Lincoln, 1994; Morrow, 1994: 53–6). Some elements of this epistemology derive from the scientific revolution in seventeenth-century Europe (Haraway, 1997: 23–9), while other themes are more recent. The splitting off of 'objective', 'rational' science from 'emotional', 'romantic' or 'idealistic' politics has been part of an understandable, but far from innocent, defence against political control, deployed against Nazi strategies for the academy and against control of intellectual life under official communism for example (Eickhof, Henkes and van Vree, 2000). It was also used, very ambiguously, by Cold War 'liberals' against left-wing dissidents in the West. 'Science for its own sake' can still seem attractive today in the face of government regulation and the marketization of the academy.

Since the 1960s, however, the idea that science and politics can be split has been increasingly criticized and the embedding of knowledge in power and culture increasingly stressed. Feminist debates have been particularly important here – not least because they were also a target for other epistemological claims, especially those of sexual minorities and Third World, black and diasporic groups (see, for example, Butler, 1999; Spivak, 1988). There is also a large body of work that, using different strategies, seeks to decolonialize research by disrupting the 'othering' process (see, for example, Bhabha, 1994; hooks, 1991; Said, 1978; Spivak, 1988; West, 1988).

Self–other relations in research take many forms, always with a psychic dimension. The researching self can express desires for the other – to merge with, to possess, to be like our objects of research – or it can take a critical distance from its others – making an 'us' against a 'them'. Researching what you hate is not uncommon. The other can even be a simpler version of the 'self' – what 'we' used to be but left behind (a developmental approach) or a 'real' us recovered. Research can be posited on a universalizing stance, in which the other is, or should be, like 'us' really. At best, perhaps, it can involve a reflective and self-transforming struggle to recognize power and differences and align ourselves politically.

Importantly, 'objectivity' is itself a form of self–other relations, still pervasive in 'science', although it is hardly recognized as such:

> There is a kind of experience of the Thou that tries to discover typical behaviour in one's fellow men and can make predictions about others on the basis of experience . . . If we relate this form of the I-Thou relation . . . to the hermeneutical problem, the equivalent is naive faith in method and in the objectivity that can be obtained through it. Someone who understands tradition in this way makes it an object – i.e. he confronts it in a free and uninvolved way – and by methodically excluding everything subjective he discovers what it contains. (Gadamer 1989: 358)

For Gadamer, to deny prejudice is to allow it to operate behind our backs with greater force (1989: 360). At the same time, he is also suspicious of empathy or imaginative recreation. 'Understanding', by comparison, recognizes the impossibility of *knowing* the other, but listens, taking on something of the reality of what is *said*. In this process, the 'I' is changed. This is close to what Michelle Fine, reviewing the contemporary debate, has called 'working the [self–other] hyphen' (Fine, 1994: 72). Gadamer also insists – and we agree – that the 'I: Thou relation' is not simply between persons, but is always mediated by language and cultural form. It is not the person we listen to exactly, but the truth of the saying (Gadamer, 1989, especially Part 3).

This degree of conscious involvement with the other of research is very different from the attitude of detachment towards society and its history that scientific objectivity prescribes. Such subjective entanglement is seen as a negative source of 'researcher bias', which undermines claims to scientific authority. This authority thus depends on what Donna Haraway calls 'modest witness'. So 'modest' are the knowledge producers that they are supposed to be crystal-clear mirrors of nature. As researchers, we are supposed to 'contain ourselves', and subordinate our emotions to reason. This 'objectivist' stance is connected, historically, with the production of gendered and racialized differences in Enlightenment thought. Haraway explores how the English gentlemen of the scientific revolution constructed their quest for knowledge as a specific form of white masculinity involving a 'culture of no culture' in which being transparent, civil, manly and rational was opposed to the feminine, the unruly and the dark (1997: 23–39).

Although the new epistemologies have shifted the ground of debate in social science, their reception has been uneven and contested, so being 'too subjective' can still be a disqualification. We have been told ourselves that cultural studies is 'only autobiography' and needs 'a more secure basis'. Much current concern with methodology within cultural studies arises from similar anxieties. Students sometimes express fears of being thought not to be doing 'proper research' when working with popular texts especially and interdisciplinary work can still be vulnerable to rigidly disciplinary examination.

One of the difficulties here lies in the persistence of the belief that rules of science can be applied generally despite the difference of objects and research aims. Objectivist assumptions continue to underlie much social science method, often as a kind of hidden standard. It is frequently assumed that there are technical solutions to researcher bias, such as good pilot-testing, avoidance of leading questions and random or accurately targeted sampling techniques. These criteria, however, derive from very specific methods with very specific aims, especially from extensive questionnaire-based surveys. These have some value in cultural analysis – even public opinion surveys can be critically (re-)interpreted. However, such methods construct the cultural *only* in terms of individualized opinions or preferences. Cultural studies treats culture as a structure or formation that goes beyond, but embraces, individual subjectivities. Large-scale questionnaires also require cut-and-dried answers so that results can be quantified, thus suppressing the complexity, ambivalence and multiplicity of viewpoints that a more conversational approach will evoke. Being a 'don't know' is the only way to express ambiguity. Finally, although surveys individualize opinion, they also construct it as a finished public discourse – they cannot tap into the layers of what is sayable and not sayable in different contexts. More generally, such methods imply that cultural determinations are unimportant or culture can be corrected for in some way. In hermeneutic terms, objectivism denies the reality of 'the life world' with all its subjective elements.

From 'standpoint' to 'positionalities'

Critical traditions concerned with knowledge and power add further themes to this 'interpretative' critique. Many of the arguments in feminist standpoint theory – our major interest here – derive from Marx and Engels' writing on ideology and from their insistence that the social position(s) and material interest(s) of the knower limit or shape what can be known (Larrain, 1983). Nancy Hartsock (1985) outlines other features of 'standpoint' theories. These are that different social standpoints are opposed or antagonistic; the socially powerful have the means to circulate their version of reality among disenfranchised others; this dominant vision is played out in the material practices in which everyone participates; and subordinated groups construct different versions of social reality arising out of their own situated experiences. The viewpoint of oppressed or subordinated groups is seen as generating superior insights that challenge the dominant. Standpoint theories insist that there are always dual or multiple versions of reality and hegemonic versions and taken-for-granted knowledges are limited and self-interested. Above all, by validating alternative visions, standpoint theories direct attention to *how* cultural dominance is secured.

Obviously, standpoint theory questions objectivity. As knowledge is always 'situated' (Haraway, 1991b), the claim to objectivity is seen as disguising or magically transcending the necessary limits of any viewpoint. It is 'the god-trick of seeing everything from nowhere' (1991a: 187). Just as Gadamer insists that knowledge is finite and within a given horizon, so Haraway insists on the 'partiality' of all knowledge. Yet, feminist critics of 'normal science' also take knowledge very seriously, while differing on the basis of claims to a new or 'successor' science.

Some versions lay claim to a new science that transcends the social determinations of ideology and is guaranteed by a correspondence with the consciousness of the oppressed. This preserves key elements of ideology theory, but substitutes women for the working class as the politically and epistemologically privileged category (see, for example, MacKinnon, 1982). These claims have some quite negative implications, however. They sideline the role of critical thinking and, ultimately, study and research. They subsume many differences into universal political categories – 'women', 'proletarian' or 'black', for instance. In the debates about these versions, women whose experiences did not fit white and Western versions of womanhood soon developed their own critiques of this assumed standpoint.

Yet, it was also argued that it was *reflection* on personal life and subjectivity and a *recognition* of partiality that made a successor science possible, especially if self-reflection was linked to dialogue with others. This argument was strengthened by the general cultural turn and those developments in identity theory that also affected cultural studies (see above). 'Positionality' was the term used (invented, perhaps) to capture, better than 'standpoint', the multiplicity and movement of identities and power, especially in relation to knowledge. There are many axes along which knowledges are formed in relation to many others, in antagonism and/or dialogue. Subjugated or marginalized points of view do not automatically carry superior knowledge, but, as a sense of partiality is forced on them, they are more likely starting points for creativity, insight or even a new kind of 'objectivity'. Critical theories and educational processes, however, also matter. As Haraway puts it 'there is a premium on establishing *the capacity to see* [our emphasis] from the peripheries and the depths' (1991: 191).

A further feature of positionality is that it involves the body and knowledge as embodied (Haraway, 1991: 200–1). The body is a locus of perceiving as well as a point of orientation. New theorizations in the anthropology of the body and its place within research practice help to overcome the shortcomings of the mind–body split involved in older conceptions of reason. This 'new' body, involved in knowledge, is itself culturally mediated. It is both the result of cultural sedimentation, of a history of meanings and practical modifications, and a source of knowing because bodily experiences – what our 'bodies-in-the-making' (Haraway, 1997: 295) can do and can feel – shapes knowledge, too.

We have travelled a long way from the modest witness of orthodox science and some reductive tendencies in standpoint theory. The new epistemologies urge on us the thoughtful recognition of our partiality and all our forms of social participation. The researchers' own positions in relation to the researched are also complex; they are not always in all respects the most powerful parties in the process, for instance. When research and (self-)education are brought so close, the aims and methods of projects are liable to shift. Researchers need more than a map of the field, they need an itinerary of where to go, an itinerary that can be revised. This orientation to knowledge can clarify the cultural studies project, but has implications for *all* aspects of research, including our claims to truth.

Making claims to truth: conventions and truthfulness

All researchers need to convince their readers of the significance and credibility of their findings. This question of truth claims is linked to matters of method. A common issue in assessment situations (in a PhD viva, for instance) is how far our methods have matched our aims and claims. We convince others, in part, by showing them that we have pursued an enquiry in a systematic and *appropriate* way. The expectations that a method will be appropriate to its object and our procedures will be clearly explained are basic in any assessment and rest on criteria shared by different epistemological positions.

A *cultural* analysis of the question of truth claims, however, must draw attention to the conventions or underlying rules (Kuhn, 1970). Contrary to one common ideal, 'the truth' does not simply establish itself. Truth*s* – rather than 'the truth' – cannot be established outside of the conventions that define them and give them legitimacy. Nor are all truth claims equal. Making truth claims is easier where there are means of legitimization that have been supported over a long period within a knowledge community. Most social science disciplines have rules of this kind, summed up, for example, as 'reliability', 'validity' and 'representativeness'. Cultural studies conventions are looser – or perhaps just more implicit.

In the methodological literature, it is common to distinguish between different approaches to truth claims – namely, the 'empirical', 'interpretative' and 'critical'. Cultural studies straddles all three sets of conventions. It is 'interpretative', with affinities to hermeneutics, because understanding our own and others' life worlds is a central commitment. The stress on power, however, aligns cultural studies with critical traditions – with Marxism and feminism, for example. Here, 'interpretation' is not enough: *why* is the world experienced so and with what effects? Research is seen, moreover, as political activity, an intervention in the situation studied and knowledge about it. Research is practice, or praxis in the strongest sense, aimed at social betterment or emancipation and seeking to overcome the splits between the subjects and objects of research and between science and politics. As Gramsci put it, 'each one of us changes himself . . . to the extent that he changes and modifies the complex relations of which he is the hub'. So that the 'real philosopher' (in the wider sense of knower) is the politically active person (Gramsci has 'man') who changes 'the *ensemble* of relations which each of us enter to take part in' (1971: 352). Finally, cultural studies engages in critical dialogues with many aspects of the empirical tradition. On the one hand, an interest in cultural determinations fosters a questioning attitude to the empirically obvious and the taken-for-granted. On the other, cultural studies has, as a tradition, been strongly empirical, attentive to and engaged with what is there. Methods of detailed observation and close reading have been important. The idea of a dialogue with the otherness of our sources, borrowed from hermeneutics, becomes a way of translating into more appropriate terms the familiar empiricist distinction between the hypothesis and the facts. Just as facts may falsify or extend our theories, so the dialogue with the other can challenge our preconceptions.

Is truth only a convention then?

This is a question that is often put to cultural analysts from empirical or realist positions. One way of replying is by defining more carefully what is meant by 'conventional'. Conventions are not fixed or sacrosanct. Making claims to truth is an active process. It engages with established truths and practices of legitimating them, challenging them and pursuing alternatives. All claims to knowledge are subject to competing interpretations, assent from some and dissent from others. There are always dissenting voices, pointing to the 'untruthfulness' of particular claims, challenging the conventions themselves and potentially cheering us on. Legitimating truths involves engaging with different positions, making alliances, marshalling support. We can also use disagreements, as we are using them here, to develop our own arguments. Making the best case within existing conventions, we can also stretch or break the conventions themselves. Are there conventions for breaking conventions, too? Perhaps. Our advice would be threefold: thoroughly know the conventions and show you know them before you break them; always seek allies, predecessors or analogous cases; and always have or give good reasons for doing things differently.

Although conventions change and are contested, they are not as trivial as the everyday connotations of 'conventional' suggests. The force of convention differs – there are stronger or weaker conventions, ones that are harder or easier to change. A thesis or dissertation, for example, may not need to have a specific chapter that reviews the secondary literature in your field of study (a weaker convention sometimes insisted on by supervisors), but work that does not show appropriate knowledge of the field (a strong convention) is open to criticism.

Showing that you know the field is vital where claims to originality are made, as in a PhD thesis.

Although we always need conventions to make a case, no set of conventions ever exhausts the truth question. We only have conventional measures of truth, just as we only have languages and other sign systems with which to represent the world. Conventions are like partiality and positionality – they are basic conditions of knowing. Truth claim conventions are another example of how embedded our practices are in our cultural object of study. However, this doesn't mean that we are anything other than serious in making claims to truthfulness or that truthfulness is a less than important value – indeed, it is, perhaps, the most important value a researcher can avow. We make claims to truth, but truthfulness also makes claims on us. In fact, truthfulness will always make claims on us that go beyond whatever the established conventions of truth might be. This is because these conventions, too, are partial and positional, limited by the horizons of the contemporary academy, for example. We make progress by recognizing the incompleteness of our procedures and the need for alternatives and supplements. Truthfulness, as a value, lies, in part, in recognizing the conventionality of current knowledges and seeking to go beyond it.

So, what might be the conventions that define a cultural studies method? As a start, we abstract three criteria from the anti-objectivist traditions reviewed so far:

- a thorough-going version of *reflexivity*
- a commitment to *dialogue* across major differences
- a particular view of the researchers' *accountability*.

'Reflexivity' versus the confessional

'Reflexivity' is a key word in contemporary methodological debates, but has different meanings (see the review in Marcus, 1994). One version starts with objectivist conceptions of knowledge and departs only briefly from these assumptions. Objectivity can be restored with properly self-reflexive procedures – that is, knowing our partialities enables us to correct our biases. Alternatively, reflexivity *informs our readers* of our partialities, so that *they* can make any necessary corrections.

The recognition of partialities and positionalities is important as a condition for openness and dialogue. Explicitness about relevant aspects of our self-positioning is important when addressing readers. Yet, if our arguments here about partiality and cultural entanglement are correct, it is not possible to transcend these conditions. There is no all-seeing godlike position available to us, no stance free from society, culture and power. This applies to everyone. We can, however, recognize *existing* forms of partiality and advance, by dialogue especially, beyond them, arriving at better, *but still partial*, knowledges. We are sceptical about attempts to restore objectivity, including claims to a second or 'strong objectivity' within critical epistemologies. Belief in objectivity seems inconsistent with cultural understanding and sociological insight. Instead, we prefer to think of various forms of distancing, estrangement or depersonalization, which do have a role in research.

A limited reflexivity can, however, encourage gestures and unpersuasive rhetoric. Relevant autobiographical features appear at the beginning of a thesis or book, never to surface again. The researcher's fore-knowledges and prejudices are confessed to but are not risked or changed. The personal voice does not guarantee that this 'I' or 'we' has given any thought to the limits of its horizons. Using 'I' insistently and without variation *can* testify to an unwillingness to learn and change.

When we refer to reflexivity, then, we are not referring to autobiography as personal confession or revelation. Self-reflection has to be about society, culture and history as well as biography. It is about others as well as the self. It is about the cultural forms we live by, that structure experience. It is about Gramsci's 'ensemble of relations'. It is about how relations of power and inequality are negotiated, represented and changed in the living. It is about the cultural forms and strategies (narratives, for instance) that autobiographers and biographers use to represent themselves within the moment of writing. Moreover, if reflexivity is about positionality and difference, we cannot lay down a general rule in favour of self-revelation. For example, it is easier, in most circumstances, for heterosexual men and women to be open about intimate relationships than for lesbians or gay men or those with bisexual, transexual or transgender experiences. At the same time, there are strategies of 'coming out' as a form of empowerment that are relevant to reflexivity in research. All we can say here is that absolute subjectivity or telling all is *not* always the answer to the objective stance!

These negative arguments suggest ways of realizing reflexivity more fully. These include awareness of the different aspects of positionality and a recognition of subjectivity as a resource in the research process – a resource, however, that is often tied up with a willingness to risk change.

Realizing reflexivity: social, spatial, temporal and cultural aspects

Social

The most familiar dimension of reflexivity in the research literature is social. How are we positioned socially in relation to the topics and subjects of our research? In what power relations especially? As we have seen, debates in critical epistemology have moved away from identifying single standpoints that grant automatic privileges in knowing. Social positionalities are multiple, complex, subject to change and very specific.

This specificity is clear from the autobiographical and biographical notes we wrote for each other early in this project. From them, we could describe our differences with brutal simplicity: three women, one man; three white English, one Indian; all middle class. This doesn't catch, however, the histories involved in being the daughter of a geographically mobile Indian Civil Service family

(Parvati) or the son of an ambitious first-generation Hull businessman sent to boarding school at the age of eight (Richard). It would not catch the contradictions of the East end of London yet also diplomatic family origins (Deborah) or specificity of lower middle class rurality (Estella) or the relatively settled lives of two of us against the others' migrations. Our common feature is specific, too – our different educational paths from the (relative) margins to a (relative) centre in the shape of jobs in the new (and relatively subordinated) sector of the predominantly white English academy!

In published debates, the older argument that subordinated knowledges do not engage with dominant ideologies has shifted to recognition of the insights gained, the 'partialities' often cruelly enforced, in lives lived in marginalized social positions. The accounts of Patricia Hill Collins, bell hooks and others have shown, for example, the complex positionalities of black women in the USA in 'domestic service' (Collins, 1990; hooks, 1981, 1984, 1991). From this point of view, white households are known from the inside, but, in the context of multiple positions, including the bars of colour, class and race. Being black or Asian and living in an old imperial metropolis or thinking with or against European philosophical traditions produces a similar double consciousness and possibilities for creativity and syncretism in popular culture and intellectual work (Brah, 1996; Gilroy, 1992; Hall, 1996a; Mercer, 1994). Though linked relations of ethnicity, nationality, gender and race have produced so much of the new thinking about self–other relations, being born into a working-class family but becoming middle-class by education and occupation, being a 'scholarship girl or boy', usually but not always white, has also been especially generative for cultural understanding (see, for example, Hoggart, 1957; Steedman, 1986; Walkerdine, 1997). All these positionalities involve social and cultural subordinations in which experience of difference has not been voluntary. The work produced has also had profound implications for those occupying more centred social positions and researchers who have chosen to study critically topics such as 'Englishness', 'whiteness', 'masculinity', 'heterosexuality' and (a still rare one this) 'elite' (as opposed to hegemonic) cultures. 'Looking back' and 'writing back' to such experiences or producing an 'oppositional gaze' have become powerful and pervasive metaphors for insight in critical epistemologies and accounts of radical educational philosophy (see, for example, Hall, 1997; Haraway, 1991: 183–201; hooks, 1992: 115–31). Learning to 'see from below' and notice your own complicities in systems of power are generative challenges, rarely wholly separate from individual lives.

Temporal and spatial

The social aspects of difference are so insistent today that other forms of positionality – our temporal positioning, for instance – are sometimes neglected. Our consciousness is formed in memory, anticipation and attentiveness to present projects (Ricoeur, 1984). As Gadamer argues, the beginning of understanding is consciousness of the traditions that form our fore-knowledges. Much of *Truth and Method* deals with the consequences of the temporal separation of researcher and researched. Gadamer is particularly critical of 'historicism' and 'romantic hermeneutics' – strategies that have sought to understand a historical period, work or author on its own terms (1989: 173–242) precisely because they exclude the researcher and the researcher's own times as part of the dialogue of reflexive researching. Again, we find that a 'disadvantage' – here temporal distance – turns out to be a *necessary condition* of knowing and, then, a way of knowing better. Chapter 7 looks more closely at this historical reflexivity.

The rise of a cultural geography and the reflexive turns in anthropology and European ethnology have focused attention on a third form of reflexivity: the geographical or spatial placings of the researcher and researched (Clifford and Marcus, 1986; Harvey, 1989; Jackson, 1989; Massey, 1994; Chapter 6 below). Cultural formations have a geographical scope and location and researchers need to understand in what kind of local world they stand and *where* they are related, in social space–time, to the others they research. Sensitivity to *relationships* between dominant and subordinated spaces is especially important in a postcolonial world.

The (qualified) dominance of Western knowledge beyond its spatial centres is a prime example of the need for such awareness. Fortmann (1996) describes how, when asked to use their own words to describe their local environment, young children in a small community in Zimbabwe paraphrased a school textbook on trees produced in the UK. She argues that this represented the legacy of British colonialism and an educational system based on memorizing 'official' knowledge. The children gave validity to an inappropriate written text even in oral recounting. She had to begin again, asking the children to write under headings such as 'what my grandmother told me about the forest trees' and 'how I feel about the forest'. Fortmann published the articles that the children then wrote as the 'Foxfire Book' and distributed copies throughout the school. This story illustrates the extraordinary transpositions of knowledges in space and power relationships and the purposeful efforts needed to grasp these asymmetries and intervene in them. It also shows how one author or teacher can turn apparently limiting experiences of geographically based inequality and power into a resource.

Cultural

We have already discussed the circumstances that make our fourth form, *cultural* reflexivity, so important. Our own entanglement in culture is one of our most powerful resources when studying culture. It is also a reason why narrowly 'social' views of power and difference (such as standpoint theory) are not enough. While there is always a relationship between 'social being' and 'social consciousness', 'consciousness' cannot simply be derived from 'being'. Whether we are in subordinated, hegemonic or complicit social positions, seeing critically is something we have to learn.

Another way of viewing this cultural entanglement is in terms of 'subjectivity'. This term is used in contemporary cultural theory to mark the effects – on consciousness, performance or (in the psychoanalytical sense) fantasies – of the images, narrative and other signs that make up any cultural formation.

Approaching reflexivity via subjectivity has been pursued by critical psychologists interested in poststructuralist theory (see, for example, Henriques et al., 1984; Hollway, 1989; Probyn, 1993; Walkerdine, 1990, 1997). Valerie Walkerdine, a critical psychologist interested in education and popular culture, has argued persuasively for a fully self-*reflexive* method in its stronger sense. She sees both fantasy (in its psychoanalytical sense) and the capacity for self-reflection as elements in *all* forms of 'subjectification' or self-making. This allows her to make two linked points. First, the importance of paying close attention to the *everyday* reflexivity of the researched, in the form of self-awareness or irony, and, second, the need to recognize that researchers are entangled in fantasies of their own. Criticizing the projection of psychoanalytical ideas about ways of seeing on to popular audiences – such as in some film theory – she argues for the complex play of selves and others in which researcher identities, too, are risked:

> What is disavowed in such approaches is the complex relation of 'intellectuals' to 'the masses': 'our' project of analysing 'them' is itself one of the regulative practices which produce *our* subjectivity as well as theirs. We are each other's other – but not on equal terms. (1990: 199–200)

We found the same stress on power and interrelated desires in Charlotte Brunsdon's account of feminists researching soap opera and its 'ordinary woman' audiences. Such an insight seems easier where there is a good deal of shared ground between researchers and researched.

Reflexivity, then, involves acknowledging the limits and specificity of the social, temporal, spatial and subjective horizons of all research, including our own. In its stronger version, it also involves subjecting the position of the knower to the same critical reflection as that of the objects of the study – who, in turn, have their own projects of self-production. It involves asking who we are as researchers and why we are doing this work. It also involves attending to the conditions under which we engage in dialogue with others, not only listening to what they tell us but also recognizing their own reflexivity in response to our presence.

A further insight, however, envisages partialities not as limits only but as opportunities, not as difficulties but as resources. Participation in the social world provides us with questions, relevant observations, memories. Even complicity in cultural forms and institutions can offer powerful clues to their subjective workings – as dominant, popular or exclusive, for example. We can therefore see how self-defeating objectivist methodology ultimately is – it strips us of skills and knowledges we already possess. This presses cruelly on researchers who wish to speak from marginalized social positions that are often silenced or pathologized in dominant discourses. This is why, as an *educational* tradition, cultural studies has, at its best, given encouragement and support to students to work on topics that are personally significant to them. This also produces good work. No one should be put off a topic because it is too close to home or they are too involved. Neither does this mean that such topics *must* be chosen, for they may be too painful to pursue.

Dialogue and difference

The stress on dialogue is shared ground between the hermeneuticists' 'understanding' and the feminist philosophers' arguments about positionality, despite their differences regarding power, gender and politics. Developments in theories of social identity have, as we have seen, complicated understandings of difference and therefore of dialogue across differences. This, together with a revival of humanistic traditions such as hermeneutics, has fed the interest in what we might call dialogue-in-spite-of-difference. Epistemologically, dialogue with others is how reflexivity is secured. In some writers it leads to a new objectivity. For Hartsock, Harding and Haraway, the point of criticizing objectivist approaches is not just to deconstruct them, but to seek a better way of grounding a science (see, for example, Haraway, 1997: 37 and 304, note 29). A consistent recognition of partiality (which needs dialogue) thus leads back to objectivity:

> So, not so perversely, objectivity turns out to be about particular and specific embodiment, and definitely not about the false vision promising transcendence of all limits and responsibility. The moral is simple: only partial perspective promises objective vision. Feminist objectivity is about limited location and situated knowledge, not about transcendence and splitting of subject and object. (1991: 190)

Later in the same text, Haraway, paraphrases Katie King: 'rational knowledge is power-sensitive conversation' (Haraway, 1991, citing King, 1987: 192).

Dialogue is key to a kind of objectivity for Gadamer, too:

> In human relations the important thing is ... to experience the Thou as truly a Thou – i.e., not to overlook his claim but to let him really say something to us . . . Openness to the other, then, involves recognizing that I myself must accept some things that are against me, even though no one else forces me to do so. (1989: 361)

In a later text he calls this 'the famous education to objectivity that makes a researcher' (1998: 68). It is because he stresses dialogue that he is so fierce with 'autobiography', which he sees as 'always much more like a story of private illusions than the understanding of real historical events' (1998: 55). It depends, of course, on what you mean by 'autobiography'. The contemporary usage of 'auto/biography' expresses the entanglement of autobiography with the biography of others and wider conditions. Gadamer's main point is to oppose 'objectivity as dialogue' with 'objectivity as mastery':

> The real criterion for whether or not the human sciences have any content is whether or not they participate in the essential expressions of human experience formulated in art and history. In my work I have tried to show that the model of dialogue is significant because it illuminates the structure of this form of participation. For dialogue is distinguished by the fact that no one participant can survey what comes out of it and then claim that he can master the subject on his own, but instead that we share together in the truth and in one another. (1998: 56)

Even if we are sceptical about 'essential expressions of human experience', we can agree that engagement with the world and others is the source of significant knowledge.

For Gadamer, dialogue is something human beings do, an essential activity. This may be true, but it also overlooks all the difficult, interrupted, unheld conversations that any research process must negotiate. Complex patterns of power and difference may inhibit researchers from asking appropriate questions or listening to answers. Power can silence respondents. Power and prejudice produces misreadings by examiners. The insights concerning power and identity that we discussed under social reflexivity above and in Chapter 2 are only now gradually being absorbed into methodological debates. By stressing difference and power, yet also insisting on shared human complicities in language and in psychic processes, contemporary identity theory strengthens the arguments for dialogue with multiple others, including the internal dialogue with fragments of the self. Language, the medium of dialogue, is itself understood as dialogic – not as a neutral tool for individual use, but, as Bakhtin puts it, 'populated – overpopulated – with the intentions of others' (1981b: 291–2).

Five main conclusions can be drawn from our discussion of reflexivity and dialogue so far.

- First, reflexivity is always, in some sense, a dialogue – with others but also within our selves and with the 'overpopulated' or social resources of language and culture.
- Second, self-reflexivity is a double movement: first 'losing' your self and your fore-knowledge in the face of otherness, then recomposing the self and its knowledge in relation to this strangeness. Gadamer writes of 'this kind of distance with respect to ourselves that opens us up to the other' (1998: 6); Ricoeur understands the critical reading process as a dialectic of 'distanciation' and 'belonging' (1991: 242).
- Third, dialogue always involves *contextualizing* moves of different kinds: contextualizing ourselves as researchers, but also contextualizing the texts, images or voices we read, watch or listen to. As Haraway puts it: 'Nothing comes without its world, so trying to know those worlds is crucial' (1997: 37).
- Fourth, we can expect that all these processes will be crossed, blocked or forced to swerve by power relations, including our own investments, material and psychic, in existing identities.
- Finally, as Valerie Walkerdine urges, one skill of successful research is to turn such difficulties and defences into something we can use for fresh questioning, knowledge and social–personal change. This may mean abandoning the desire for the last word and acknowledging the partiality (Haraway) or finitude (Gadamer) of our most exciting discoveries.

Accountability and responsibilities

Accountability is linked to partiality and the critique of objectivity. It is hard to be accountable for your own truths if you see yourself as only mirroring or discovering nature or a given social order. Discovery is split off from value and from choices about the future. This is why critics can say that objectivist science is 'irresponsible'. It does not make explicit, let alone debate, the values that always inform scientific enterprises.

Accountability is especially important in critical traditions of research such as feminism and cultural studies where truth is not only about representing a reality but also changing it. Indeed, the practical effects of a theory in action constitute part of the proof of its truth. This insight from dialectical materialism has been given a significant new twist in contemporary cultural theory, especially in some versions of poststructuralism. Here, knowledge is seen as actually *constituting* social differences and power, as being intrinsically political in this sense (for example, knowledge of the sexual in Foucault, 1979). Thus, Haraway and others can argue that the scientific revolution did not merely reflect the European male masteries of the day but also contributed to their constitution, positioning both masters and servants. Values, responsibility and accountability are embedded in the nature of scientific practice itself. Haraway can envisage a time when 'questions about possible liveable worlds lie *visibly* [our emphasis] at the heart of our best science' (1997: 39).

In much of today's academic world, accountability is interpreted more narrowly. It is as accountability of academics and students to academic institutions (or their corporate managers), responsibility of academics to students (but only as customers) and accountability to funding bodies representing governments and tax payers that it is generally used. Thesis and dissertation writers are made accountable to examiners in vivas and examination rooms in the sense we mean here, but they do not reach this point unless they have the courage to follow through an agenda of questions that they make their own. Our first responsibility as researchers is therefore to our own agenda and process of research as a fully self-reflexive practice. Important, too, are accountabilities in relation to the subjects or objects of research. The minimum responsibility is simply put but hard to practice: to *listen* or *read* in the full sense of the term dialogue that we have discussed. A third form of accountability concerns writing – we are accountable to those whom we address as readers of our work. Minimum responsibilities include having something to say and saying it explicitly and with clarity in ways that offer insight. Finally, there are responsibilities that follow from the social embeddedness of knowledge and go beyond older claims to academic autonomy from political control. Long-term social accountability has also to go beyond immediate utility as enforced by governments and business corporations, questioning and extending their criteria. This means clarifying our own ethics and politics in social and cross-cultural dialogues. This is the other side of 'partiality' in Haraway's work. 'Partiality' points to the incompleteness of any point of view (including the dominant), but also to the necessity of taking sides – 'of being *for* some worlds but not others' (1997: 37).

Conclusion: the logic of combination

The focus of this chapter has been on clarifying the approach to method that informs much cultural studies research. We have drawn on feminist critiques of objectivity and hermeneutic conceptions of relations of self to other in research. We have stressed the pervasiveness of cultural processes within cultural research itself. We have advocated a strong or more elaborated form of reflexivity that recognizes issues of power and the contexts of space and time and may precipitate personal changes in researchers themselves. We have stressed the real pressures that come from empirical others in research – whether these are actual persons we meet or cultural texts we read. We have emphasized a wider social participation and the importance of responsibilities beyond the academy.

These broad orientations make sense – or show the logic – of our running theme of the combination of methods. A strong version of reflexivity points towards the importance of critical self-awareness – therefore, of auto/biography – in all forms of cultural research. Cultural studies has often combined auto/biography with different ways of studying the cultural worlds of others. There is a continuum, indeed, from the cultural study of immediate worlds and the engagement of worlds more distant in space, time or social experience and auto/biography shades into ethnography and history. Our argument also shows, however, that even critical auto/biography is insufficient, however, because there are formations that have not touched our lives and times or, if they have, have done so only indirectly. Even when research is closer to home, we have to check whether or not others' experiences really do resemble our own.

Other methods in the combination arise from the all-pervasiveness in culture of language and representation. In any dialogue, the *reading* of what is said is crucial, which is why so many different ways of reading have been devised. If we had to sum up cultural studies methods in a single word, 'reading' might be the strongest candidate – especially if given its full hermeneutic weight of understanding, translation and the risky transformation of the reader. Reading, like reflexivity and dialogue, is a political and ethical category as well as a bundle of methods. This is because it implies that texts or other people have something important to say that we need to hear. Attentiveness to text, voice and image are values that imply empirical methods and we need techniques for listening to what is said.

Our discussion also suggests the importance of 'disciplines of context', a term used by E. P. Thompson to describe history (1972). For us, context includes the spatial, social and cultural and psychic/psychological, too. Neither reflexivity nor dialogue are possible unless we know enough of the context to see the whys and wherefores of subjective worlds. Moreover, one of the 'big' explanatory theories in cultural studies is that cultural formations express, re-present and produce relationships of power. This embedding of culture in power and everyday life requires dialogue about method with all the 'social disciplines', including social history, social geography, ethnology/ethnography, sociology and political economy – all disciplines associated with strongly empirical or realist epistemologies. This is why in Part II we look not only at theory in relation to empirical research, but also at history, geography and political economy – three key settings for the cultural. First, however, in Chapter 4, we want to develop our argument about method by considering closely the different 'moments' in the practice of research.

4 The research process: moments and strategies

Choosing and developing a topic	**63**
Starting	**64**
Managing time	**65**
Working with others: supervisors and peers	**66**
Reviewing the literature, mapping the field	**68**
Developing research proposals	**71**
General models of researching	**73**
Starting from a source not data?	**74**
Sources and questions	**74**
Research, analysis and textuality	**75**
Contextualization and creating distance	**77**
Writing as a moment – functions and forms	**78**
Diversity in the writing process – planning and writing	**80**
Writing and the autobiographical voice	**81**
Writing ethics and politics: authorial power and its deployment	**82**
Conclusion	**84**

In this chapter we focus on what Michael Green, in a similar project, has called 'working practices' (1997). We hope it will be useful to researchers and their teachers as 'advice literature'.[1] As Diana Leonard argues, literature of this kind usually tends to favour 'modest safe efforts' rather than 'research for pleasure, significance and originality' (Leonard, 2000: 186 and 2001; Philips and Pugh, 1994, and, in the USA, Sternberg, 1981). So, our second, and hopefully more enlivening aim, is to explore the implications for practice of our arguments about method. How do we develop topics, review secondary literature or prepare a research proposal, for instance, in the light of arguments about 'situated knowledge' and 'dialogue with the other'?

Particular practices acquire pressing importance at particular times in a research project, but by calling them 'moments', rather than stages or phases, we want to suggest that they recur throughout, in different forms and combinations. We therefore organize this chapter according to these key moments in the research process – from choosing a topic to writing down our observations.

Choosing and developing a topic

Researchers are commonly asked 'What are you working on?' or 'What is your topic?' These are awkward questions, threatening exposure, especially early on. We may know little about our subject – not even, in any developed way, what 'it' is. Yet, the terms of such questioning are themselves instructive about our dilemmas. 'Topic', 'subject' or 'object' are everyday words, but they signal different epistemologies and ontologies. 'Topic' foregrounds the researcher's own choices and the ways in which they constitute an object or field. 'Subject' denotes an agent as well as a discipline, an other who is capable of answering back. There is a pressure to think of this 'subject' as an 'object', which gives it some presence and stability – as a good solid object out there, we can work on it. The anxieties that can gather around these terms, however, suggest confusion or embarrassment about the reality or ontological status of our studies. Are they silly or trivial? Do they correspond to anything real?

Such feelings are understandable and normal, for research involves the production of something new. Projects start with an idea – a question, concept, hunch, feeling of anger or identification, half-grasped experience, or a difference or strangeness evoking curiosity or wonder. Choosing and developing a topic is a true 'moment' in the research process and has particular urgency at the beginning of a project. Yet, research – especially in the humanities, perhaps – centres on the *progressive* clarification of aims and objects. Research supervisors often ask – even of a penultimate draft – 'What is this project/dissertation/thesis *really* about?' implying a lack of focus. Oscillations between relative confusion and relative clarity are also normal. A period of empirical immersion – in fieldwork, say, or media texts or archives – may confuse us and lead us to find that we are asking the wrong questions. Our initial questions seem unanswerable from the sources the otherness of which tells of something different. Confusion can also arise from encounters with new ideas or challenges in our everyday lives that change our questions and suggest new frameworks. Then, as the frame shifts, the terms of the dialogue change and a different pattern emerges.

Confusion is not just normal, it can indicate a good response. It can mark the point where we take in the reality of other people's lives or the truth of other's sayings. We digest something new, struggle with what it means for our existing knowledges, even for our leading questions. Old questions or knowledges do not have to be thrown away, though – we can enlarge or extend them. This requires reflection, introspection. We engage with otherness as fully as we can and this involves looking away from our selves, but then we have to turn and look *to* our selves, as effective researchers and citizens of the world. This explains the rituals all researchers develop to help thinking, from going for walks to deserting the computer for pen and paper.

In moments of confusion, it is useful to recover the nature of our initial interest. Ask yourself, 'What was bugging me about this topic anyway?' or 'How did I get into this?' Autobiographical methods may help here, from lists and jottings in your research diary to more elaborate memory work (see Chapter 12). There are always pragmatic reasons for topic choices, especially in the context of educational institutions. These include getting a grade, securing funding, getting through the course, pleasing a teacher, proving something to or for our family, even beating the system. If we have one rule about topic choice here, it is the importance of a personal attachment to the topic itself. Subjective engagement with a topic is what keeps us going, whether on a four-month dissertation, three – or four-year PhD or a book project like this one. It follows that researchers need to 'own' their topic, which implies responsibility as well as possession. Supervisors (and institutions), by contrast, must know how *not* to possess a topic. They must identify with it, nurture and develop it, yet *never* make it their own or compete for it. This is a politico-ethical as well as a pedagogic principle in cultural studies because of the importance of keeping studies open to what is emergent, hidden or currently unsayable in the world. The spirit of our advice here runs against some current academic tendencies, which impose a narrowly pragmatic, utilitarian and often masculinist conception of research, centring on 'completion rates' or 'outputs' (for a critical account, see Leonard, 2000). We have to take account of these pressures but they do not have to be internalized or constantly invoked.

Starting

Starting is hard, even when a topic is clear. Three strategies are often useful, here. First, start from what we know already, then, second, prioritize key elements and, third, bracket others out. We have already argued that all cultural researchers are entangled in their subjects of study. They may have memories and reflections relevant to the topic. Recovering these and giving them a more formal shape is one place to start. Reflexivity is especially important at the outset of a project because it may suggest trajectories of research and elaborate and contextualize our hunches.

Even so, there is always too much to do. This can be paralysing, so prioritizing is important. Asking what the essential tasks are, whatever direction the project takes, is useful. We can do these first. Bracketing out goes along with prioritization. It is not the same as dropping, repressing or even procrastination! It keeps items on the agenda until their pertinence is clearer. Practical short-term planning like this builds up our judgements of significance and value. Recorded and reflected on in dairies, talked through with tutors, such decisions both concretize and realize our aims.

Another common place to start is with bibliographical searching and reading around a topic, which is discussed in full below. Often, tutors of shorter projects will suggest beginning with 'three key texts in the area'. Where academic work is thin, a small-scale pilot study is a good way to get going, generating themes for later work. Where the literature is richer and the project is longer, using hunches to read a way into a body of ideas is appropriate.

Managing time[2]

Research involves organizing our daily lives, creating time, space and claiming rights to do this activity in the face of everyday pressures, including making claims on others. The right to own time or leisure tends to be a masculine preserve, but all researchers need a strategy and support for managing time and space to complete their projects. Research involves spatial removal (to office, spare room or library) and some isolation from ongoing social relationships. While acknowledging the guilt that researchers often feel, it is not helpful, in our view, to represent research as somehow selfish or unreal. It has a longer cycle of social return than face-to-face engagement, but it is social participation nonetheless.

Most research is a part-time activity as we have lives to lead as well as other work to do. This impacts differently on researchers depending on their positioning and the kinds of dependence and autonomy involved. For this reason, learning to use time in bits is often essential. Productive work is not only that done in a whole day devoted to it. Even writing can be done in shorter bursts, especially once a section has been planned. However, some traditional modes of student working – concentrated bursts when up against a deadline – are not appropriate for larger projects, except, perhaps, when polishing them off in a final spurt. Dissertations and theses involve more sustained work – an accumulation of bits of time, preferably each day or week.

Time is also manageable when it is tackled with a strategy of long-term pacing. Thesis and dissertation work lacks structure, even when there are deadlines. In thesis work, it is useful to construct a framework of three main phases:

- a phase of reading around and defining questions and methods leading to a proposal or research design
- a phase of more intensive research activity
- a phase of writing for presentation.

If, after a year of full-time registration, a PhD researcher has reviewed the literature and mapped the fields of study, clarified leading questions, reviewed the approach and methods to be used and perhaps started on a pilot study, this is good progress. If most of the research has been completed by the end of the second year or just into the third, this is good progress, too. In part-time study, even a loose schedule such as this may be too rigid. A useful alternative (also applicable to full-time study) is to divide a thesis into separable projects (which may correspond to chapters or parts) and complete the reading, research and first writing for each in turn. Such drafts can only be provisional, as ideas will develop later on in the chapter sequence and so rewriting will be necessary. With different quantities – weeks rather than months – these proportions and strategies may apply to MA or first degree dissertations of 10–20,000 words as well. MA dissertations involve particularly tight schedules that can limit ambitions and enforce a certain pragmatism.

'Rational' planning of this kind, however, is never enough, nor fully possible .It is also important to follow lines of pleasure, desire and interest. It is essential to aim for days of work – and of non-work and varied forms of work – that please in process and satisfy in outcome. All good strategies recognize other intrusive demands and build in ways of not blaming ourselves for those times when things don't go quite to plan.

Working with others: supervisors and peers

We have stressed how research involves dialogue with others – with sources and readers, for example. We are also in dialogue with a larger cultural context, which includes academic knowledge. The acknowledgements in most academic texts touch on this social character of all knowledge production. In cultural studies, there is a strong tradition of group work and co-authorship, especially among teachers and postgraduate students, though this arose from 'conditions . . . which would seem to have almost vanished' (Green, 1997: 195; see also Clare and Johnson, 2000). All academic relationships, however, involve discussants, tutors, supervisors, readers, critics or editors in face-to-face relationships, while informal intellectual networks, circles and partnerships are everywhere important. These install forms of dialogue at the centre of the research process (Johnson, 1998). Here, we shall focus on two aspects: working with a supervisor and dialogue between student peers.

There has been much discussion about research supervision as an aspect of postgraduate research (see, for example, Delamont, Atkinson and Parry, 2000; Salmon, 1992; Winfield, 1987). Institutions can and should establish a framework of expectations and entitlements in this area and ensure that this information is known to all participants. Many institutions have guides or handbooks and some have ways of monitoring progress and/or the adequacy of supervision. Compared with the neglect of the past, these developments are helpful. Here, however, we want to address researchers directly as *managing their own supervision*, offering norms to aim for, while recognizing the reality of academic power.

At all levels of research, meetings with supervisors or specialist tutors should occur before and during the project with feedback on achievements at the end. Some institutions specify a required minimum (sometimes also a maximum) of supervision hours or meetings. We advocate meetings of about two hours a fortnight for writers beginning a thesis, but this could well reduce to once a month in later phases or even less for periods of fieldwork. Frequency should increase again when final drafts are being discussed. E-mail and/or telephone contact is indispensable, but, if done conscientiously, it involves extra work and does not match the responsiveness and nuanced commentary possible face-to-face. Times and a rough agenda for the next meeting(s) should always be arranged jointly before a meeting ends, as part of a summing-up process.

Researchers, not supervisors, should actively set the agenda for such meetings, especially latterly, but presenting a draft chapter should not be necessary for a meeting to happen. Meetings can discuss progress, debate readings or tackle points of difficulty. Sessions should be prepared for and it is helpful for supervisors to have warning of what may come up.

The minimum expectation researchers should have of a supervisor is that the project is recognized and engaged with knowledgeably, sometimes critically, but not dismissively or destructively. *Not* getting recognition or not getting engagement are sound reasons for changing supervisor – for which institutions should have a procedure that is safe for the student. In our view (which may be contentious), good supervision, even at a PhD level, does not necessarily require a close-in expertise on the particular topic involved. The best supervisors may have done similar or parallel work, know some of the literature and/or have used similar sources or methods. Where students are supervised by panels of two or even three research supervisors they should sometimes meet together.

Support from student and researcher peers in seminars or course modules or informal self-organized workshops or even in a common room or shared study facility is crucial. It avoids the intellectual isolation that can follow from working on your own. Reading and discussion groups and day schools are also a good way of sharing ideas and giving mutual support.

Theories of dialogue throw useful light on all these processes. Supervisors, for example, are doubly involved in dialogic relations. They recognize and encourage the researcher's project, but must also take the position of the examiner, advising on what is rather gruesomely called 'submission'. Dialogue is here entangled with the power relations of the academy, though there may also be significant other readers beyond tutors and examiners. Research may have professional applications, policy implications or be designed to uphold and empower a particular group or movement, for instance.

From this analysis, we can see why relationships between supervisors and researching students can be traumatic and restrictive as well as supportive and enabling. When a supervisor is worried about the level of the work, it is hard to shift from one supervisory voice to the other. The researcher needs both voices – the critical supporter's voice and the quasi-adjudicatory voice. Our own strategies as supervisors differ, but certain features seem more consistent with our view of cultural studies than others. Given our stress on students' agendas, critical, thoughtful recognition of the project, in its best form, has priority while recognition of extra-academic motivations, personal and political, implies a certain distance or instrumentality towards the academy and its conventions.

The absence of adequate recognition in terms that are valued by the researcher is a common reason for failure in the form of non-completion. Yet, researchers also need realistic advice about the likely consequences of breaking academic rules of all kinds and about the relative malleability and rationality of these rules, depending on the circumstances. When student or topic are socially marginal, the centrality and (supportive) institutional power and intellectual status of a supervisor is needed as much as the identification with marginality.

Reviewing the literature, mapping the field

Dissertations, theses, research projects and monographs are genres with their own distinctive conventions that researchers need to know. One clear convention is that the researcher should be able to give an account of existing work in the field(s) of the research – extensive and analytical in doctoral or postdoctoral work, more selective in first degree projects and dissertations. This is one element that makes the difference between a dissertation and an essay, which is the main form of writing in the humanities and social sciences in universities in the UK. As a piece of research, a dissertation or thesis must engage with existing knowledge and produce something fresh. In PhD work, reviewing the field(s) of research is linked to the requirement of 'originality', which in turn is linked to publishability. A PhD thesis must show how existing work is extended, qualified or critiqued.

The need to review existing work fits our own stress also on dialogic relationships and social participation. Understanding *is* engagement with the work of others. The accuracy and care of our own interventions also depends on knowing the other positions in the field, just as the ethics of interpretation involve doing justice to others' work. Mapping the field is part of being effective as an intellectual.

Attentive reading of a few key texts – with their acknowledgements as well as bibliographies – can quickly construct something of the character of academic fields and networks. 'Snowballing' from text to text, however, may need to be accompanied by broader scans, less limited by the starting point. The following further processes are involved in broad scan or expansive literature searching and review. They all involve conceptual as well as technical issues.

Deciding on keywords for searching

Keywords for bibliographical searching can be too broad, producing floods of titles, most of them quite useless, or too narrow, producing very little. Refining the search involves practical ingenuity, producing combined categories and building in negatives. At the same time, as Raymond Williams' *Keywords* (1983) clearly shows, selecting categories is a conceptual operation that takes us into their historical construction and surrounding meanings. Our keywords for the literature search may be a first conceptualization of the main threads of our topic. *Relationships* are important here: it is one thing to list books under headings or aspects, another to map the conceptual relationships between writers or themes. Diagrams may be more useful than lists. Here, for instance – in Figures 4.1 and 4.2 – are two diagrams used in the initial stages of literature searching for an essay on 'Mourning Diana' (Johnson, 1999). These diagrams are recreated (with a little tidying) from the pages of a research diary.

The version in Figure 4.1 drew attention to a pivotal role of celebrity as the point of intersection of the main themes, especially of constructions of the nation, and of the social-psychic processes of grieving and its media representation. Thus, 'celebrity' proved a more useful entry point for

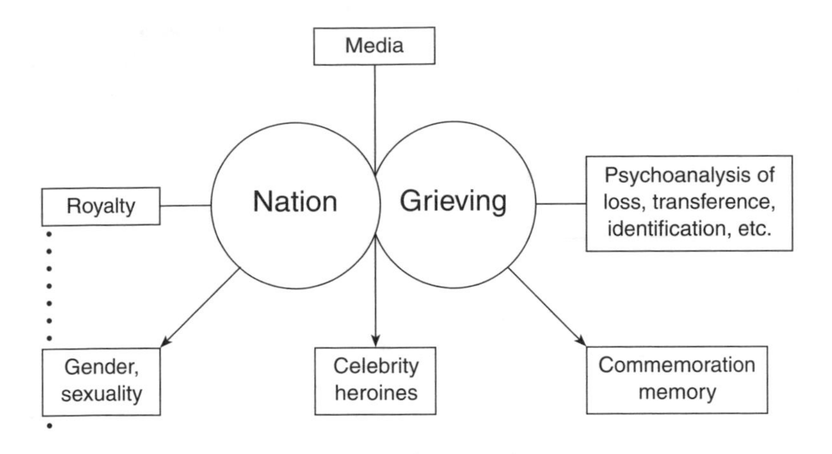

Figure 4.1 Mourning Diana, version 1
(*Source*: Adapted from Johnson, 1999b)

bibliographical searching than either 'nation' or 'grieving', which produced large and heterogeneous listings. In other ways, however, this initial mapping was quite descriptive.

The diagram in Figure 4.2, which appears later in the same research diary, does a better job of representing certain key relationships.

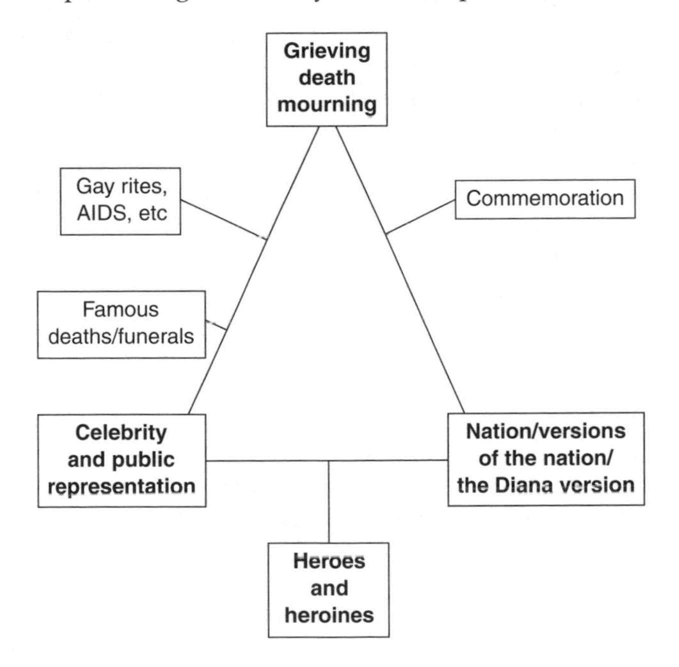

Figure 4.2 Mourning Diana, version 2
(*Source*: Adapted from Johnson, 1999b)

It helped thinking about the relationships between the three points of national identity, mourning and (media-based) celebrity and identify further search topics along the poles between them.

Searching, recording and reviewing

Searching involves technical issues – from choosing appropriate search engines to deciding whether to keep lists in notebooks, on cards or in computer files, perhaps with the help of a programme such as Endnotes. It soon throws up patterns of absence and presence, the shape of our topic as a field of discourses. A project on schooling and sexuality that involved looking at different media as informal sex education, for instance, threw up little on this topic, but a flood of material on 'children and violence'. As listings accumulate, we can check out patterns of this kind, to both refine our searches (entering 'not violence', for instance) and describe the topic's public anatomy.

Reading secondary texts

In reading the secondary literature, it is important to read widely, according to a plan, and also actively. Again, prioritization helps, but so does not deferring reading tasks that may seem intimidating. It is often a good strategy to reserve a body of reading until later in the process, but, if it keeps coming back to view, it may be important to tackle it and end what starts to look like procrastination.

Reading actively means recording your own feelings and comments about a text, as well as taking notes from it in a more passive sense. It is a useful guard against unconscious copying to use particular orthographic conventions to mark off quotations from the text (quotation marks and an exact reference), paraphrasing (for which, again, you should note page numbers and source details) and your own commentary (by, for example, putting it in square brackets). It is likely that reading, especially in a longer project, will change from the relatively passive or absorptive – with lots of quotation, paraphrasing and noting of dates and names and relatively little comment – to a much more opinionated or critical mode of reading later in the project. Initial reading tends to focus on recording and interpreting empirical materials of different kinds – biographies, chronologies and bibliographies especially – but also on mapping of themes and theories. As we read more critically, however, we are often interrogating the frameworks within which instances are given meaning, transposing the cases to our own frameworks with the stress on appropriation and critique.

It is also worth mentioning a common researcher's myth – that somewhere, in a major library we haven't visited or on an obscure shelf in our own library, sits the one book or article we need for our research that will tell us what we still don't know. More often than not, this item does not exist and is, in fact, the work we are writing ourselves.

Developing research proposals

Writing a proposal

Writing a formal proposal is standard practice in applying for doctoral and postdoctoral awards and for a place to study on a research degree, registration and transfer and approaching publishers. Even undergraduate dissertations begin with a proposal of some kind. Proposals are the communicative aspect of research design and planning and setting up a research project of any kind. Though versions differ according to the project and institutional requirements, such plans tend to have standard components:

- a title, which should be informative, interesting and concise (cultural studies researchers should resist the temptation to construct double meanings at any cost!)
- a clear statement of aims.
- a rationale for the project, including comments on existing approaches and the value of the project – this will include claims to originality for doctoral and postdoctoral proposals (in the latter case, funding bodies are often interested in outcomes and plans for networking with colleagues, often internationally)
- an account of both method, in the larger sense, and methods of research and analysis to be used
- a time schedule
- References and bibliography.

Clarifying aims

Many projects begin from a broad empirical description that has the character of a capacious box holding many different contents as yet unsorted or even identified. Designating a media genre (talk shows, say) or an author or genre of literary fiction (feminist science fiction, for example) or a site of social interaction (the school or youth culture, for instance), or even a theme (such as heterosexuality or aspiration) are 'boxes' of this kind. Boxes provide starting points for literature searching and discussions with a tutor and can proliferate different file headings for sorting materials, but they are not really adequate for starting research. They do not provide a way in. They encourage a stamp-collecting, scrapbook outlook to research. Collection, sorting, classification and arranging are real but essentially descriptive research skills.

Formulating research questions

Research projects properly take off when they generate a set of questions, a problem or a contradiction. Being interested in 'sexuality and schooling' is one thing; focusing on the key contradiction that schools are both desexualized and hum with sexual interest is another. To ask how this contradiction arises, how it is manifested, how it is managed and what its consequences are for pupils and teachers gave this particular project dynamism and direction. Actually, many choices of topic occur because there is a contradiction of this kind, often in the researcher's own experience. If not, the reading-around process may offer clues to an angle. There may be a key absence that structures research so far. Sometimes it is the encounter with the 'other' of research that stimulates or changes the question.

It is important not to have too many research questions pointing in too many unrelated directions. To have one main question and some subsidiary questions is one way in which to compose a project. The following are the questions that animated the schooling and sexuality project (Epstein and Johnson, 1998):

- What is the *particular* role of the school in the formation of sexual identities among young people? (This was the main question, pointing not only to sex education but all aspects of formal and informal curriculum and peer interaction in the school.)
- How do the authority dynamics of schooling affect the sexual cultures of students and teachers? (This specified the first question more tightly. The dynamics of control and response between teachers and pupils are main features of formal schooling, so that sexuality becomes a kind of 'playground' in opposition to the official desexualization of the school).
- Why is the school an especially difficult place to come out in, as lesbian or gay or some other conspicuously different to sexuality to the most insistent forms of femininity and masculinity? (A generative question from a particular point of view.)
- How is sexuality in the school regulated and policed externally? (This led to questions about legislative controls on sex education, press and political campaigning and the roles of schools' governors, parents and others.)
- How are schools affected by or implicated in aspects of the larger national sexual culture? (For example, anxiety over teenage pregnancy, rates of divorce and the growing visibility of lesbian, gay and transexual identities).
- Where are the other social spaces and cultural processes where young people learn about sexuality and sexual identity? (such as commercial popular culture, girls' magazines.) How do these relate to schooling?

This was a five-year project with two main researchers and several others involved, but, even so, the last two questions were not adequately addressed and functioned as a context for the main enquiry. This project would have been too ambitious for a single researcher, even at PhD level. The commonest reason for difficulty is that projects are too ill-defined and, therefore, undoable or fated to remain entirely imaginary. The ideal, perhaps, is to combine generous aims with careful prioritization and phasing.

General models of researching

The remaining moments concern 'research' and 'writing'. What research is, is by no means self-evident. Four main models can be distinguished, if not more.

- The dominant model of researching identifies three main moments: the gathering of data, analysis of data and writing up of findings. This is also the order of presentation. After an abstract or introduction, there are sections that review literature and/or theories, describe methods of research, present the data, analyse or comment on it and reach findings.
- In a second model, research is seen in relation to sources or traces that remain from past processes. Research is the discovery and critical interpretation of these sources or traces.
- In a third model, the researching process is the reading and interpreting of texts – from literary works to symbolic actions.
- Finally, research can be conceptualized as a dialogue between the researching self and some other, distanced in time, space, culture and/or social relations.

These models are related to different epistemologies and disciplines. Data gathering and analysis derive from quantitative models of social science research – often transferred, not always appropriately, to qualitative methods. The idea of a source or trace makes most sense within historical enquiries where the archive, as a form of public memory, shapes our view of the past with some power. Text reading as research is especially characteristic of literary and linguistic approaches (but also of musicological and visual disciplines), including cultural studies. The dialogic character of research is most dynamically realized when an enquiry involves face-to-face communication with another person or group. These models also prioritize different moments of enquiry. The languages of 'data' and 'source' direct us to 'searching', 'collecting' or 'gathering' as stages in research, while 'reading' and 'dialogue' centre on interpretation or analysis.

Each model offers something for cultural researchers, pointing to the value of methodological combination. There is always some human agency (as well as technical and other means) in the sources, which we treat as things (texts or data). This human agency is always unfamiliar (other) in different ways. It is hard to conceive of a source that *cannot* be 'read' like a text. It has to be made to mean something, even if it is a symbolic practice or an embodied sign or gesture. All sources (persons or things) have histories of production and survival; all call for the historian's critical eye for their specific provenance (where the source comes from) and the partialities of the archive (the dependence of memory and voice on power). Even the notion of data has value within a cultural approach because there is always a sense in which our sources are given, or found, and have an objectivity beyond us, even while we produce them. These different models are not always competing or contradictory, many elements are complementary and can amount to a broader, sharper picture than would be possible if they were left out.

Starting from a source not data?

One difficulty with the notion of data is that it starts too late in the research process, telescoping many moments. It pre-empts the sequence of research acts we have discussed so far, especially the formulation of questions. Like all empiricist accounts, it assumes a direct relation to a real world as data is found or gathered rather than produced or re-presented. Moreover, the idea of 'gathering' data skates over the work of recording and translating, whether this means the process of producing a transcript from an interview or paraphrasing a literary or philosophical text. The active role of the researcher is also erased. 'Source', though, starts further back in the process as we only have data, facts or evidence *from* a source if we have recorded, read and interpreted it. In its most interesting connotation, a source is something for someone who 'thirsts' – for water, perhaps, but also for knowledge. This conveys the agency of the researcher, though not of the source giver.

At the same time, there is something important about the idea of a source as being found or given and existing independently of the researcher. Finding sources, which may be rare and inaccessible, is a basic experience of research. Without them, nothing works. More accurately, perhaps, there are always two poles of this source relation in researching. They may be described as:

- finding an appropriate source for a question
- finding an appropriate question for a source.

Sources and questions

A source may be produced or found in order to answer a question. This involves ingenuity – a key virtue of researchers – and trial and error – an inevitable cost. It may involve tracking along historical processes in order to decide where some trace of a process – in documents or memory – might remain.

In her study of female fans of Hollywood films in the 1940s and 1950s, Jackie Stacey writes directly of her experience of this process of trial and error:

> In retelling the story of this research I am aware of the temptation to represent the research project as a seamless narrative in which the next step seems inevitable. The dead-ends, the U-turns, the frustrations and the despair tend to get written out as the logic of the research project is imposed retrospectively. (1994: 50)

Stacey discusses the less fruitful avenues she encountered. Her questions – especially 'What do spectators bring to films from their specific cultural and historical options which then determine their reading?' – led her to the Mass Observation archive at Sussex University, readers' letters in the contemporary film magazine, *Picturegoer,* and the British Film Institute.[4] Having unsuccessfully written to stars to ask if they or their fan clubs held collections of fan mail, she also placed advertisements in four major women's magazines with readerships of an age group coinciding with the period she was interested in, asking for respondents to an open-ended qualitative questionnaire. The success of this strategy transformed the project: she received over 350 responses, including long letters as well as requests for the questionnaire, and 238 long questionnaires were returned. These were so rich that she abandoned her intention of using published sources of the time and based her work on respondents' memories instead.

The emphasis on fandom and spectatorship she encountered in this material raised questions of personal desire and identification that were absent from the public sources that had survived from those decades. 'Found' sources are always framed and limited by the conditions of their production and preservation – in this case by the national politics of Mass Observation and the dominant rhetoric of a film magazine. The solution was to produce or evoke sources where none could be found, drawing on memory as a resource – and as a challenge. Stacey's study also shows how sources feed back into research questions, methods and ways of writing, as, in this case, she found that she needed to include a fuller treatment of issues of identity, fantasy and memory. Clearly, sticking with our questions and pursuing different sources rather than retreating from our ambitions in frustration can be fruitful.

Research, good research, does not always work in such a question-led way. The source may be found by the researcher or find the researcher first. Before the research process begins, we may already be fascinated by a particular author or life by reading the author's works or hearing them talk. We may have a passion (or hatred) for a particular genre – literary, televisual, filmic. We may identify (or not) with a particular social group or cultural space or milieu. An initial encounter with what becomes a source may produce the thirst we mentioned earlier.

In source-led modes of research, it is important to be clear about the researcher's side of the dialogue, especially where the source is rich and multilevelled. In question-led modes, the absences and frustrations of sources may demand a change to the questions in the end. As projects develop, as a dialogue, the distinction between the two modes breaks down. Even so, differences of emphasis may not altogether disappear, as shown by continued tensions between more inductive and more theory-led approaches in the literature on method.

Our own preference is to reflect on research as a dialogue between the researching self and the researched other. In what follows we explore three aspects of this exchange – textuality, power and context – and the inner dialogues of the researcher.

Research, analysis and textuality

It is hard to imagine a form of cultural research that does not produce its source as a text. As texts, cultural forms *appear* relatively fixed and stable so that their complexities can be analysed and represented. Such textualization, however, also involves costs. For example, it accentuates the abstraction of the text, as an object or commodity, from its conditions of production and its social use and, in some versions, from the world of other texts that surround it. This applies as much to the interview transcript as to the literary work or media message, yet we do need to fix the fluidity of an interview dialogue in order to reflect on it. If we don't do this in a transcript or notebook, it will happen anyway, more selectively and less systematically, in our memories.

Cultural research is often seen as text work – a work on texts – but it can also be seen as a production of texts in relation to other texts, or as a work on and with *intertextual relationships*. Reading and writing are here understood as forms of dialogue or, more technically, as forms of intertextuality. These intertexts are realizations of the dialogue between the texts we study and the texts we make. Self-consciousness about this double process is the best guard against a particular kind of objectivism and cultural determinism in research that is associated with structuralist and other language-led approaches. From our own preferred point of view, researching is a process that involves the creation of many different layers of representation, related textualities of many different kinds.

This textual layering begins as soon as we confront our sources. We read or listen or watch, but we also take note as we take notes. Such observations may be mental at first in face-to-face encounters, then written later. They may be marginal notes on the edge of a written or printed text, underlinings, highlightings, exclamations, summary points. These notes are the beginnings of our answers to the questions posed to us by the texts we read. They are also rephrasings of our own questions in the light of answers given – or withheld – by the texts. In a further layer, our notes may become more formal or extensive. We quote, paraphrase, comment, reflect, reorder, juxtapose, read across the different texts. In a project on the post September 11th 2001 speeches of the British Prime Minster Tony Blair (discussed more fully in Chapter 10), for example, a collection of extracts was compiled and organized under such themes as Us ('the civilized world' and 'our' way of life) and Them ('terrorists') and the handling of this difference in the form of ethical absolutes and a lack of moral ambiguity. Juxtapositions from different speeches brought out the main themes and tropes, including absences and elisions. As hermeneutic and dialogic theories suggest, reading is always such a process of translation or appropriation – an appropriation that also changes the reader. Our readings, like all our knowledge, are going to be partial, yet it is our reading that makes our source live again and capable of yielding some answers. At the same time, texts or situations exercise a real pressure on our reading. We cannot make of them just anything we like.

So, processes of research can be understood as movements between these different layers of representation or forms of textuality. The writing side of this makes it clearest. Having processed our (textual) materials – translated them perhaps into many different forms of representation – we may write a first draft, largely from memory, one step removed from our detailed research materials, mediated perhaps by yet another textual layer – a plan. Getting away from the detail in this way can free up our writing, but, in revising the first version, we have to return to our other texts, checking details and quotations, sometimes going right back to the first version – the source where it is still available – to see if we have quoted accurately or will bear the interpretation we wish to give it. If not, we have to change the writing.

Contextualization and creating distance

Even so, intertextual dialogue remains, in our view, too narrow an account of the cultural research process. Research also involves grasping the nature of the differences and forms of power that circulate around the self and the other in a dialogue and are actively produced within and around key texts. These are not necessarily available even as a result of a critical reading of the text in question. In research on contemporary cultures, this context is often supplied initially by our existing knowledge, which we may have then to check and extend. Up to the time of writing this chapter, for example, Tony Blair did not make any mention at all of 'oil' in his post September 11th speeches, yet, as we will argue in Chapter 10, the missing contexts of the political economies of oil and the environment make a new sense of his political rhetoric. The movement from text to (more or less hidden) context is crucial for cultural research and involves a different kind of dialogue. It will be a major consideration in all our chapters on reading (see Part III).

Contextualization is one of the ways in which a first or surface reading of texts is relativized and a distance achieved that allows a critical reading. In a first reading – of a political speech, for example – we are positioned as the subject of the rhetoric and agree with hermeneutic traditions that this is an indispensable moment. It is one that deliberately takes the pressure of the rhetoric, suspends scepticism and allows itself to be persuaded by what the text explicitly has to say. A second contextualizing reading is different from this. It returns the text to context and to our own positionalities and interrogates our responses.

Dialogue, then, is also in a sense *internal*. It certainly occurs between the researching self and sources of different kinds, but it also happens within the researcher, in the dialogues of different readings and writings. In effect, we make an object of our previous understanding and critique and revise it. The self-reflexive self is always a split or multiple subject, capable of making an object of or creating some distance from its own and others' knowledge and, indeed, trying out readings precisely to relativize them later. Gadamer, in discussing the difference between understanding a text and 'reconstructing the way it came into being', states many of our themes of researching in their interrelations:

> One intends to *understand the text itself.* But this means that the interpreter's own thoughts too have gone into re-awakening the text's meanings. In this the interpreter's own horizon is decisive, yet not as a personal standpoint that he maintains or enforces, but more as an opinion and a possibility that one brings into play and puts at risk, and that helps one truly to make one's own what the text says. I have described this above as a 'fusion of horizons'. We can now see that this is what takes place in conversation, in which something is expressed that is not only mine or my author's, but common. (1989: 388, emphasis as in original)

While agreeing with much of this, we note again how such hermeneutic accounts seek to *resolve* differences. In contrast, sometimes we may have to hold 'horizons' separate to grasp differences more clearly.

Although researching is dialogue between self and an other, via sources, texts, meetings and sayings, this does not, cannot, mean vacating our own self, our own times, our own evaluations. On the contrary, our horizons, traditions and knowledge of contexts are crucial in the reading. Yet, any reading also *risks* our own horizons or has an experimental character to it. Different possible readings, as much as layers of representation or writing, constitute the tissue of research. In these ways, a dialogic relation to source, its textual character and attention to its and our own contexts interact in the reading and writing processes.

Writing as a moment – functions and forms

The practice of writing is often taken to be concentrated at the end of a project. At our university, students completing a PhD are officially described as 'writing up' and pay appropriately reduced fees. Yet, the 'writing up' model, where the researcher leaves most writing to a final phase, is not one we would recommend. Our best advice, in a nutshell, is to 'write, write and write as an aspect of research' (for other useful discussions, see Ely et al., 1997; Green, 1997). Leaving writing to a final stage can be both a symptom and a cause of writing blocks because starting to write can loom as a moment of crisis, rather than a continuation of a usual activity.

More positively, writing and researching are, as we have suggested, intimately connected. We write in order to appropriate the materials and ideas of others, critique them and to develop our own ideas. As we have argued, writing is a part of 'active reading', where we jot down comments as we read. Writing has different qualities from those of oral performance or, indeed, the inner speech of thought or image. In particular, it can fix ideas and impressions and structure them into arguments and sequences. These allow for them to be filed away, a possibility enormously enhanced by electronic technologies. Such materials can be systematically recovered and reworked – rethinking actualized. Writing aids the ways of starting we suggest above – the generative case study or engagement with theoretical ideas. If the manipulation of texts in their relations is at the centre of cultural research, creative work can hardly begin until we start to write.

Writing is also the main form of communication in humanities and social sciences and is still – despite the growth of work in video, photography, performance and film – the dominant medium in cultural studies in the universities. Orally based dialogue has many virtues, but the forms of dialogue our method envisages also require writing – for supervisors, student peers, 'submission' and wider readerships. It is a key form, too, for developing inner dialogues with ourselves. Many researchers write too little and are therefore not as aware as they might be of the internal processes that constitute their creative thinking. Cultural research is also advanced by writing because being a writer (or other specialist creator of representations) teaches us a lot about cultural forms and processes. In fact, cultural studies could itself be seen as an attempt to make more visible and teachable skills usually carried in implicit forms of cultural capital. As Hammersley and Atkinson have remarked, 'there is no more damaging myth than the idea that there is a mysterious "gift" or that writing is a matter of "inspiration"' (1995: 239).

Research involves different forms of writing or 'writings'. Many are for no one but ourselves. This applies to research diary entries, notes on reading, bits of analysis or argument, annotations to transcripts, plans, headings and computer files for future chapters. This layer of 'record' (which already includes analysis) is the basis for other layers of writing that are more reflective, developmental or productive – the main purpose being to organize material conceptually or develop the concepts themselves. These may consist of note-like draft chapters or sections, early drafts, working papers and so on that may go to supervisors and other readers. In later stages – when we 'write up' rather than 'write down' – the emphasis shifts from recording and development towards presentation and communication. This involves stronger conventions and schematization – in the thesis or dissertation genre, for example.

The transition from writing for research to writing for presentation can be enabled or troubled in different ways. Writing for presentation always has to reach back into the textual layers of writing for record, reflection or explanation. There are some technical solutions here, which include working to plan from the beginning of a project or as soon as a chapter structure emerges, storing material and drafts, including quoted text, in separate files for each chapter or theme and under subheadings that help to form the argument. However, dialogics and power relations are involved, too. One common failing of supervisors is to look only at finished texts, complete with references. This limits their engagement with the dynamics of writing and makes the transition from development to presentation harder for students, especially when a supervisor is very critical or pedagogically rigid. Ideally, there should be a manageable progression from the liminality of diary-writing, fieldwork notes and general note taking and drafting, where the intended readership is 'just me', to the elaborated writing for draft and final presentation for academic or other audience(s).

These later stages are distinguished not only by addressee, but also by the conventions necessary in order to secure some credibility with our readers, such as referencing and literature reviews. The discursive space in which research is produced is defined by the textual conventions of the past, by what we read as well as what we observe and experience. In Clifford and Marcus's (1986) collection *Writing Culture*, for example, the authors emphasize that all forms of research contain distinctive conventions of writing or 'poetics'. These conventions consist of rhetorical structure, modes of authority and processes of suppression and omission. They have been highly influential in determining the authority to represent cultural realities. Writing is always a process of coming to terms with convention in this representational sense – one closely related to our earlier discussion of credibility and truth claims (see Chapter 3). It is helpful if supervisors support and validate this as a complex process and the struggles it involves, as well as engaging with the final product. Supervisors also need to recognize – which sometimes they do not – that students are very differently placed in relation to these conventions and the academy (in national variants) as a whole, according to their biographies, educational experiences, cultural codes and social and geographical journeys.

We have found it helpful to realize – and teach – that not all the functions of writing have to be met at once: writing can be accumulative in more than one way, with particular attention to arguments and intellectual results at one stage and in one draft and close application to presentation and readership in another. Writing difficulties often arise because all the different anxieties that attend the writer are concentrated in a single moment – the writing up of something that must please a tutor and convince an examiner. These difficulties are more than intellectual – academic writing is also a challenge to perform a new identity, which can be painfully at odds with past self-presentation and current loyalties.

Diversity in the writing process – planning and writing

At all stages, researchers write in different ways. A persistent difference is between planners and writers. Year after year in the groups we teach, this difference emerges, though often to different degrees. Planners produce detailed plans or notey drafts before they write – often in great detail, indicating even quotations and references to be used. They find it hard to write until this is done. Then they start at the beginning and go through to the end. 'Writers', on the other hand, seem to do a minimum of preparation. They start writing with a limited plan or a broad aim alone, arguing that discoveries occur in the writing. They may not begin at the beginning, but instead with some key idea or problem. They may produce many fragments of this kind and only order them later.

It it useless or worse to try to win writers away from the writing method they use. When the differences are not recognized, conflicts with advisers may contribute to writing blocks. Many academic advisers favour planning, as does good supervision practice, because it allows for fuller communication in the early stages. The research proposal formalizes this preference, for educational and regulative purposes. A better strategy, however, is to enquire into individual writing processes and seek to enhance them. By the third year of a degree, students are experienced writers and many have developed practices and rituals providing comfort in a stressful activity. Yet, both routes to writing processes, often developed in essay writing, have their own limits, especially when applied to theses or dissertations.

Minute planning can kill creative discovery and produce stolid plods through a predetermined subject. It can be associated with the setting of inhibitingly high standards for a first draft. It helps to remember that replanning is likely and that, with modern word processing programs, a text can be revised and manipulated many times if necessary. This can take the pressure off 'version one' and encourage creative departures in the writing. Writers are in danger of losing their way in a long piece of work, so planning episodes during writing – writing, reflecting, then rewriting – can be useful. It may be that best practice moves towards mixed forms, combining spontaneous and rougher writing, planning episodes and extensive revision, including movement back and forth from sources.

Writing and the autobiographical voice

The classic voice of science bids for authority by showing the detachment of the researcher (Latour and Woolgar, 1979). However, this will not work in writing that is informed by an understanding of cultural processes. Writing is both self-production and 'produces' readers, too, but there is no obvious single answer to constructing a preferred rhetoric in cultural studies, except to say that the personal voice, which recognizes its own *produced* subjectivity, is appropriate here as one strategy among others.

An additional twist, however, is the difference between the permitted voices of traditional humanities and social science. In the humanities, it is acknowledged that writing itself is a mode of discovery. Interpretation is central, the literariness of writing is acknowledged and the use of metaphor, for example, more permitted and freer than in the social sciences. Interpretative approaches encourage writing that incorporates personal responses and reflections. Literary criticism, theoretical polemic and the essay form can all be intensely personal – this has all been well represented in cultural studies.

This old-style humane personalism is not, however, the same as the kind of self-reflexivity that we have been advocating. The old voice can be very complacent and monologic. The main reason for recognizing our own partiality and subjectivity is to make way for dialogue with others whose voices, therefore, should be a presence in our text. However, these will still have to include versions of our own voice, appearing sometimes as an 'I'. As we argue that subjectivity is a resource, not merely a liability, this may sometimes include extended auto/biographical work. This involves two 'I's': an 'I' who *presents* autobiographical episodes as ways of studying, say, subjectivity or memory, and an 'I' who *comments* on the first autobiographical voice. Similarly, the 'I' who starts a project is never quite the same 'I' who concludes it and this can be represented in the writing. Critical auto/biography, which is a strong movement in both cultural studies and sociology, provides resources for dealing with these issues.

In general, then, while we favour writing oneself into the project, we think that this implies more than opening confessions of partiality or a paragraph on reflexivity in the method chapter. It has implications for the whole work. In theoretical review or 'overview', for example, it suggests that positions should be mapped from a clear perspective, which itself can change. Some of the dislike of reflexivity and auto/biography that we notice in the literature on research may be a response to the cultural superiority of some humanist approaches, refurbished no doubt by newer kinds of arrogance. We agree with Les Back that reflexivity can 'degenerate into solipsism and self-absorption, where social researchers are continually examining their own discrete and sometimes stale professional culture' (1998: 292). Commitment to dialogue with others, accountability to subjects and readers and an openness to difference and change are rather different. It is because it involves others in this way that writing is never just about poetics – it is about politics and ethics as well.

Writing ethics and politics: authorial power and its deployment

Student researchers often feel subordinated in the moment of writing because of its association with assessment, so it is hard to realize that writing is itself a form of power. Writing creates a little world where the author has command over structure, the power to organize the material, pulling together different threads into a coherent story. This includes the sayings and doings of others, according to their chosen form of analysis and theoretical frame (Hansen et al, 1998: 60). Editorial authority has the power to cut, paste and tidy up others' words from texts and interviews and frame and gloss their meaning. If a single dominant authorial voice is produced, other voices can be silenced and othered, reduced to objects of scrutiny or the gaze. This isn't just a personal power as it depends on the author's own social positionalities and the discourses employed in writing. The asymmetrical relations of different social groups to the academy – with its predominantly male, white, middle-class character and conventions mean that writing is very different, as an act of power, especially for differently positioned authors. Yet, critiques of such power are now trenchant in cultural research. Classical ethnography, for instance, has been criticized for being ethnocentric and androcentric (Moore, 1988), with authors implicitly speaking on behalf of the societies they research (Hammersley and Atkinson, 1995).

Our view of research as a dialogue with others has many implications for these issues of authorial power. It points towards practices that make visible not only the partialities of the author but also the nature of the relations with others we enter into when researching. In some ways, these are familiar issues in traditional scholarship, though contemporary postmodern discussion suggests further possibilities. We are thinking of practices of careful quotation and referencing especially. It is worth spending a little longer on both these practices, reframing them in terms of our own concerns.

Referencing

Citing the work of others via references in the text or in foot- or endnotes can buttress authorial power in quite negative ways. It can be a kind of academic name-dropping. It can reproduce the idea that knowledge is individualized, that it is a form of property. It can reinforce the academic colonization of knowledge by omitting to reference non-academic sources; it can nurture cliques, social exclusions and celebrity reputations. Significantly, perhaps, it is often a source of anxiety among new academic writers.

Yet, referencing is also a way of expressing relations of indebtedness and difference. It represents and develops the dialogue with the work of others, positioning our own arguments in relation to them. If we try to be clear about these relations – and clear in our communications in general – then it is easier for others to join in. There is a case for thinking hard, in relation to any project, about the choice of referencing conventions, especially between the footnotes or endnotes favoured in humanities and the rather truncating Harvard system, as used in this book. Sometimes the more fully dialogic recognition of sources, possible in footnotes, is preferable to the curt '(Smith, 1997: 12)'. References and bibliographies can be seen, and designed, as means of access to a discussion for new readers. There are few aids more useful when starting a project than a thoughtful and thorough bibliography or literature review.

Many voices – quotation, dialogue and multiple authorships

Traditional scholarly practices of careful quotation and paraphrasing of the work of others fits, in many ways, with our own stress on dialogue and writing-as-research. Choosing a quotation and commenting on it is a key moment of learning in dialogic writing. It is a key moment for readers, too, because they can see what we make of something they can also read.

Beyond this, however, there is much contemporary enthusiasm for multiply voiced texts and mixed- or multi-genre writing – combining, for example, poetic, autobiographical and analytical forms – though there is also some scepticism. We favour experimentation of this kind, which draws on postmodern ethics and aesthetics, especially where it breaks up the privileging of masculine and middle-class modes of representation over more marginalized points of view and where multiplicity and difference are visibly negotiated on the page. Yet, willingness to *read* in an equally experimental way is not yet widespread among academic assessors and is uneven across the disciplines. As we argued earlier, thought has to be given to particular circumstances (of assessment especially) when risking breaking of conventions. Even using multiple voices, moreover, does not efface (though it may disguise) the orchestrating power of a partial author.

Sharing research and authorship is another writing strategy (for a fuller commentary, see Johnson, 1998). This can be very transformative for all concerned, but it is important to recognize that differences in power relations and fields of knowledge are always brought into such collaboration. Negotiations are especially complex when the subjects of research also become its authors. Decisions still have to be made, for example, about whether to aim at a relatively unified authorial voice – our choice in this book – or represent differences within an authorial group and how to do this. Moreover, these decisions are closely related to questions of audience. In her work on Mexican women in the rainforest, Janet Townsend (1994, 1995) shared authorship with her co-researchers, but the ways in which the dynamics of that sharing were manifested shifted with the different types of texts. Townsend herself worked with the commissioning editors of the series of which the academic text became a part, but, when the Spanish edition of the book was used to lobby the Mexican government, that power balance shifted towards her co-authors.

In our view, finding a voice is one of the most complex and taxing tasks of single *or* composite authorship. In writing, we have to negotiate our relationships with the principal others who are the subjects in our research, with our readers, imagined and real, and all the significant others who crowd our pages or peer, in ghostly form, over our shoulders as we write.

Conclusion

This chapter concludes our laying out of some of the groundwork of method in cultural studies. Research always involves a combination of practical activities including reading, refining our thinking, talking to others and writing. We have sought to show that these activities are not discrete and need to be managed in combination. Thus, not all reading around is done at the beginning; not all writing is done towards the end. We have tried to encourage an open, experimental practice that is aware of the conventions and rules, but also of their limits, and is reflective about the processes and conditions of working. Just as every project has to find its method, so all researchers have to find a process that works not only for their topics but also in the conditions of their lives.

These features of openness and self-reflection are linked to the dynamic nature of cultural research. In contemporary studies particularly, we are often caught up in the shifts of cultural formations and political events as part of our own social, spatial and temporal contexts. In Part II we look at some of these settings or contexts of research, settings that, in most cases, are also an aspect of the subjects of study themselves.

Notes

1 This chapter is mainly based on our own practices as supervisors and teachers of method, which is why there are relatively few references. We would particularly like to thank the thesis and dissertation writers with whom we have worked over the years, especially successive student groups on the Research Practice programme in the Faculty of Humanities at Nottingham Trent University, whose work and dialogues have strongly shaped this chapter. The chapter is also shaped by our rethinking of these practices, as represented by the early chapters of this book and our reading cited there.

2 We are especially grateful to Pat Noxolo for her discussions and writings on this theme.

3 For what it's worth, we favour computer files – especially as the size and divisions within a bibliography grow.

4 Mass Observation was a British experiment in popular anthropology set up in 1937. It encouraged participants to record their thoughts and views on everyday life in the form of diaries, letters and essays that later formed the basis for the collection. These were, however, documents aimed at a public readership and tended to express that in their articulation of specific kinds of knowledge and pleasure.

Part II
SETTINGS

Introduction

This part of the book is organized around some features of human life that enter into all our studies. These include the processes of thinking or abstraction (Chapter 5), our involvement in power and social relations (Chapter 8) and the organization of our existence in space and time (Chapters 6 and 7). Culture is always produced in such settings, but they are also settings for our practices of research. As we have seen in Chapter 3, space, time and social relations are key aspects of our positioning as researchers, our relations with others in our research and the partiality of our (and their) points of view. An understanding of settings or contexts and the ways in which they pressure or limit knowledge and cultural production, is important, therefore, both for our reflexive practice and our dialogue with others.

These ontological features, or basic aspects of human life or being, have a very interesting relation to academic disciplines. The disciplines often focus on one feature. We could say, for instance, that, while history deals primarily with the medium of time or temporality, geography is preoccupied with place and space. Similarly, if there is one discipline especially concerned with questions of thinking, it is probably philosophy, while social relations and power are shared among the social sciences. Academic disciplines, in other words, tend to make a specialism of ontological features. This has certain advantages and disadvantages. It focuses intense attention on one aspect, but also limits and contains enquiry. Issues of temporality, for example, tend to be narrowed to 'the study of the past' – one not very adequate definition of the subject of history. Philosophy, in its anglophone traditions especially, can become very technical. However, if our general argument is right, these features are too important to be left to specialists and so non-specialist reappropriations are necessary.

Cultural studies is an interdisciplinary project where such appropriations are very common and, in this part of the book, we make some of these dialogues explicit. In Chapter 5, we stress the importance of conceptualization or relatively abstract thinking, but also its limits, especially in relation to the more empirical moments in research. Cultural studies, according to this view, is marked by conceptual explicitness and adventures in thinking, but it is also committed to detailed research that can recast or qualify our abstractions. The practical problems of securing this dialogue between levels or kinds of knowledge are addressed centrally in this chapter.

Chapter 6 focuses on the ways in which space and place influence the research we do and how an awareness of spatial issues can enrich our understanding of cultural processes. As this very popular metaphor might suggest, the borderlands between cultural studies and cultural geography are among the busiest and most exciting spaces in the study of culture. This chapter argues, however, for cultural research that takes a less metaphorical and more material view of space and place. It also engages with the key contemporary issues of the global and transnational.

Chapter 7 turns to issues of time and temporality and the longstanding but somewhat interrupted dialogue with history-writing and research. A principle aim of this chapter is to refresh a dialogue that became wearisome as a result of quite acrimonious debates about theory in the late 1970s. Since this time, like other disciplines, historical studies have taken a decisive (though not exclusive) turn towards culturality – that is, towards a concern with cultural forms and processes. There are now major convergences between cultural (and other) histories and historically informed cultural studies. This chapter aims to foster that connection while identifying what might be distinctive about a cultural studies view of the temporal.

In Chapter 8, we address the settings of power and social relations. The picture is more complex here as many disciplines take this as a principle focus. Forced to select, we decided to take the long and somewhat repetitious debate with political economy as our key example, though we make some reference to 'social theory' – one particular style of sociology. In truth, the engagement with issues usually tracked by the social sciences, is too extensive to be contained in a single chapter. Much of this book can be read as a dialogue with sociology (see especially Part IV), just as it can also be read as a long argument with literary and textual studies (see especially Part III). The issue of 'economy and culture', however, has assumed such importance in contemporary debate and research that we dedicate a chapter to it.

5 Theory in the practice of research

Theory, fear and loathing	**87**
Theory as opposed to practice	**89**
Theory and practice as praxis	**90**
Theory and the empirical	**93**
Reading for theory as a method	**97**
The argument so far	**98**
Theory as abstraction	**98**
Levels of abstraction	**99**
Kinds of abstraction: strengths and limits	**100**
Conclusion: theorizing as a practice	**102**

In this chapter we discuss theorizing as a practice in order to place it within the research process. We approach this first by addressing some commonly encountered fears about 'doing theory'. We then map some differences in expectations about what theory can deliver. These differences seem to arrange themselves along two major dimensions, suggesting four contrasting poles. The first dimension concerns the relation between theory and practice and runs from their separation and opposition (theory versus practice) to their fusion (theory as practice). The second dimension concerns the relation between abstract thinking and empirical research and runs from strongly theory-led epistemologies, where key concepts are held to determine the direction of research, to strongly empirical conceptions of knowledge, where explicit theorization is kept to a minimum.

In describing these four positions – and locating them diagrammatically – we argue for a position of our own, which takes something from each pole. This position is summed up halfway through the chapter (see below under the heading The argument so far). We then turn to the idea of theory as abstraction – our own preferred approach, which allows us to argue for the close interconnections of different levels of abstraction. We conclude with some rules of thumb for 'doing theory' without theory 'doing' us.

Theory, fear and loathing

The word 'theory' can instil awe or fear, which can slide, in other contexts, into suspicion. It can also be promoted as a kind of master narrative, so that to be thought 'a theorist' is both to excel and carry burdens of envy, distrust and the power to intimidate. In *Keywords*, Raymond Williams identifies a long-term suspicion of theory in English culture dating back to the seventeenth century. Theory has been linked with speculation, fantasy and dreaming and, indeed, is still often opposed to empirical science and being practical (1983: 316–18). In politics, it is often placed in opposition to 'practice' or being 'realistic'. These tensions – so different from the high value placed on '*theoria*' in ancient Greek culture or German humanism (see Gadamer, 1998: 16–36) or the prestige accorded to philosophy in France or Scotland – resurfaced in the debates about theory in history and cultural studies in the late 1970s. It was at this time that the turn towards culture seemed to install a canon of cultural writings that acquired a reified character and an overvalued celebrity status. Within the restricted world of academic reputations, empirically led researchers often felt devalued.

Even today in the academy, the word 'theory' often represents ideas at their most complex, abstract and difficult. It is sometimes hard to see the point of a particular theory on first reading and without an adequate context as theoretical abstraction can segregate ideas from the particularities they refer to and the social experiences that generated them. In more ordinary learning situations, 'theory' slides into meaning the already known – what is already in the archive, written, stored and reproduced in books and journals – and, by implication, already carries a higher value than our own work. Students struggle to relate what *they* know or can find out to the theories that they find in the libraries and hear from the mouths of tutors.

Theoretical writing has also deployed particular forms of language. In anglophone cultural studies it has often come to us in translation, from French especially, and the anglophone reader may not know its original cultural context. Long sentences, translated from another language and intellectual tradition, make ideas that are already complex still harder to grasp – they have a kind of hidden otherness. The allusions of such writing when it appears in English can be a problem, too. Because what counts as 'theory' is most commonly generated within academic institutions (though not necessarily so), it can position the reader as someone who doesn't yet know but will, presumably, learn. In all this, it is terribly easy to lose sight of the relationships between thinking, reading and writing and everyday practices and to fail to see ideas as the result of a process.

We have already argued that we see theory and its practice as a crucial aspect of cultural studies. Certainly, theory is intrinsic to research activity. Research is as much about thinking and reflecting as it is about carrying out surveys, conducting interviews or reading texts. At stake is the acquisition – or not – of capacities for critical thinking and writing that is self-reflective and communicative because it is conceptually clear. It is important both to think and know what we are thinking. So, against the put-downs and the fear that theory generates, we want to insist that (to retranslate Gramsci) 'everyone is a "philosopher"' (1971: 323). We *all* develop theories to make sense of the world, narrow choices by following a set of principles and provide coherence in our lives. Theory in this sense is everywhere; it is not restricted to the academic domain. Theories are embedded in political programmes, strategies and manifestos; they organize the details of narratives and descriptions. When we think, we always have recourse to some structure of assumptions about the world, however implicit. Theories in research may be more complex and fully articulated than the theories we need to get through the day, but this is a difference of explicitness, scope and coherence, not of kind.

To take these points further, it is useful to sketch some of the main ways in which theory has been conceptualized, especially in relation to practice and empirical research. We will assess the limits of each of these approaches, but also be seeking to carry forward some elements from each position in order to clarify our own point of view.

Theory as opposed to practice

Theory can be seen as a self-validating activity that is opposed to practice. As such, it entails curiosity, witness, contemplation, interpretation or understanding – intellectual labour in the purest sense. In an essay entitled 'Praise of Theory', Gadamer upholds this view of theory, which he first derives from classical Greek thinking about *theoria*. He uses it to question the modern organization of science, especially the subordination of theory to practice or theory's allocation to 'a modest sanctuary' of 'pure science'. He stresses 'its proximity to mere play, to mere looking and wondering at something, far removed from all use, profit and serious business' (Gadamer, 1998: 17). As always, he stresses the virtues of striving to understand something that is other, that which is not ourselves. Of course, as he argues, the same splitting of theory from practice, with the values inverted, is also a way in which research is sidelined and subordinated, not simply to practice but to specific conceptions of what is useful.

At the end of *Praise of Theory*, in a partial deconstruction of his own arguments, Gadamer shows how intertwined theory and practice are. There is a *practice of theorizing*, and practice itself is inadequate without what he calls 'the self out-stripping question' (1998: 12).

> Just as the individual who needs relevant knowledge must constantly reintegrate theoretical knowledge into the practical knowledge of his everyday life, so also a culture based on science cannot survive unless rationalizing the apparatus of civilization is not an end in itself, but makes possible a life to which one can say 'yes'. In the end all practice suggests what points beyond it. (Gadamer,1998: 35–6)

It seems important to carry forward into our own approach some elements of this 'praise of theory', especially those that go beyond instrumental motives for finding things out. Anyone who embarks on a substantial piece of research knows that it takes more than calculated pragmatism to finish it, and finish it well (see under Choosing and developing a topic in Chapter 4). We stress 'some elements', however, because liberal humanist justifications are also associated with elite entitlements and a certain social irresponsibility. The praise of theory can become an overidentification with academic ways of thinking and claims for autonomy. Cultural studies, as part of the critical academy, has not been exempt from intellectual exclusiveness of a paradoxical kind, in which competence in theoretical codes and ideas become prerequisites for entry to the field. Interest in theory may start from a desire to explain culture with due complexity, but can end up excluding from debates those very groups implicated in the research. Tensions between excitement about a new way of looking at a problem and accessibility or usefulness can be acute. There has been a strong strand of intense seriousness about intellectual work in cultural studies, linked to a hope of its long-term social usefulness. This has often provoked a more popular tendency to debunk such pretensions.

We conclude that there are actually good *social* reasons for refusing to internalize the narrowing of ambitions, both in education and in research, that is a marked feature of governmental and corporate control today. Gadamer's main theme – the pleasures of the effort to understand, akin to appreciation of the beautiful – should perhaps be celebrated more. We can all experience the pleasure of seizing on a new idea, making it our own and recognizing how it changes us, too.

> When we understand a text, what is meaningful in it captivates us just as the beautiful captivates us. It has asserted itself and captivated us before we can come to ourselves and be in a position to test the claim to meaning that it makes. What we encounter in the experience of the beautiful and in understanding the meaning of tradition really has something of the truth of play about it. (Gadamer, 1989: 490)

Theory and practice as praxis

Mainly, however, cultural studies has been associated with a version of the theory–practice relation that is at the opposite pole from classic humanism or its utilitarian inversions. A key word here has been 'praxis' – a term the specialized modern sense of which is Hegelian or Marxist. As Williams puts it, 'praxis is practice informed by theory and also, though less emphatically, theory informed by practice'. In a typical Williams formulation (note the 'whole's in the quote that follows and the resistance to abstraction) praxis describes 'a whole mode of activity in which, by analysis but only by analysis, theoretical and practical elements can be distinguished, but which is always a whole activity, to be judged as such' (1983: 318).

Praxis makes sense of many aspects of cultural studies – the emphasis on power, links with the agenda of social movements, stress among advocates on '*doing* cultural studies' (Ang, 1998; du Gay et al., 1997) and even the quotations from Gramsci and Marx (see for example those from Marx's 'Theses on Feuerbach' in Suchting, 1979). Our own foregrounding of research practice and research processes, the social *relationships* of research and (alternative) forms of accountability are also attempts to develop research and method as praxis (see the Introduction and Chapters 3 and 4 especially). What, then, are the implications of the praxis position for the practice of theorizing?

Theory as embedded

All researchers are *already* theorists. We consciously and unconsciously draw on a range of resources, including texts of various kinds, social practices, our experiences (including hunches and assumptions derived from particular beliefs or allegiances) and what we have inferred from the experiences of others. These starting points include 'theories' in several different senses. They include our prior mining of public archives in libraries and on the Internet, but also our own premeanings and assumptions. They include what Gramsci (1971: 323) calls 'common sense' ('the "spontaneous philosophy" which is proper to everyone') and the more self-conscious and elaborated theories (which Gramsci calls 'philosophy').

Theory as explictness and critique

'Theory' is also about making these pretheories more explicit and open to challenge. From one point of view this is an aspect of reflexivity that we have already discussed. The need for theorizing that is (self-)critical, however, also arises from the relationship between knowledge and power. Critical theory is necessary because the operations of power are not always directly *observable* and are often hidden. Although the most powerful people or groups – or their intellectuals – create the ruling ideas, they have the capacity to remove themselves and their instruments of power from interrogation or study. Structures of power can also be taken for granted because they define everyday realities for most people most of the time. Certain aspects of injustice or domination may not be visible from some points of view. The immediate experience of workers does not directly include the machinations of international finance capital. Many citizens of First World states do not have experience of the poverty and displacement endemic in other parts of the world. Of course, some of these limits to knowledge can be overcome by better observations, dialogues across major differences and political alliances, but specifically cultural processes are also involved here. These make social appearances *seem* 'natural' – if not fair, then necessary and impossible to change. In the best reading of Gramsci, hegemony works not by persuading everyone to think the same, but by convincing enough people that there is no alternative. In Foucault's terms, systematic knowledges – contemporary neo-liberal economics, for instance – construct their own 'regimes of truth', have their own 'reality effects' and, in fact, construct realities as a result of discourses, policies and practices of their own (Foucault, 1980). Anyone who has sought to conduct interviews with relatively powerful people can bear witness to such combined effects – the difficulties and intimidations of access in the first place, the problem of getting behind the persuasive self-justifications or the official line, pressure to become complicit with a dominant viewpoint, the struggle to find questions that halt the flow and open up contradictions and the force of appeals to what is real, realistic or works, given existing power relations.[1]

However, the *effects* of power *are* observable – and they are material to our own positioning within these structures. Once we recognize that our theories are situated, too, we can see the value of critical questioning, especially where it draws on subordinated points of view, our own or others'. If we are in relatively powerful positions ourselves, we can avoid a complicit dialogue with the powerful by also talking to subordinated groups. In any case, we cannot depend only on our own experiences to construct our theories. It is crucial to be open to the experience of others and to engage effectively with different theoretical voices. An explicitly theorized critical framework enables us to work with the visible aspects of a power structure (such as the hierarchical structures of state bureaucracy or the patterns of ownership of media corporations) in order to develop an analysis that explores the less visible parts (from secret agreements between organizations or states to the production of consent).

Theory as extending experience

It is important not to reduce theory to *anybody's* experience or essentialize it. No one's experience offers a direct route to adequate theory. To theorize, we have to reflect on experience and do so through a theoretical lens. The lens will magnify certain elements of the material, clarify its structures and relationships and help us to focus on significant elements. Reflection is a necessary stage in the development of a fully theorized account. As we shall argue later, reflection involves abstraction but is rarely a purely cerebral process. Thinking, knowledge and feeling are closely bound up in complex ways. Our emotions inform and shape our intellectual processes, they are not outside them. The relationship between the intellectual labour of theorization and emotional labour of politics is particularly close in cultural studies. It follows that a certain emotional literacy – if not a theoretical knowledge of identity and emotional processes – is important, too, in theoretical work. It is not surprising, perhaps, that this is one of the areas of growth in cultural studies (see Chapter 14 below).

Theory as practice, practice as theory

It is not enough to question our existing positions, enable dialogue and reveal structures of power, though much critical intellectual work, including our own, ends with this at best. The idea that theory is tested by practice is sometimes seen as involving pragmatic closures, an overpoliticizing of knowledge and the abandonment of questions of truth. This is not necessarily the case, however. Praxis implies responsibilities for the practical effects and implications of our knowledge and research processes. It implies internal dialogues between our theories and other modes of acting in the world. Praxis means taking our own and other's theories seriously enough to seek to act and live by them, letting what is learned in the living also test and develop the theories. Drawing theory closer to practice may bring knowledge to account at the bar of politics (where it already has a place as witness), but also summons politics to the bar of knowledge and truthfulness. We can be intensely practical, yet critical of short-sighted utilitarianism or knowledge that *only* expresses wishes (important though wishes are). Praxis applies with special force to ways of being a teacher, student and citizen of the academy as a form of polity or public sphere activity, but it also applies to more private or everyday sites – and to 'big P' politics. A really good theory doesn't only understand or explain, it suggests strategies and tools to either change things or defend things that are good. Only in difficult struggles for consistency of this kind do the practical and theoretical cease to be antithetical positions and become embedded in each other.

The relationship between 'theory' and 'practice' is therefore a double articulation. We make explicit and think about our assumptions, for these influence what we see and do. We also allow what we see and do to challenge our theories and provide a better basis for our thinking. This is why empirical engagement – which hermeneutics sees as the understanding of 'alterity' – is also critical for theoretical work. As Stuart Hall has put it, 'Until you go to cultural studies through these structures, not from within cultural studies itself but from these externalities, you don't really translate it, you just borrow it, renovate it, play at recasting it' (1996d: 397).

Theory and the empirical

The second polarity in defining theory concerns its relation to empirical research. In cultural studies, this opposition has often surfaced in polemics around structuralism, postmodernism and empiricism (see, for example, Edward P. Thompson, 1978), but the issues are important generally in the human sciences.

Concept-led approaches

In rationalist or theory-led epistemologies, knowledge depends on the framework of categories that selects the questions posed. Any particular framework of assumptions allows us to ask *some* questions, but silences others. Different terms are used to describe such structures of assumptions, in part according to discipline. 'Paradigm' (Thomas Kuhn, 1970) is a sociological version, 'problematic' (Althusser and Balibar, 1970) a philosophical or conceptual version and 'episteme' (Foucault, 1974) a more historical version. Althusser's version, influential in cultural studies, is worth quoting at length. He and Balibar are discussing Marx's critique of political economy and the 'epistemological break', or fundamental theoretical shift, that distinguished Marx's analysis from political economy, Hegelian philosophy and Marx's own early work:

> This introduces us to a fact peculiar to the very existence of science: it can only pose problems upon the terrain and within the horizon of a definite theoretical structure, its problematic, which constitutes its absolute and definite condition of possibility, and hence the absolute determination of *the forms in which all problems must be posed,* at any given moment in the science. (1970: 25, emphasis in original)

These authors work very hard to argue that the force of a problematic lies in the effect of the concepts themselves – a typically structuralist view. It is not a personal point of view or a social positionality that constitutes the frame of a problematic but the concepts themselves as a structure or field. Possibilities for change thus come from within a theoretical problematic, itself. 'A revolution in an old theory' starts from a new answer without a question. This is a symptom of a question that cannot be posed within the old frame. An example is Marx's development of the theory of surplus labour, which appears in classical economics but is not theorized there.

> These new objects and problems are necessarily *invisible* in the field of the existing theory, because they are not objects of this theory, because they are *forbidden* by it – they are objects and problems necessarily without any necessary relations with the field of the visible as defined by this problematic . . . and that is why their fleeting presence in the field when it does occur (in very peculiar and symptomatic circumstances) *goes unperceived*, and becomes literally an undivulgeable absence – since the whole function of the field is not to see them, to forbid any sighting of them. (Althusser and Balibar, 1970: 26; emphasis in original)

A particular kind of reading is needed to make the absences – which structure much of what goes on in a theory – fully explicit. This method is called 'symptomatic reading' because it divulges the undivulged event in the text it reads. At the same time, it relates this event to a different text, as yet unwritten, where the answer will eventually find its question. Thus 'surplus value' comes to be a linchpin in Marx's theory of exploitation and the reproduction of capital (for further discussion of this method, see Chapter 11).

Empirical objections

It is easy to see why Althusserian and similar epistemologies are a provocation to those who hold to strongly empirical forms of research. The empirical is secondary here. Sometimes it is hard to see what contribution it can possibly make to knowledge as the conceptual field determines all observations. 'Research', indeed, is a key absence in Althusser's own problematic. Similarly, the symptom or anomaly that stimulates critique and can transform what Kuhn calls 'normal science' is a textual or conceptual event, not an event in the world outside the text. It is not produced by a change of point of view or movement in history itself or new set of observations – as we would argue it often is.

Empiricist difficulties

In terms of cultural theory, conceptually led epistemologies are a form of cultural determinism. Yet many objections to an Althusserian method have themselves depended on notions of fact and evidence that are reductionist in that they ignore or underestimate the relational dynamics between researcher and researched and their mutual entanglements in cultural forms. We agree with E. P. Thompson that conceptually led epistemologies do not allow for or subordinate the dialogue of 'concept' and 'evidence', 'hypothesis' and 'empirical research', thought and 'its object' (1978: 229–42). They are not forced to face 'the others' of their thinking. However, the idea that facts or evidence are somehow given or already there to be interrogated (Thompson, 1978: 220–1) is itself a defensive fantasy that is very limiting when it comes to thinking about method. In empirical critiques of rationalism such as Thompson's, we are rarely told much about the *process of reading* sources, as texts or otherwise – something that must occur before facts are established. Generally, the role of conceptualization is limited as theories are mainly questions or hypotheses that have little power until tested or grounded. Theory here is mainly a *prerequisite* for producing knowledge. Going much beyond hypothesis or analysis to further abstractions is liable to mislead.

Against this tendency, we insist that happenings only come to be facts in the context of theory. Our reading, hearing, seeing and remembering is already influenced by presuppositions. Our theories affect how we define our research, locate our sources, choose our texts, analyse and interpret and, of course, how we write. While there is a real world (ontological realities), we can only have access to it via a self and mental apparatus (concepts as well as a mind) that are located, positioned and culturally produced. We can only describe this real world by means of theories of what constitutes the real, modified by encounters with others and objects, including those we treat as evidence or source.

Let us revisit Figure 3.1, reproduced here as Figure 5.1, representing the circuit of research as a cultural process, to make these points in another way.

The small circuit (the circuit within the circuit) is only a part of the larger circuit of research. The small circuit affects the larger circuit, but the larger circuit encloses and feeds into the smaller circuit. There is an inner dialogue of self–other, theory–object that it is at the heart of research. Without this dialogue,

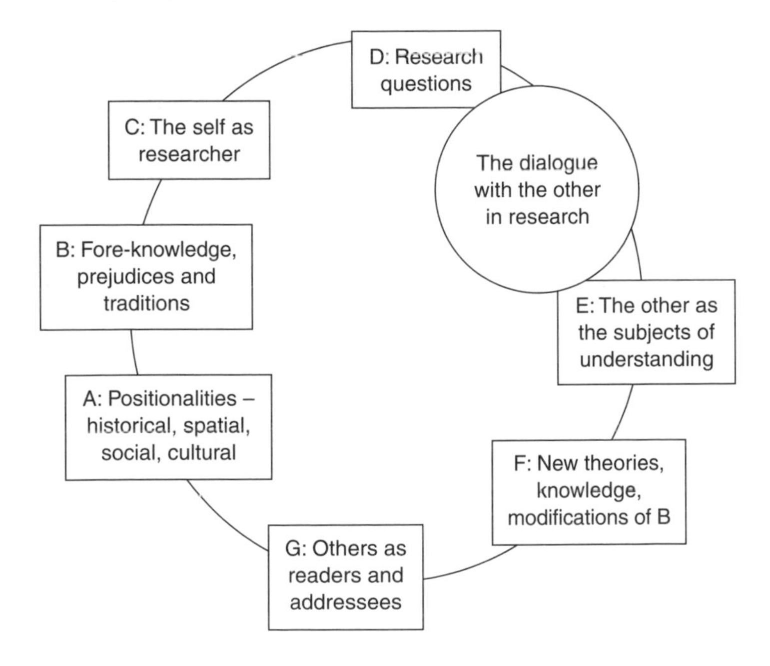

Figure 5.1 Cultural research as a cultural circuit

which involves self-distancing and changes of horizon, it is not clear how learning, or what Ricoeur calls 'refiguration', can occur.

As the circuit suggests, however, not all learning comes from the dialogue that is empirical research. We may also encounter a new theory. We may engage in a new movement, or with a new social group or be caught up in cultural currents new to us. We may be challenged, politically and personally. Significant learning may happen independently of our researching activities, feeding back into our studies. There are also serendipitous events, hard to theorize except as accidents. We often experience shifts of perspective during our researching lives that stem from social movements and new forms of politics. Most professionalized epistemologies separate specialized learning from ordinary living or even from broader non-disciplinary intellectual activity – our general reading and teaching, for instance. A cultural approach to method, which draws on feminist insights, has to repair these splits.

Similarly, it is not the case that the only product of our research is a new empirical account or the proof or falsification of a hypothesis. New work can help to qualify or extend a body of theory – on racialization, patriarchal relations or capitalism's globalizing dynamics, for instance. Conceptually informed empirical research typically allows us to develop *intermediate* categories, concerning, for example, the combined structures of race, gender and class, or genres and subgenres of text or speech or different practices of consumption.

The empirical as other

We would argue, against Althusser, that change in a framework may not be so complete or sudden as his notion of 'epistemological rupture' prescribes, though moments of realization do often *seem* sudden. They may be based, however, on a slower accretion of empirically based knowledge that erodes the credibility of old frameworks. Surprise, however – which hermeneutics calls 'otherness' – is a crucial generative moment in research. Again and again, researchers return to us from the field exclaiming that it was not as they expected. It is possible to be jolted out of your existing knowledge and frameworks. Such experiences can be quite disorganizing, but become the basis for a more systematic rethink. Otherness, of course, can also take the form of a new conceptual framework that may also throw hitherto neglected observations into high relief because, as Althusser argues, they were already anomalies in the old framework. The idea that a critical change of framework comes about when we find answers to questions that are not posed in our existing framework has considerable *practical* value.

It is important to add that, in cultural studies, the empirical moment of the other is very often a matter of ideas. We may encounter others, in their sayings or texts, in the form of new ideas. Furthermore, all projects involve the mapping, assessment and critique of others' work in the fields of research. It is to this process – and the value of 'problematic' within it that we want to turn next. First, however, Figure 5.2 presents a summary of the different approaches to theory that we have discussed.

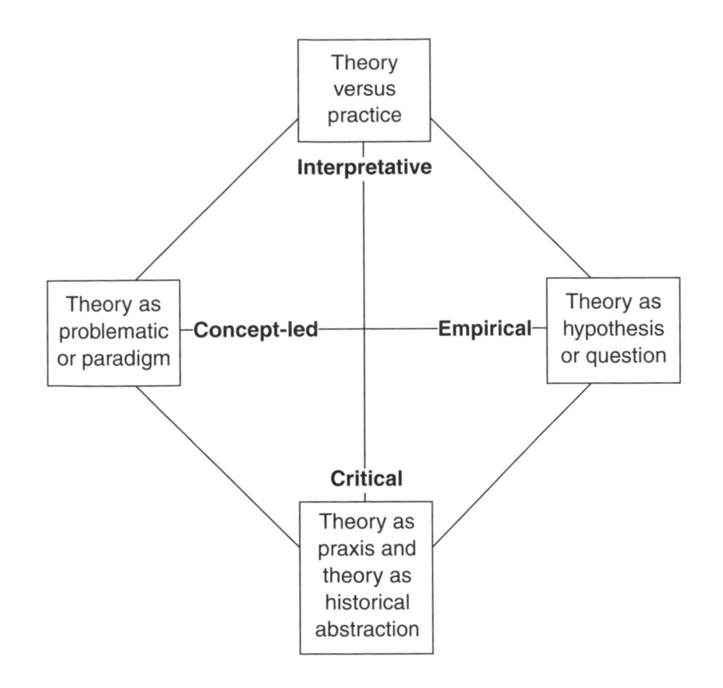

Figure 5.2 Approaches to theory

Reading for theory as a method

Theorizing develops in 'conversations' with other people's ideas. This is a further reason for not only talking about our research in everyday situations but also systematically reviewing the conceptual character of our field of study (see under the heading Reviewing the literature, mapping the field, Chapter 4). Reading for theory is a method that corresponds to this process of mapping. It involves not only identifying theoretical approaches around the topics that we choose to study but also engaging with them, thinking them through or critiquing them. It is here that the idea of theory as 'problematic' or organizing framework is useful in practice. To fully engage with the theories in our field we need to identify problematics or paradigms not in order to label or dismiss them but to lay out the different approaches and think through our own position in relation to them. A critical reading will seek to identify the standpoint of the authors or speakers and trace the conceptual framework that underpins the key questions and how this framework affects the substantive account. Presences and absences create patterns characteristic of specific formations.

One of the limits of the Althusserian version of theory, however, is that it is insensitive to the *historical* character of concepts and *social* circumstances of their production that shape and limit their use (Edward P. Thompson, 1978). Any theoretical problematic, like any literary genre, is both a formal structure and an historical event. This is why the history of conceptualizations – of theories of culture and power – is so important, not least as a guide to the scope and relevance of the categories themselves. In educational studies in the UK, for example, educational history was commonly presented in terms of a progressive and incremental struggle for more effective public provision. This was a framework associated with social-democratic and progressive educational politics that was only seriously questioned after the neo-liberal assaults on education policy during the 1970s. After that time, it was no longer possible to think of the extension of state schooling as fairly automatic and necessarily progressive. All theoretical approaches have a history and geographical, social, temporal and conceptual conditions of existence. We will return to theory and history in Chapter 7 and to the spatial conditions of thinking in Chapter 6.

The argument so far

So far, we have seen that theory is understood differently within different epistemologies and each version has implications for practice. Traditional humanistic approaches uphold theory as curiosity and openness against pressures towards the short term and utilitarian. While questioning the underlying assumptions of this view, we agree that intellectual work must have something of this character to be of any value. In strongly empirical epistemologies, theory is mainly limited to a question-posing function – the real knowledge being extracted, it is often not clear how, from source, evidence or fact. This is almost inverted in strongly rationalist approaches where concept-building is the key practice and the dialogue with evidence is hidden.

We ourselves draw on all these approaches, believing it is possible to combine paradigms, rearticulating elements from different sources. Rationalist epistemologies show how culture forms our thinking, right down to our (selective) observations. Empirically rich traditions insist on engagement with concrete other worlds, even though this engagement can never be transparent and direct. However, we locate our version of cultural studies mainly on the ground of praxis, where theory and politics, conceptualization and engagement with others are all aspects of research activity. What remains evasive, perhaps, is how we define theory and what its strengths and pitfalls might be. Some further answers are yielded by viewing theory as abstraction[2] and this is the emphasis of the rest of this chapter.

Theory as abstraction

All thinking works as a result of a process of abstraction, by which means details are simplified and links and relationships made more apparent. Abstraction is a kind of empirical disembedding, a move away from the complexity of the concrete, a shift from the particular to the general. This movement is not just logical simplification. Useful abstractions are abstractions from more particular circumstances already grasped in other ways – as a narrative, for example, or as a reading of a text or transcript. In fact, when we read or tell stories, we already abstract from a 'real' that is more complicated than we can possibly tell. So abstraction is a kind of editing in and editing out, choosing those elements that are relevant to our framework and leaving aside or, better, temporarily bracketing out (so not forgetting) those that are not.

Abstraction is not avoidable in intellectual work, but we can either do it unconsciously or more explicitly, being aware of the basis of our selections – our questions and their theoretical presuppositions. Being aware of theory, we can justify our choices and see their effects and make these visible to others. In this sense, too, intellectual work is always theoretical and never simply a kind of unprocessed taking in of the real. Questions are more than ways in, they select what we shall see.

On the other hand, our thinking may be more or less abstract or more or less concrete. 'Concrete' (a difficult word) can be used in two ways. It can mean the real – the actually existing – or it can mean a feature of *thinking* about the real. In concrete *accounts* – narratives and descriptive reportage, for example – we keep as much of the detail in play as possible, even at the expense of muddle. Such accounts are often called 'rich', but we can bracket out a lot of what we observe. We can take a single episode (one kind of abstraction) or abstract a single relation from a number of episodes (another kind). We can 'jump out' gendered interactions or read stories told to us in interviews as examples of the same narrative forms. So, it is useful to talk about levels of abstraction and note that abstractions take different forms. We discuss each of these in turn.

Levels of abstraction

The term 'theory' is usually reserved for higher levels of abstraction, for the more abstract accounts. 'Empirical' often refers to less abstract accounts. We are happy enough with this as a starting point, with two provisos. First, that less abstract accounts are also theoretically organized and are *accounts* (which is why we can abstract a theory from them). Second, that higher or lower levels of abstraction are not in themselves truer or more false. Theory isn't superior to description *in itself*, just as there are limits to being concrete. Both kinds of account refer to the real world and, depending on qualities that are not only to do with abstraction, may say things we need to know. Abstraction can achieve a certain clarity, especially for explanatory purposes; it can give a tight description of features of form or certain social dynamics. Concrete accounts can show how different features interact and convey something of the feel of a situation. We do not need to privilege either moment.

Intellectual work almost always involves different levels of abstraction. What matters most is how we manage the movements between the levels. An example of this process is when we decide whether or not to use an example in an argument that we have been putting in quite general terms. Is it to be an example only – an illustration of what we already know – or do we treat it as an item that generates further knowledges, more a generative incident, complete with its own surprises? Both ways of working are legitimate in our view, depending on our purposes, but they are different ways of handling levels.

If theory makes it possible to be clearer about a small set of relations, we should not confuse this abstraction with more concrete representations. A salutary example is Marx's theory of capitalism – one source of our thinking about abstraction in this chapter. In *Capital*, Marx develops a theory of capitalist development that stresses its radical instability and contradictoriness as a system of production and social relationships. Some readings of *Capital* (and sometimes Marx himself) present this in terms of 'laws of development', which include an inevitable social revolution. Marx has been proved right about many features he identified, but the 'laws' were an extrapolation that broke his own rules of method. His 'laws and tendencies' are not the same as a concrete history. They may have some predictive value, but leave out (abstract from) many strategies and forms of power relevant to predicting the future, especially the cultural forms and subjectivities embedded in particular capitalist regimes and the cultural and political conditions for successful transformations. The problem of some readings of *Capital*, then, is that they mistake the levels of abstraction in the work.

If we know that our more abstract thinking *is* theoretical, we also know that we have to return it *back* again to the more concrete account from which we abstracted it – or to equivalent cases. We can then establish its explanatory value. Moving between levels includes re-embedding our theories in the denseness of the particular, so that our understanding of the particular is enhanced. Theorization, therefore, involves a double articulation – a move away from the complexities of individual instances to relatively simplified concepts and then a move back to the concrete with our explanations enhanced. This process of explanation or concretion can be as exciting as the initial bright idea. In concretion, our theory finds further correction or elaboration. The *whole* circuit is necessary, which means it doesn't help to privilege one level or the other, except sometimes strategically.

Kinds of abstraction: strengths and limits

Levels of abstraction are linked to the scope or range of reference of the categories. A very thin abstraction, such as 'youth', can be presented as quite general – a stage of human life that appears universally. (If we said 'teenager', this apparent universality would be dented rather.) Thin or simple abstractions are often necessary – 'culture' and 'power' are cases in point – to demarcate a certain terrain, but they have only a very limited usefulness and carry certain perils. The opposite case is where an abstraction encompasses many relationships, perhaps too many – a form of abstraction that Marx called 'chaotic'. Chaotic abstractions attempt to grasp great complexity without analysing the different elements. Marx's favourite example was 'population', which includes everything! Many recent discussions in the media in the UK have focused on the problem of teenage sex and the phenomenon of single motherhood.

Commentaries and editorials claim interest in the welfare of young mothers, but offer opinions that demonize and castigate them. 'Single parent' as a category (almost always a mother) is linked to teenage pregnancy and, thence, to moral decline or youthful fecklessness. Everything is bundled together, without critical analysis, into single categories carrying a high moral charge. This kind of chaotic abstraction assumes that the determinations involved in sexual behaviour are simple, obvious and ahistorical and does not prompt empirical encounters with young pregnant women of a kind that might challenge the commentators' values.

The more abstract or thin a category is, the wider its scope of reference is likely to be. However, universalizing categories that ignore historical and spatial specificities, including their own, are notorious for being sources of exclusion and dominance. L.T. Smith (1999) points out that Eurocentric theories – of class or identity, for example – do not provide an adequate framework for understanding the lived experiences of Maori populations in New Zealand. Ien Ang observes how the globalization of cultural theory has involved the universalization of highly specific models of race produced in the particular context of America and the UK, but used to understand racialization in many other contexts, including Australia:

> The category 'black' in Australia refers to Aboriginal people, whose history of dispossession and genocide and whose resistive indigenous attachment to 'the land' have little in common with the African diasporic history of forced transatlantic movement. (Ang, 1998: 22)

Many other general categories travel uneasily, so, like 'youth', they are not nearly as universal as they seem. This is why intermediate levels of abstraction are especially important in research work, often marking points of originality and complex understanding. Such concepts allow us to grasp historical and geographical variations in the cultural handling of age stages or different forms of racism.

Another way of putting this is that good theory involves *historical* abstraction, categories that define and explain change over time and grasp coexisting patterns of difference. Marx gave to this idea of historical abstraction the force of a realist theory, arguing that it is only because the forms have developed in reality that we are able to grasp them in the mind. Abstraction, therefore, has a double character: it is both the way we think and a relation between thought and the social world to which that thinking belongs. Abstraction happens *in* thinking, but is a social process, too, on which thinking is based. By this argument, for instance, it becomes possible to think abstractly about education or media at the point where they emerge fully as separated institutions. This bold argument informs our own in several ways, especially our suspicion of universals. It is also why a general suspicion of abstraction (on the grounds that everything is always part of everything else) is at best only a partial insight or a valid wish.

Conclusion: theorizing as a practice

What, then, does theorizing mean in practice as an aspect of writing a project, dissertation or thesis? Of course, this, too, is a question that can be answered more or less concretely, more or less abstractly.

At the beginning of a piece of work, it is quite usual to be overwhelmed by the theories we come across and the extent of our ignorance generally. One way of countering this is to write a review of a key text, author or theory early in the research – a review that may become a section in the project or dissertation or a chapter in the thesis. We can start to develop our own position by working out how it differs from some main positions in the field. A theoretically informed literature review helps us to do just that as we can engage with the existing positions, decide on those we want to take on and those we side with. It also helps to bring out supporting positions and provides the basis for challenging others. As we have argued throughout, challenging others and being challenged by them is also a way of easing out what is particular and questionable about our own starting points, our own theories in this sense.

A theoretical review chapter or section, however, is not the only way in which to deal with the existing map of theories in a more extended piece of work. It is possible, for example, to begin with minimum statements of engagement, acknowledging our starting points and the dialogues that brought us to where we are theoretically. We can 'do theory', however, throughout our text, engaging with other writers at appropriate points, moving through the different levels.

How we incorporate more abstract conceptualizations into our research will vary with our purposes. Some dissertations or theses are primarily theoretical – they aim to develop concepts or argue with philosophers or cultural theorists. They may be reading for problematics all the time. In this case, lower levels of abstraction (not inferior, remember) may function as illustrative examples. Examples of this kind, chosen for their appropriateness to the argument, are essential for clarity. They enable the reader to grasp a point of theory in another way, via a richer set of associations.

In other types of work, we may want to work the other way across the different levels of abstraction. We may want to present a concrete instance first in narratives or rich descriptions, then tease out some notable features from them, analysing and commenting further, building our own theory.

The most important advice, perhaps, is not to view theories as starting points only, clustered at the beginning of a work. In teaching, we often find dissertation and thesis writers have difficulty in getting to their own work, feeling that they must first review what everyone else has been saying. This can marginalize work that is fascinating and original and ought to be foregrounded and is, in any case, new work. If we also place theoretical discussion towards the *end* of our piece, we ensure that we bring our findings back to the existing debates and show how our work may modify them. Theory is not a starting point only – it is not what someone else produces – it is part of our own production.

In conclusion, then, we can summarize – now more abstractly – what theorizing might, in practice, include.

- **Reflecting**
  Being aware of our own theoretical presuppositions (in a practical or more explicit form) and the ways in which they affect our research process and detailed accounts.
- **Reading**
  Reading the work of others critically with an eye to presuppositions and frameworks.
- **Mapping**
  Distinguishing different approaches in a field of study, where they clash and converge – not only in their observations or obvious forms of partiality but also as competing frameworks.
- **Abstraction**
  Using abstraction self-consciously as a deliberate simplification in order to be clearer about specific aspects of a problem or cultural formation without mistaking theory for the concrete.
- **Concretion**
  Moving between levels of abstraction in the course of our work, whether this is manifested as using examples for theoretical arguments or theories as explanations for what we have observed and represented in more concrete forms.
- **Theorizing**
  Producing new ideas, sometimes by extension or critique of others' work, sometimes by abstracting from research, sometimes by combining ideas usually held separate.

Not every piece of work can or will include all these aspects. In academic evaluations today, there is a tendency to rank such features and treat them as separate skills, albeit high-level ones. In our view, however, these aspects of theorizing are closely linked. They form a texture rather than a pathway – a texture that is independent thinking.

Notes

1 Having said this, we recognize that there are levels and layers of power involved here, and that power is differentially produced and experienced.

2 What follows is largely based on work done at the Centre for Contemporary Cultural Studies (CCCS) at Birmingham University in the early 1980s on the role of abstraction in Marx's method, partly to work through the problems encountered in the two-sided dialogues with Althusserians and Marxist historians (see especially Hall, 1973a – an important source text – and Johnson, 1982). All these ideas, however, have been re-thought in the collaborative writing of this volume. We are grateful to Mariette Clare for discussions on abstraction, pathways and texture.

6 Make space! Spatial dimensions in cultural research

Bringing place and space into focus	**105**
Complex spatialities	**107**
Theoretical tools for researching spatiality	**108**
Spatiality as a metaphor for power	**110**
Virtual spaces, technologized places	**112**
Complex places	**113**
Bringing it all together again: transdisciplinary integrations	**117**
Conclusion: the return of abstraction	**118**

In Chapter 5, we highlighted some of the ways in which theory is always both spatially and temporally located. The issue of temporality is explored in Chapter 7, in this chapter we shall focus on the ways in which spatial locatedness influences the research that we do and how spatiality can be used as a tool of analysis. We argue for the spatial locatedness of all studies, however implicit, and the importance of the linked ideas of place and identity to cultural research in particular. Recognizing the particularities of the places we study – and where we study them from – implies the need for reflexivity about the ways in which all places are spatially produced. This is why we look at some of the conceptualizations of the spatial that have been productively reconfigured by theorists, especially geographers. Space and place have long been explicit objects of research in certain areas of cultural analysis, such as heritage, tourism and the analysis of urban cultures, but it is the *interface* between geography and cultural studies that has been particularly theoretically productive and on which we focus here. We conclude by connecting up our arguments with those at the end of Chapter 5, suggesting that there is a need to concretize all our theoretical abstractions, not only in time but also in space.

We want to argue here that issues of space and place are inherent in every project. Recognizing and taking account of this spatial embeddedness has important implications for the way in which the project is approached. This chapter, then, explores how a sensitivity to the *geography* of our topic and practices can help us in our research. Indeed, geography has been one discipline in which conceptualizations around space and place have been most highly developed, so it is to the work of those researching within that field that we mainly turn. However, geographers have themselves increasingly taken up agendas, theories and methods from cultural studies, so our own moves here are an example of the borrowing and returning that we envisage and advocate as an aspect of transdisciplinarity.

Bringing place and space into focus

Positionality as spatiality

Issues of spatiality and place are always present in research, although they are not always foregrounded. As we discussed in Chapter 3, the 'researching self' is a spatially located self and every moment of the research process is inflected by this fact. Such locatedness will influence the kinds of questions asked, texts drawn on and, most importantly, forms of cultural knowledge that are available. Being self-reflexive about it is therefore crucial.

One significant element of this locatedness is the shared, culturally sedimented and implicit knowledge that frequently shapes and mediates everyday practice in highly localized ways. We can call this folk knowledge or, following Gramsci, 'common sense'. Such knowledge will inform not only customs and practices but also expectations and desires. It is knowledge that is rarely outwardly projected, operating in the form of taken for granted assumptions about the world or social relations that are also very particularly placed. Because cultural studies aims to make such knowledges *explicit*, by bringing their particularities into focus and exploring their wider dimensions, our specific relationship to the local is an important, though relatively unacknowledged, dimension of research.

Engagement in the particularity of this spatial locatedness means that cultural studies researchers often focus on forms and practices with which they are already familiar. For example, clubbing and club culture have been appealing topics of research for UK students precisely because they speak about lived practices or draw on cultural knowledge with which they are familiar. Such knowledges may be available even to those who do not participate in the specific activity of clubbing because they are widely circulated, mediated and reproduced in popular culture, including television, newspapers and magazines, and would probably shape the kind of research questions being asked. However, although club culture appears to be widely dispersed as part of the more general globalization of youth culture, it is important to recognize that the practice of clubbing may carry with it a very different set of meanings in Rio de Janeiro to those produced in Manchester, so the research questions that arise in each context will reflect quite divergent experiences of youthful sociability. To extend Gadamer's analysis, developing a spatial consciousness therefore involves recognizing the *locationally* specific cultural frameworks that we often implicitly use.

We also need to be aware that the process of making such sedimented and implicit cultural knowledges available is only possible when we recognize otherness. It is spatial alterity, the dialogue between 'I' and 'thou', that makes understanding and self-questioning possible. Recognizing the knowledges that are implicit to our spatiality is not enough – they also need to be made explicit, brought back again and again into dialogue.

Issues of power, including the spatial constitution of power, are a crucial aspect of this critical engagement. Space is 'where discourses of power and knowledge are transformed into actual relations of power' (Sharp et al., 2000).

Critical interventions that seek social change need to grasp that place is itself a producer of meaning and changes in spatial practices always have cultural implications.

Identity and locality

Although work in cultural studies in the UK from the 1950s onwards always carried meanings about space and place, these were rarely foregrounded, either by the authors or by readers, for whom the category of class was the primary analytical formation. It is largely with a contemporary sensitivity to place and locatedness that we can recognize and appreciate the ways in which the specificities of localities are inherent in, and often formative of, these early narratives. Thus, we can now see that the relationship between place and identity is crucial in the work of Raymond Williams, Richard Hoggart and Edward P. Thompson. Not only is their writing very vividly located in particular neighbourhoods, regions or areas (albeit with wider implications for similar and contrasting processes elsewhere), but the places themselves have produced the processes, identities and cultural formations that are written about. Raymond Williams' 'border' identity and commitment to the margins, for example, was clearly linked to his own upbringing in the Welsh marches – a place between England and Wales that is itself uncertainly located – and issues of space and place were to become increasingly explicit themes in his work from *The Country and the City* (1973) to *The People of the Black Mountains* (1990). Likewise, E. P. Thompson's *The Making of the English Working Class* was strongly shaped by West Riding sources and experiences (1963: 13–14).

In a similar fashion, Richard Hoggart's *The Uses of Literacy* (1957) nostalgically describes working-class life in the Leeds suburb of Hunslet during the 1930s, comparing its 'authentic' cultural forms with what is characterized as an Americanized and decadent mass culture of the 1950s. The book has been read largely in terms of its concerns with class and popular culture, but it is also a study of a place – Hunslet – and how meanings about cultural identity are produced in a specific location as well as at a particular time. For Hoggart, the organic popular culture of working-class Yorkshire life is threatened by cultural forms that are 'out of place' – that is, the inferior and inauthentic popular music and films imported from the USA. Yet, the author represents this cultural encounter primarily in terms of time rather than place – his understanding of social change is temporal and linear rather than spatial, even though his object of study is geographically bounded. Nonetheless, it is important to see that the social relations described and Hoggart's conception of an organic community are dependent on ideas of boundedness that are clearly about place. His account of Americanization is thus tied to an argument about the breakdown of located collective identities. With hindsight, we can see that this idea of community refuses the possibility that the social formations and new forms of collective identity produced as a result of change might also be valued.

For Hoggart, then, regional identity is crucial, yet not fully acknowledged. Indeed, there is a strong implication that Hunslet is representative and its cultural patterns generalizable, although this is not explicitly theorized. The development of a whole body of critical work around space and place, spatiality and locatedness in the last 20 years, however, means that we now have a set of analytical tools with which to read his work in ways that he may not have anticipated. It has also provided the means whereby an alternative approach to the kind of study of working-class communities that he pioneered can be developed.

This approach recognizes the complex relationships between identity and locality in a globalized world and draws on a range of theoretical paradigms to develop accounts of lived cultures in particular places. For example, Darren O'Byrne (1997), in a study of a predominantly white working-class housing estate in Roehampton in London, explores the impact of globalization on local communities. Drawing on a range of cultural and social theories, O'Byrne examines the ways in which ideas of place and identity are lived in Roehampton. In contrast to Hoggart, with whom he engages in a critical dialogue, O'Byrne is able to situate local communities in relation to changing and fluid social and cultural processes and problematize the idea of community itself. Class is not part of the discourse of locality used on the Roehampton estate, it is deployed by O'Byrne to interrogate these local identities in the context of global processes: '[l]ocality and local solidarity and loyalty become the central concepts in inclusion and exclusion . . . Inclusion may rest upon involvement in the local community, and an acceptance of the values associated with that host community', (1997: 80). Similarly, although the estate is ethnically diverse, discourses of localism seem to be more important than those of race.

If O'Byrne's work makes the community he describes both concrete and real, and Hoggart represents working-class life in poetics and metaphor, much research that explores space and identity effectively does so by combining the two positions. Cultural research has therefore been able to become much more engaged with questions of space for the following reasons. First, because of the relatively recent development of complex theorizations of spatiality and, second, because of the application of existing cultural theories to work on place and space. Both the theorizations of spatiality and our relations to space have thus been radically re-centred.

Complex spatialities

The focus on spatiality has at least in part been driven by the desire to turn away from the tyranny of time – the temporal modes of structuring thought and narrative that have dominated Western thought. Sometimes this has also involved exploring the relationships between temporality and spatiality. For example, Foucault (1967) maps the emergence of a discourse of insanity that is both historical and spatial. He argues that, in the 'age of reason' – during the eighteenth century – those who were deemed irrational and unreasonable would be *spatially* segregated and confined in specialist institutions. The lunatic asylum can be understood as emerging from the specific social relations that existed at the time, which were also spatialized. Foucault's identification of the spatial dimensions to this process suggests that the spatial is crucial to the production of power.

The focus on spatiality in cultural research has also been driven by a recognition of the necessity to move beyond the particularity – the uniqueness – of places to an exploration of the ways in which they are constructed. Doreen Massey's influential essay about the power geometries of this process, 'A Global Sense of Place' in Massey (1994), showed that these are neither static nor homogenous. Writing about the London suburb of Kilburn with its rich and varied population and history, Massey points out that:

> the specificity of place is continually reproduced but it is not a specificity that is produced from a long internalized history . . . There is the fact that the wider social relations in which places are set are themselves geographically differentiated. (155–6)

As she observes, the globalization of social relations is a central element in the production of place. Massey's relocation of Kilburn into a globalized context marks a significant shift in the theorization of space and place. Far from opposing the global to the local, Massey insists on their relatedness and, in so doing, reconfigures the significance of spatiality in the construction of place.

This interrogation of place has several methodological implications. First, it suggests the need to move away from the description of local particularities in order to see *how* place is spatially produced. Second, it helps us to question the assumed homogeneity of locales as well as their implicit boundedness and suggests that cultural research needs to reflect more explicitly on the relationship between knowledge and spatiality.

Social and cultural theorists working on these issues have highlighted the extent to which space and spatiality is at least an implicit – and often an explicit – analytical category by means of which thought has been structured (Crang and Thrift, 2000). Here, we outline some theoretical conceptualizations that we can use in our research to understand how space is conceived, perceived and utilized. The analytical tools we offer are only a part of a set of possible points of departure in the analysis of spatial relations, but the theorizations that we draw on may be particularly useful for *cultural* research. Such theories offer us a method – in its broadest sense – with which to pursue our research agenda.

Theoretical tools for researching spatiality

We can begin by considering how the work of Henri Lefebvre provides us with a paradigm for conceptualizing different spatial tropes, the various forms that 'space' takes in social life (Lefebvre, 1991). Lefebvre argues that the interplay of space in all its forms, including buildings, streets and towns, must be articulated by a theorization of the processes involved and that, by examining the spatial practices of everyday life, we can develop an understanding of the meanings produced around 'ordinary' spaces. In order to understand the production of space, Lefebvre differentiates between three categories: representations of space, representational space and spatial practices. 'Representations of space' refers to the space constructed by the practices of professionals, such as planners, developers, architects and engineers – the buildings and roads, usually produced in 'official' or public space, that, for Lefebvre, reproduces dominant ideology. 'Representational space' is the experiential space of everyday life – it is felt rather than thought, often chaotic and therefore elusive. 'Spatial practices' relates to the routes and networks of everyday life, such as journeys to work and patterns of play that structure the reality of daily life. Lefebvre thus offers us some conceptual tools to understand how space is conceived, (re)produced and (re)presented.

These abstractions can be used, for example, to understand the ways in which the British city of Birmingham recast itself spatially in the 1990s. Driven by the radical changes taking place in local, national and globalized economies during the late twentieth century that had begun to destabilize British manufacturing industry and the cities built around it, Birmingham was effectively remade (primarily by the local authority but in tandem with other interests) not as a provincial industrial city in the UK, but as a European city with a cultural focus. The city re-imagined itself as a spectacular space of international business and culture and was then reconstructed to fit this design. As part of this project, the city centre was literally rebuilt to express the ambitions of its re-imagined purpose. The space outside the town hall was reconstructed with fountains and paving in the style of a properly 'European' public meeting place. A new square was forged out of the area around the repertory theatre and was filled with public art that both commemorated Birmingham's industrial past and marked its new identity as a cosmopolitan city. An international convention centre was built next to the refurbished old canals, housing a concert hall and conference spaces, and the streets surrounding it were transformed into pedestrianized squares with apartments, art galleries, cafés and restaurants. This process of reinvention therefore involved the recasting of hitherto industrial spaces – the canals, warehouses and factories – into leisure spaces dominated by the service and retail industries.

It also entailed a move in the assumptions made about those who might legitimately use and occupy the reconstructed spaces – a very specific, but also imagined, figure of an international (but white, male and middle-class) businessman. We can therefore use Lefebvre's ideas to understand this as a change in the representation of space, as public structures, which are expressive of the dominant order, are changed as the order itself shifts. In the case of Birmingham this meant the public reconstruction of the city's meaning, moving away from its previous one of an industrial manufacturing centre and towards that of a cultural centre within a European, or even global, context. Interestingly, as part of the recasting of Birmingham's image, the city's recent history as the destination of very different kinds of cosmopolitan traveller – those who emigrated there in the 1950s and 1960s from the old Commonwealth countries – was exploited. In a final twist to this particular tale of the city, Birmingham's large settled populations of peoples of African-Caribbean and Asian origins were largely represented in publicity about the city either as a tourist spectacle of multiculturalism or as servicing the needs and desires of the business classes in ethnic restaurants. They thus served both an immediate economic function within service industries and an ideological one of presenting Birmingham as a multicultural space.

Indeed, Birmingham's re-imagining of itself in multicultural, but also highly commodified, terms involved a further spatial shift – the casting of the inner-city suburbs of Sparkbrook and Balsall Heath as a 'balti belt', an area retailing 'authentic Indian food' in authentic Indian (actually Bengali) cafés and in 'genuine' karahi (the metal, wok-like pot the food is served in). This involved the overt and official commodification of already existing spatial practices (in Lefebvre's terms) that had developed in the area. The routes and networks casually involved in the consumption and retailing of balti meals were recast as part of the official geography of Birmingham.

As we can see, the example of Birmingham shows us that we need to take account of the way in which the spatial production of meaning is organized in historical and cultural processes, which may then be commodified in the economics of cultural exchange or tourism. If we choose to make place and space our primary objects of research, then, we must recognize that they are produced as a result of the meanings we attach to them. These meanings are imbued with power, especially those of the people who have the authority to imagine and direct the organization of space and those of the people who utilize and experience that space. The case also exemplifies one way in which we can use Lefebvre's ideas to theorize material and cultural spatiality.

Spatiality as a metaphor for power

The growing importance of space and place to cultural analysis has been accompanied by the increased appearance of geographical concepts, such as 'mapping', 'boundaries', 'borders' and 'cartographies', although some of these – 'mapping', for example – have a longer history of such deployment in cultural studies. Arguably, social relations themselves have been partially reconceptualized by a rhetorical intervention in which spatial metaphors have helped to clarify issues of power, enabling complex relationships and structures to be enunciated in new and important ways. For cultural studies, the most important contribution has been the recognition of the existence of oppositional spaces and the questioning of dominant spaces by means of the specific use of terms such as 'marginal', 'peripheral', 'central' and 'metropolitan'. These relatively abstract concepts highlight places as *relational* and emphasize such relations as being about power. Connections between places and across spaces are both structured and riven by power differentials that are themselves productive – not least for identities and subjectivities. Metaphors of space and place, such as marginalization or displacement, help to address these differentials by means of terms that evoke spatial relationships and describe – and act out – resistance and opposition. Once we understand the constructedness of space, we can see how it may be struggled over and *claimed*, rather than being 'just there' or 'given'.

Claiming space and recognizing our complex relations to space – as in claims to 'marginality', for instance, have become important theoretical-political strategies for academics and activists alike. Margins can be seen as places of particular creativity – a tendency evident, perhaps, in our own discussion of positionalities and cultural studies in Chapter 3. However, some of the most interesting writing, from margins of multiple and different kinds, has stressed instead the double-binds of representations from the edges and the problems of speaking from, or speaking for, subordinated positions produced by powerful discourses. Anyone who writes a dissertation or thesis that involves taking up a position of marginality as a deliberate strategy – of solidarity with oppressed groups, for instance – faces these ambiguities. Often, indeed, to continue the productive spatial metaphor, the demand from the margin has been that the centre should speak about itself, only in a new and more critical way – perhaps about masculinities, whiteness and Englishness and other Western or First World identities (see, for example, Hall, 1996b; Spivak, 1988, 1990). To do this is to activate – or respond to – the kinds of dialogue across difference that we have discussed before.

Another way of playing with this metaphor has been to consider 'the spaces in between' that may become resistant 'third' spaces – those in which a challenge to dominant cultures may be produced, often by migrant cultures. Post-colonial theorists such as Homi Bhabha deconstruct the ready notion of binary spaces that tend to operate in Western cultures and have highlighted the productivity, political possibilities and fruitfulness of 'liminal' spaces (on the threshold), arguing that they become the location for alternatives to such binaries:

> Minority discourse sets the act of emergence in the antagonistic *in-between* of image and sign, the accumulative and the adjunct, presence and proxy. It contests genealogies of 'origin' that lead to claims for cultural supremacy and historical priority. (Bhabha, 1994: 157)

Bhabha's argument has important implications for political interventions in the conceptualization of space. If we understand the process of production of marginal spaces as one that inevitably also involves the production of resistance within those spaces, we can reconnect Bhabha's largely metaphorical model to the politics of materiality.

As these arguments about the nature of space demonstrate, it is difficult to conceive of the spatial only as a given, concrete reality. Indeed, by making use of metaphorical conceptions of the spatial we are already acknowledging that the idea that there is a 'real world' waiting to be described is less convincing than a model of the world that recognizes the role of discourse and discursive processes in its production.

Michel de Certeau's *The Practice of Everyday Life* (1984) takes this recognition further. He conceives of urban space not as metaphor but as 'metonymy' – a term derived from literary analysis in which parts of a thing stand in for the whole in linguistic exchange, as in 'the crowned heads of Europe'. De Certeau applies this concept to his understanding of the city as fractured and fragmented. Because the process of moving through a city, whether on foot or by car or bus, is also a trajectory in a more abstract sense, meaning about urban space may be produced by means of a series of connections that are not always linear or structured. Crucial to this process is memory, which for de Certeau forms what he terms an 'anti-museum' – a set of fragmented knowledges that are dislocated and dispersed. These memories return as part of our experience of urban space and become part of the constitution of 'the city' as a site of haunted geographies (Crang, 2000).

Methodologically, de Certeau's ideas return us to a textual model of the city, in which the 'reading subject' – the walker or rider through the streets of the metropolis – is the agent of meaning. De Certeau's deployment of ideas drawn from psychoanalysis leads him to insist on the centrality of imagination and individual particularity in the production of our own 'spatial grids' – the idea of the relationship between different parts of the city that shapes our understanding of it. He thus demonstrates the profound spatiality of narrative.

Virtual spaces, technologized places

New kinds of spatialized narratives are pivotal to the contemporary cultural forms produced by contemporary technologies. For instance, space is often the organizing principle of computer games as the primary narrative of such games involves entering and conquering new territories. Such games, according to Henry Jenkins, help children to be 'virtual' colonists 'driven by a desire to master and control digital space' (1995: 262). At the same time, the rapid development of extended media technologies, especially the Internet, has meant that empirically grounded notions of spatiality are insufficient for contemporary theorization. Perhaps one of the most challenging of these spaces has been cyberspace, which operates as both a metaphor and as lived practice. William Gibson (1984), in his novel *Neuromancer,* describes it as a consensual hallucination that is not really a place, and not really space, but *notional* space, a space that is produced discursively. The idea of 'cyberspace' thus occupies and describes spaces that are both real and not real.

Following Lefebvre, we can conceptualize this dislocated area as a representational space, but also as a space of representation. Commercial or institutional websites and search engines operating via the Internet, for example, constitute a version of Lefebvre's representations of space as they are constructed by professionals and operate as a form of official or publicly legitimated discourse. The official website for Nottingham Trent University, where we are based, includes information on the courses offered by the institution and also staff biographies, but the latter come in the form of public knowledge about individuals and their lives, professional careers and titles, rather than personal relationships or desires. In contrast, the way in which we *use* the Internet is more akin to the idea of representational space as it is both driven and potentially chaotic. However, unlike the representational space of the physical environment, our use of the Internet seems to both stretch and render more fluid our experience of spatiality and physicality. It includes the real physical space of the computer chip and the neural networks that make up the Internet, the real physical space where we are situated (perhaps sitting at a desk at a computer) when we connect up to the Internet and also the *imaginary* space of our relationship to communication. Moreover, by producing a sense of simultaneity, cyberspace disrupts our conventional notions of time. Indeed, the cultural products of cyberspace, the chatrooms and e-messages, present themselves as more ephemeral and less authoritative than the printed book with its accumulation of cultural authority. They also offer the possibility of a kind of two-way communication between the text and its audience that exceeds the way in which printed media works. Cyberspace may thus be spatially separated yet also socially conjoined. It stretches space while also helping to create new virtual communities. This process also makes room for more and different kinds of individualization and, perhaps, for the sensation of chaos noted above. As Cheater points out, 'conceptualizing global processes and their social results as chaotic involves concentrating on individualized irregularity, in preference to older assumptions that, by definition, some form of social collectivity must be involved' (1995: 127).

In this way, cyberspace also provides us with interesting methodological problematics and possibilities. Because our access to the sites involved is highly mediated by technology, our experience of them is dependent on social infrastructure, economic capital and cultural competence, without which we cannot begin to surf the net or even open our e-mails. The specific locatedness of the cultures *producing* cyberspace (whether they are in California or Bangalore) cannot, therefore, be wished out of the equation or treated as though they really are floating free beyond the reach of critical interrogation.

Complex places

While place influences our research, we have to engage 'at least implicitly, and . . . [preferably] explicitly, in dialogue or tension with non-ethnographically composed constructions, narratives and representations' (Marcus, 2000). We have to *think* space within our own culturality in order to develop a constructive engagement between the places we study – and those we study from. When reaching for sources and tools with a spatial thrust in order to study culture, we must also understand the cultures within which they have been fashioned. As terms such as mapping, cartography, borders, travelling or nomadic cultures become increasingly common in the parlance of cultural analysis, having outgrown, in an appropriate metaphor, their disciplinary 'home', we need to be alert to the specific aspects of *their* culturality as well as our own.

Sites

As we discussed in the introduction to this chapter, the site of much early cultural studies research was largely conceptualized in terms of the power relations of class rather than locality. However, recent feminist and geographical critical interventions have helped to foreground space and place as much more than an empty framework for the playing out of classed, gendered or raced struggles. 'The field' has begun to be recognized in cultural research as a particularly constituted element in the practices and formations being studied, one that carries meanings that are themselves significant.

It is, however, also effectively constructed by the researcher in the process of their research. 'The field' is what – and where – we define it to be. As Mary des Chene points out:

> the very task of defining a site or sites for research raises a number of questions. If one's work concerns events that have taken place in many locales, what renders one of these the primary site for research. If one's focus is on historical processes, what makes a geographically bounded residential unit the obvious object for study? If one's work concerns the lives of people who have more commonly been in motion than stationary – refugees, migrant workers, colonial district officers, academics – what makes the place where one happens to catch up with them in itself revelatory of that mobility and its meanings? (1997: 71)

Scales

The questions that we set ourselves also influence the scales with which we work. It is therefore necessary to foreground and reflect on the models of spatiality that we use. Most research carries with it an implicit assumption about the scale and scope of the study, but this has not always been acknowledged, as we have seen. In the example from the work of Richard Hoggart cited above, it is noticeable that the author locates his study within a specific community that is actually quite clearly defined by place and spatial relations but that these elements remain relatively submerged or are coded in discourses of class. As the spatial is always structured by the political and vice versa, the scale that we deploy in our research is linked to the scale in which we imagine social and political boundaries.

If our work is structured and partially determined by a sense that the boundaries of the nation state are real borders, for example, our research will articulate this. The use of the nation state as a defining unit of spatiality has implications both for the sources we draw on and the theorizations we are able to make. Indeed, it may work to reify structural relations that are, in fact, more fluid than some conceptual models allow. As such scales are always in process – emergent or residual rather than fixed and absolute – the tendency to treat the nation state as a given will work to limit what can be said. This has been a particular problem for some of us working in cultural studies in the UK because we have often concentrated on specific national formations without fully foregrounding the implications of spatial boundedness. The scale of the local has, however, been one area in which a highly particularized and politicized body of knowledge has developed.

In more recent years, this scale has also expanded, from national to European and to the more generally international as the global has become pressing in contemporary research. More importantly, various theoretical interventions, including theories of globalization and post-coloniality, have forced us to recognize that *all* the scales we deploy in our research – from those of the body to those of the wider political economy – are interrelated. Because lived practices are themselves produced via and across these differing scales of nation, region, continent and so on, they cannot be reified as only belonging to one particular site. The global acts in local places; the local can be made across global spaces.

This relationship across scales is particularly apparent, indeed emphasized, in the genre of travel writing. In the latter part of the colonial history of Western Europe during the nineteenth century, this genre was developed as part of the discourse of colonialism, working to articulate the legitimacy of Western territorial accumulation by means of narratives of exotic and dangerous travel. Such accounts described the landscapes, traditions and practices of local peoples in the authoritative discourse of imperialism, in which the relationship between the colonizer and the colonized was naturalized by spatial as well as racial differences. However, the authorial expertise ascribed to the travel writer has never been wholly uncontested and this becomes particularly evident in the work of female adventurers and travel writers, whose problematic relationship to the dominant masculinities of the imperialist tradition renders their work ambivalent (Blunt, 1994). Mary Kingsley, for example, strongly resisted attempts to map her journeys in linear terms, arguing that her lack of authority as a woman made it impossible. Instead, her writing is characterized by a strategy of metaphorical mapping that locates her both inside and outside the imperialist model of exploration and conquest.

Scapes

Arjun Appadurai (1990) suggests that we can use the idea of 'scape' – as in 'landscape' – to express the fluidity of social formations under conditions of global cultural interconnections. He coins terms such as 'ethnoscape' to describe the emergent landscape of constantly moving people and social groups, including migrants and travellers in the postmodern world. For Appadurai, it is the landscape itself that is shifting and not just the communities inhabiting it. This model highlights the fluidity of place and of the spatial relations that structure it and involves a shift from the relatively concrete conceptualizations of place found in early studies of the landscape to an abstracted notion of spatiality. Such a process of abstraction enables Appadurai to develop a theoretical understanding of landscape that takes account of larger social and political formations and movements and represents a postmodern approach to the theorization of space and place. By moving away from models of national or geographical determination, we can deterritorialize spatiality, refusing or reworking fixed and stable conceptualizations of land and peoples.

Appadurai's theory is clearly linked to the elaboration of other postmodern concepts such as indeterminacy and fluidity. One way in which cultural geographers have represented movements through these fluid spaces and 'scapes' is in the use of mental maps, which represent our *relationship* to the material rather than its concrete form, rather like de Certeau's notion of 'haunted geographies' noted above. The use of a term such as 'mental map' also helps to highlight the way in which mapping as a representational process is profoundly discursive. Furthermore it is by focusing on the local scale that we can see clearly the extent to which maps are discursively produced.

Maps

Development practitioners working in the Third World have frequently utilized mapping exercises in order to understand local perceptions of space and develop possible project activities. For example, in one such exercise, villagers in Sindhupalchowk in Nepal were asked by workers for the charity, Actionaid, to draw maps of their village in the damp soil it stood upon (Participatory Rural Appraisal, 1992). When examined, it became clear that these maps did not simply describe *what was already there*, they also represented *what ought to be*, including proposed new communal buildings and different uses for the land. They were intended to be used as tools for bringing about social change. This form of activity explicitly recognizes that location shapes both what is known and what can be represented and that mapping is always a discursive process. In such projects, while local knowledges are always already defined as 'alternative' knowledges, they can also be understood as being at least equally as valid as the knowledge produced by official, often Westernized, sources.

However, the recognition of such knowledge may also involve the reproduction of localized forms of dominant power, even while it problematizes Western models. Thus, the voices of men, those of higher castes or classes and the urban elite may be more powerful and dominant in the local context.

When maps are explicitly used in the service of power, they can often be surprisingly, crudely ideological. Official maps and charts produced by government institutions are important representational strategies for the purposes of claims to ownership and military surveillance. For example, maps produced by the British Royal Ordnance Survey during the hey-day of the British Empire explicitly represented the ownership and control of territories around the world by means of the cartographic rhetoric of pink shading. Less overtly ideological the conventional model for representing a three-dimensional object – the globe – on a two-dimensional plane has been through the Mercator projection. This projection magnifies the temperate latitudes so that Europe and North America are disproportionately large on the map, thus naturalizing their global economic and social power and presenting (in cultural studies terms) a preferred version of the world in which post-imperial global power relations are represented discursively. It is therefore important to recognize, and be critical of, the fact that official maps legitimate official discourses when using such a document as a resource for cultural research.

Bringing it all together again: transdisciplinary integrations

The combination of the cultural turn in geography and development of spatial preoccupations in cultural studies has led to a range of complex conceptual tools becoming available to explore questions of culture and spatiality. These two turns, we argue, have together transcended disciplinary boundaries – emphasizing the overlaps, not the differences, between researchers across disciplinary divides. In the examples below, we outline the ways in which a complex understanding of space, spatiality and place is politically embedded in feminist research as well as being grounded in our understanding of the past.

Cultural studies has a strong tradition of critical engagement with the lived practices of modernity and this interest has often returned cultural researchers to the very locus of modernity – cities and urban spaces. In addition, tracing the history of urban spaces and re-emphasizing their spatial dimensions in terms of power differentials has been an important project for feminist and cultural historians (Nava, 1996; Samuel, 1994). They have explored the ways in which women's use of urban space and the gendering of space in the city has been culturally produced and mapped. Walkowitz, for example, draws on a range of contemporary documents from the 1880s and 1890s, such as police reports, club minutes and newspaper articles, in order to explore the different ways in which discourses of gender, desire and space were negotiated by men and women in late nineteenth-century London. She offers a detailed case study of the Jack the Ripper murders of 1886 in which she argues that the management and control of space in London throughout this period was organized as a response to the fear of crime, especially among women. The circulation of various discourses around the Ripper murders therefore worked to police women's use of public space, in both formal and informal ways.

These concerns about the control of women's space and the division between private and public spheres continue to engage researchers today. For example, Johnston and Valentine (1995: 99–113) point out that public space is more problematically constituted than is normally assumed and that, for lesbian couples especially, public space may also include the home. They argue that such space continues to be a site of moral policing:

> despite the greater freedom to perform a lesbian identity within the boundaries of a 'lesbian home', it is still a location where this identity comes under the surveillance of others, especially close family, friends and neighbours. It is not necessarily a place of privacy. (1995: 112)

Methodologically, such work combines the archival documentary model of history with the theoretically driven concerns of cultural analysis in order to understand a spatial form. The question of sources is central to such work. As a cultural historian, Walkowitz depends on the appropriateness of her sources to substantiate her claims. In other words, the nature of the analysis we undertake depends on the kinds of sources we use. If the primary object of our research is spatial, the sources we use should be sensitive to, or determined by, spatiality. However, although the focus of such a study is a spatial form, the analytical lens that we use could well combine many theoretical and methodological perspectives. In the example above, historical and feminist models were combined in order to produce an account of the meanings that are attached to, or produced by, space.

Conclusion: the return of abstraction

To conclude, then, we return to some of the issues raised in Chapter 5 about theory and abstraction in order to understand this necessary process from a spatial angle. We argued there that theoretically informed research involves a double articulation – the abstraction from empirically located work and the return of theory back to the original case and/or other concrete cases. This articulation includes the recognition that theories derived from one instance may be challenged and extended by thinking about other instances. Most of the terms of this argument are given fresh inflections if we attend more fully to spatial dimensions. The scope of reference of categories is always spatial or geographical as well as temporal and social. 'Universals' are not just categories that refer to 'the human' or to 'all history', but are, literally, a spatial claim, about the world. Interestingly, however, the term itself reaches beyond the world – or at least our bit of it, Earth. We are led to wonder if this is only a metaphorical reference that the language makes or if the invocation of the universal involves its own symptomatic exaggeration of the impossible scope of general categories. Merrifield's argument, then, sums up many of our themes:

> Theory must render intelligible qualities of space which are at once perceptible and imperceptible to the senses . . . It will doubtless involve careful excavation and reconstruction, necessitate both induction and deduction, journey between the concrete and the abstract, between the local and the global, between self and society, between what's possible and impossible (2000: 173).

Furthermore, for Doreen Massey, the important issue 'is not the spatialization of the temporal . . . but the representation of space-time' (1999: 269). By holding out the possibility of an open temporality, space itself can be re-imagined as the sphere in which stories coexist, meet up, affect each other, come into conflict or cooperate. This space is not static, but disruptive, active and generative.

Finally, when we speak of research as located, we really do mean in a place. In general, as with historical knowledge, geographical knowledge insists that the tendency to reach for the universe should be matched by a return to the particular. Our view is that cultural studies, too, should take a cue from these two disciplines of context.

7 Time please! Historical perspectives

Thinking about time 120
Writing cultural histories part I: radical popular histories 123
Writing cultural histories part II: history's cultural turn 124
The argument so far: history and cultural studies – convergence and tension 126
Public representations of the past and popular memory 127
Thinking historically: historicizing theory 129
Historicizing the present 130
Conclusion 134

In this chapter, we explore the setting of time or temporality in human life and cultures and engage with history – a discipline that seeks to understand times past. This is not, however, a chapter on methods for historians, on which there are many useful books. Instead, our focus is on the strange medium of time, which, like the spatial dimension discussed in Chapter 6, imposes some requirements on the study of culture but also adds further resources for pursuing it.

Our dialogue with history as a discipline is more complicated than that with geography. The convergences with history-writing, though clear, are at present less noticed and perhaps less valued than those with geography – on both sides. There is a legacy of tensions and defensiveness, especially around the issues discussed in Chapter 5 (see Johnson, 2001). So, in what follows, we seek to define the distinctiveness of the handling of time in cultural studies, compared with historians' approaches. This allows us to say different things to different groups of readers. It upholds a form of contemporary history. It insists that non-historians can work historically, too. It argues that cultural studies has not been historical enough. It suggests how to 'historicize' further. In all this, history is as important a resource as geography has come to be.

We start the chapter by identifying different orientations to time. We use the ideas of Paul Ricoeur as an aid in this, while questioning the universality of his account of the basic features of temporality. Ricoeur's ideas, however, help us to clarify the different ways in which time figures in history and contemporary cultural studies. We then look at different strategies for studying culture historically within and alongside history. These include:

- the writing of cultural history – in at least two different modes
- an interest in public representations of the past – including historiography – and individual and collective memory
- the project of historicizing theory (picked up from Chapter 5) and some of the methodological issues that arise

- the construction of 'histories of the present' as practiced by Michel Foucault and those influenced by genealogical method
- the practice of 'contemporary history' or historical cultural studies, including a new engagement with the emphasis of folklore studies on cultural continuities and change.

We end by arguing for the (re-)historicization of cultural studies based on the strong convergences between cultural history and historical cultural studies.

Thinking about time

In *Time and Narrative*, Paul Ricoeur applies the 'arc' we introduced in Chapter 2 to the understanding of temporality, starting with Western puzzles about time first explored in the Confessions of St Augustine:

> Augustine, in this famous treatise on time, sees time as born out of the incessant disassociation between the three aspects of the present – expectation which he calls the present of the future, memory which he calls the present of the past, and attention which is the present of the present. From this comes the instability of time; and, even more so, its continual disassociation. (1991: 31)

Time, as experience, is a kind of movement or passage. Augustine's and Ricoeur's rather difficult term is 'distention', from *distentio*, which is best retranslated as 'stretching asunder', by which they mean that the mind is stretched and dislocated by time. Attention has to pass from anticipating an event to experiencing it as happening to remembering it. These three actions may address the same phenomenon, but it changes as, first, it is anticipated, then it is involved in our actions in the here and now, then it is remembered. There is something fundamentally unsettling, perhaps unknowable, about time (Ricoeur, 1984: 5–12).

This phenomenology or basic experience of time corresponds to the 'prefigurative' level in Ricoeur's circuits of representation. Here, time is 'narratable' but not yet narrated (1984: 54–64). It is only when we 'configure' or represent temporal experience that particular cultural conventions come into play. Ricoeur is fascinated by different forms of narrative. Narrative is not a simple representation of events in sequence; it is a sense-making process, an ordering, a grasping of events, together, as a whole. It is configuration. The key configurational device is 'emplotment', which is the construction of events, characters, values and so on into a plot or storyline. Emplotment involves 'schematization' (a selection of events) and it also draws on a history of traditions and genres of narration. Narrative counters the disorders of temporality. Although it cannot smooth them over entirely, it can make sense of events, explain them and compose a basis for action (1984: 64–70)

Ricoeur's summary version is decisive: 'the historicity of human existence can be brought to language only as narrativity'. Further, 'this narrativity can be articulated only by the crossed interplay of the two [particular] narrative modes' – that is history and fiction (1991: 294). The realist narratives of conventional history-writing and the fictional narrations of literature allow us to grasp different aspects of the temporal. Fiction creates imaginary worlds, while always retaining, according to Ricoeur, a representational aspect, a reference to the real. History aims at factual accounts, but can only represent the past indirectly by construing sources. History doesn't stand alone as the guardian of time and is more closely related to fiction than is usually admitted. History, we could say, is not the same as historicity in general.

We have reservations about Ricoeur's approach. He draws on the structuralist analysis of narrative (see our critical comments in Chapter 14) and tries to repair its failures to grapple with time, authorship, readership and everyday practice. Yet, when he presents a universal experience of time, or does not qualify his starting point culturally, alarm bells start ringing. Is there a level of abstraction problem here of the kind we discussed in Chapter 5? Just how universal is narrative or the sense of time passing as a linear stream? Certainly, time is culturally variable. After all, Augustine's inquiries were motivated by his early Christian interest in eternity – a belief that, like a faith in reincarnation, must make a difference to experiences as apparently universal as death and dying. 'Clock time' has only relatively recently been unified. Feminist accounts and non-Western frameworks suggest that time is also experienced cyclically, as in menstruation, the crop cycle, the waxing and waning of the moon and the seasons (Kristeva, 1986). What difference does a cyclical experience of time make to ways of configuring past, present and future, to remembering, initiative and anticipation?

Nor does Ricoeur's scheme grasp time as imposed or contested, such as in struggles over 'time discipline' and the inculcation of capitalist working rhythms (see, for example, Thompson, 1993: 352–403). Western conceptions of narrative may also be imposed on other patterns of narration (Rigoberta in Carr, 1997). Time can be seen as layered and differentiated, not as a unified progression.Taking account of diversity and power in temporal relationships opens up fascinating spheres of enquiry, historical and comparative (for a lively iconoclastic introduction see Griffiths, 1999). Awareness of temporal diversity – and our own positioning in versions of the temporal – is an important aspect of reflexivity.

Nonetheless Ricoeur's approach allows us to disentangle differences within Western public temporalities. In particular, we can distinguish the time orientations typical of history-writing and cultural studies. An example may help us here.

An example of temporality in history and cultural studies: Raymond Williams and Raphael Samuel

On his death in 1988, Raymond Williams' work was reviewed by Raphael Samuel, a New Left colleague and key organizer of radical history networks in the UK:

> Raymond Williams was not a historian. His point of address was to the present and his touchstone of learning was relevance to contemporary debate. When he wrote about

> the past it was as a novelist and autobiographer, or critic and theorist, rather than as a self-conscious practitioner of the historian's art. (Samuel, 1989: 141)

The review goes on to appreciate Williams' 'historical intelligence', 'archaeological imagination', fascination with continuity and change, 'historian's sense of the deceptiveness of tradition', 'peculiar immediacy of his encounters with the past', even 'page on page of dense historical analysis'. Samuel thus draws a paradoxical picture of Williams: a not-historian who took account of temporality all the time.

Ricoeur's categories help to name the difference here. Historians are characteristically interested in the past or the present of the past. Williams' work was engaged with the present of the present and the present of the future. His view of the past was also present- and future-oriented. In closing his review, Samuel himself defines the difference:

> He was not interested in history for its own sake, or even, to judge by his writing 'as it happened', but rather in how it could be used, the 'basic meanings' it could be made to yield, and above all, the principle of hope that could be discovered in it. (151)

Williams' reading of the past for the future, for anticipation or hope, can be seen in his treatment of traditions of pastoralism in *The Country and the City* (1973) or of English social criticism in *Culture and Society* (1961). It informs his theoretical work, too, his commentaries on hegemony in *Marxism and Literature*, for instance, and key categories such as 'the residual' and 'the emergent' (1977: 121–7).

The residual is not what is old and dying; it is the way in which older elements are worked into contemporary hegemonies or into social alternatives and opposition. The residual is active in contemporary formations and may point to the future. Nor is 'the emergent' only new or fashionable; it includes elements silenced within the currently dominant formations, but indicating other possibilities. It is often underarticulated or implicit. Williams even referred to the 'pre-emergent' in ways that remind us of Ricoeur's 'prefiguration' and Althusser's answer without a question. This emphasis was associated with his political engagement, socialism and working-class loyalities and, perhaps, with his ideas of progress. However, 'emergence' can be applied to hitherto unspeakable or newly articulated currents of many different kinds – to women's movements or struggles over racism and social essentialism or the great sea-change of environmental consciousness and anti-capitalist questioning today. This past–present–future continuum is most active within history-writing with an emancipatory impulse such as feminist history, some histories of sexuality and some post-colonial histories of imperial relations. Ricoeur often formulates this continuum, arguing against the usual historians' objectification of the past in ways reminiscent of Edward P. Thompson's *The Making of the English Working Class* (1963: Preface, 12–13). He links historical reflexivity – the 'consciousness of being affected by the past' – with the need to keep an open view of it, as the memory of possible futures:

> We must struggle against the tendency to consider the past only from the angle of what is done, unchangeable, and past. We have to reopen the past, to re-vivify its unaccomplished, cut-off – even slaughtered – possibilities. (1988: 216)

Cultural studies has typically been about anticipation, which is not quite the same as prediction. It has often taken the form of contemporary history. It has focused on what is new or emergent in politics, youth cultures, media products, discourses concerning sex and gender, new ethnicities and the new racism, forms of consumption, scientific practices and, indeed, new cultural theories. On its boundaries with sociology, it has pursued the modern, the postmodern and the global and other aspects of 'new times'. These are all ways of being historical. They are justifiable as well as seductive, yet they also risk losing the handling of time in depth, which Williams so often managed. The memory of cultural studies (about itself as well) is often too short, just as the memories of historians are sometimes depleted, as Ricoeur argues, by seeing the past as finished and gone.

Some strategies for making cultural studies more historical can be borrowed directly from history – the writing of cultural histories, for example. Other strategies draw on both orientations – the study of representations of the past as a feature of contemporary culture, for example. A third set of strategies starts off from cultural studies' concerns – with cultural theories, for example – but historicizes them. Finally, there are different ways of attempting to work along the continuum of past, present and future.

Writing cultural histories part I: radical popular histories

In the UK, the United States and parts of Continental Europe, the middle decades of the twentieth century saw the flourishing of a new kind of radical popular history that came from similar political, educational and intellectual impulses as cultural studies and centred on the histories of subordinated groups and classes. They were written against conservative nationalist histories while preserving some of their features. Communist and socialist historians identified (with) rebellious peasants, slaves and small producers and early working-class movements from medieval times onwards (see, for example, Hobsbawm, 1959; Edward P. Thompson, 1963), but they also developed ways of writing history that were both critiqued and adopted by historians connected with the social movements of the 1960s and 1970s, who also had their own intellectual traditions to draw on (see Hall, 1998; Scott, 1988).

This social history was cultural in the sense we discussed in Chapter 2 – it focused on the ways of living and forms of struggle of particular social groups or movements. Orthodox economic history and other reductions were criticized and moments of popular creativity recovered. These currents ran strongly within the history workshop movement in the UK, a meeting place, as it were, for feminist and oral historians, with offshoots and equivalents in other countries that made it a point of contact for radical historians internationally (Henkes and Johnson, 2002).

This 'History From Below' raised issues of method that resound today, changing many historians' horizons. It drew attention to the social exclusions of the archive and the favouring of dominant social groups – male, white and middle-class – in history and official memory. It achieved a revolution – or, rather, successive revolutions – in what counted as a historical source, a significant historical event, as history, indeed. It changed, and multiplied, the social points of view, the kinds of partiality from which history was written. The critical or political epistemologies that we discuss in this book are, in many ways, the result of a reflection on these same transformations across all the different fields of study, including history.

If we abstract from a very wide range of histories of different groups and movements, three features form a common ground of methodological innovation. The first was to read the documentation produced by ruling groups as evidence of power and partiality – as ideology, for instance. The second was to read the same texts against the grain of their moralizing discourses, so that they yielded up evidence of popular behaviour and belief. State or legal records on disturbances, for instance, can be read for the social composition and symbolic actions of the crowd. A third resource was to produce completely new historical sources or surviving materials as sources for the first time. Texts such as radical popular newspapers from the early nineteenth century, 'chapbooks' and printed ballads, slave narratives, working-class autobiographies and folklore collections started to be used as history for the first time. Feminist research validated whole new classes of sources, including diaries, devotional literature, family scrapbooks and correspondence, magazine miscellanies and household and etiquette guides. Such material was often produced by or for women and had not been considered a serious historical source before. The most spectacular example of source creation was, however, the oral history movement discussed below, which radically extended the social range of the archive by recording the memory narratives of successive generations.

This politics of the archive often inspired developments in cultural studies because history was a leading discipline in the radical mix. It is now difficult to accept cultural history written from the texts of public culture only, without acknowledging their limits (though such history is still done), because everyday life or local differences are often overlooked, misrecognized or actively stigmatized in many public representations. The source-based ingenuity of the histories from below remains a model for cultural studies, though methods and readings may differ.

Writing cultural histories part II: history's cultural turn

Discussing Raphael Samuel's work shortly after his death, Luisa Passerini reflected on 'the big transition we have been through in the last 20 years'. She described this as having 'gone through this culturality':

> And it was the transition from – in the profession – social history to cultural history which involved me very much. I think the book [Samuel's *Theatres of Memory*] expresses it

> very well . . . from an approach which tried to reflect experience of the underprivileged classes, to an approach which takes into consideration that every experience is culture really . . . and therefore also to the possibility of not looking for an 'authentic' culture, not looking for 'the' subjects of the revolutions, but of finding the signs of the historical movement everywhere. It could be in the elites or in the masses, in imagination as well as in a strike. But always with an eye . . . to what connects the legendary, the imaginary . . . to agency and subjectivity and experience . . . (Passerini, Fridenson and Niethammer, 1998: 256–7)

In other words, history, like geography, has had its own cultural turn – one that has involved a shift in questions, reception of new theories, changes in the practice of history and opening up to other disciplines.

The shift from social to cultural history was part of the same broad movement discussed in Chapter 2 as a change of objects within cultural studies. Early radical social histories had focused on the culture and agency of subordinated social groups. In the 1980s, this broadened to an interest in relations of dominance, subordination and emergence in larger socio-cultural formations. Once the category 'woman', for example, ceased to be anchored in history-writing in a common-sense way, attention passed to how to theorize and research gender relations, especially as qualified by other relationships. The question of the relation between public cultures and everyday feelings and meanings or, as Passerini puts it, between 'culturality', 'agency' and 'subjectivity' was also posed. It was in the course of attempts to theorize these relationships (around 1979) that the debates on theory became so polemical.

'Going through this culturality' involved methodological change in history-writing, too. The cultural turn foregrounded its role as a cultural practice. It drew attention to history as a representational medium. It connected historians to the larger work of social or public memory (see, for example, Centre for Contemporary Cultural Studies (CCCS) 1982). The new political epistemologies, such as the stress on positionality and reflexivity, together with the new cultural theories, highlighted the 'situated' character of history-writing and its resonance with contemporary issues.

There are many examples today of cultural history as critical cultural politics (just as there have always been conservative cultural projects in history-writing). National identity, ethnicity and race are key issues everywhere in the paradoxical contexts of globalization, migrations, multiculturalism and heightened local identities. In the UK, this has stimulated new histories on at least three fronts. There has been an emergence of a 'four nations' history in which national and cultural differences within the British Isles have been highlighted in relation to nationalist revivals and tendencies to devolution (see Kearney, 1989, and, for a review of debates, Samuel, 1998: 21–75). Multicultural, anti-racist and post-colonial agenda have stimulated historical work on the shaping of dominant English identities and practices (masculinities and femininities for example), through imperial relationships and episodes (see, for example, C. Hall, 1992b, 1996; Hall, 1996c; Ware, 1992; and, differently, Samuel, 1998: 74–95). Perspectives from outside or across national and continental boundaries have redrawn the implicit spatial maps of history and cultural studies. The idea of 'the black atlantic' is a redrawing of this kind, whether the object is slavery and the slave trade itself, engagement of diasporic black intellectuals with European philosophies (Gilroy, 1993a) or cross-class, black-to-white transatlantic histories of popular cultural forms. In such work, exchanges between cultural studies and historical enquiry have been especially close.

'Culturality' draws history closer to literary studies, psychology, cultural geography, the study of the visual, linguistics and philosophy in addition to cultural studies. Dialogues are sometimes provoked by common theoretical encounters – the debates between cultural materialist approaches and new historicism for instance. While cultural materialists are interested in supplying the contexts of hegemony and the social relations of class and other relations, new historicists are interested in reconstructing the discursive field in which texts were produced and read (Veeser, 1989). This latter strategy shades into another – that of using key texts as a way into past cultural formations or what Foucault calls 'the archive' of historical discourses (Foucault, 1972). Such strategies, explored more fully in Chapter 11, are now used by historians of political ideas, literature and the theatre, colonial relations and subjectivities and sexual, especially homoerotic, formations. Disciplinary boundaries break down here (though they are also recomposed). It would be hard to say whether Edward Said's *Orientalism* (1978) or Eve K. Sedgwick's account of 'the closet' (1990) are literary criticism, cultural history or historical cultural studies, or perhaps all three.

The argument so far: history and cultural studies – convergence and tension

So far, we have suggested a distinction between the general condition of living in time – temporality or historicity – and particular orientations to past, present and future. Historicity is like culturality, spatiality and an awareness of power and difference: it is a transdisciplinary perspective relevant to all our studies. All intellectual work, not just historical study, needs to be historically sensitive and give thought to how time is schematized and how social change and continuity are conditions of human life. We would further suggest that there are marked convergences between cultural studies and history, especially histories alive to the political significance of the past. Ricoeur's arguments, Williams' practice and trends in history-writing show that future-oriented contemporary studies also need open-ended, reflexive histories of the past. This convergence should help to open up the resources offered by critical history-writing to more historical cultural studies.

This doesn't mean that there are no tensions. History-writing retains a stronger sense of studying the past for its own sake and, therefore, a deeper investment in the archive and empirical research than cultural studies. In more orthodox versions, this is still associated with the suspicion of abstraction ('theories') and explicit politics ('bias'), as well as a resistance to 'presentism', in which the past is judged in relation to today and can, it is implied, be made to mean anything we like. The harder kinds of historical objectivism persist within some professional common sense: bright ideas are all very well, runs the argument, but we should get on with finding out what really happened (Elton, 1967: 1–8). Historians can still understandably object when theorists seem to identify history with fiction (Hayden White, 1973; compare Ricoeur 1984: 161–74). What does this do to the vital myth-slaying functions of critical history (Hobsbawm, 1997)? Ricoeur's *Time and Narrative* suggests that this fear is misplaced, while his later work on ethics and politics elaborates on historical debts and the perils of forgetting (1996: 3–39). Fiction also references the real and there is nothing about history's use of representations (such as forms of narrative) that disqualifies its claims to truthfulness or explanatory power. Rather, the contrary is true – it is the combination of ambition to represent the real and reflect imaginatively on what it means for present and future that gives to history-writing its temporal scope and reach.

Nonetheless, these tensions can tug at us in personal and practical ways. How do we justify an intense, curious, time-consuming gaze on past time when present problems call so insistently? Can we afford time in the archives? Are truth and relevance always to be in conflict? These feelings fuel the search for present- and future-oriented forms of historical work.

Public representations of the past and popular memory

Our second historicizing strategy more explicitly combines elements from historical studies and cultural studies as well as other disciplines. Representations of the past of all kinds can be studied as aspects of contemporary culture, closely related to collective identities and individual and group subjectivity.

Once history began to be recognized as a cultural practice or practices, it was a small but significant step to broaden out the study to representations of the past more generally. Raphael Samuel in the UK and Pierre Nora and his school in France have studied particular *'lieux'* (Nora) or 'theatres' (Samuel) of memory – the former concentrating on the national or civic, the latter on unofficial knowledge and popular memory (Nora, 1997; Samuel, 1994, 1998). From the early 1980s, work in cultural studies focused on representations of the past in relation to national identities, television and film, memorial practices, museums, heritage sites, landscapes, school books, popular fiction, public sculpture and political rhetoric (see, for example, Centre for Contemporary Cultural Studies (CCCS) 1982; Wright, 1985). The controversial growth of 'heritage', as a pervasive retrospective mood, a branch of capitalist business and as a state ideology during this period, fuelled these studies, as well as older legacies of trauma prompting critical questions about the relationship between history, popular memory and power. Does 'heritage' express and extend popular historical consciousness or does it commodify history, promote conservative identities and limit ways of connecting with the past? Whose heritage is it anyway? Are these safe stories enough? Do we need the risky stories, too (Clare and Johnson, 2000; Hall, 1999–2000; Johnson, 1991; Kuhn, 1999)?

Oral history has approached similar questions from a different angle, more aligned to individual and group memories than public representations or official practices. Initially developed in connection with the popular radical histories – crucial in feminist history, for example – it has also connected with an earlier interest in life history, so that biographical approaches have become a persuasive way of structuring feminist histories, including, for example, histories of feminism and migration. Oral history continues to have a role in the rewriting and 're-righting' of history (Samuel and Thompson, 1990; L.T. Smith, 1999), but can also be more than testimony, important though this is. It can be an alternative to mainstream history. As Smith points out, the desire of indigenous peoples to tell their own histories arises from a powerful need to name a land and the events that raged over it, to restore a spirit and bring back into existence a world fragmented and dying. 'The sense of history conveyed by these approaches is not the same thing as the discipline of history, and so [our] accounts collide, crash into each other' (Smith, 1999: 28).

Oral history has continued to be inflected towards subordinated social groups and themes, but it has also been recast in the turn to culturality. Life stories are interesting not only as evidence of past events but as events in themselves that represent the narrators' imaginary relationships to the past (Portelli, 1990). Memory stories are forms of narrative, composing identities and subjectivities (Passerini, 1990a). As we explore in Chapter 14, the theme of self-narration crosses over many disciplines, including life history, critical auto/biography, memory work, discursive or cultural psychology and questions of subjectivity and identity in cultural studies and sociology. The methodological issues overlap with those of fieldwork (see Chapter 12). Here, we underline the great value of oral history and auto/biographical methods. Life stories are a way into the cultural repertoires of the past. They are evidence of past subjectivities or mentalities. They provide examples of the subjective work of memory as our stories position us in the present as well as the past. They are prime sources for contemporary self-production in relation to others. The relationships between our present selves and our past selves, are, after all, another form of self–other relations. In the form of memory work or auto/biography, this self–other relation can be both a means of conscious self-reflection and source of empirically grounded insights central to research, as we have stressed (Chapters 3 and 4).

The importance of a fully historical cultural analysis can be illustrated by the problems and opportunities of using inherited ethnographic collections in the contemporary museum. These problems have a particular edge and poignancy in ex-imperial countries, such as the UK, France and the Netherlands, and in white settler societies, like the United States, Canada, Australia and New Zealand, where first nations were subordinated or subjected to genocidal extermination. Such collections were often acquired as plunder in the course of colonizing activity. They have often been displayed and interpreted according to the rules of nineteenth-century anthropology, which mobilized versions of human evolution that justified colonial conquest and rule. They are displayed today in post-colonial and multicultural contexts, sometimes in the face of claims for repossession of the objects (see, for example, the African and Indian collections at the British Museum in London). Our argument suggests that reframing these objects with liberal values, stressing, for instance, how different cultures have handled similar life experiences, is not enough as this merely serves to hide the complicated past of these objects. Against this, some critic-practitioners advocate research that brings the history of collection to view, producing for the museum visitor a fuller recognition of the legacies of colonization – that is, the oppressive forms of power but also the intimacies and ambivalences (Legene, 1998; Subden, 1998). Such historicized cultural readings of appropriated treasures (where they are not returned or returnable) then provide resources for rethinking identities in their contemporary relationships, fully recognizing what Ricoeur calls 'the entanglement of our stories with the stories of others' (1996: 10; compare Lidchi, 1994; Hall, 1999–2000).

Thinking historically: historicizing theory

We have argued already in Chapter 5 for being more aware of the histories and limits of our abstractions. A starting point is to recognize the historical content of all theories, including our own. This is not quite the same as the 'background' or 'context' of ideas. Rather, it is to see that the categories themselves (including the problematics of cultural theory) always carry or encapsulate the needs and demands of their times. It follows that there is always something to learn from widely circulating ideas, but also that they do not necessarily apply equally well to all times and places. It also follows that, though new ideas are often significant and therefore fascinating, they do not necessarily invalidate the old, in so far as these still tell us something important about current realities and are necessary in practice. The older categories may continue to refer to persistent social features that are being rearticulated in new combinations. Thus, those forms of feminist theory that focused on Western versions of patriarchal relations of power need to be rethought today, especially in relation to the political claims and debts that grow from class oppression and global racist structures. This is not to say, however, that gender theory is redundant or feminism is dead. In other words, one way to historicize categories is to treat them as aspects of wider historical cultural formations and, therefore, as emergent or residual, too.

Awareness of the legitimate historical scope of reference of a theory or category is another way of thinking more historically. It is an important resource against those universalizing tendencies that are as common as ever in social theory today. Our questioning of Ricoeur on time is a case in point. This example also shows, however, why we should not – indeed, cannot – avoid universal categories altogether, even while suspecting their hidden partialities. We need such thin or simple abstractions to demarcate a sphere of understanding and praxis. Shelter, food, environment, gender, class, racism, sexuality and culture are some politically indispensable categories of this kind. However, universals – especially their ethical aspects and relative prioritizations – must be held provisionally, with qualifications and particularities that remain to be specified.

Theorizing or abstracting from particular historical cases is a way of building more complex theories that can grasp particularities, especially historical or spatially organized differences. As Sharon Sievers has pointed out, 'it is the burden of feminist theory to account for the asymmetry, dissonance, and, yes, oppression women have faced. Precisely for this reason theory can become a historical enterprise' (1992: 322). Feminist theorizing is always 'an eclectic, cross-pollinating enterprise that reflects back and forward in time' (329). Theory and research often produces intermediate categories that capture complexity but relate it to the formations already described more generally. Sex and/or gender systems, for example, vary widely, in relation to cultural contexts and forms of power. These differences can be understood as variant structures or, more loosely, differently articulated practices or discourses. Empirical research and the otherness of new cases can thus exercise pressures on our first ways of thinking, qualify our universals and make our theories more complex and mobile. The more we historicize our theories, the more we solve the history versus theory problem. More importantly, perhaps, the better we really grasp differences, historically and otherwise, the nearer our universals – rights, justice, humanity, for instance – will approach inclusiveness.

Historicizing the present

Finally, then, we look at ways of thinking about the present and future in historical ways, relating our analysis to the past. This inevitably takes us into the whole huge area of philosophies of history. We can usefully look at two broad positions and some of their implications here: Michel Foucault's 'history of the present' and a cultural materialism that centres on the contemporary.

Histories of the present: Foucault's genealogies

Foucault's work is explicitly engaged with issues of method, but it turns upside down many terms that, in their common uses, suggest strong historical continuities. These include 'archaeology', 'history of the present' and 'genealogy'. 'Genealogy', for example:

> does not pretend to go back in time to restore an unbroken continuity that operates beyond the dispersion of forgotten things; its duty is not to demonstrate that the past actively exists in the present . . . Genealogy does not resemble the evolution of a species and does not map the destiny of a people. (Foucault, 1986: 81)

Instead, Foucault defines 'effective history' as that which shows the radical discontinuities between past and present:

> History becomes 'effective' to the degree that it introduces discontinuity into our very being – as it divides our emotions, dramatizes our instincts, multiplies our body and sets it against itself. 'Effective' history deprives the self of the reassuring stability of life and nature . . . It will uproot its traditional foundations and relentlessly disrupt its pretended continuity. This is because knowledge is not made for understanding; it is made for cutting. (88)

Disparity, difference and surprise are found at the origins of social movements and institutions: 'their essence was fabricated in a piecemeal fashion from alien forms' (78). In redescribing heritage, Foucault reaches for a favourite metaphor – that of 'archaeology': heritage is thus 'an unstable assemblage of faults, fissures and heterogeneous layers that threaten the fragile inheritor from within or from underneath' (82). These are risky stories indeed! In his histories of sexuality and crime and punishment, he shows how contemporary discourses – of medicine or criminology, for instance – were formed in surprisingly indirect ways. In *Discipline and Punish* (1977), he draws on examples from French history to argue for an absolute discontinuity between a regime in which torture was a public spectacle and one where prisoners are locked away and reformed. The modern regimes make sense not in a continuous history of punishment, but as transpositions of the regulatory regimes of factories, schools, asylums and clinics and as effects of the knowledge and power nexus of the human sciences. Even the body is 'totally imprinted by history' (83). If history has an 'essence', it is not some smooth development towards the present, it is 'the endlessly repeated play of dominations' (85).

Foucault is also interested in 'emergence', but it is the surprising emergence of modern forms of regulation in the past that fascinates him, not emergence towards a future today. He is also more playful about time than most critical historians, fascinated by recurrence and repetition and suspicious of the linearity of conventional historical accounts. This is one reason for his preference for writing histories with different temporal schema, not a unified time. An important effect of Foucault's version of history-writing is its opening up to questioning the naturalness or necessary developmental logic of linear accounts. It has had a widespread influence on historical-cultural studies in areas where denaturalizing the present and questioning modern science has been important, such as in the histories of sexuality, social policy and forms of governmentality, law, the body, ethics and conduct and, more generally, subjectivities, performance and the production of the self.

Foucault's genealogical method is an extended critique of forms of history, especially teleological constructions of past to present relations in which the past unfolds towards the present, losing its capacity to shock or surprise. In conservative histories of nations and histories of moral development, the past is narrated as a journey to the high point of contemporary values or enlightenment. Of course, all critical histories question these central narratives and most feminist history is much more explicit than Foucault about its standpoint, partialities and methods. Yet, the question Foucault puts to radical history-writing is a telling one: how far do you simply replace one teleology and one form of mastery with another? Foucault's 'counter-memory' offers a different way to handle past–present–future relationships. Paradoxically, by showing that politically effective history can be written without the fatally wounded grand narratives of progress, Left or Right, he restores a certain faith in historical work itself.

Contemporary histories: Ricoeur, Gramsci and folklore

A second way of historicizing the present is to understand contemporary situations as moments in ongoing historical processes. In these processes, which are not always or inevitably progressive, human beings are both formed by the past and, as active agents, make the future. Historical consciousness is vital in the making of futures and must embrace both continuity and change.

Ricoeur on Foucault

In *Time and Narrative*, Ricoeur reviews Foucault's *The Archaeology of Knowledge*, comparing his 'effective history' with Gadamer's belief that contemporary consciousness is historically formed, but also capable of reflection on this process. Ricoeur sees Foucault's stress on discontinuity as an attempt to emancipate himself from the effects of history and, like Gadamer, he sees this as impossible:

> Taking a distance, or freedom as regards transmitted contents, cannot be our initial attitude. Through tradition, we find ourselves already situated in an order of meaning and therefore also of possible truth . . . Research, then, is the obligatory partner of tradition in as much as the latter presents truth claims. (1988: 223)

This criticism is linked to our feminist-inflected critique of Foucault – that he does not fully acknowledge the standpoint(s) from which his histories of discontinuity are written. Moreover, as Ricoeur also argues, because there is innovation and preservation in historical processes, to describe the present in terms of the past is not necessarily ideological or an act of mastery. Historical memory is not simply a practice of fixing identities in an evolutionary groove. It is always a struggle with historical effects, which include forgetting and loss:

> The notion of a historical memory prey to the work of history seems to me to require the same decentering as the one Foucault refers to [as 'genealogy']. What is more, 'the theme of living, open, continuous history' [Foucault] seems to me the only one capable of joining together vigorous political action and the 'memory' of snuffed out or repressed possibilities from the past. (219)

History and its traditions, like our social positionalities and initial questionings, are where we have to start from in making something new. This also brings us close to Williams and Gramsci, for both are fascinated by the existence of the past in the present and weave this into their understandings of contemporary domination. In all three thinkers, perhaps because they are all influenced by

Marx, tradition is the cultural space where what is historically already produced ends and contemporary praxis (which Ricoeur calls 'initiative') begins.

Gramsci and cultural sedimentation

Gramsci is especially interesting on the cultural aspects of continuity and change:

> Every social class has its own 'common sense' and 'good sense', which are basically the most widespread conception of life and man. Every philosophical current leaves a sedimentation of 'common sense': this is the document of its historical reality. Common sense is not something rigid and stationary, but is in continuous transformation, becoming enriched with scientific notions and philosophical opinions that have entered into common circulation. 'Common sense' is the folklore of philosophy and always stands mid way between folklore proper . . . and the philosophy, science, and economics of the scientists. Common sense creates the folklore of the future, a relatively rigidified phase of popular knowledge in a given time and place. (1985: 420–21)

If everyday culture is a kind of sediment laid down, added to and stirred up in different historical times, it follows that, in order to understand the present and gauge possible futures, we need longer-term histories of cultural forms and ways of living.

Gramsci's comments are also relevant to one of cultural studies' most neglected interdisciplinary dialogues – that with folklore studies or ethnology. He does not argue for the authenticity of popular common sense – a constant temptation in folklore studies (for an excellent review and introduction, see Bendix, 1997). Rather, common sense and folklore are mixed up with modern knowledge and futurist perspectives (1977: 324). Our argument points, then, towards another methodological combination – that of cultural studies, folklore studies and cultural and social history. Such a combination would allow us to explore the circulation and transformation of cultural forms, spatially and in time, identifying innovations and continuities, including those of the present (Henkes and Johnson, 2002).

W.T. Lhamon's study of 'black face' performance is an interesting example here (1989). Lhamon shows how minstrelsy crosses racial barriers. Its typical gestures begin in black performances that are taken up by poor white youth in the docklands of North America in the nineteenth century. Elements of this black repertoire are recognizable but transformed in subsequent white appropriations and performances, such as Al Jolson's in the 1920s and in later histories of black performance, such as the dance steps of hip-hop performers in the 1980s. Though 'blacking up' involves racist constructions, Lhamon insists on the presence of positive significations of blackness, right through this folkloric cycle. His argument resembles Paul Gilroy's on the intellectual cycles and cultural syncretism of 'the black Atlantic', but with a different methodological mix that includes folkloric recovery and theory.

It also raises interesting questions about ways of writing in historical cultural studies. These are related to some of our earlier reservations about Ricoeur's approach to time, our appreciation of temporal play in Foucault and our discussion of the diversity of temporal schemes. A dominant feature of historical writing remains a rather determined plod through a unified chronology. Yet more open and fluid movements between past, present and future suggest innovatory possibilities in this way of ordering accounts. Historical cultural studies can also play more with time. It can move between different temporalities or tenses, past, present and future, our own times and others' times. It can also visit, from time to time, the present of the study, our own questions and working.

Conclusion

Far from being displaced by considerations of spatiality, the time dimension remains an essential perspective in cultural study and social theory because time and space–time (in speed and communications) remain crucial loci of control and contestation, difference and imposed 'time-accountancy' (Griffiths, 1999). Debates about globalization, for example, are centrally about space–time and its compression. In dealing with these temporal dimensions, the relations with history as a discipline are especially important. The convergences between cultural studies and history-writing that we have explored are typical examples of the new transdisciplinarity in the study of culture. On the cultural studies side, we have argued for careful listening to the historians, especially, but not exclusively, to those who have themselves taken a cultural turn. We have explored a range of different strategies of convergence throughout this chapter, arguing, in the end, for a stress on both continuity and rupture in our actual and imaginary relations to the past.

At the same time, there are likely to remain differences between historical cultural studies and cultural history. Cultural studies is likely to continue to be concerned, especially, with the emergent and the new. Yet, as understanding the present and the future involves opening up again the possibilities of the past, we want to advocate a much stronger return to the historical and to work in history within cultural studies.

8 Culture, power and economy

Cultural studies 'versus' political economy: failures of dialogue 136
Baselines: separating power and culture 137
Ideology analysis 139
Representation and the limits of ideology critique 140
Power and culture: expanding the agenda 142
Where does power lie? The popular and the dominant 143
Starting elsewhere: economies as culturally embedded 145
Economies as representation and discourse 146
Cultural and economic circuits: overlap, interdependence, identity? 148
The question of consumption 149
Cultural conditions of economic systems 150
Changing determinations: the economy as culture 151
Conclusion 152

In this chapter we consider relations of power as a further setting of cultural processes. While the connection between power and culture is a central concern of cultural studies, there are different ways in which power can be defined in relation to culture, each with implications for method. In particular, we want to argue that, in most cases, it is better to see cultural processes as actually constitutive of power relations than as separated from them. Culture is always a setting of and for power, just as power is a setting of and for culture. Methodologically, this implies close dialogue with those disciplines that have made a specialism of studying power relations. The picture here is more complex than for space and time. All the social disciplines deal with power relations and every discipline has responded, more or less, to the redefinitions of power coming from social movements – the extension of the question of power to the personal and domestic, for instance.

In cultural analysis, the relationship with sociology – arguably *the* discipline of the social – has been as generative as that with literary studies. Its complexity, however, calls for separate study (Johnson, 2001). In this chapter, we focus instead on critical political economy and some strands in macro-social theory. These approaches have in common the ambition of grasping the main social dynamic of the contemporary world, whether these are seen as economic or socio-cultural in character.

In the first half of this chapter, we address some starting points in the debates between cultural studies and political economy and some points of difference in the ways in which questions of social power have been addressed. We argue that difficulties have arisen from the tendency, on both sides of this dialogue, to separate questions of economy and culture, when the study of power requires that we view these aspects in the closest of relationships, while giving due weight to the cultural aspects of social processes. We suggest some alternative starting points, drawn from early New Left theory and history-writing. We argue that it is not enough to simply add cultural studies to political economy as two perspectives. Rather, each approach has to be transformed in relation to the other.

In the second half of the chapter, drawing on a wide range of research on cultural economy, we identify five main strategies for recomposing the culture/economy distinction and going beyond the terms of an outdated polemic.

Cultural studies 'versus' political economy: failures of dialogue

Cultural studies and critical political economy share a point of departure in Marx's writings on capital, power, the state and ideology, yet arguments between them have been particularly repetitious. Dialogues with social theory – on questions of modernity and postmodernity, for example – have been more productive. There is, however, a tension between any large-scale analysis of systems – including 'reflexive modernization' (Beck, Giddens and Lash, 1994), societies of 'risk' (Beck, 1992) or 'McDonaldization' (Ritzer, 1993) – and a concern with social differences and detailed cultural meanings. Some unease with cultural studies informs Ferguson and Golding's *Cultural Studies in Question* (1997), which criticizes its 'failure to deal empirically with the deep structural changes in national and global political, economic and media systems through its eschewing of economic, social or policy analysis' (1997: xiii). If we take this critique as also defining the writer's own concerns, 'political economy' (and perhaps 'economic sociology') describes this position well.

We can identify six main features, some methodological, of such an agenda. First, there is an ambition to locate the most powerful – typically capitalist – dynamic of social change. Second, accounts are relatively abstract, dealing in systems or structures. Third, there is an interest in periodization – modernity/late modernity/postmodernity; 'reflexive modernization'; Fordism/post-Fordism, for example. Fourth, there is a concern with the global or the international that contrasts with cultural studies' early parochialism (in critical communication studies, for example, Schiller's 1968 critique of 'American Empire'). Fifth, such accounts are likely to depend on statistical data, drawn from official sources. Finally, there is a preference for 'critical realist' or strongly empirical epistemological frameworks.

Differences between this approach and that of cultural studies have often emerged in competing versions of media studies. Here, cultural studies is criticized for an overidentification with postmodern theory, a departure from epistemological realism, a preoccupation with text and literary methods at the expense of social research, a failure to engage with public policy and evaluation more generally and a neglect of production or the economic. These criticisms connect with the concerns around 'cultural populism' discussed below. Taken together, the critics say or imply that cultural studies lacks politics of any kind.

The preferred remedy is to recover concerns with economy, institutions and public policy found in Raymond Williams' work, for instance (see, for example, Murdoch, 1997). Jim McGuigan argues that cultural studies needs to scrutinize issues of production, ownership, the control and power of institutions and the shaping of the meanings of cultural products by the production process. He recommends that the complicated relationships between production, texts and audiences be explored in more detail and that issues of cultural policy be addressed (1992, 1996, 1997). Douglas Kellner (1997) suggests, as we have seen, a 'multiperspectival' approach, bringing together the study of political economy and textual models of cultural analysis. Such criticisms are frequently made from within cultural studies (see, for example, Angela McRobbie, 1997; Morley, 1997) but, typically, the argument stems from a concern with media institutions, which finds in cultural studies only a text-based approach to the media or popular culture or consumption. The long-term concern with dominance in cultural studies apparently drops out of view.

The categories used in this debate – 'textualism' and 'policy', for example – need serious critical examination. Furthermore, to try to restore the one to the other, unchanged, is no solution to the separation. As we have argued (Chapters 2 and 3), *combining* methods means risking change. If cultural studies takes on board political economy and vice versa, *both* traditions will be transformed. To do just this, however, is an important project. It corresponds to what is often seen as a kind of cultural turn in daily life, matching that in the disciplines. As Paul du Gay and Michael Pryke (2002) have argued, there are two ways of viewing this turn. Some social theorists have argued for a kind of epochal shift or historical stage in which the economy is systematically being culturalized, relying more and more on signs and symbols (see, for example, Castells, 2000; Lash and Urry, 1994). Others, especially in cultural theory and cultural studies, have argued that economies have always been constituted culturally – not necessarily all of a piece, but assembled in ongoing practices, all involving knowledge, power, meaning and identity (du Gay and Pryke, 2002). This second view – the economy as more contingent, piecemeal, ramshackle even – allows room for challenge and change. It allows us to grasp 'the economic' as being always *more* than *capitalist* social relations – including forms of power around gender difference or racialization, for example, and non-capitalist forms of production and use (see, for example, Gibson-Graham, 1996).

Baselines: separating power and culture

Both political economy and cultural studies started out, on their different routes, from a theory in which economic relationships were separated from cultural processes – an explanatory strategy inherited from Marxism, though it is not the only reading of Marx. Engels, interpreting Marx, argued that the economic base is not the only determining element, but that the interaction of all elements that determines the course of historical change. Nonetheless, 'the economic movement finally asserts itself as necessary' (Engels, 1962: 488, and compare Marx, 1962). In much Marxist theory, this separation is retained. Power resides primarily in the state and economic relations, often condensed in the idea of the capital relation where the worker depends on capital and vice versa. The main dynamics of change are seen to lie outside a cultural domain, but affect how consciousness is organized.

This perspective allows some important critiques of contemporary mass communications. These centre on the uneven distribution of power in and between societies, the relations between the media and the state and the domination of the economy, including communications, by giant corporations (see, for example, Downing, Mohammadi, Sreberny-Mohammadi, 1995; Stevenson, 1995). Mass media are studied first and foremost as an *industry* that empowers some groups over others, in terms of access, institutional control, financial returns and the selection and framing of messages.

One example is work on media deregulation that took place during the 1980s and 1990s (see, for example, Garnham, 1990). Under the sway of neo-liberal theory, governments privatized media, relaxed controls and reduced restrictions on ownership. At the same time, by investing in regions where labour unions were weak, labour cheap and profits high, multinational corporations were able to expand and flourish. Deregulation enabled media tycoons such as Rupert Murdoch to achieve a kind of global power unimagined a hundred years ago. Murdoch now owns Twentieth Century Fox, BSkyB, Star TV in Asia and the publishing company HarperCollins. His newspaper empire embraces the Australian national newspaper, as well as the *New York Post* and *The Times*, *The Sunday Times*, the *Sun* and *News of the World* in the UK.

It is possible to add to such an analysis an account of cultural products and even of ways of reading, following round the circuits that we outlined in earlier chapters. The Frankfurt School theorists Adorno and Horkheimer developed their theory of the culture industry as a form of 'mass deception' during the 1940s and focused on the industrialization of culture exemplified by the 'Fordist' (that is, in the mode of Ford car assembly lines) mass-production processes of the Hollywood studios and the music industry (1972). The culture that is produced by profit-oriented corporations, they argued, is wholly formulaic and standardized in order to guarantee both audience and profits. The culture industry claims to be democratic and individualistic, but is authoritarian and manipulative. Film, radio, music and magazines seem diverse and individualized, but are standardized and conformist, a form of mass culture that is inferior, predictable and mass produced – not *by* the masses, but *for* them.

More surprising are arguments found in the early work of Roland Barthes (see, for example, 1972). Barthes' semiology is often taken as a model of textualism (see, for example, Connell, 1995), yet his early account of myth as a type of signification is accompanied by a more familiar argument about bourgeois cultural production and its ideological effects. His analysis of myth seeks to reveal how capital's exploitative power is concealed. The design of a French car of the 1960s – the Citroën DS, for example – was so stylish and sleek with such smooth, flawless contours that it seemed to have dropped from heaven rather than off a production line, with no connection to the sweated labour of workers. Barthes' extension of literary analysis to advertisements, wrestling matches, food and architecture was a basis for later textual cultural studies, but he did not question Marxist orthodoxies about the cultural effects of capitalist production. Rather, *Mythologies* created a space *away* from the analysis of economic power and ideology for closer inspection of the specifically cultural. This space of signification – like the space of culture in British cultural studies – sheltered, but also enclosed, much later work. The relationships of semiological to economic processes were not properly attended to until later.

The difference it can make, not least to evaluative judgements, if we combine attentiveness to both text and context in a less tightly systemic analysis can be gauged in the case of deregulation and the Turkish minority population living in Germany. The development of satellite television gave them access to the proliferation of new channels that had begun to appear in Turkey in the 1990s, some of them precisely with these diasporic viewers in mind. Not only was watching these programmes preferable to jostling for minority space on German television, these channels brought a greater variety of images and identities of Turkishness than the mainstream Kemalist version that had prevailed in Turkey until deregulation. The national cultural order in both Germany and Turkey was challenged as a result (Robbins, 2001).

Ideology analysis

Political economy, however, is associated with a form of cultural critique – often called 'ideology analysis'. In this view, cultural products exercise power by hiding or misrepresenting reality – sometimes, in more postivistic versions, conceptualized as 'bias', 'distortion' or 'negative stereotypes'. Social relationships lie behind these ideological versions and determine them: ideology expresses this reality in some way, but distortedly (for a complex review and development of this tradition, see Hall, 1977).

Ideology critique has had a chequered and changing relation with media and cultural analysis. It has held up best where representational codes are realist (as in news and documentary) and the forms of distortion or bias are gross. Criticisms, once made, may then gain wider assent. The pioneering British studies on television news by the Glasgow Media Group is a case in point (1976, 1980, 1982). The group identified bias in the television coverage of war reports, including the conflict between the UK and Argentina over possession of the Falkland Islands, and industrial disputes. After extensive analysis of 'large samples' and by observing media producers and talking to trade unionists, they showed how television presented a view of the latter in which workers were blameworthy, the public illegitimately inconvenienced and management, government or police exonerated. Such biases, they argued, stem from the nature and control of media institutions, including the social (mainly class) backgrounds of media professionals. In its most polemical version, as *Really Bad News*, the group insisted on the pro capitalist, middle-class character of television news and the class bias behind UK television's ideologies of neutrality and balance (Glasgow Media Group, 1982).

Arguments about misrepresentation have been important in critical media studies. Significant absences, imbalances or hostile or reductive representations are often easy to demonstrate once a critical position has been adopted. Experiences of misrepresentation, feelings of injustice about something that is just not true, are catalysts for a fuller knowledge of the power of representation – including starting out on a cultural studies project. The ownership and control of media institutions do have palpable effects on media products in terms of pressures to generate profit or competitive advantage, while the specific interests of owners and producers will influence agenda. Demonstrating the ideologically framed nature of media is important, politically and educationally. Moreover, realist models of understanding have a strong hold on everyday consciousness – and for good reason, despite contrary currents in philosophy and epistemology. In our own work, and in this book, we retain the term 'ideological' to mark an unacknowledged partiality. We prefer to use it at the *end* of an analysis that includes the textual identification of specific ideological effects (for these methods see Part III, Readings, as a whole).

Representation and the limits of ideology critique

Yet, ideology critique is a limited model for cultural research and, ultimately, for understanding power. Interestingly, the term 'ideology' itself accumulated many new meanings in the 1970s, (Barrett, 1991; Larrain, 1983). These went far beyond earlier definitions of ideology as ideas or knowledge that are more or less false or true. It was as though this one term now carried too great a burden of meaning, had too much to say. Partly in response, new terms proliferated in cultural analysis in the 1980s. Representation or 're-presentation', which became the more favoured (and apparently neutral) general term in cultural studies is not restricted in the same way. For one thing, representation is everywhere – in everyday communication and self-knowledge, as well as in publicly mediated forms. Similarly, reading these representations is an everyday activity.

Both representation as a process and reading as an ordinary practice are sometimes overlooked in the critique of textualism that is associated with realist premises. Against this, we would argue that textuality and reading are elements in *all* research, cultural or otherwise. We never have direct access to reality, it can only appear via cultural means – language, discourse, theories, frameworks of meaning – and these are all *part* of 'the real'. While we can read for the 'what' of representation, we can only do this intelligently or critically if we understand our dependence on culture and cultural skills in doing so. All forms of representation call on *means* of representation, the rules of which form, limit and shape each version. As Volosinov argued, it is hard to express even such a basic desire as hunger without some moral or ideological intonation, some expression of feeling and meaning (1973: 87). Sometimes empiricist and epistemologically realist positions work against adequate cultural analysis, because all the energy goes into finding out what really happened, as though there were a single answer that existed outside the realm of cultural understanding. The *making* of meaning – with all its contradictions, emphases, absences, formal rules and codes – is given too little space in such conceptions of the real.

This relatively narrow model of ideology and 'the ideological' leads to an equivalent methodological issue in the use of sources that are seen as tainted, biased, trivial or inappropriate forms of evidence in serious research. Cultural studies researchers use such ideological sources all the time, risking raised eyebrows. Scandalous stories in tabloid newspapers and celebrity magazines do not hold up to conventional academic criteria of truthfulness. They may, however, offer us important insights into social relations and, indeed, models of reality that official or approved sources ignore. The sensationalist UK Sunday newspaper *News of the World*, for example, continues a long tradition of sexual news, going back to the seventeenth century at least. Such lurid documents tell us a lot about sexual construction – about the pervasiveness of discourses of (hetero-)sexuality as fun or liberation and the contradictory association of pleasure with secrecy, risk and disclosure, for example. We can also use them to highlight press power in regulating sexual mores (see, for example, Epstein and Johnson, 1998). Putting such sources into a special 'unreliable' category misses all this and can imply that somewhere there is a source that is transparent and direct and not in need of critical interpretation.

It is often tempting to infer the character of a cultural product from its conditions of production – as a capitalist commodity, mass formulaic trash or gutter journalism. The risks are especially high with entertainment forms. As the Glasgow Media Group put it, 'The tedium and repetition of formula Westerns, detective stories and comedy shows comes because they have in the end to be basically the same' (1982: 139).

Yet, while popular genres do share 'basically the same' elements in order to meet producers' and advertisers' requirements of profits and audiences, they are frequently more complex and varied than such reductions allow (see Chapter 9). The economic pressures are real, but then so are the readings of those who enjoy (or hate) these popular forms. Viewing Westerns or situation comedies always involves a *second* production of these products that is not predictable from their first production. Our circuit model from Chapter 2, reproduced here as Figure 8.1, may help to clarify this.

We cannot infer C (the text) and D (the readings) and A (the intersections with the everyday life of viewers) from an account of B (the moment of production). Moreover, the effects of the *whole* circuit feed back to production (B) and shape it all the time. Popular (and elite) forms may or may not be aesthetically problematic, but such judgements – when we need to evaluate – require us to read texts carefully and also to attend to the lives of readers (See Chapter 10).

It is also not always easy, though it may be important and worthwhile, to ground a more truthful alternative to biased accounts convincingly. The increasing sophistication of many media forms, including their incorporation

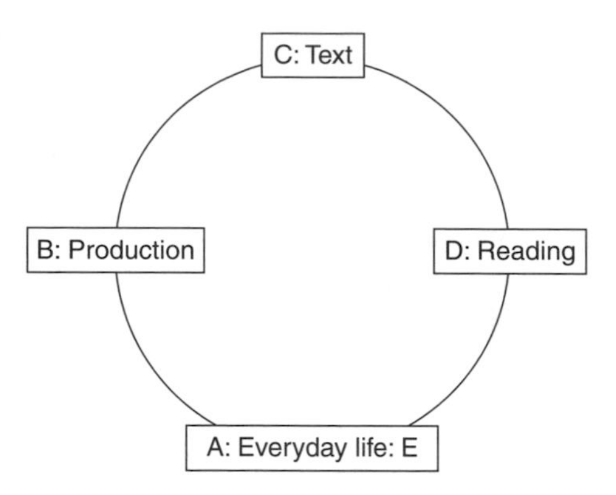

Figure 8.1 Cultural circuit

(and recuperation) of some oppositional positions, has also to be reckoned with. There are ways of doing cultural studies that serve to confirm our dearest wishes and least inspected beliefs – gratifying, but terribly limiting. Yet, once we have let the genie of ideology out of the bottle and acknowledged its pervasive power, we cannot neglect what it tells us about our *own* truth claims and evaluations. This is why we adopt a modified form of 'standpoint epistemology' in this book (see Chapter 3 especially). What we see and how we see it always takes the pressure of *who* we are, *where* we are and *when* we are – our social, spatial and temporal positionings. These settings are *general* conditions of knowing; there are no convenient exceptions.

Power and culture: expanding the agenda

The limits of ideology analysis become clearer when we consider all the other forms of culture-as-power. Bidding for political leadership, claiming the high ground morally and setting agendas of significance for others are all forms of power-in-culture. It is not only ideas that are powerful but also pleasure-seeking and emotions, such as hating, admiring or desiring. Power relations attend the formation of identities and subjectivities, individual and collective. As the cultural version of psychoanalysis teaches, psychic relations are power-laden (Benjamin, 1990; Frosch, 1987).

Moreover, claims to truth and falsity are themselves kinds of power. It is not so much the truth of knowledge that matters here, but what Foucault called its 'truth *effects*' or 'regimes of truth' – the ways in which they secure credibility (1980). Knowledges produce or incite new subjects or social identities – 'citizens', 'clients', 'customers', for instance. Similarly, power works by producing systems of inclusion and exclusion in cultural representations of 'Us' and 'Them'. Versions of a nation, for example, act differentially on different groups or practices, so some are central or exemplary, others are marginal or can only belong on certain conditions. Some groups or practices are not only excluded, they are explicitly produced as the 'other', whether hated or admired. The lines may be fine but the pressures are real. When, after September 11th 2001, George W. Bush and Tony Blair insisted that Muslim peoples were welcome as members of their 'multicultural societies', they also implied that full belonging depended on good behaviour and that mosques and neighbourhoods would be watched (Johnson, 2002).

If cultural representations are constitutive of power relations, then, the concern with text and reading as a method are not diversions from the question of power, but, rather, are one way of investigating and challenging such relations.

Where does power lie? The popular and the dominant

In an influential critique of cultural studies, Jim McGuigan has identified a tendency to 'cultural populism' as 'the main trajectory' of cultural studies:

> *Cultural populism is the intellectual assumption, made by some students of popular culture, that the symbolic experiences and practices of ordinary people are more important analytically and politically than Culture with a capital C.* (1992: 4, emphasis as in original)

In this view, 'cultural populism' involves an overoptimistic or depoliticized view of the consumption of media forms under capitalist conditions. Power in institutions is neglected and working-class survival strategies are misrecognized as resistance (for a different version, see also Walkerdine, 1997). A sentimental affiliation to the world of 'the people' (or a particular subordinated group) stands in for independent appraisal and action. Yet, this criticism ignores the fact that much cultural study is neither about 'Culture with a capital C' nor appreciating the 'popular', but, rather, appraising the dominant. In Chapter 10 we explore what this means for method. Here, we question the dominant/popular division itself.

Constructing cultural boundaries or distinctions – perhaps around 'popular culture' and 'culture with a capital C' – is one way in which power works – a process explored with great resourcefulness by the French cultural sociologist Pierre Bourdieu (see, for example, 1986). Dominance, however, is a *set of relationships* that are *everywhere* in cultural *transactions*, cutting across the social divides, hinging together cultural spaces. It is certainly not confined to official knowledge, political practices or economic relations. The dominant and the popular, like the economic and cultural, are often mixed up together, in the same texts, practices and institutional spaces (schools, for instance). Dominant ideas, discourses or power relations often work via popular forms in contradictory ways. The emergence and globalization of MTV, for example, involved the development and refining of a rock aesthetic linked to the video together with the creation of an international audience (or audiences) for Western pop and rock music. The music videos MTV played – and even MTV itself – represented ideas about youth and freedom, but also American global cultural power.

The question of populism also foregrounds the evaluations that cultural critics make and the sides they take, morally and politically. It is lazy analysis simply to turn upside down the old elite judgements of 'high' and 'low' and make 'the popular' automatically good. The popular is itself a construction and differently constructed versions of 'the people' have different relationships to hegemonic forces. The popular may be oppositional (as in new social movements or the social forums they create) or it may be linked to dominant interests (as in the moral majority of Reaganite politics). The popular can be divided, split all ways, by racism, xenophobia, the subordination of women or gays. A sentimental populism, allied with a purely negative conception of power, can also be disabling. If power in itself is always bad, there can never be a popular or oppositional 'we' with the power to change anything.

There are, therefore, limits to the dominant/popular couplet itself. The plurality of terms in English for describing cultural 'superiority' shows how complex cultural hierarchies are: 'dominant culture', 'middle-class (or 'bourgeois') culture', 'elite culture', 'high culture', 'Culture with a Capital C', 'hegemony'. Some of this complexity is already present in one of the earliest texts of the culture-as-power tradition – Marx and Engels' *The German Ideology*, written in 1845–46. Here, we find, side-by-side, two ways of thinking about 'ruling ideas'. In the first, more famous formulation, 'the ideas of the ruling class are in every epoch the ruling ideas'. Dominant ideas, in other words, are those possessed and produced by the ruling class (and its agents). However, the ruling ideas are also, 'nothing more than the ideal expression of the dominant material relationships, the dominant material relationships grasped as ideas; hence of the relationships which make the one class the ruling one, therefore the ideas, of its dominance' (1977: 64). Here, dominance has to do with *relationships*: relationships between ideas and everyday living, relationships between rulers and ruled. Ideas do not 'express' a single ruling group's way of living, but do express their relationships with other groups.

This more relational understanding of dominance is closer to what Gramsci meant by 'hegemony', as complex relations of force between social alliances (1971). It also speaks more adequately to the mixed and puzzling cases that typically face cultural analysts today. In considering the popular mourning for Diana, the Princess of Wales, for instance, we are not obliged to identify the public figure of Diana uncomplicatedly with ruling ideas. Rather, strong popular identifications with her as a rebel were mixed up with reassertions of royalism. Diana grew to challenge some gendered definitions and recognized gay sexualities, but she also confirmed narratives of heterosexual romance in her 'fairytale wedding' and in circumstances of her dying. Many forces and points of view fought for dominance in Diana's global story (Kear and Steinberg, 1999). Even Diana's own (personal) relationship to culture and power was contradictory: she was an aristocrat but with popular tastes rather than the 'legitimate' ones that Bourdieu ascribes to the upper classes.

Even so, as related questions, popularity and dominance do not go away. Culture came to matter when it entered into the concerns of critical agents –

socialists (especially of the various brands of New Left), student radicals, feminist critics, black activists, anti-colonial intellectuals, sexual dissidents, disability campaigners, environmentalists and so on. Those who seek emancipation need to know what is holding the dominant way of living in place. This has gone along with the need to represent ourselves, find a voice, shape emerging collective identities and revalue them positively. In other words, changing the dominant and representing the popular are linked tasks. So, for instance, practices of black self-representation in the United States and Europe are best understood against the larger histories of colonialism, slavery and racism. Pride in blackness or syncretic cultural creativity within a black historical tradition are forms of popular assertion and self-representation. Protest against unjust institutions (including images) and self-representation underlie a wide range and long history of cultural practices, including black cultural studies (Hall, 1996a, 1996b; Hooks, 1991, 1992; Mercer, 1994).

Once we realize that 'the popular' is not a single category and has no necessary aesthetic value or liberatory tendency, we can develop a sensitivity for those forms of the popular that are important as resources for the future or a differently organized social order. This is not a matter of fully formed alternatives, but, rather, a different standpoint and popular agency. Subordinated standpoints relativize dominant standpoints and provide the basis of critique – a repeated process in the history of cultural study as new social movements forge new academic agenda. Most recently, for instance, the representation of experiences of being disabled has led to a widespread questioning of able-bodiedness and the question of the body and embodiment more generally (see, for example, Butler, 1993; Grosz, 1994).

Being sensitive to the precise forms of the popular is also related to questions of political agency. The criticism of cultural populism and advocacy of culture as a 'reformer's science' (Bennett, 1998) sometimes suggests that significant social change can only come from above, perhaps from cultural experts advising state policymakers, managers and politicians. Popular agency, in its diverse forms, is sidelined. Cultural critics may sometimes mistake strategies of survival for resistance, but holding on to the idea of resistance as a productive force is important if we are not to lose sight of agency itself. In an era of what the US government's strategic advisors call 'full spectrum dominance', the questions 'Who resists?' and 'Who can secure change?' press very hard.

Starting elsewhere: economies as culturally embedded

We have seen how New Left analyses opposed not only economic determinism but also the separation out of the economy or culture or any other social aspect. Formal abstractions such as 'base and superstructure' were seen to be problematic because economic relations are always embedded in those of law and culture. In his discussion of law in early modern England, Edward P. Thompson insisted that 'law did not keep politely to a level but was at every bloody level'. It was 'imbricated within the mode of production' as much as it was found in John Locke's philosophy. Thompson thought that even the Marx of *Capital* was too much the 'political economist', too formal, too abstracted (1978: 288). Raymond Williams, similarly, in his literary history and theoretical commentary, always insisted on the (inter)dependence of particular practices within larger social processes:

> we cannot separate literature and art from other kinds of social practice, in such a way as to make them subject to quite special and distinct laws. They may have quite specific features as practices, but they cannot be separated from the general social process (1980: 44).

'Practices' are a crucial idea in Williams' appropriation of Marxism. He constantly alerts us to the dangers of fixing the properties of variable processes into physical entities by categorizing them (see, for example, Williams, 1977: 82).

There are, however, problems with resistance to abstraction when it is made into a general principle. We argued in Chapter 5 that abstraction is a necessary editing out of some of the complexity of situations in order to think about them more clearly. Of course, these theories have to be distinguished from the concrete. Moreover, abstraction does not only happen in thought but is a feature of social relationships, too. Certain social practices do become separated out into institutions such as 'literature' or 'schooling' and so acquire a sort of autonomy. The printed or electronic text stands free, for a moment, from its conditions of production. Schools are very particular institutions. We have to be careful that, by opposing abstraction entirely, we do not make it more difficult to think effectively about our split-up world. In this spirit, we pursue our two main abstractions in this chapter so far – first, culture's *constitutive* role in making power relations; and, second, the embeddedness of power, including economic power, in cultural relations.

In what follows, we review five main strategies. Each can be illustrated by recent work. They are:

- reading economies as representation, signification or discourse
- tracing the overlaps and interdependencies (perhaps identities) of cultural and economic circuits
- focusing on material culture and the question of consumption
- exploring the cultural conditions of economic processes
- tracing the contemporary emergence of a (more?) cultural economy

Economies as representation and discourse

Economic life is itself a process of representation, signification or discursive construction. There are, however, versions of this insight that are more or less radical, depending on how culture itself is conceptualized. Helen Grace (1991), for example, draws on textual models to explore how business is a form of spectacle, entered, perhaps, via the business pages of daily newspapers. Stockmarket crashes are here visually represented by photographs of hysterical floor traders, which grab public imagination more effectively than do charts and graphs. Such images signify a spirit of energy and virility that is linked to the market's freedom and openness. Indeed, advocates of monetary theory, such as Milton Friedman, themselves appropriated aesthetic symbols – 'Monetary theory is like a Japanese garden' – to give form to their ideas (Friedman, 1979 cited in Grace (1991)).

Money is, in any case, an abstract value that works by evoking ideas beyond itself. It is, as Grace notes, the 'classic fetish in many ways because it stands for something else, it replaces the object which it ostensibly represents' (117). It is exchangeable not only for commodities but also its own negation – debt. In considering this world of economic reality, Grace finds fictional entities everywhere – futures trading (futures being commodities that do not yet exist), junk bonds (the greater the risk, the greater the return), credit (which is actually debt) and the terrifying reality of Third World debt, which threatens the North as well as the South as a result of over-extended credit and non-payment.

> Clearly, then, a world of high fiction is observable, a daily soap opera, full of the most extreme occurrences. Everyday economic life has become a fiction of terrifying realism, a horror scenario with such convincing special effects, that at times, you really feel you too are there, in the middle of it. (119)

Grace is using classic cultural tools here, such as Vladimir Propp's account of narrative structure in folk tales (See Chapter 9), which is intriguingly appropriate to City 'heroes' and 'villains'. Women ('princesses'), however, are notably absent from the story, with young, lean, fast-moving men doing anything to stay on top. Grace's use of a formal textual analysis thus reveals much about the fictionalized constructions and precarious self-belief of a world where immense power is wielded in global markets.

We can extend cultural analysis of the economy further. From a Foucauldian perspective, the economy appears as a set of determining rules or discursive formations with its own history and way of producing subjects or social identities – workers, managers, supervisors, customers, consumers, the unemployed. Such an analysis includes attention being given to the truth effects of contemporary neo-liberal economists, such as Friedman, but also many other forms of expert practice: information technology, financial risk management, pension fund management and money-tracking systems, for instance, and the professions of accountants and auditors, management, public relations and advertising. We can also explore how processes of privatization, individualization and the marketization of knowledge are producing distinctive economic and social subjects or identities: There is the infinitely flexible worker, for instance – pursuing lifelong learning and continual self reinvention.

Reading the economy as a representation or discourse has some limits, though. It may not include more everyday aspects of living as they structure, and are structured by, capitalist and other conditions. The public representations of the economy that appear in media or academic texts leave out its hidden sides and subjugated standpoints. They may therefore produce too deterministic (and fixed) a view of a system rather than seeing economic relationships as conflicts that lead to change. Major changes in economic life have often sprung from popular movements and worker resistance – movements for factory regulation or shorter hours forced capital to find new ways to make profit, trade union strength and social-democratic state policies in Western countries forced company relocations to 'Third World' nations. For this reason, a larger historical contextualization – therefore, a mix of methods – remains important.

Cultural and economic circuits: overlap, interdependence, identity?

The version of cultural circuits that we have used in this book was derived from Marx's accounts of the circuits of capital, especially from Stuart Hall's reading of Marx's *Grundrisse* or 'Notebooks' (Hall, 1973a). In the predominantly capitalist world of today, circuits of culture and circuits of capital overlap and intertwine as they are interdependent parts of the same social processes. In a recent Open University course text, a group of authors, including Stuart Hall himself, show how a similar circuit throws light on a particular cultural commodity – specifically, the Sony Walkman personal stereo (du Gay et al., 1997). They analyse the role of cultural objects in everyday lives, but also the structures, strategies and the culture of a global commercial enterprise. They examine the way Sony represents itself as a unique company. They explore the strands that make up its site of economic and cultural production – namely, the individuals who set up the company, its relationship to the United States, its Japanese features, the economic expenditure and the targeting of consumers for the product. They also include the stories and meanings that have shaped its invention, design and manufacture – production in the larger sense.

Like many companies, Sony deploys discourses of national identity in its image making. The hierarchy of occupations within the company, the idiosyncratic rituals, the idea of a 'job for life' and employee loyalty are presented as authentically Japanese. Yet, the company also developed a hybrid culture of production, poaching management and engineering staff from other firms, employing bright eccentrics prepared to take risks and adopting US work practices of delegating responsibility to small design teams alongside the core Japanese hierarchy. Sony's assembly plants employ a predominantly female workforce who work in military-style rows for the numbingly rigid and routinized tasks of assembling the Walkman, while men do the creative design work in small teams. A powerful image is used in the study: a photograph of the rows and rows of women on the assembly line, bent over their workstations. This image contrasts starkly with the chic young people using the gadget in Sony advertisements. The women constitute the invisible labour concealed in each Walkman machine.

Production and consumption are brought together by a study of Sony's marketing, public relations and feedback systems. The actual take-up and use of the Walkman was more individualistic than initial advertisement and design (dual headphone jack sockets and joint listening) anticipated, so the design was changed accordingly (du Gay et al., 1997: 58–9). In general, the Sony study shows the interdependence of moments in the circuit, but also explores how production, distribution and consumption are at once economic *and* cultural processes.

The question of consumption

Critics are right to point to the concern with consumption in cultural studies, but this is not a diversion from economic and political analysis. Contemporary stress on the materiality of consumption places it as central both to capital's circuits and the production of identities and social life (see, for example, Lury, 1996; D. Miller, 1987). This builds on longstanding feminist recognitions that political economies are gendered and consumption (like the division of labour) constructs gendered differences and relationships of power (see, for example, Brunsdon, 2000; Coward, 1984; Gray, 1992; Winship, 1987). The trivial pursuits of the mass consumer have often been constructed as predominantly feminine, for example. At the same time, the commodity system depends absolutely on the saleability of its products and the cultural work of producing popular needs and desires and shaping ways of living. The circuit model highlights the interdependence of each of the economic/cultural moments, but each moment has something specific to it, too, so that consumption cannot be understood from the viewpoint of production alone. In Marx's analysis, consumption involves both 'exchange value' and 'use value'. The former concerns the abstract nature and exchangeability of commodities and money, the latter the concrete uses that commodities come to have for groups of people. Some theorists argue that use value vanishes in 'late capitalism', but we argue for retaining this idea as the relay between cultural and economic analysis. It is in consumption (as well as production) that capitalist dynamics and popular ways of living intersect (see also D. Miller, 1987). Here, as elsewhere, the popular and its cultivation – always gendered, ethnicized and class aligned – are decisive.

An interesting example of this is the failure of digitalized commercial television in the UK in 2002, which foundered because of the lack of a cultural content that people would actually buy despite massive advertising and technical development. A huge financial deal between independent (not BBC) television companies and the Football League (representing the non-premier football teams) collapsed because the programmes did not draw audiences. The history of commodified cultural production provides many more examples of failure than of spectacular successes, such as McDonalds, Coca-Cola or Nike. So, studies of consumption, pleasure, desire and popular culture are important, in part, because economic understandings are inadequate without them. Commercial popular culture is a crucial site for the formation of social identities of all kinds, but these everyday social practices also put pressures on commodity production itself.

Cultural conditions of economic systems

A third strategy is to explore the cultural conditions on which economic systems depend, including the forms of human subjectivity that are preferred or presupposed. Economic arrangements are often treated as inevitable and fixed, but integrated cultural analysis can bring out their specificity and the possibility of economic ways of life based on different values. Economies depend on material resources and scarcities, but also on how different groups of human beings imagine progress or betterment. Culture is more than a *product* of economics, it *founds* economies in different ways.

Cultural histories of the relation of economics to other theories – to aesthetics, for instance – bring out these connections (see, for example, Gagnier, 2000). We need to know how neo-liberal economics became hegemonic today, nationally, regionally, globally. 'The system' does not automatically produce its own subjectivities and ways of life; these are an aspect of hegemonic politics and cultural work. Gramsci, whose theories remain a resource here, shows how hegemony is about securing cultural and institutional conditions that support *new* forms of production as well as securing consent to the old. His analysis of Fordist mass production – fully achieved in the USA but not in Italy in the 1930s – suggests ways in which to integrate economic with cultural analysis while marking out popular ways of life and cultural leadership as being central to these connections (Gramsci, 1971, especially 277–318). These conditions were not guaranteed; they had to be struggled over.

Some forms of empirical sociology, the new economic geography and socio-historical studies offer researched examples here. Bourdieu and his school have theorized the ways in which cultural capital (distinctions of status and taste) and social capital (networks and personal connections) can be converted into economic capital. They have empirically investigated the specific forms of class-related distinction in France (Bourdieu, 1986) – work taken up very widely in cultural studies and cultural sociology. Financiers and entrepreneurs use their cultural competences as well as their long-standing relationships with each other, to make money. The financial hub of the City of London was originally located in the 'square mile' because proximity helped to cement the cultural capital necessary for trust between trading partners. Thus, the *culture* of the City was what made it function as an economic centre.

Similarly, ethnic minority entrepreneurs in the UK today deploy shared understandings of economic needs that are culturally determined. When Islamic shops sell particular products – such as the stand on which copies of the Quran are placed – they are drawing on specialized cultural knowledge that is transformed into economic enterprise. They seek to strengthen Islamic culture, while making money, uniting cultural necessity and economic strategy in the product. In this way, large-scale cultural conditions or different versions of the global – such as religious traditions and transnational movements – may underpin the base of economic life rather than being themselves determined by it.

Changing determinations: the economy as culture

A final strategy for rethinking economic–cultural forms of power is to focus on the so-called 'new economy'. We draw attention here only to one main theme in accounts of contemporary economic change – a kind of inversion of Adorno and Horkeimer's (1972) earlier argument about 'the culture industry': if culture is 'industrial', is not industry increasingly 'cultural'?

This 'culturalization' is perceived as taking place in many sectors (Castells, 1994) and especially perhaps in service industries (Lash and Urry, 1994). Management gurus, it is argued, have become celebrities, with their faces on the front covers of magazines. Businesses are increasingly about the meanings and lifestyles (not just functions) that are attached to brands. Thus, Nike sells identities, not just sports shoes. Consumer culture and advertising feed into and feed off such identities, not only among consumers but within the business world itself. If culture became a commodity for the Frankfurt School, knowledge and meaning are taken to be productive forces today.

Thus, social interconnections no longer operate from base to superstructure, along a single line of causality. Cultural arrangements are more chaotic and less predictable. Development is decentralized and non-linear, connected in an interlocking network fashion, like a rhizome or the roots of a tree (Deleuze and Guattari, 1988: 15). There are new forms of organizational restructuring, too – away from rigid vertical bureaucracies to horizontal, flat structures and, thence, to more open, flexible networks. The Internet is both paradigmatic and strategic here. It creates strange reconfigurations of public and private spheres via websites, chatrooms, and mailing lists by using the technologies of telecoms, Internet service providers and web agencies.

These 'big pictures' are fascinating, but need filling out and questioning in 'local' terms. Too intense a focus on 'the emergent' (see Chapter 7) means that they lack historical perspective. Economies have *always* been 'cultural' (D. Miller, 2002) – even business heroes are not new. Careful evaluation is therefore important, avoiding the 'wow' or 'ugh' of technophilia or technophobia. More detailed researches – often involving exchanges between geographers, anthropologists and students of culture – include biographies of cultural objects (see, for example, Lury, 1996), the mapping of the symbolic economies of cities, with battles over access and branding (see, for example, Zukin 1996a, 1996b); interest in new cultures of working and networking (Wittel, 2001) and the study of the new gendered and class subjectivities in neo-liberal and 'Third Way' political economies (Rose, 1996, 1999; Walkerdine and Johnson, 2003). Production, too, is being recast, so aesthetic values, cultural codes and information are as much means and conditions of production as are material capital and physical raw materials. The subjective aspects of labour itself are important – knowledge, skills, psychological adaptability, willingness to serve, a certain feminization. Nor are economic developments divorced from formal politics. A *cultural* analysis of Blairism and other 'Third Ways' is as important today as analysis of the New Right was in the 1980s (Johnson and Steinberg, 2003).

Conclusion

Our argument that culture is an embedded aspect of social power has many implications for method. It points to transformative encounters between cultural studies, political economy and social theory. *Specifying* the cultural conditions, aspects and consequences of large-scale systems or dynamics are vital moves. Here, also, cultural studies can bring the sociological abstractions and historical research closer together. Yet, treating sources *only* as cultural texts is not enough. As we argue throughout Part III, which follows, this has many implications for the ways in which we read texts, especially when we are interested in power relations.

Part III
READINGS

Readings and meetings

In the next two parts of this book, we turn from questions about the broad basis of method and methods (Part I) and the relationship of cultural analysis to the contextualizing disciplines (Part II), to the two great clusters of methods, usually taken as the central tools of cultural study. The first cluster approaches the other via textual means, most typically by reading texts that are already available in the public sphere. This cluster of methods is often termed 'textual analysis'. This can be distinguished from methods that involve direct encounters and interaction with embodied cultural practitioners, often termed 'ethnographic'.

In what follows, we seek to do justice to the value and indispensability of these methods, but also show their limits, the points where combination is necessary. It is our belief that, ultimately, the division between text analysis and ethnography is a misleading one and that the best work goes beyond it in different ways. As we shall see in Chapter 14 especially, a developed method in cultural studies needs to find other ways of doing justice both to the textual organization of culture and to its embeddedness in social relations and practices. Each of the chapters in Part III press in different ways beyond the conventional division, albeit from the side of the text.

Reading as method, method as reading

Reading is a skill that all of us engaged in research have learned, intellectually digested and internalized. It is a form of cultural capital that enables us to gain access to the (limited) power that academic knowledge offers. Yet, because the precise mechanisms of reading are so familiar to us, we tend to naturalize them and the ideological processes involved in their acquisition. For example, the widespread availability of reading material has helped to inculcate a print culture that is hegemonic throughout most Western societies, a culture in which the printed text has been linked to national identity and the power of the state – dominant power – and has assumed a degree of reified authority. Knowing how to read became a skill associated with particular kinds of power and specific forms of official knowledge. One of the most important aims of the chapters that follow, therefore, as of this book as a whole, is to make as explicit and accessible as possible, practices of reading that have tended to become means of exclusion and privilege.

There are diverse traditions of reading in literary and cultural analysis. Cultural studies initially took its reading methods from humanist models of English literary studies, especially from Richard Hoggart's application of 'close reading' to new objects, including working-class streets, interiors and faces. Later work drew on a parallel tradition in the work of the French semiotician Roland Barthes, who made a similar extension of literary methods to such objects as wrestling, motor cars and fashion (for example, Barthes, 1972). More recently textual analysis has been applied to such subjects as 'cities', 'bodies', 'silence' and 'the political actions of disabled people' (Parker et al., 1999). There is still some tension between these and other approaches to reading. Barthes' structuralism has made it possible to understand meaning as being produced as a result of forces outside the conscious or deliberate intent of an individual author. This opened the way for a more elaborated cultural analysis. On the other hand, it now clear that these gains were made at the expense of the possibility of well-grounded evaluative judgements of cultural forms, judgements that may be political, ethical or aesthetic, or a mixture of each. A second aim of the chapters that follow, therefore, is to pursue our more general preference for combining methods by working *across* traditions of reading, especially those influenced by structuralism and Marxism, as well as other emancipatory theories that retain some sense of human agency.

Different ways of reading offer different entries into the text, produce different versions of the text and, thus, have their own strengths as well as limitations. Structuralist models (see Chapter 9) can offer a way of opening up the narrative for analysis by reading for structure, genre and narrative conventions. However, structuralism ultimately returns meaning to textuality or texts as they relate to other texts. A more dialogic approach, such as that which informs our own approach to method, emphasizes the relationship between the text(s) and a community of readers. As Meaghan Morris argues, cultural studies is 'a political theory of contexts', it 'works to understand how contexts are "made, unmade, and remade" . . . [and] . . . are always dynamic' (1997:44).

Plan of Part III

In Part III, we explore in turn three clusters of reading methods, bearing in mind another of our arguments, that methods are related to objects, and that there are many ways of reading, far more than we can cover here. In Chapter 9, we explore the strengths and limits of using a literary–linguistic and structuralist model of reading for texts of popular entertainment, especially film and television. In Chapter 10, we look at overtly political texts, employing a broadly Gramscian method. In this chapter, we also consider reading as a research process, with its own stages and moments, returning to some of the procedural and practical themes of Chapter 4. In Chapter 11, we engage with the reading of historical fictions from two different methodological traditions – those of cultural materialism and of the new historicism.

We are interested throughout Part III in how cultural readings can offer us a way of understanding power relations in more complex and nuanced ways than is possible from a narrowly textual approach or a sociology or an economics that does not engage textually at all. The formal, concretized character of texts is often what enables us to identify the traces of power dynamics, but the relationship between text and context is also crucial. The 'articulation' of texts and contexts – the ways in which cultural forms and practices may be both joined and separated, speaking and silent, hinged together while also swinging apart – helps us to understand the history or histories that produce a text as well as the text itself. To read a text, then, is also to read its contexts.

9 Reading popular narratives: from structure to context

Structural readings: textual strategies 158
Structural readings: contextualizing strategies 162
Beyond structuralism: poststructuralist approaches 167
Combining methods 168
Conclusion

In this chapter, we consider how we can apply a culturally inflected version of 'structuralist' readings to particular texts in order to pull out the underlying meanings that may be embedded in a narrative or generic tradition. We also seek to show how it is possible to link this to the wider contexts that are involved in textual production and reception. This is to follow our broader agenda about the combination of methods, which we see as typical of cultural studies. The kind of detailed analyses described here are, importantly, more than a simple consideration of 'content' – a method that may be used initially to review and survey what we find in texts but does not consider questions of how textual meaning may be produced. A reading for structure makes explicit the *relationships* between texts by foregrounding the way in which meaning is not innate or absolute but is always produced in relation to other meanings. We begin, therefore, with the structuralist model. As structuralism is itself a complex tradition, with its own breaks and 'posts', we choose to focus on one analytical strategy: narratology, or the analysis of texts as narratives. Again, method follows object – not all texts are narratives, but the kinds of texts we are especially interested in often have a narrative form.

Our emphasis here is on those film and television texts that largely belong in the realm of the popular – that is, as commodified forms of mass entertainment (especially those produced by Hollywood studios or media conglomerates that are distributed, if not globally, then certainly internationally) and as 'well liked by many people' in Raymond Williams' (1976) formulation. It is these texts that have perhaps been most debated, struggled over and problematized in cultural research. They were reviled as a form of 'mass deception' by some of the Frankfurt School critics in the 1940s, celebrated for the possibilities they offered for resistance in the 1980s and returned to as a source of interest and fascination by cultural scholars in the years between and since precisely because of their popular status. This chapter is not concerned to engage with the extensive debates about 'the popular'. We do want to insist, however, on the legitimacy and value of studying popular texts and genres. They are clearly crucial in the context of consumption (see Chapter 8), the construction of hegemony (see Chapter 10) and identity formation. Popular texts also take us deep into those issues of value that constructivist readings (including structuralism) have repressed. We therefore want to return questions of 'value' to the agenda of cultural researchers and address this issue towards the end of the chapter. Our own interest in positionality and self-reflexivity has implications for an old debate between a literary humanism that puts value first and a structuralism that explores how meaning is produced. While a priori value judgements (those that exclude the popular as 'low' or 'not art', for instance) should not limit our objects of cultural study, we do need to make our own complex evaluations of both popular and elite forms more explicit and develop criteria for this purpose. There is an odd kind of complicity between a residual academic objectivity among many cultural researchers and the scientism or abstract objectivism of classical structuralism. We need continually to remind ourselves of the emotional and cultural investments that are always at stake in popular formations and, crucially, in critical work itself.

Structural readings: textual strategies

The range of structuralisms that developed in the mid-twentieth century tended to share a highly formalist approach to cultural artefacts and practices, together with a preoccupation with the search for meaning and a commitment to what was seen as scientific objectivity in their analytical methods. This focus on the structural dimensions of culture – the formal, narrative and generic elements of a text, for example – moves us away from humanist concerns with value and truth (as well as individual agency) and thereby allows us to explore the complex processes of representation. There are various versions and traditions, developed by the cultural analyst, Roland Barthes (see, for example, 1967), by the folklorist, Vladimir Propp (see, for example, 1968), the anthropologist Claude Levi-Strauss (see, for example, 1968), the Marxist Louis Althusser (see, for example, Althusser and Balibar, 1970) and the film theorist Christian Metz (see, for example, 1974). Underpinning all these approaches, however, is Ferdinand de Saussure's (1974) theory of linguistics, developed between 1906 and 1915, which distinguished between the system of a language – its rules and conventions – and individual use. This distinction is important because it offers a way of theorizing the difference between what might be called structure and performance and entails attention to both the inner workings of a cultural form and its relationships to a larger set of meanings. Classic structuralism proposes that all cultural forms operate as a kind of language system. Because meaning is produced through the *relationship* between texts identifying the 'rules' or codes of the sign system becomes a way of determining what the meanings are and how they relate to each other.

Organizing meaning – narrative

Narrative structuralism thus begins with the 'bones' of books or films and looks for the underlying, deep structure of a text – the determining elements that shape it yet are not immediately apparent or are so taken for granted that they seem invisible.

When we examine texts that tell a story in some way, identifying the characteristics of narrative structure can help us to uncover the process of signification, or, how meaning is produced. Beginning with an intensive examination of one text can, then, give us clues to the larger structures that shape it. For example, most conventional mainstream popular narratives tend to work using the following linear structure – first identified and analysed by Roland Barthes (1977):

order → disruption → complication → resolution

Narratives begin by establishing order by means of a scene-setting process in which the main characters, location and social relationships are clearly established. This is then disrupted by an event, such as a crime, sexual awakening, mysterious appearance or disappearance, that leads to conflict. The rest of the narrative is devoted to the development of the disruptive event and its eventual resolution, with (social) order – albeit modified – firmly re-established at the end. In other words, mainstream narrative texts work by foregrounding and resolving a relationship between order and disorder that is itself culturally produced.

In his account of popular film genres, Stephen Neale (1980) argues that this involves a balance between equilibrium and disequilibrium, a drive towards closure and pleasure in process. For a text to work effectively, it must therefore balance the revelatory process of plot development with other kinds of pleasures, which may be more spectacular or discursive, such as a song or dance routine in a film musical. In addition, narratives work by means of two further codes according to Barthes (1977): those of action and enigma. Action codes will often advance the narrative in shorthand ways – simply showing a flashing blue light in a television show will 'code' the police and therefore a dramatic event without showing the police car, officers and so on, for example. The enigma code works by setting up problems or uncertainties that will be resolved during the course of the narrative.

The American comedy series *Friends* works very closely within these 'rules' in terms of its structure, despite its innovatory aspects, such as its move away from the nuclear family as the primary focus of situation comedy. As Jane Feuer (1992: 148) observes, in form at least the television sitcom is particularly static – characters can never completely change the 'sit' that produces the 'com' without overturning the basic premise of the programme. This relative rigidity makes it easy to decode the narrative strategies employed. Equilibrium or social order is indicated in every episode by the use of the opening establishing shot of the outside of the friends' apartment building or the café where they habitually meet, Central Perk. This is followed by a scene in the semi-public space of the café or the private space of one of the apartments where the episode's main plot strand, together with the central enigma ('Will Monica and Chandler have a baby?', 'Will Joey get a job?'), is set in motion. This central narrative event is complicated by later turns in the plot and is usually only resolved in the penultimate scene. The final scene (sometimes coming after the end credits) will then return the characters and the viewer to the equilibrium and 'normality'.

This equilibrium (and the characters' relationships) is never fundamentally changed in a regular television comedy series – even by the most dramatic shifts in plot, such as the marriage of Monica and Chandler: the friends remain locked forever into the 'comedy situation', playing and replaying the underlying structural problematic, until the programme is cancelled. Interestingly, the order–disruption–complication–resolution model also structures individual segments of *Friends* (often indicated by the repeat of the establishing shot and the insertion of snatches of the theme tune) within the larger narrative. The successful achievement of resolution, then, points to the way in which, in fictional texts, all the elements are strictly controlled and managed. For Barthes, this 'hermeneutic code' works to close down some possible meanings as well as enabling others to be articulated. Such closures are linked to questions of power in the production of meaning.

Organizing meaning – plot and story

The organization of meaning in the process of storytelling is not, however, limited to the relatively simple linear structure outlined above. For example, the structuralist critic Gerard Genette (1972) argues that there is a difference between the 'story' and the 'narrative' of any text: the former is the events, in temporal and causal order, before they are put into words or told to the reader, while the 'narrative' is the written or represented version of those events, including the order in which the story is related, the emphasis that is placed on certain elements and the presentation of the characters. This distinction between story and narrative is particularly clear if we look to the example of classic detective fiction as such work depends on precisely this difference in order to sustain suspense and the reader's interest in the outcome. The story is effectively what we know at the end of the book or film – in the case of detective fiction 'whodunnit', why and how – while the narrative is the means by which that knowledge is offered to us. To put it slightly differently, David Bordwell argues that in a film, the crucial difference is between 'story' and 'plot'. A conventional linear plot organizes the story around four nodal points – 'an undisturbed stage, the disturbance, the struggle, and the elimination of the disturbance' (1985: 157). This drives the narrative towards closure as the point at which the story's meaning becomes evident. We can only know what the story is – and is 'about' – once these nodal points have been passed.

These formal structural dimensions to a text become especially important when we contextualize them by considering how they are imbued with ideological dimensions, as it is at this point that the relationship between differential forms of power and their cultural expression becomes apparent. The structure of the classic detective story is not culturally innocent – it works to regulate both the development of narrative and the particular meanings about criminality, social roles, property and so on that may be offered to the reader. The revelation of the criminal will also mark the restoration of social order. A 'reading for structure' is then almost inevitably also a reading for culture-as-power or ideology as identifying the ways in which a text has been constructed also invites us to consider why and how it appears in that form.

Organizing meaning – character and location

In another version of the structuralist narratological model, Vladimir Propp (1968) argued that traditional Russian folk tales shared a common set of underlying narrative structural features, although each of the stories was quite different at the level of its surface detail. These features comprised the range of character roles used (the hero, princess, helper) and what he called the functions, which shaped the tales themselves in quite specific ways. For Propp, even the most individualized characters are no more than functionaries whose purpose is to enable the story to unfold, while the 'deep structure' of the functions and their sequence is unchanging. Applying this model to Ian Fleming's James Bond novels, Umberto Eco (1979) draws on Propp's categories to show that the same plot moves and basic character roles (the girl, foreign villain, supportive second agent) appear over and over again, superficially individualized – as Blofeld or Goldfinger, for example – in each story. Graeme Turner (1988) also points out that *Star Wars* (1977) exhibits a remarkable fit with Propp's model, perhaps as a self-consciously contemporary kind of folk tale. These repetitions suggest that the structuralist proposition – that narratives are shaped by underlying and deep conventions – can be a useful tool for identifying the powerful cultural assumptions about heroism, masculinity, power for instance that they seem to naturalize. Crucially, such meanings are not, for structuralist theorists, about the deliberate intent of a single author but part of a wider set of signifying practices.

This also means that characters, situations and locations tend to be organized around underlying binary structures that are represented in oppositional (rather than complementary) terms. These might include nature versus culture, the country versus the city, the wilderness versus civilization, men versus women and, of course, good versus bad. Such binary oppositions not only work to structure the development of the narrative and the values that are assigned to particular characters or spaces but also help to naturalize the way in which meanings are offered in conflicted terms. The drive towards narrative resolution noted above thus becomes explicitly linked to the reconciliation of binaries or, more probably, the assertion of the superiority of one element in the opposition.

For Rick Altman (1989), the deep structure working beneath the surface of a text that informs the storytelling conventions of Hollywood musicals reveals the unconscious operation of cultural meaning and this is always coupled with a set of binary oppositions. For example, in an analysis of the Fred Astaire and Ginger Rogers musical *Top Hat* (1935), he explores the operation of what he calls 'paired dualities' around the idea of social conventions and expectations versus freedom from constraint. He shows how, from its opening in a London Gentleman's Club to its joyous musical ending, the film works to assert the superiority of Astaire's American 'new world' attitudes towards freedom and pleasure over Rogers' European 'old world' stuffiness. In so doing, it also naturalizes the cultural superiority of Astaire's masculinity, which is represented as the site of democratic ease and openness. This process is staged by means of the various dance routines that mark the journey from restraint to freedom, thus offering moments of pleasurable spectacle that 'stop' the plot, while simultaneously working to assert underlying cultural values and expectations.

Altman's work points up the centrality of ideological discourses to what is still frequently seen as 'just entertainment', as though such texts operated outside ideology. It is worth asking if contemporary popular texts such as *Friends* also mobilize this kind of deep structure of binary oppositions in which America stands for youth, democracy and freedom and 'old' Europe for tradition and conformity. It is also worth asking how the articulation of these kinds of binaries informs other mediations that may be more overtly and therefore more recognizably 'ideological', such as those that structured the political discourses underpinning President Bush's speeches after the attack on the Twin Towers in September 2001 (see Chapter 10).

Structural readings: contextualizing strategies

Genre and intertextuality

Having examined some of the elements of a text that seem to be intrinsic – especially the narrative codes and structure – we can begin to ask questions about the extrinsic elements, including its relationship to other texts. Here, recognizing 'intertextual' relationships or 'intertextuality' becomes a key contextualizing strategy. This approach was developed especially in the work of Julia Kristeva, a French poststructuralist feminist critic who was influenced by the theories of Mikhail Bakhtin and the Leningrad circle of the 1920s and 1930s, themselves early critics of de Saussure's, linguistics which they called 'abstract objectivism' (Kristeva, 1984; Volosinov, 1973). Genre analysis, for example, must inevitably focus on intertextuality because the effective organization of the tension between sameness and difference is how generic belonging is understood and defined. Examining the specific ways in which a particular text manages the pleasures of process and closure by means of the manipulation of the various known conventions of a genre – the romance, thriller, horror or Western, for instance – together with the inclusion of surprises or unconventional elements, can tell us much about how texts manage meaning. Such an analysis must also situate those texts within the wider cultural context of manufacture and circulation in order to make sense of genre as a dynamic form of cultural production.

Indeed, it is worth noticing how genres actually appear *across* different media, making it possible not only to consider the formal relationship between, for example, detective narratives in film, television and popular fiction but also enabling us to foreground the wider cultural and political dimensions to genres (Clarke, 1992), including the difficult question of stars and the meanings attached to them (see Dyer, 1979, 1986). Such a reading will almost certainly invite a consideration of the relationship between textual and consumption practices. It would be impossible to claim, for example, that a film genre existed without the consent of a cinema-going public able to recognize and enjoy it. Reading for genre thus involves recognizing both the industrial processes involved (marketing, the star system, the studios) and the role of audiences in the development of generic conventions. Not for the first time, we note how a successful cultural analysis involves taking account, in some way, of all the moments in cultural circuits.

Reading approaches must also take account of the specificities of the cultural form being analysed. For example, cinema not only deploys the narrative and generic conventions discussed above, such as the distinction between plot and story, it also depends on visual and non-representational signs to produce meaning, such as the mise en scène (all the elements within the frame of a shot) sound, editing and specific camera angles. James Monaco explores the interaction of these dimensions in a discussion of the famous shower scene in Alfred Hitchcock's thriller *Psycho* (1960) and forcefully makes the point that the dominant meaning of a film – or a single scene – is complexly determined:

> the specifically cinematic codes in Hitchcock's one-minute tour de force are exceptionally strong . . . Hitchcock manipulates all these codes to achieve a desired effect. It is because they are codes – because they have meaning for us outside the narrow limits of that particular scene: in film, in the other arts, in the general culture – that they affect us. The codes are the medium through which the 'message' of the scene is transmitted. (1981: 148)

These filmic codes are crucial mechanisms in the production of textual meaning, working to shape and inform our understanding of what we are seeing. Indeed, they are in some senses intertextual as they depend on a systematized deployment across cinema as a cultural form for their effectiveness. By identifying and critically interrogating such techniques, we can begin to see how meaning, far from arising naturally in a scene, is itself wholly constructed or put together. Because the systematization and institutionalization of such codes and conventions in cinema and television practice has helped to naturalize them, we need to 'make them strange' again in order to bring the meaning construction process into focus. Critically examining some of the narrative and representational conventions of realism – the dominant mode of narrative in most mainstream film and television texts – is one way in which to do this.

Problematizing realism

In all forms of narrative realism, the social world in which the action takes place is richly and extensively detailed – it looks realistic – and individual characters are offered as emotionally rounded and multidimensional – they resemble real people. Such narratives feign transparency – they create an illusion of real life by means of seamless editing and the use of camera shots that insert the spectator into the narrative and thus invite the viewer/reader to recognize them as a 'true' representation. The realist narrative is usually told in the form of an authoritative voice of a third person, as in the narrator of a novel or, more complexly, in the assembly of scenes in a film, both of which construct a position from which meaning is deduced. Colin MacCabe describes these elements, which are very common in popular forms, as a 'hierarchy of discourses', arguing that, together, they constitute the system of classic realism, in which the truth of a story is located in the 'meta-language' of the author's prose voice or the final cut of a film. It is, he says, a system that favours the production of a single meaning in a text and thus claims 'direct access to a single reality' (1974: 10).

Of course, there are exceptions to these general conventions – first-person narratives, the film flashback, genres such as the gothic melodrama that demand a more contradictory identification with the heroine and moments in otherwise realist texts that deploy non-realist conventions, such as dream sequences. Yet, such exceptions frequently work to alert us deliberately to the troubling presence of alternative narrative positions and may, therefore, help to confirm realism's neutrality. By identifying the conventions of realism, then, we are using a contextualizing strategy that helps us to distance ourselves from the truth of the text and be critical of its meanings and claims.

If we follow MacCabe's version of structuralism, we can focus on how classic realist narratives are propelled by the highly ideological assumption that social agency – or the power to 'make things happen' – belongs to particular individuals rather than social groups. In Alfred Hitchcock's film, *Vertigo* (1958), for example, the plot is driven by the desire of the hero, Scottie, for the enigmatic Madeleine. The agency of the (white) male hero is either offered as a given (he has a natural right to social power) or is made the subject of the text's problematic (he must recover his right to social power). The latter is, in fact, the problematic of *Vertigo*, in which Scottie's fear of heights becomes a pivotal factor both in the plot and the text's construction of his agency. By locating agency with individuals who must act heroically in order to intervene in the world, realism represents wider social forces primarily in terms of their localized expression and differences of power largely in terms of personality or natural characteristics. The ascription of agency to men, for example, both naturalizes male power and tends to render the desires or motivations of female characters mystified or marginalized. *Vertigo* even depends on this mystification in order to develop its central enigma ('Who or what is Madeleine?'), although it is also very knowing about how this is achieved.

In classic (Hollywood) films, this process is usually reinforced and systematized by means of the convention of the 'point-of-view' shot – an image that shows the audience what the hero sees as though we are looking through his eyes – which, according to Laura Mulvey (1975), privileges a 'male gaze' that positions female characters as desirable or threatening objects rather than knowing subjects (see Chapter 14). In *Vertigo*, a complex sequence of scenes works to produce Madeleine as the mysterious object of Scottie's gaze as he follows her through the streets of San Francisco, and the film spectator watches her 'with' him in shots that frame her from his point of view. The hegemony of these conventions as they appear in realism is, then, closely related to wider social and cultural structures.

However, McCabe's somewhat monolithic theoretical model of realism's dominance in film and television has been contested and problematized both by the appearance and popularity of unconventional, non-linear texts, such as *Pulp Fiction* (1994), and the recognition that its structures and codes do not always operate in predictably ideological ways. Christopher Williams, for example, argues for a differently nuanced understanding of realism's conventions. Realism, he says, articulates 'the aspiration towards a structure of cognition, which is the desire to identify the deeper structures which determine reality' (Williams in Gledhill and Williams, 2000: 216). It is these aspects that help to make realist texts pleasurable and familiar and also invite us to go beyond a reductive model of realism's relationship to discourse and ideology.

The persistence of deep structures in organizing meaning is crucial to our understanding of social relations in a wider sense as they seem to contain and manage what may or may not be known about the world in important ways. However, the objective textuality of classic structuralist theories presents two problems. The first is the way in which quite complex cultural practices are reduced to their formal elements, which may mean that we lose sight of the specific pleasures (or problems) that they offer us. The second is the ahistorical character of structuralist frameworks. If we return to de Saussure's original model briefly, we can see that the emphasis on synchronic analysis – that is, the study of a text or sign system as it appears at a given moment in time, not as it develops historically – potentially excludes wider temporal frameworks. Together, these tendencies make structuralist approaches very determinist.

Social and cultural formations

Reading, therefore, is not simply about the mechanistic identification of formal elements or functions: it is also about tracing the ways in which textual formations are linked to larger cultural formations. As our circuit model and discussion of settings suggest, texts are always part of larger cultural processes and connected to social relations of power via the production context and the economic relations involved (those of the publisher, studio or television channel responsible, for example) and the context of the text's appearance and reception by particular audiences at particular times and places. For example, a collection of essays about the Hollywood romantic comedy during the 1980s and 1990s (Evans and Deleyto, 1998) links the development of the genre to changes in social attitudes to romantic love, sexuality and gender identity. Genres mutate, stars lose popularity, texts shift in style, new kinds of texts and cultural forms appear, technological innovations transform mediatory possibilities. A key contextualizing question would therefore be, 'Why *this text* now?' or even 'Why this text *now*?'

This move towards the cultural and social environment of a text is not so much a matter of shifting *away* from text to context as an attempt to hold the two in tension. For instance, the use of theories of language to explain wider cultural phenomena becomes a methodological device, a means of entering the form under discussion without losing ourselves in their familiar pleasures. Theories derived from other structuralisms may be used in similar ways. The cultural anthropologist Claude Levi-Strauss argued that, in folklore, individual myths always express an underlying structure driven by a common set of precepts and codes – the 'unconscious foundations' of a society. Myth, he claimed, helped to 'magically resolve' material contradictions by means of symbolic resolution (1968: 229).

This universalization of the idea of myth is problematic as it does not recognize what is particular in social, spatial or temporal terms, but we can still use some of Levi-Strauss' ideas in a more qualified way. For example, the idea of the magical resolution of 'real' ideological contradictions at a symbolic level has been found in contemporary popular romances addressed to women in which *narrative* closure is also the point of *ideological* closure. Such stories represent marriage or the production of the stable, monogamous couple as the magical resolution to the 'problem' of heterosexual desire and as a utopian space in which women especially can find fulfilment (Modleski, 1982; Radford, 1986). Richard Dyer draws on a similar model to show how the deep structures of racism operate in Anglophone cultural forms but are temporarily resolved in narrative (1997).

A rather different take on the idea of myth as a structural determinant in culture appears in Roland Barthes' mischievously titled *Mythologies* (1972), which emphasizes the cultural connotations or associations that sign systems utilize and the taken for granted practices of the culture in which texts are produced and read. By considering both the immediate and the connotative meanings that operate in contemporary and commercially mediated 'texts' as diverse as advertisements, food traditions and cars, Barthes shows not only that semiotic analysis depends on cultural knowledge but also that such knowledges are themselves culturally located. Unlike Levi-Strauss, 'myth' for Barthes is linked explicitly to the political or ideological production of meanings, though, as we argue in Chapter 8, he did not integrate his semiological and ideological analyses.

Culturally inflected structural readings should, then, always involve a consideration of the wider social and cultural relations that a text seeks to represent or to which it refers. One way in which to explore this is to return to genres, which are lived narratives as well as sign systems – they inform the stories we tell ourselves and each other in all kinds of contexts, both fictional and factual, including, perhaps, personal narratives about our own heroic or romantic lives! As Bakhtin (1981) argues, genres are made up from 'thousands of living dialogic threads' that are woven together in a cultural encounter. They thus work to organize and interrogate our understanding of social identities by formalizing both what can be represented and how it can be configured. Although the codes may be played with, shifted, reinvented or subverted, genres are also culturally, temporally and spatially specific.

Recognizing the historical nature of genres becomes critical if we are to understand how and why they secure their audiences and how (and where) those audiences are produced, configured and reconfigured. Popularity is, after all, constructed within time and space. This does not mean, however, that it is wholly embedded within the constraints of one *particular* time and place. For example, while the American television sitcom *I Love Lucy* is clearly a product of 1950s America and tends to articulate the values and assumptions of its moment of production, its generic pleasures also exceed that historical and spatial locatedness. *Lucy* continued to secure audiences in India during the 1970s precisely because the generic tropes remained sufficiently powerful and recognizable to audiences rather differently configured and situated to those who watched it in Ohio in Eisenhower's era.

Beyond structuralism: poststructuralist approaches

Structuralism's analytical emphasis, together with its combination of linguistic and psychoanalytical insights into the production of culture, has been important as a kind of intervention into the arguments about cultural value. It enabled a space to be cleared in which cultural criticism could address other important questions. Indeed, Steven Cohan (2000: 54) argues strongly and convincingly for the continuing usefulness of structuralism as a *method* as a way of 'opening up [a] narrative for interpretation' in an essay on *Singin' in the Rain* (1952). However, the tendency to determinism and to 'return' the reader to the text, together with its own underlying ideology – the commitment to scientific or objective knowledge – means that classical structuralism is largely useful to cultural criticism when it is expanded, subjected to an internal critique – in the form of poststructuralism – and combined with other approaches.

An example of this can be found in Yvonne Tasker's study of the action movie *Spectacular Bodies: Gender, Genre and the Action Cinema* (1993), in which she uses a combination of poststructural and cultural analysis to situate films such as *Die Hard* (1988), the Rocky series (1976–90) and *Lethal Weapon* (1987) within the specific context of Hollywood in the 1980s. Drawing on a range of theoretical work, including feminist accounts of representational strategies in film portrayals of gender and Judith Butler's work on performativity (see Chapter 14), Tasker points out that, far from simply endorsing or reproducing dominant ideologies of masculinity and binary structures, action films play with such categories and with the idea of gender as performance. In this way, although she uses some of the conventional elements of film structuralism to identify the preliminary generic codes, Tasker is much more interested in the polysemic possibilities of a poststructuralist reading, one that allows for multiple meanings, fluidity and contradiction.

The production of textual meaning in poststructuralist accounts is, then, a process of continuous deferral rather than fixed oppositions and this potentially allows for the agency of audiences in the interpretative process, although most poststructuralist theory remains highly 'textual' in its approach to meaning. However, if we wanted to go further and critique action movies from a more overtly politicized position, we would have to engage in a more detailed argument in which their aesthetic and political value would be addressed. It would be possible to ask, for example, how far such forms add to a critical understanding of the construction of masculinities and whether or not they offer alternative or different ways of being a man or transgressing gender limits. Such questions would have to be posed for popular audiences and not merely for critical critics. It is important to have such debates about value. It is also important to recognize that our positions may offer only a partial understanding that needs to be in dialogue with that of others.

Combining methods

This emphasis on the dialogic can be found in feminist research on specifically popular supposedly women's texts, such as romantic fiction, soap opera and women's magazines, which is often exemplary in its practical use of method combination, eschewing methodological purity, yet producing important insights (see, for example, Hobson, 1982; Winship, 1987 and, for an overview, Brunsdon, 2000). Although about texts, such work does not only employ textual analysis. Instead, it combines the detailed exploration of texts with research into audiences, often prompted by auto/biographical experiences, offering us a much richer understanding of the process by means of which texts acquire meaning.

Janice Radway's work in *Reading the Romance* (1984) uses such a combination of methods, arising from her desire to fully engage with the experiences of women and their use of popular culture. Radway renders her methodology both open and explicit in her introduction:

> Since I was assuming from the start with reader theorist Stanley Fish that textual interpretations are constructed by interpretative communities using specific interpretive strategies, I sought to contrast the then-current interpretation of romances produced by trained literary critics with that produced by fans of the genre. (1984: 7)

In this focus on interpretative communities, Radway moves away from the structuralist model and towards an approach that reinserts the audience for popular culture. Even so, she admits that it was only when her field group – the women of 'Smithton' in the USA – repeatedly talked about romance reading as an *activity* rather than the books as texts that she began to conceive the project differently. It is this explicit concern with methodology as a determinant of interpretation and the combination of fieldwork (including questionnaires, group discussions and face-to-face interviews) with textual analysis and psychoanalytical theory, prompted by her acknowledgement of her own locatedness as a feminist researcher, that makes Radway's work interesting for us here. By combining these elements, Radway produces a piece of work that effectively extends textual analysis beyond the confines of the text.

Conclusion

As we have argued in Chapter 2, texts, like other cultural formations, are complex constellations of elements and therefore require a complex approach to reading them. Such an approach involves the recognition that textual meaning is very far from a singular or monologic entity and that readings are diverse, often contradictory and may well challenge our prior assumptions or those of our critical sources. Our emphasis here on positionality and self-reflexivity is underpinned by a desire to develop a nuanced understanding of both popular and elite forms in which the emotional and cultural investments involved are made explicit. The abstract idea of the text, as an object or commodity, away from its conditions of production and its social use, can be countered by the strategies of contextualization identified here. As researchers, therefore, our own reading should, then, be a *close* reading not a *closed* reading.

The contextualizing strategies explored in this chapter offer us ways in which we can take account of the different groundings texts may emerge from, occupy or be linked to, while a combination of methods enables us to take account of the 'fore-meanings' brought to them both by reading communities and the researcher. These multiple methods of reading texts may be variously syncretized, depending on the research questions being posed, in order to produce a method for the research. The refusal of a break between text and practice also marks an interesting convergence between theories of dialogue, the audience as a subject of research, cultural analysis as a politics and anti-objectivism as an epistemology. Together, they form a congregation of concerns that continue to be central to cultural studies.

10 Reading texts of or for dominance

Reading texts of dominance: a possible reading path 171
Why (not) texts? The value of a textual approach to an analysis of anti-terrorism 173
How much text? 176
Which texts? Dialogue and dominance 178
Opening the text, starting the dialogue 179
Elaborating a (theoretically informed) reading 182
Moral absolutes, the 'other' and unconscious processes 183
Making a reading convincing 184
Conclusion 185

This chapter is about methods of reading texts as a way of studying power relations.[1] As we have seen in Chapter 9, structuralist language theory and methods of analysis focus on meaning as carried in textually encoded languages and conventions. However, while making crucial contributions to cultural analysis, insufficient attention is paid to historical, spatial and social contexts, the dialogic properties of language and the setting of power relations. An interest in culture-as-power, therefore, forces us to go beyond structuralist readings while not abandoning their main resource, which is a careful address to textuality and its conventions. In particular, we need to pay greater attention to context or setting.

A further set of themes are carried forward from Chapter 8, where we argued that critical methods of reading are not a secondary practice in analysing relations of power but a vital, primary one. In this chapter, we advance this theme along a more methodological path, outlining the different moments in the reading process, just as in Chapter 4 we reviewed the different moments of research overall.

To engage properly with practice, we need a main example. We have chosen a rather obvious contemporary body of texts: the speeches of President Bush and Prime Minster Blair in the months following the attack on the World Trade Center (the Twin Towers) on September 11th 2001. These have figured in studies by group members (see, for example, Johnson, 2002; Tincknell, 2004) and so are reasonably familiar to some of us. Apart from convenience (which always is a factor) there are real dilemmas in such a choice. On the one hand, these are very obviously texts of dominance as they are precursors and accompaniments to powerful military and diplomatic projections across the world. By contrast, the most original contribution of cultural studies has often been to show how relations of power are present in the most innocent places – schools or forms of entertainment, for instance, including the film and television texts discussed in Chapter 9 and the historical fictions explored in the next chapter. Yet, cultural studies is sometimes challenged for not being political enough or not engaging with formal politics. This is a charge that overlooks many studies of politics, even in the narrow sense (see, for example, Centre for Contemporary Cultural Studies (CCCS) Education Group 1980, 1991; Epstein, Johnson and Steinberg, 2000; Hall et al., 1978; Hall and Jacques, 1983) and cultural turns within the academic discipline of politics itself (such as Laclau and Mouffe, 1985; A. M. Smith, 1994), but certainly cultural analysis can and should attend to explicitly political moments of power, including state policies and the machinery of government.

Perhaps it can contribute most by exploring the informal cultural processes that undergird political success or failure in the narrower, electoral sense. This extends the limits of standard political science as a discipline that concentrates on power as defined by political systems and the state. Comparisons of published studies of New Labour or Blairism show this difference clearly (cp. Johnson and Steinberg, 2003; Selden, 2001; Ludlam and Smith, 2001). In our example, then, we seek out the *cultural* work of speeches by Bush and Blair.

What are the strengths and limits of text reading in such an enquiry? What are its methodological moments, aspects or stages? We list these moments in advance, as a kind of reading pathway. We hope this will suggest ideas for similar enquiries, though with caveats from our earlier discussion of 'moments'. In the real life of a particular project, the order of enquiry will differ, the moments of analysis folding back on each other and recurring (see Chapter 4). There is a logic to *our* order, one possible reading path, but it is not the only one. In the rest of this chapter we look, selectively, at some issues our pathway serves to open up.

Reading texts of dominance: a possible reading path

Why text-reading? Assessing the strengths and limits of text analysis and deciding on a methodological combination

Why is text analysis an appropriate method here? What might its limits be? What are its strengths? How do we deal with 'context' in this case? Is context a matter of reading *other* texts or reading the same texts in another way? Are other methods involved, in combination?

What texts? Choosing the range of sources

What texts are appropriate for this enquiry? How could we justify choices made? How far are individual texts discreet identities anyway? What about dialogue and 'intertextuality'? (See Chapters 4 and 9 especially.)

How many texts? Rethinking sample sizes for cultural studies

Should we analyse a smaller range of texts – a single speech, a fragment – intensively or sample a wider range? Should we compile compendiums around themes? Should such approaches be combined and, if so, how? Does it make a difference to the size of the sample that our object is cultural? Does representativeness as a criteria of selection work in the same way as in more social approaches?

What are our questions? What are the key contexts? Reflexivity in questions and their framing

Are we as clear as we can be at this stage about the questions we are starting from – even if these will change in research? Do we have an adequate preliminary grasp of key settings and contexts that depend in part on our questions? If reading (for power relations) is a movement between text and context, how should we manage this?

How to read? Opening the text, starting the dialogue

We start to read but all reading is dialogic. What hunches do we bring to a text that is obstinately 'other'? Reading is an empirical procedure – the text has its own reality, which limits and pressures our reading. What features or silences strike us first? First impressions are important. We record them – in underlinings or highlightings or marginal notes.

How to reflect? Clarifying and reformulating questions, reaching for an argument

Moving away from the text again, what have we learned? Are our hunches confirmed or confounded? How must our questions change? What's the relation between our impressions so far and the ideas we have used or learned before? Is our knowledge of context adequate? Does the pressure of the text and our preliminary reading suggest different questions, more appropriate, more compelling, more answerable? Is an argument emerging? With ourselves? With our text? We might start to sketch an argument in bits of writing or headings.

How to elaborate a reading?

Moving back to the text again, but now with a developing *argument*, how do we elaborate, substantiate, extend it? We start to think about writing strategies – of quoting and commenting, paraphrasing or translating into our own terms, juxtaposition of aspects of text and context. What passages will we use for these purposes? We are becoming more active or interventionist as readers, less passive or receptive.

How to make a reading stick? Validity and representativeness rethought

How do we validate a reading? How can we *show* our reader that our reading is valid, interesting, convincing? More generally, what kind of validity do we seek? What kind of ('interpretative'? 'critical'?) truth can we claim? *Who* do we want to persuade or interest or entertain?

Writing – first drafts

We write an account, or fragments of an account, primarily to develop our ideas, fix our thinking (see Chapter 4).

Preparing for later drafts – contextualizing again

Now we take the results of our readings to other texts, other practices, existing knowledge. Do we agree? Do we have something new to say? The dialogue widens to include others who have worked on the topic or have a stake in it. We may get feedback from readers of our first writings. We think about audience and genre, our own addressees and how to address them.

Writing for presentation

We write an account for presentation with particular readers in mind.

Why (not) texts? The value of a textual approach to an analysis of anti-terrorism

Political speeches are performances with a peculiar collective authorship and particular conventions, designed to persuade, exhort and argue. Why start here? Surely the real action is elsewhere. Why not start with what governments are doing in the global context of economic power?

From this perspective, speeches may seem the worst place to start, disguising intentions, masking actions. Aren't they just public relations, propaganda or spin? In this framework, as we have seen, the speeches would be analysed – if analysed closely at all – as an ideological misrepresentation. As we (presumably) have access to what is represented by other means, the speeches are not even a reliable source. They might, however, provide clues about the larger picture and show the distortions of political rhetoric.

This is quite a familiar approach to half of our subject – Blairism or New Labour. The politics of New Labour have emphasized presentation and spin has been seized on as a distinguishing feature. We are not arguing *against* studying presentational techniques or the rhetoric and, yes, the speeches *should* be placed in the context of other political actions and their conditions. Nonetheless, 'Blairism-as-spin' allows only a *reduced* account of culture and politics.

Indeed, the public rhetoric of key politicians can be extraordinarily revealing, for it often says more than is intended. After September 11th 2001, the Bush and Blair speeches were useful in at least four ways. First, it was possible to puzzle out government *strategies* from the speeches at a time when they were just emerging. Second, the speeches themselves, as performances, were part of the pursuit of these strategies, whether bidding for consent at home or coalition-building abroad. Third, putting strategies and political processes together, the comparative strengths and limits of the Bush and Blair projects could be identified. Finally, analysis of the speeches and their changing settings provided a way of finding a critical perspective on contemporary events at a time of great confusion.

In what follows, we say enough about our findings to illustrate a process of research, but our main aim is to reflect on methods of reading and the issues they raise.

(Anti-)terrorism and the Bush presidency

Bush is often caricatured as a stupid man and an ineffectual politician. Reading his speeches, however, suggests that the Bush team, at that time, projected a successful, populist politician who addressed his own American audiences with some accuracy, spoke their language and articulated many of their concerns. Bush's presentation is populist, bellicose, very masculine, clipped, brutal even, holding the emotion aroused by events in quite a tense and rigid body, close-set eyes almost hidden. This can be compared unfavourably with Blair's wide-eyed, winning and rather idealistic appeals, but Bush is also direct, popular, commonsensical. His themes are national and patriotic, evoking a nation that is fearful as well as fearsome, hurt as well as vengeful, ready for war but compassionate. Bush mixes and jokes with ordinary people without condescension, especially men. He recognizes local preoccupations. He draws on the religious movements with which he is politically affiliated and that see him as 'serving this country' with 'godly leadership' (see, for example, Bush, 4 December, Meeting with Displaced Workers). Even his famed inarticulacy and anti-intellectualism may not be disadvantages here. He habitually includes *himself* in phrases such as, 'while *we* will go about *our* business *of going to World Series [baseball] games* or shopping, *travelling to Washington DC*' (Bush, 31 October, underlining supplied). His baseball performances and fanship promote this self-presentation as a very North American kind of man. His jokey intros to his popular performances are notably homosocial:

> And I want to thank Jim Bunning. He was telling me he thought my fast ball, when I threw it at Yankee stadium, had a little zip in it (Applause). Nothing like his fast balls (Laughter). (21 November, sharing thanksgiving with troops and families at Fort Campbell.)

Baseball is a multi-ethnic, cross-class sport in the USA with a family following that includes girls and women as spectators. Baseball spectators use score cards or programmes that include photos of team members. Bush has let it be known that he keeps a score card of leading Al-Qa'ida figures and crosses them off as they are captured or killed (Bush, quoted in the *Guardian*, 4 February 2002). This is only one example of how a popular national sport provides the cultural forms in which victories against terrorism are celebrated and Bush's identities as an exemplary American man and a patriotic leader are fused. Bush emerged, for a while, as a great 'patriot president', every speech weaving an alliance with ordinary baseball-playing, shopping, working – and suffering – Americans. In this way, the Bush speechwriters and Bush as performer constructed a popular version of the nation that recapitulated a long history of American manhood (Kimmel, 1996). They seized the opportunities offered by the bombing of the Twin Towers and Pentagon and continuing fears of fresh terrorist acts (such as the possible anthrax attack) to create a popular and nationwide presidency. This was an urgent project politically, given its barely credible electoral beginning and narrow geographical basis. September 11th offered the chance of extending Bush's Southern American political base, right into the multi-ethnic, often liberal or sceptical Eastern seaboard. His official opening of the baseball World Series, not in Arizona but in New York itself, was emblematic of this Southern/Eastern-seaboard alliance.

Analysis of the speeches, in context, also suggests major weaknesses, however. The temporary hegemony of the Bush project is essentially conservative, passive or non-transformative. Bush asks Americans only to defend what they have, to be what they are. A rich and powerful man as well as being the president, he reassures Americans that they have power and influence in the world and are good, compassionate people, who help each other and aid strangers, too. Bush's alliance, however, seems especially vulnerable to the fortunes of his central anti-terrorist strategy. Sustaining this campaign also involves many cultural conditions, including the reproduction of vengeful feelings, the successful othering of a range of enemies and the articulation of these feelings to forms of masculine identity that are historically far from secure. Indeed, the Bush Junior Presidency marks a point of US *vulnerability* as much as strength.

Second, Bush's strengths at home are also international weaknesses. From almost any position from outside the United States, the limits of US exceptionalism and arrogance are obvious, as is the very dangerous edge it turns towards the rest of the world.

Blair and the international

It is harder to see Tony Blair as a convincing football fan, though he can head a football and play rock guitar. Mainly, Blair comes across as a middle-class English family man, reasonable, respectable, a bit intellectual, not really a sporting type, certainly not a lad. His own voice isn't quite identified, however, with this paragon of hard work and responsibility. He can rise a little above it all, give us an overview in a style of sensitive masculine intellectuality that is modestly personal, too. Blair tries to embrace his audiences by wooing them by means of reason. (For an interesting account of Blair's rhetoric and discourse more generally, see Fairclough, 2000.) He has to work hard to convert his high moral tone, global ambitions and professional address to a popular–national appeal. It is arguable, indeed, that, by 2002, Blair's own very personal international ambitions and the alliance with the Bushites had become a liability in home politics.

Blair's strengths and weaknesses are in some ways the inverse of Bush's. Methodologically, here, we might note the value of *comparison*, of working across materials and cases that are in some ways similar, in others different. Strong at home, Blair can use his domestic base to marshall a wider international coalition, largely supportive of US positions. He relies heavily on reasonable arguments and moral appeals, partly because the British state lacks the military and economic clout of the USA. Most of his 'international' speeches, post September 11th, are about how 'we', members of the international coalition or 'community', can defeat the terrorists, but also 'reorder this world around us' (Blair, 2 October, 2001). Blair is limited by his inability to deliver militarily and by the danger of eroding his own national base. How far will the nation, even the party and the government, join him in his apparently unquestioning support for US policy? It is not surprising perhaps, that the Bushites and Blairites entered into a tactical alliance – an old alliance, of course, but with a certain complementarity in their positions – different national hegemonies, different levels of material power and moral force, different possibilities in the world.

Such an analysis depends in large measure on a knowledge of political and other settings in which the speeches were delivered and received. As we are talking *contemporary* history here, the sources are all around us. They include the national (and sometimes international) press, television news (chiefly BBC and CNN) and, importantly in this case, alternative media sources on the Internet (such as Znet, at *www.zmag.org*). In addition, much was learned from the work of Michael Kimmell (1996) on masculinities and politics in the United States and from discussions with friends interested in the politics of masculinity or knowledgeable about US politics. A timely holiday visit to a baseball match in the Seattle Mariners' stadium was also a source of insights! Where contemporary cultural studies is concerned, the effectiveness of textual analysis depends on a *general* engagement in the world as well as the collection and careful reading of key texts.

What does *not* appear in speeches, or speeches to particular audiences, is also important. The question of oil did not appear in any speeches about September 11th, yet oil arguably formed the rhizome that linked the necessities of war, the character of the Bush regime, the political economy of the United States and its allies, the interest in Afghanistan, and the defence of a cultural way of life. Nor would anyone use the speeches – especially the stress on US compassion – as a guide to how the war in Afghanistan and Pakistan was actually conducted in terms of its costs to civilian populations or breaches of humanitarian codes. Analysis gains its critical edge by combining critical reading with a knowledge of what is absent or silenced (for an elaboration of this method, see Chapter 11).

How much text?

'The size and nature of the sample' is often a question in social science research. 'When have I done enough?' is an issue for every researcher, especially those in tightly defined work for dissertations or projects. The fact that we study culture does not make this question redundant, but it does affect how the question is addressed.

Cultural methodologies are related to theories of culture. We can approach culture, for example, as though it were just a matter of the attitudes or beliefs of individuals. This is a common starting point in the psychological disciplines and underlies public opinion polls and market research. These methods gather data from individuals – usually by means of large-scale surveys – then code, count and statistically manipulate the findings. The relationships between our sample and the relevant total population is very important here and so is the focus of concerns with reliability of the method, validity of claims made and the representativeness of the results.

Such methods, however, are *anti*-cultural in an important sense. If we define culture as the production of shared meanings and social identities, it doesn't make a lot of sense to approach it by means of individuals. If culture consists of historical formations or 'structures of feeling', it doesn't only pertain to individuals. It makes more sense to study social groups or cultural spaces in face-to-face meetings (the ethnographic strategy) or to read the texts that in context, carry or embody the cultural forms. The circulation of cultural forms also suggests that the location or 'moment' is more important than quantity. What matters most is *where we break into cultural circuits*, not, so much, how many individual units we amass.

Reading speeches is, thus, one way in which to break into the cultural-political circuit around the 'war on terrorism'. Tony Blair's speeches, as well as the writings of Peter Mandelson (see, for example, 2002) or Anthony Giddens (see, for example, 1998) are a significant point of definition of the politics and culture of 'the Third Way'. We are looking at more than Blair's personal ideas here. We are tapping into a complex political–cultural process or formation, at a place – and, hopefully, in a way that is appropriate to our purposes.

This may help to explain the preference in cultural studies for methods that are small-scale and intensive, but there is another, more compelling reason for this, which has to do with the complexity of cultural materials. All close cultural analysis involves some abstraction because it would be impossible to analyse *all* the possibilities of meaning in any elaborated cultural text. However, surveys radically decontextualize cultural materials, seeing only a few isolated answers to very structured questions. This method cannot catch the coexisting meanings, implications, contradictions, ambiguities and silences of cultural performances. Methods that are informed by skills of literary, linguistic and visual analysis and sensitivity to bodily performance begin to match the complexity of the human communication of meaning.

So, it is likely that a cultural analysis will end up looking in quite minute detail at quite a small range of materials. We can learn a lot about cultural repertoires from analysing small textual units: single episodes of a situation comedy or soap opera, the climax in a film, an iconic star performance, the announcement of a new campaign.

In the event, we read all the speeches on international issues coming from the White House and No 10, Downing Street between September 11th and the end of 2001, partly because this corpus was relatively small and easy to access via government websites. Though there were interesting shifts within it, there was much repetition and duplication. There was a formative period for political rhetoric and strategies in the weeks and months immediately after the attacks, for example. By Christmas, the formulae used by both men – especially Bush – had become familiar. One of the answers to the question 'When have I done enough?' is 'When you are learning nothing new'.

It is also useful to combine different levels of analysis – relatively intensive and relatively extensive. A few key speeches did emerge in the post September 11th study. Blair's speech before the Labour Party conference in October 2001, for example, pulled together many of his national and international themes. However, selection was based on reviewing the whole corpus in order to build a picture of the typical themes, discursive formations, kinds of narratives and so on that make up a typical Blair or Bush speech – namely, particular genres with their own forms of masculine embodied performance. This allows a kind of representativeness, too, but it is based not on number but on an understanding of context and form.

Which texts? Dialogue and dominance

If dominance involves relationships (see Chapter 8), the most revealing texts might be those with more than one voice. Some of the material for a wider Blair study is dialogic in this obvious sense. For instance, Downing Street's website has transcripts of Blair's answers to listeners' questions on a BBC breakfast programme of 30 July 1999. The highly ritualized exchanges of the House of Commons are also available on television and in *Hansard*, online and in print.

One more multivoiced type of text we considered for this chapter came from material distributed by international charities on the softer side of international power, which often construct giving in personalized terms. Donors in the rich countries can, for example, 'adopt' a child or a 'granny'. In the publicity for such schemes, Western-based charity headquarters frame the exchanges and produce the material, but named community activists and beneficiaries are often represented as 'speaking for themselves' (in highly mediated and translated ways, of course). There is a strong pressure to present beneficiaries as (ex-)victims who are now happy and grateful, but, even here, something of the specificity of hopes, needs and resources comes through in the literature – such as concerns with livestock and marginal access to land, strategies of survival and resistance. These are texts of dominance to be sure, representing gross wealth discrepancies and power relations; but they are still dialogic or multivoiced and so susceptible to more than one reading.

All texts are dialogic to some degree as this is the nature of language. Also, all language negotiates relationships and never simply belongs to the speaker as sole author.

> In point of fact, *word is a two-sided act*. It is determined equally by *whose* word it is and *for whom* it is meant. As word, it is *precisely the product of the reciprocal relationship between speaker and listener, addresser and addressee*. (Volosinov, 1973: 86, emphasis as original)

Bakhtin's later formulation is even more striking:

> language, for the individual consciousness, lies on the borderline between oneself and the other. The word in language is half someone else's . . . [I]t is populated – overpopulated – with the intentions of others. Expropriating it, forcing it to submit to one's own intentions and accents, is a difficult and complicated process. (Bakhtin, 1981b: 293–4)

What applies to the word or individual sign also applies to rhetorical figures, elements of discourse, jokes, anecdotes and epigrammatic phrases. Speeches produced in democratic political processes are notably dialogic in form and content. They are in dialogue with the positions of political opponents, with the faithful, with disgruntled party activists, with professionals in the public services (including the military), with press, television and other media. As we have seen, speeches marshall a version of the people-nation as workers, consumers, voters and other identities, putting the citizens in their places, addressing them differentially, but trying to pull an alliance together as a single will or political direction. To do this, the speaker must neutralize, disorganize or ridicule other positions and agents. Blair's speeches are particularly argumentative. His speeches on globalization, for example, not only inform his national audiences about realities out there, but also answer the arguments of anti-globalization movements and critics of neo-liberalism. Hence, in speech analysis, it is especially important to attend to the audience *as a context of performance*. It is surprising, for instance, how revealing Tony Blair can be about his domestic aims when speaking, 'off-island', to elite audiences in countries other than the UK.

Opening the text, starting the dialogue

As a method, text-reading is an empirical procedure that is itself also dialogic. It may be useful to remind ourselves here in Figure 10.1 of Figure 3.1, showing the research process in general.

In approaching a text, our lines of questioning come initially from our interests, our fore-knowledge (B) and our positionalities (A) in the wider contemporary context. So, we approached the Bush/Blair material reeling from the shock of the attack on the Twin Towers, but also from the ferocity of the response, especially the violent translation of a criminal act of terror into a cause for full-scale war. However, in the central dialogue of research, the inner circle of the diagram between D and E, we have to open ourselves to the speeches themselves, listen attentively, read in context, take the pressure of the texts.

There are two ways in which to open texts like these. We can read a whole speech to get a view of its movement, pattern and themes. We can divide it into segments, to mark movements in form, topic or tone. We can name these segments to give ourselves a sense of structure and movement. A second procedure is more piecemeal. It involves highlighting or underlining particular words and phrases that seem interesting, that jump off the page. Especially striking in this case were differences between the two sets of speeches and the televized performances of the two men. These stimulated a lot of interesting thoughts – first about different

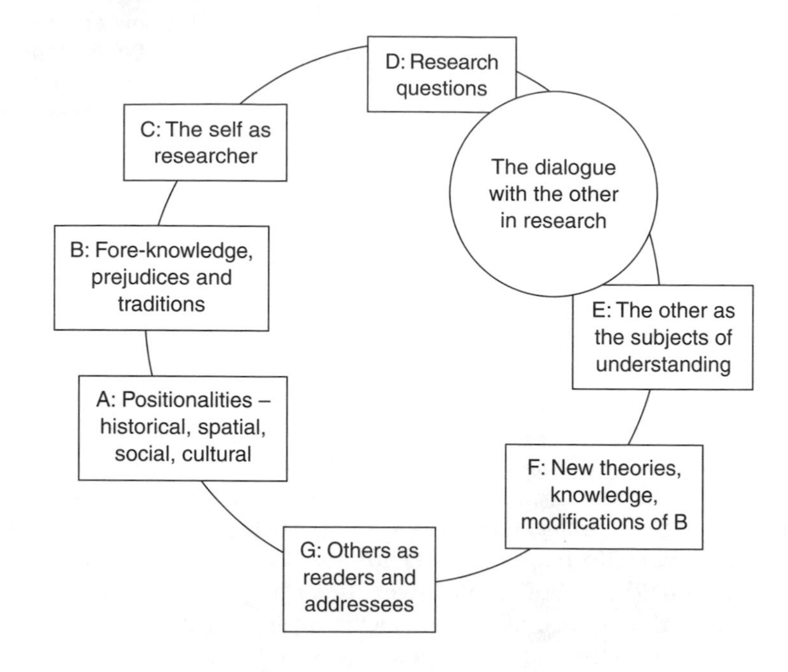

Figure 10.1 Cultural research as a cultural circuit

kinds of masculinity, then about the different situations and resources of 'Bushites' and 'Blairites' – the two main political forces involved. On the first reading, the repeated phrase 'way of life' also jumped out, especially in Bush's speeches. This suggested an interpretative entry point. What did they mean by way of life? How did this idea work in the speeches?

In Bush's populist address, 'our way of life' figured primarily as a terrorist target:

> The object of terrorism is to try and force us to change our way of life, is to force us to retreat, is to force us to be what we're not. (Bush, 23 October)

Vulnerability began with the people who died in the Twin Towers, the planes and the Pentagon, but it extended to 'our way of life' and to the identity of the nation. Together with the absolute evil of the perpetrators (see below), it justified an equally aggressive response, extended global warfare, expressed in a rhetoric that itself pounces, pursues and punches:

> The only way to defeat terrorism as a threat to our way of life is to stop it, eliminate it, and destroy it where it grows. (Applause.) (Bush, 20 September)

Bush did not ask Americans to change their way of life. Rather, he urged them to 'go about their daily lives' as usual, especially to carry on working and shopping. Fears about the fortunes of the capitalist economy, globally and nationally, are very audible here:

> We need to go back to work tomorrow . . . And tomorrow the good people of America go back to their shops, their fields, American factories, and go back to work. (Bush, 16 September)

> The most important thing is that we *carry on* with *confidence* in the *basic strength* of the economy and in our *basic way of life* because the *actual objective fundamentals* of the economy have not altered . . . and there really is no reason why we cannot *carry on* being *confident* in the *basic strength* of our economy and in the things that we normally do. (Blair, 27 September, emphasis supplied)

Blair sounds more confident, but his choice of words and their reiteration – 'objective', 'fundamentals', 'actual', 'confident/ce' (twice), 'carry on' (twice), 'strength' (twice), 'basic' (twice) – suggests a mobilization of resources (political and rhetorical) against major anxieties.

By late October, Bush was admitting that 'consumer confidence is down', but he had already woven economic recovery and his own government's measures, into a heroic narrative of a national mission: the war to defeat the terrorists. This involved exaggerating the terrorist threat at every level, so that his speeches end up expressing anxiety and vulnerability:

> When terrorists struck our homeland, they thought we would fold. They thought our economy would crater. That's what they wanted. (Bush, 24 October)

> We fight a war at home; and part of the war we fight is to make sure that our economy continues to grow. (Bush, 24 October)

So, in both countries, the 'way of life' is a potential victim that may reveal itself as a source of strength. Bush himself emerges, in his rhetoric at least, as the national hero who expresses the hurt the folks are feeling, but who stands up with them, their pugilist, their world player and their (baseball) pitcher.

A little later Bush starts to philosophize in public about his own version of Americanism and then campaigns around it. 'How should we live', he asks, 'in the light of what has happened?' (Bush, 8 November). 'Our way of life' is now a kind of mission and something that can be displayed as an example, to the wider world. Its moral aspects are now stressed. We can 'show the world the true values of America through the gathering momentum of a million acts of responsibility and decency and service' (8 November). Tracking down terrorists and exterminating them, as well as showing love and compassion, becomes an American vocation, 'the calling of the twenty-first century' (29 November):

> This country will define our times, not be defined by them. As long as the United States of America is determined and strong, this will not be an age of terror; this will be an age of liberty, here and across the world (20 September).

Elaborating a (theoretically informed) reading

We have stressed throughout the importance of fore-knowledge in processes of research (A and B in the circuit). One of the reasons for 'way of life' jumping out of the text is that it is a familiar and a founding category for cultural studies (Williams, 1961, 1965, 1976). It remains interesting today because, unlike 'civilization', it resists instant and fundamentalist claims to superiority, yet does not abandon evaluation entirely. Moreover, 'way of life' is a bridging category. It bridges the materially sustaining or economic practices of daily living and the more particularly cultural features – systems of meaning, forms of identity and psycho-social processes – by means of which a world is produced as meaningful. Way of *life* also includes the crucial bio-social interspecies aspects of living on this Earth.

It is always important to distinguish between particular *versions* of 'our way of life' as they are deployed in hegemonic versions, such as Bush's and typically in forms of nationalism, and the diverse ways of living that coexist, interact, interweave and may conflict in any social space. Conservative cultural theories work with the idea of cultures as bounded, homogeneous and entire – 'whole ways of life', in short. Yet, they are always extremely selective in their invocations. 'Our way of life' assumes a new significance when it is deployed in waging terror, war and peace across the globe. Both Bush and Blair seek to attach elements of popular living, tradition and belief to the waging of a war of a particularly total kind, a war that will itself permeate and reorganize everyday life. It may involve sacrifices – of civil liberties, for example.

'Way of life' connects with other ideas based in a reading of Gramsci's *Prison Notebooks*. We have already used terms such as 'hegemony', 'alliance', 'national–popular', 'collective will' in this chapter. The idea that every hegemonic formation involves inequality or 'putting citizens in their places' is very Gramscian. Even under dictatorial regimes, such as the fascism Gramsci faced, power goes beyond simple coercion. Ruling or rising groups must secure some measure of popular consent, must connect with popular 'common sense' – a Gramscian category as close to culture as 'way of life'. The popular and the dominant are intertwined realities of power or, to put it another way, power is profoundly relational and dialogic.

The Gramscian focus on the nation is less helpful in understanding the international and global aspects of the crisis – evidence, perhaps, of a new form of empire (Hardt and Negri, 2000). The national dimensions don't dissolve, however, but interact with the international or global. National governments can use domestic success to add to their weight in international negotiations and assert leadership abroad. They can bring the status gained from international statesmanship back home, but they must also suffer the domestic consequences of disastrous international defeats or humiliations.

In some ways, a more serious challenge to Gramscian analysis is the particular way in which distinctions between us and others, between citizens and terrorists, between good and evil, were drawn by Bush and Blair.

Moral absolutes, the 'other' and unconscious processes

Gramsci was very interested in the 'ethico-political' aspects of hegemony or the assertion of a *moral* leadership. Both Bush and Blair work with very strong moral distinctions, even with a certain fundamentalism or moral absolutism. Lines between good and evil are very firmly drawn. However, this is not simply tactical or strategic – something more is going on.

In the speeches, the enemy, the terrorist, is absolutely external and other. Al-Qa'ida is presented as having no past and no connection with a longer history in which the UK or USA could be involved. As Blair puts it, 'this mass terrorism is the new evil in our world' (Blair, 2 October). Bush says that America is 'learning about terror and evil' (Bush, 24 October) as though US history was not itself quite violent. For Bush, terrorists are 'the evildoers', 'evil people', even – Biblically and essentially 'the evil ones':

> They're evil and so dark and so negative, they couldn't realize that there's going to be such good that comes out of what took place in America. (Bush, 4 December)

'They hide in caves' (Bush, 16 September). They are 'an enemy who can only survive in darkness' (7 November), but we will 'smoke [them] out of their holes' (16 September). They are also absolutely blank or null: they are 'people who have no country, no ideology' (17 October). These are images of the inhuman, the animal and, of course, the devilish.

To understand this making of demons, we can turn to psychoanalytical traditions and contemporary theories of identity (see especially Chapter 14). With their human faces blanked out, darkened or racialized, it becomes possible to project on to Al-Qa'ida and the Taliban aspects of British and American ways of living that are themselves discomfiting. The threatening figure of 'the terrorist' is thus internal to the culture in more than one way. His expulsion and destruction, as a psychologically invested figure, then becomes part of the contemporary production of British and US identity. It may also be that Blair and Bush stress the superior morality of their position as a more or less conscious defence against Islamic fundamentalist views of Western moral decadence.

Such processes are especially difficult to pin down in ways that will convince the sceptical – those who see the political, for example, as simple self-interest and 'realism'. However, as Freud argued a long time ago, there are aspects of speech and memory that are best explained as interruptions of rational behaviour by emotions that are unconscious but active (Freud, 1973: 39–87). Bush does often seem to speak of his own 'madness' when he is describing the enemy:

> We see the same intolerance of dissent; the same mad global ambitions; the same brutal determination to control every life and all of life. (Bush, 6 November)

His famous slips of the tongue (which even survive the official transcript) reveal more than is intended:

> I think the best way to attack – to handle the attacks of September 11th is to fight fear with friendship. (25 October)

His theme, here, is how to deal with the Islamic world, which he is at pains not to criticize as a whole. He seeks to 'fight fear with friendship' – a slightly odd manoeuvre (why 'fight' if you want to reassure?) However, it is certainly inappropriate to call this 'the best way to attack'. So, when this phrase pops out, unbidden and surely unscripted, it is quickly changed to 'to handle the attacks'. Analysis, however, must hold on to this slip a little bit longer. The violent and attacking qualities clearly don't all belong to Al-Qa'ida, yet it is important that they appear to. Anti-terrorist measures, not to mention Western ways of life, must not appear morally ambiguous – the terrorists must bear the full weight of moral blame. Bush's slip, however, shows what is involved here emotionally. A lot of the hate and anger that Bush is feeling himself, and which fuels the vengeful responses, is projected on to Al-Qa'ida, but it finds expression, nonetheless, in the slip.

Another way of showing the irrational elements here is to focus on the 'absolutism' of the moral stances. As Blair puts it for a British Islamic audience:

> I don't think there should ever be, though, any moral ambiguity about this. I mean, what happened in the United States of America can never be justified, no cause could ever justify it, no set of circumstances could ever justify it. (27 September, address to leaders of 'the Muslim communities')

Later, Blair closes out the possibility, even, of 'understanding':

> There is no compromise possible with such people, no meeting of minds, no point of understanding with such terror. Just a choice: defeat it or be defeated by it. And defeat it we must. (2 October)

Al-Qa'ida has thus not only committed a terrible crime, but is truly beyond 'understanding'. In this way, the terrible, shattering acts of September 11th are not allowed to prompt any questioning about the West and Western ways of living – or of fighting. As we noted in Chapter 3 and will explore further in Chapter 14, this stress on the formative nature of self – other relations is a keynote in contemporary approaches to identity and subjectivity and, while sharing in his dialectical way of thinking, take us well beyond Gramsci's subtle Marxism.

Making a reading convincing

In this section, we would like to explore three more general reflections on the credibility of readings. First, we aren't claiming that reading a text in terms of 'dominance' is the only credible reading, even within a framework of concern with power. Our approach in this chapter is only one approach. Another would be to look at the deployment of different discourses or forms of knowledge-as-power – the discourses of war and criminality, for instance. A third approach would be to analyse patterns of public remembering and forgetting in the speeches: Bush's use of memories of Pearl Harbor, for instance, or Bush and Blair's common 'forgetting' of Western involvement in the origins of Al-Qa'ida and similar networks during the Cold War. Of course, we can also combine all these readings, or elements of them, while being conscious of their different presuppositions (see Chapter 5).

Second, our questioning of a text always comes from particular research agenda and this agenda is always partial. To quote Haraway again, 'The only way to find a larger vision is to be somewhere in particular' (1991: 196).The 'somewhere in particular' in this chapter has been an interest in texts and power and, more particularly, an unease with anti-terrorism programmes. In this case, as so often, research was a way of *finding* a political position, *exploring* a moral doubt. This involved not 'finding what we wanted to find', but seriously addressing texts that were 'other' or strange. The recognition of the partiality of starting points is the condition for proper dialogue with others about our readings, readings that do have a real object out there, even if any one project can only grasp parts of it.

Third, this dialogue has an evidential aspect. The reading of texts is an *empirical* procedure, though a tricky and complex one. Any (convincing) reading must return, again and again, to the text itself. In presenting an analysis, it must make available by quotation or paraphrase (or as an appendix) the segments, sentences, words and moments of absence on which the reading (in the larger sense) is based. We have to *offer* a reading – 'This is how it reads to me', from this point of view, taking account of these contexts but also ask 'What do *you* think?'

Conclusion

In this chapter, we have focused on a form of reading that is allied to political analysis in the most obvious sense, but integrates a cultural dimension into the analysis of power. The close reading of strategically chosen texts can be a crucial resource, an entry point into, in this case, popular–dominant dynamics or bids for hegemony on a national and international scale. Such texts, as we argued in Chapter 8, are marked by complex power relations as well as the deployment of cultural resources.

Again, we note how readings differ depending on the nature of the textual material and the aims of the analysis. Chapters 9 and 10 offered two very different sets of readings of very different texts. There is a sense in which all research projects have to develop their own reading procedures. On the other hand, all textual analysis involves certain choices and decisions and we hope, in this chapter, to have clarified some of these procedures in ways that offer something of use for very different kind of projects. In the next chapter, we ask what difference it makes, if any, if the texts we read are, more overtly, historical fictions.

Note

1 This chapter is based on research that was an early attempt to understand post-September 11th global politics and its fundamental reordering of political forces. It was written before the Iraq war, the 'defeat' of the Ba'athist regime and the, in our opinion, illegal and chaotic occupation of that country by US and British forces. It preceded the growth of global popular opposition to the war and the subsequent political vicissitudes of Bush and Blair. Analysis of this episode today would have to be informed by the signal failures to win consent to the war, both nationally and globally, especially outside the United States, and by a reading of the counter-hegemonic discourses that grew up around the crisis of political credibility and more general opposition to global injustice. It remains to be seen how deep this crisis in neo-liberal hegemony will become and what its implications will be for both 'Blairism' and, more broadly, New Labour politics in the UK (30 July 2003).

11 Reading fictions, reading histories

Fiction and/or history? 187
Cultural materialism: rereading literature 189
'New historicism' and historical discourse 193
Staging and silencing: explicit and implicit meanings 194
Elementary, my dear Foucault 197
Beyond a (national) boundary: post-colonial encounters 198
Conclusion 199

In this chapter we will be looking at various approaches to fictional texts that foreground the historical, social and cultural contexts of their production. Sometimes such approaches refer to the larger historical context in order to (re-)interpret the fictional text, sometimes fiction is used as a way into the cultural formations of a particular time and place. In disciplinary terms, as we suggested in Chapter 7, such approaches move between historical literary studies, cultural history and historical cultural studies. The texts chosen for such analysis 'speak to' or allude to the social debates and anxieties of their time – perhaps implicitly – while often articulating dominant discourses. As all texts are generally also marked by their contradictions and silences, a critical reading can also involve the identification of those absences or the text's struggle to reconcile contradictions, by means of 'magical resolutions', for example, which work to erase the differences of power.

A *cultural* analysis of a fictional text is nearly always concerned with the relationship – the dialogue, even – between the (apparently) intrinsic elements – its formal structure, characters, themes – and the (seemingly) extrinsic aspects of context, especially those concerning the social moment of production and the articulation of power relations. We say 'apparently' and 'seemingly' here because, in the course of such an analysis, the text/context distinction itself tends to break down as contextual elements appear in the text, either directly or as symptoms, while the text itself comes to appear as a particular concrete instance of the wider cultural field. The chapter is divided into sections that trace the different ways in which the intersections between fiction and history (discussed in the section below) may be theorized.

Fiction and/or history?

Although literary historical studies are a particularly flourishing area of interdisciplinary work today, conventional academic practice has often insisted on the maintenance of disciplinary boundaries – between 'literary studies' and 'historical studies', for example – as well as on an absolute difference between documentary or factual sources and the histories based on them and fiction. Yet, as we have seen, all texts effectively participate in the production of beliefs and ideas and so will bear traces of their historical moment of production. Paul Ricoeur has argued that history-writing and literary fiction are in many ways complementary narrative forms by means of which the temporal dimensions of living are grasped. The first seeks to represent a social world but can only do so indirectly by interpreting surviving texts and sources and the second, while presenting itself as an act of imagination, always refers to the social world (Ricoeur, 1991).

It is important in politics and ethics to insist on boundaries between truth and falsehood, forgetting and remembering, 'covering up' and 'being open', but it is also important not to confuse these vital differences with the conventional distinction between fiction and history. Here, as elsewhere, truth-seeking may have to recognize conventional distinctions but also push beyond them (see Chapter 3 above). In all this, it is also important to take the position of the *contemporary* – that is, twenty-first century – reader, for whom reading historical fictions is not only a route to the past but also a means of reflection on the present and future.

This is well illustrated by the case of one of the characters in the work discussed below – Sherlock Holmes, himself a great truth-seeker. Holmes is an example of a significant cultural figure whose fictionality seems to be only precariously maintained and who clearly 'exists' at some level outside the confines of the written text. Holmes is a potent symbol, standing as he does for the triumph of rationality, science and gentlemanly superiority over the threat of various others and it is this that, arguably, has enabled him to exceed the boundaries of the Conan Doyle stories. A cultural analysis of the Holmes stories can thus move *between* text and context in order to understand the complex relationship between a fictional figure such as Holmes, his moment of appearance in the imperial UK of the 1880s and our own responses to him now. This is not simply about setting the character against a historical background that is itself taken to be fully formed, fixed and stable, but, rather, about using the Holmes figure as a way into the world of the 1880s and our knowledge of that world – from its other texts – to further understand Holmes, both in terms of his time and today.

In such an account, the specific historical and social contexts in which a text appears, is read and understood becomes itself increasingly visible and important to the meanings we find within it. This is especially interesting if we consider the temporal pressures that will lead to a text being written in a particular way or addressing a particular audience. We are not, however, looking here at historical fiction – stories produced deliberately and often self-consciously about the past; our interest is in the contemporariness of texts – the way in which they address their own present and our present, too.

So, we want to argue here that it is possible for fiction to be a form of history and for history to be a kind of fiction as both will offer a story of some kind, operate in a particular register or idiom that is itself constructed and will inevitably articulate a range of discourses that are ideological in one way or another. Within the terms of Gadamer's view of historical consciousness in *Truth and Method*, a dialogue with historical fictions has many aspects: it involves grasping values and perceptions very different from our own; leads us to revise or rethink our own tradition and can change our horizons today. Ricoeur would add, characteristically, that studying the imaginations and unrealized possibilities of the past can directly feed our own imaginings and actions towards a better future (1984, 1985, 1988). The figure of Holmes, for example, can be a focus for reflection on such related themes as masculinity, science, rationality, otherness, Britishness and the Empire. Such reflection can form a part of a contemporary politics of nationality, identity or science.

Cultural materialism: rereading literature

As we have seen, cultural approaches to reading have been developed that constantly return the text to its context – to its moment of production or consumption, to the processes and ideas that attend that exchange and the social relations that help determine it. Cultural analysis in this sense can be used to interpret literary or canonical texts just as effectively as it can address popular texts. Some of the earliest examples of such analyses can be found in the work of Raymond Williams.

The classic text and structures of feeling

Williams developed what he came to call a 'cultural materialist' model of analysis. As we have seen, he was critical of the classic Marxist proposition that the economic base of any society was the key determinant of its social and cultural superstructure (see especially *Marxism and Literature*, 1977). He developed a range of critical categories by means of which literary and other cultural forms could be viewed as part of larger cultural formations, subject to the 'pressures' and 'limits' of social processes that included economic change and class dynamics. His concept of the 'structure of feeling' is one of his most complex and difficult ideas, but was an attempt to grasp the shape and organization of ideas and sentiments at particular times and in particular contexts, focusing especially on 'emergent' elements, often only partially articulated. A good example of Williams' method can be found in *The Country and The City* (1973), his study of English literature's representation of the rural and urban from the sixteenth century to the twentieth, though it is important to note that this text precedes his engagement with the ideas of Gramsci – a key dialogue in *Marxism and Literature*. In terms of Williams' own emergent knowledge, *The Country and the City* catches him somewhere between his early class- or group-based view of culture(s) and later concern with cultural formations (see Chapter 3 above).

Crucially, in *The Country and the City*, Williams sees 'literature' as a *changing* social practice, one that represented the shifting social and cultural values of a specific, often highly privileged, group of people:

> It is a truth universally acknowledged, that Jane Austen chose to ignore the decisive historical events of her time. Where, it is still asked, are the Napoleonic wars: the real current of history? But history has many currents, and the social history of the landed families, at that time in England, was among the most important. As we sense its real processes, we find that they are quite central and structural in Jane Austen's novels . . .
>
> Darcy, in *Pride and Prejudice,* is a landowner established for 'many generations', but his friend Bingley has inherited £100,000 and is looking for an estate to purchase. Sir William Lucas has risen from trade to a knighthood; Mr Bennett has £2000 a year, but an entailed estate, and has married the daughter of an attorney, whose brother is in trade.

Having established his topic in those specific material relations that underpin Austen's work yet so frequently go unremarked on or taken for granted, Williams goes on:

> To abstract this social history is of course to describe only the world of the novels within which the more particular actions begin and end. Yet it must be clear that it is no single, settled society, it is an active, complicated, sharply speculative process. It is indeed that most difficult world to describe, in English social history: an acquisitive, high bourgeois society at the point of its most evident interlocking with an agrarian capitalism that is itself mediated by inherited titles and by the making of family names. (1973: 114–15)

Here, then, Williams' project is the relocation of Jane Austen's novels back into their social context in order to demonstrate their particularity to that history and their narration of it in ways that are profoundly ideological. In contrast to (some early examples of) structuralism's claims to 'scientific' neutrality, Williams' analysis is clearly political – and he is setting out to demonstrate the profoundly political dimensions to fiction. For Williams, Austen's stories are not the source of universal values or truths and are certainly not simplistic assertions of the triumph of romantic love, but, rather, representations of a specific historical moment. As he points out, far from ignoring the material or economic sphere, Austen's work is wholly concerned with it: her novels document income and social status in minute detail and with great precision. They do this not only in order to establish individuals as characters but also to assert their legitimacy as *subjects* (in both senses) of the novel as it was being developed in the early nineteenth century.

The landed gentry, upper middle classes and aspirant merchant classes are, in Williams' own phrase, 'the knowable community' of Jane Austen's world. As he goes on to say in the same book, 'What she sees across the land is a network of propertied houses and families, and through the holes of this tightly drawn mesh most actual people are simply not seen. To be face-to-face in this world is already to belong to a class' (1973: 166). Here, Williams shows that great literature does not occupy a sphere above economic and material concerns, but, rather, that those dimensions are central to what it has to say and that this is an ideological process.

Importantly, Williams' method of reading is a critical one, rather than one determined by reference to theory. Although his analysis is shaped by his Marxist beliefs (and also by his Leavisite background), Williams rarely references Marx directly in order to support his argument. Yet, it is clear that a version of Marxism informs his reading, albeit in subtle ways. Williams' attention to the pressures of class identity and class relations is one aspect of this. So, too, is his awareness of the importance of economic power to the maintenance of other kinds of status. Yet, he demonstrates this to us by means of a rigorous and detailed reference to the literary text combined with a discussion of society in early nineteenth-century England rather than by means of repeated referral to Marx's work.

Cultural materialism has been one of the main approaches to fictional texts in cultural studies and Williams' work has been highly influential in all kinds of ways. In contrast to the traditions of work on the political economy of culture, however, it is primarily driven by a focus on the 'small units' of cultural production, specific texts, rather than on the larger structures and processes. It is also explicitly engaged in an exploration of how particular forms of consciousness – rather than particular kinds of economic structures – come into being and are accorded the status of truth.

Popular fiction and hegemony

As the model has developed, it has become more explicitly grounded in a theoretical framework, drawing especially on the work of Antonio Gramsci, in order to understand fictional texts as the sites of struggles over meaning. Because Gramsci developed a highly nuanced model of political analysis, his work is particularly useful as a way into the relationship between the politics of the public sphere (Parliament, political parties and world events) and those of the culture of everyday life, especially at a given historical moment. This critical framework thus becomes a contextualizing strategy that can return the text to its historical moment while also enabling us to pull out threads or tensions that are not explicit. Cultural materialists have used Gramsci's theory of hegemony as a cultural process and his arguments about the relationship between common sense and ideology to explore the ways in which popular texts may articulate struggles for cultural power and shifts in belief systems, between dominant and subordinate social groups or forces.

For example, Roger Bromley does just this in his analysis (1986) of two highly popular (and highly gendered) British novels of the 1930s, Daphne du Maurier's gothic romance *Rebecca* and Geoffrey Household's *Rogue Male*. Bromley uses Gramsci's concept of hegemony to read *Rebecca* as a novel that works as a response to the economic and political crises of the 1930s: the Depression and the growth of fascism. For Bromley, *Rebecca*'s romantic plot is bound up with its class politics. The novel attempts to deal with the contradictions raised by changes in class power in the UK during the 1930s by means of a combination of nostalgia for a stable past, located in the aristocratic English country house, and an implicit recognition that such stability conceals complex tensions around sexual desire and social power. Bromley explicitly links these tensions with the public sphere of governmental politics, pointing out that *Rebecca*'s publication in 1938 coincided with the wider articulation of anxieties about class relations being expressed, especially by the upper classes, with the election of the first Labour Government in the United Kingdom (1986: 162).

He goes on to argue that the political and social crisis of the 1930s produced a response in which the lower middle classes were deliberately incorporated into a particular model of Englishness and, alongside that, the project of capitalism. He identifies *Rebecca* as a text that is part of this hegemonic move by the 'ruling bloc' – that is, the alliance of the gentry and the bourgeoisie in order to secure power. As he points out:

> Maxim loses his country house (a reference to a specific historical reality recognized by the text) and gives up many of the functions, political and social, consequent upon its ownership, for a personal life relatively confined and austere, and in some ways rootless. What he recovers and retains, through the fusion and assimilation of his 'lowly' second wife, is a transfusion of ideals and values, and a *style* with an important ideological function, that of the gentleman, signed by a morality of fair play, selflessness, courage, moderation and self-control, independence and responsibility. All of which can be summed up by the word *authority*, commanding deference. (1986: 163)

As we can see, Bromley is using Gramsci's theories here as a kind of prism through which he interprets du Maurier's novel. In contrast to Williams, his arguments are expressed in highly theorized terms and with specific reference to Gramsci's model. Moreover, his vocabulary – 'the bourgeoisie', 'progressive forces', 'the ruling bloc' – discloses his own Marxist intellectual framework and concerns; he wants to show how popular fiction operates to *secure consent* to the political beliefs and interests of a ruling minority by offering narratives and characters whose desires and concerns are naturalized and legitimated by the text. By linking the underlying ideas that shape *Rebecca* as a popular romance to the wider issue of the cultural dimensions of political hegemony, Bromley shows both that no text – however apparently innocuous – is innocent and that all texts are historical documents of one kind or another.

This approach also owes much to the historicist ideas of Walter Benjamin. 'There is no document of civilization which is not at the same time a document of barbarism' (1992: 248), he argues, meaning that even the 'cultural treasures' of all societies, such as the canonical texts valued by critics and scholars, will be marked by the particular ideologies of the dominant class, race or other social group in any given historical moment.

It is important to stress that similar methods can be used on contemporary popular fictional forms. This is the approach that was adopted in a study of the popular family saga in the 1980s (Tincknell, 1991). The study grew out of political concern about the success of the project of Thatcherism and the New Right throughout that decade and sought to explore some aspects of its specific address to women. This was attempted by means of a detailed textual analysis of a particular genre – the 'blockbuster' saga, by writers such as Barbara Taylor Bradford and Danielle Steel – situated in the context of the 'conjunctural moment' of the 1980s. Such novels specifically addressed a female readership and featured a tough, proto-Thatcherite heroine fighting her way to the top of a business enterprise despite male opposition and female jealousy. Because they worked to naturalize class and gender differences by identifying their heroines as 'exceptional' women, they helped to secure consent to the ideological imperatives of Thatcherism and 'made space' for women in the ideology of entrepreneurial capitalism, albeit in limited ways.

Like Bromley, this project drew on Gramsci's theory of hegemony to explore the success of these stories, together with a focus on them as sources of pleasure for women, akin to the approach adopted by Janice Radway discussed in Chapter 9. Indeed, it is sometimes easy to lose sight of the particularity of texts and the specific ways in which they work if we ignore 'the pleasure question' or reduce texts to their ideological dimensions. By exploring the ways in which material pleasure in clothes, food and interior decoration are foregrounded in these novels, it was possible to argue that the books helped to develop and organize the growing emphasis on consumption that was so central to Thatcherism's hegemony during the 1980s.

New historicism and historical discourse

Cultural materialism has important theoretical continuities with the critical practice of what has been termed 'new historicism' – a tendency in the more traditional arena of literary criticism. New historicists, such as Stephen Greenblatt, Alan Sinfield, Richard Wilson and Richard Dutton, have explicitly positioned their understanding of the work of Shakespeare especially as part of a return to history in literary criticism, emphasizing the role of the literary text as the bearer of historical meaning, as a vehicle for politics and the expression of dominant power relations (Sinfield 1992: 1). For such critics, as for Williams and Bromley, the relationship between text and context is not simply an extra dimension but central to the very operation of the text itself.

Greenblatt's now seminal essay, 'Invisible Bullets', for example, explores the relationship between power and subversion in a range of Renaissance texts, including Shakespeare's *Henry IV, Part One*, and argues that they articulate *both* the dominant beliefs of the age and the subversion of those beliefs in a complex play of meaning. However, he concludes that, ultimately, 'subversiveness is the very product of that power and furthers its ends' (1981: 41). For Greenblatt, the Renaissance machinery of power is self-validating and totalizing, even where it appears to allow for contradiction or subversion, so that all the texts he explores are finally and, in spite of their formal differences, texts of power.

This tendency to re-present literary texts as always and in every way articulations of dominant ideology, or as totalizing and wholly recuperative documents able to simultaneously forge and defuse dissent or political subversion is importantly at odds with the emphasis of some cultural materialist work on the potential for resistance in cultural formations. Indeed, as John Brannigan points out (1998: 65), Greenblatt's apparently loose yet monolithic conceptualization of power and its operation led to vigorous criticism of his approach among other literary scholars, who accused him of a lack of historical specificity and an overdetermination of the operation of dominant power, discerning its machinations in every poem, every play and every prose document produced during the sixteenth century.

Even so, Greenblatt's emphasis on power as an organizing mechanism in textual production and articulation is important. It is related to Foucault's conceptualization of history as a set of discursive processes as well as his emphasis on power's complex and strategic dimensions. For researchers in cultural studies, however, it is the tendency among new historicists to confine their critical work to the relatively familiar terrain of the established literary canon – the 'great texts' – that limits their account of the historical-textual dialogue.[1]

Staging and silencing: explicit and implicit meanings

Staging: class and history

We have already mentioned the way in which all texts operate by means of the production and organization of meanings that are both explicit and implicit, and we will now look at this proposition more closely in relation to fictional narratives. Any narrative will be openly about a particular topic, offer a theme or set of concerns and be structured by virtue of a plot that develops those issues: these are its explicit meanings. However, texts also do something else. They operate via implicit meanings, meanings that are suggested, implied, alluded to and invoked, perhaps by metaphor or imagery, perhaps by the way in which the narrative is structured. These meanings are also important to an interpretation of a text, but they may be harder to 'fix' or prove. Such identifications are important because they help to expose what is offered as truth as partial, limited or ideological.

The French philosopher and literary critic Pierre Macherey developed a model of implicit and explicit meanings (1978), exploring the importance of the 'silences' in a text in relation to what it actually claimed to say:

> The speech of the book comes from a certain silence, a matter that it endows with form, a ground on which it traces a figure. Thus, the book is not self-sufficient; it is necessarily accompanied by *a certain absence*, without which it would not exist. A knowledge of the book must include a consideration of this absence. This is why it seems useful and legitimate to ask of every production what it tacitly implies, what it does not say. Either all around or in its wake the explicit requires the implicit: for in order to say anything, there are other *things which must not be said.* (1978: 85)

Macherey's argument draws on the work of the Marxist critic Louis Althusser, whose theory of ideological address – or 'interpellation' – was profoundly influenced by Freudian accounts of the unconscious. Althusser was an important and very controversial figure in the development of cultural theory, primarily because of his contributions to rethinking such categories as ideology, the state and 'determination' (see, for example, his essay 'Ideological State Apparatuses', 1971). However, Althusser's *method* is interesting, too, because he foregrounds the *practice of reading* as a key element in the development of a theoretical understanding of Marx. Indeed, he focuses on Marx's *own* reading of Adam Smith's economic theory in *Capital* in order to develop his argument that the task of critical practice is to deconstruct the problematic of a text – the dense weave of assumptions and discourses that make it up and also set the boundaries of what it can or cannot say. Because ideology is a closed system, he argues, it can only set itself the problems that it can answer and must remain silent on those questions that go beyond those boundaries. This way of reading texts had a strong influence on the practice of mapping theories that we discussed in Chapters 2 and 6, though it was also criticized as being insufficiently historical.

A problematic is produced by what is absent as well as by what is present and can only be identified by means of the procedure of a 'symptomatic reading' – that is, a reading for the symptoms that express these absences and the underlying tensions and contradictions inherent in an ideological position. In terms of our dialogic model, a problematic may not only rule out certain questions, it may produce answers that have no question, which appear in the text as symptoms. Marx, says Althusser, undertakes just such a symptomatic reading of Adam Smith:

> Like his first reading, Marx's second reading presupposes the existence of *two texts*, and the measurement of the first against the second. But what distinguishes this new reading from the old is the fact that in the new one the second text is articulated with the lapses in the first text (1969: 28).

This symptomatic second reading is effectively a double reading in which both the manifest text – the text that is there – is read and also the *latent* text – the text that is produced by the lapses and absences. Althusser's method of reading, therefore, is one that seeks to go beyond the visible text in order to identify what John Storey (1993: 113) calls the problem struggling to emerge in it. All of this may seem excessively complicated when it is explained, but actually 'doing' a symptomatic reading is not so hard and can be very rewarding.

For example, Macherey follows Althusser in arguing that the silences and absences in a text are as eloquent as what it actually says and are part of its ideological dimensions. He then demonstrates this by a symptomatic reading of Jules Verne's novels including *Around the World in Eighty Days*. He argues that this novel effectively *stages* the contradictions of French imperialism in the late nineteenth century by means of its elaborate plot and the series of cultural encounters it describes. These encounters become more fantastic in each episode of the story. Macherey argues that the book does this not as a result of the conscious intent of its author or because of a coherent and simple set of intended meanings, but because it contains multiple meanings and conflicting discourses. He uses Freud's analysis of dreams to show that there may be a gap between what a text *tells* and what it *shows*, between what it wants to say and what it actually does say. The *staging* of what cannot be spoken is part of what Frederic Jameson later calls the 'unconscious' of the literary text and it is this that can be revealed by critical reading.

Silencing: gender and history

To clarify this approach further, we can return to the Sherlock Holmes stories mentioned at the beginning of this chapter. In her highly influential book *Critical Practice* (1980), Catherine Belsey draws on the work of Althusser and Macherey to offer a brief case study of the Holmes stories in which she demonstrates a symptomatic reading of a fictional text. Belsey argues against the assumption that the tales simply express an ideology of scientific rationalism and goes on to suggest that they operate at two levels:

> The project of the Sherlock Holmes stories is to dispel magic and mystery, to make everything explicit, accountable, subject to scientific analysis . . . Nonetheless, these stories, whose overt project is total explicitness, total verisimilitude in the interests of a plea for scientificity, are haunted by shadowy, mysterious and often silent women. Their silence repeatedly conceals their sexuality, investing it with a dark and magical quality which is beyond the reach of scientific knowledge. (1980: 111–14)

Belsey uses a Machereyan reading of the short story 'Charles Augustus Milverton' combined with a feminist analysis that is specifically gender-sensitive (and in contrast to Macherey himself) to explore the interplay between the explicit declaration of belief in logical deduction and reason and the stories' evasiveness over the nature of women's sexuality. We might extend her argument a little by pointing out that this way of representing female characters as both mysterious and mystified is not confined to texts produced in the late nineteenth century and it is one that only works successfully while the centre of consciousness and the implied reader is assumed to be male. As Belsey says, 'In the Sherlock Holmes stories classic realism ironically tells a truth, though not the truth about the world which is the project of classic realism. The truth the stories tell is the truth about ideology, the truth which ideology represses, its own existence as ideology itself' (1980: 117). The stories' 'silences' over women, sexuality and desire also indicate the impossibility of a fully sexualized masculinity.

Belsey's interest in the worldview offered by a very particular type of fiction, the realist novel, is important to our discussion here. Important because almost all popular fiction – and most classic texts for that matter – deploy the conventions of realism, whether in its literary, cinematic or televisual form (see Chapter 9). If this model seems to be perfectly natural – a reflection of how things are – it is worth addressing the question of the realist text's silences and absences as well as its presences and emphases. For example, the social realist film comedy *The Full Monty* (1997) is also a textual construction of the recent past. Its historical realism includes the relocation and closure of the British steel industry from the 1980s to 1990s and the nostalgic invocation of the 1970s as a decade in which manufacturing industry was healthy, employment readily available and the relationship between men and women reassuringly stable – an account invoked by the use of a soundtrack of vintage disco music from that decade. This implied contrast makes the limited choices open to its male characters in the 1990s seem starker, more disturbing and perhaps more unnatural than might otherwise appear. The film is silent about the inequalities of the past and very noisy about men's disempowerment in the present, its central trope of the striptease the men perform becoming a symbol of the reversal of social norms. *The Full Monty's* representation of recent history as a narrative of decline, with the 1970s cast as a golden age, assumes also that men's experience is itself more central and more legitimate as a truth about reality. (See Tincknell and Chambers, 2002)

Elementary, my dear Foucault

It is worth returning to the example of the Holmes canon and considering more fully how the cultural materialist focus on history may be combined with other approaches. Derek Longhurst offers a materialist account of how the Holmes stories helped to articulate the conflated masculine identities of class, gender and nationality via the figure of the English gentleman – a figure whose remodelling as the apotheosis of civilized humanity in the late nineteenth century was central to the cultural hegemony of Englishness. Longhurst focuses on the stories' representation of London's public and urban spaces as the primary site of criminality and links the appearance of Holmes as the master detective in the 1880s to the development of other kinds of narratives about the urban working classes in the same decade (1989: 53).

He argues that the emergence and enormous success of the symbolic figure of Holmes must be read in relation to the material determinants of the stories – anxieties about a criminal urban working class, the assertion of London as an imperial metropolis, the threat of Germany's growing power – and he links these to the stories' operation of 'magical resolutions' to the problems posed by the specific crimes described (1989: 53). In this way, he combines the cultural materialist model discussed above with some of the narrative analysis we looked at in Chapter 9. Longhurst goes on to say that, 'one of the fundamental pleasures of the Holmes narratives is to construct a tension between the inexplicably enigmatic and the reassurance of total closure. As such, they are "magical narratives"'(1989: 65). Longhurst does not ignore the formal properties or structures of the stories, but then neither does he privilege them at the expense of the wider social dimensions. Instead, he shows that the two things are coterminous and that the ideological meanings articulated by the Holmes stories are produced out of the formal narrative structure as well as the stories' content.

Jon Thompson (1993) takes this model of methodological combination further by linking a genre analysis (of the kind discussed in chapter 9) with a detailed reading of the social and political dimensions of the Holmes texts. This analysis is coupled with a post-structuralist emphasis on the relationship between institutions, power and knowledge, which draws on Michel Foucault's theory of discourse and discursive formations elaborated in *Discipline and Punish* (1977) and *History of Sexuality* (1979).

In contrast to Althusser, Gramsci and Macherey, Foucault's account of power is not defined in terms of class or even of a specific social group, although he is interested in organizations and institutions and his theory of the unspoken rules of discourse resembles Macherey's model of implicit meanings. For Foucault, power is a strategic terrain and the site of a relationship between the powerful and the powerless; it is wielded via the discourses of various institutions (such as the law, medicine and, of course, education) and operates by means of a process of definition and exclusion. A discursive formation thus defines what can be said, written about and acted on regarding a particular subject by virtue of a complex network of unwritten rules. Thompson mobilizes Foucault's account of the discursive relationship between power and knowledge in order to interrogate Holmes as a powerfully symbolic cultural figure:

> Sherlock Holmes' knowledge, his ability to unravel the most intractable puzzles, gives him the power to penetrate the mysteries of London. The same form of knowledge that ultimately produced the Empire also produced the figure of the empirical detective hero, Sherlock Holmes. (1993: 76)

Once again, then, the method here is to move from textual specificity to historical specificity in order to demonstrate the material relations between the two. We might note, too, that Thompson explicitly links the colonialist imperative to empiricist forms of knowledge and ways of knowing in a way that helps us to consider the problematic aspects to a nationally bounded approach to texts.

Beyond a (national) boundary: post-colonial encounters

We can explore this move in a slightly different way by looking at Edward Said's *Culture and Imperialism* (1994). This is an extensive analysis of the complex relationship between the aesthetic traditions of European – especially English – literature and the discursive formations of colonialism. Said expands from Williams' concern with class and nation to consider the ways in which Jane Austen's novels, specifically *Mansfield Park*, are suffused with an often implicit set of assumptions about colonialism and empire.

He is, however, emphatically *not* saying that Austen's work is an apology for imperialism or that she should be judged, anachronistically, as somehow 'politically incorrect'. Instead, Said reads the novel closely and meticulously, pointing out the centrality of the links between England and the Caribbean to the workings of the text:

> Take . . . the casual references to Antigua, the ease with which Sir Thomas's needs in England are met by a Caribbean sojourn, the uninflected, unreflective citations of Antigua (or the Mediterranean, or India, which is where Lady Bertram, in a fit of distracted impatience, requires that William should go . . .) They stand for a significance 'out there' that frames the genuinely important action here, but not for a great significance. (1994: 111–12)

As he goes on to argue, 'The Bertrams could not have been possible without the slave trade, sugar, and the colonial planter class' (1994: 112).

Said thus moves between the literary text and its social moment in order to make visible the relationship between Jane Austen's moral framework – her irony and delicate precision of observation – and its economic foundations. As he says, 'the task is to lose neither a true historical sense of the first [power], nor a full enjoyment or appreciation of the second [irony], all the while seeing both together '(1994: 116). His method combines interpretation and close reading with references back to the empirical evidence of colonial exploitation. Said's work is both post-structuralist in approach – in the sense that it comes after and refers to, but is not confined by, the rigidity of structuralism – and post-colonial in its focus – in the sense that it relocates Jane Austen's work (and that of other canonical writers) into an historical context in which the global relations of power and identity produced as a result of imperialism are laid bare. In such a reading, fiction's role as a site of discourse is crucial: it becomes clear that, while there remain important (and closely policed) boundaries between 'fact' and 'fiction' or 'documentary' and 'literature', the circulation of ideas, beliefs and meanings is not confined by such categories.

Conclusion

All of these are examples of approaches to reading that are both intensive and extensive analyses. That is, they couple an historicized and contextualizing account of a text's appearance as part of a specific social or political moment with analysis of the narrative structure, language and style of the story. This approach to fictional texts as sites of discourse also allows for the idea that meanings may be multiple and contradictory and that there can be no single answer to the question, 'What does this text mean?' Methodologically, it also moves us away from the fairly rigid scientism of structuralism and towards a more playful way of reading. Perhaps most importantly, by using a literary text as a way into a larger cultural formation, the distinction between text and context is almost eroded – the literary text becomes a moment or nodal point in the larger formation. Reading a text thus becomes a way of doing cultural history (albeit with a firm eye on the specificities of form and structure) or an exploration of imaginary or imagined geographies. The London of the Holmes stories can then be understood as a discursive cluster as well as a real place, while the texts themselves appear as spaces of contradiction, encounter and dialogue.

Note

1 Having noted this, we recognize that much of the work done by new historicist writers such as Greenblatt, Alan Sinfield and Jonathan Dollimore is on texts that effectively predate the largely nineteenth-century industrialization and commodification of culture and cannot be simplistically assigned to 'popular' or 'elite' categories.

Part IV
MEETINGS

Meetings, fieldwork, ethnography

We use the term 'meetings' to describe methods that involve direct engagement between the self and others, or, indeed, between different aspects of the self. We have chosen this term because it is wider than the usual terms in use, which include 'fieldwork', 'ethnography' and 'ethnology', and because it draws attention to the relational or dialogic aspect of this engagement. 'Meetings' includes fieldwork, of course – a term that draws especially on anthropological and ethnological practice. It implies not only a single I–thou encounter, but entry to a whole cultural world or scene. This has often involved going into 'fields' that are relatively unfamiliar, though this initial strangeness has been less common in cultural studies than in anthropology or geography. Cultural studies has most often focused on modern urban ways of life, turning a defamiliarizing gaze on contemporary cultural forms and practices, especially aspects of mass culture. Its researchers have appeared as observer-participants in contemporary cultural practices – much less often as collectors of memories and folk forms in the manner of folklorists or ethnologists.

'Ethnography' most commonly indicates a method where group life is observed and perhaps entered into for the purpose of study. For Clifford Geertz, it is 'the representation of one sort of life in the categories of another' (1988:144). Confusingly, it is also used more broadly (as in cultural studies) to indicate any method that involves talking to people. We prefer the term 'meetings' here because it avoids this elision with more specialized anthropological meanings, while incorporating all kinds of face-to-face encounters, including thematic interviews and focus groups, and the longer, less structured conversations that are a feature of oral and life history.

Ethnography and Auto/biography

Within our own approach to method, ethnography, fieldwork and meetings in general are rethought in relation to auto/biography. This follows from our stress on self–other relations in research, in both their hermeneutic and feminist versions. Ethnography, which is a study of the other, also always involves awareness of the role of the self. Auto/biography, which is the critical, self-reflexive study of the self, always involves awareness of relations with others. In fact, all the 'eth-term' methods or disciplines have recently become alive, sometimes in disorientating ways, to this deeply relational nature of representation and research. As Alan Jabbour argues in the context of US folklore studies:

> Most of us who have worked in the field have had searing experience of this us vs them dilemma. Is it ourselves we are studying? Is it somebody else? Is it the interrelationship between the two that we are studying? . . . That powerful growing together of us and other seems to me typical of folklore past and present, and I think it will remain typical of folklore in the future. (1983: 242–44, quoted in Bendix, 1997: 219)

If we face this confusion squarely, not just as an incidental byproduct or difficulty of method, we are forced to recognize that there is a continuum of methods running from full-scale autobiography, via individual or group memory work with its production of written fragments, to oral history, life history, biography, other interview-based methods and to ethnography and ethnology in their classic senses. We call this 'the auto/ethno continuum'. This parallels the coinage of the term 'autoethnography' by others to describe fused or combined forms of writing in academic, fictional and crossover genres.

From the point of view adopted in this book, this auto/ethno continuum is a range of strategies for handling the I–thou relationships of dialogue that are fundamental to all research. These strategies are often used in combination and, as 'autoethnography' suggests, may even be fused to make something rather new. Thus, in her interviews with women scholars who worked on soap opera, Charlotte Brunsdon puzzles over the question of whether her interviews are autobiography or ethnography. On the one hand, the interviews (conducted with friends and colleagues with common enthusiasms) are elicited autobiographies or passages of intellectual life history, but, on the other, Brunsdon herself analyses the interviews rather in the manner of an ethnographer. To make matters even more complicated, the interviews are often about both the researchers' own involvements in soap opera and the ethnography of the audience. They therefore 'hover between autobiographical and ethnographic modes' (2000: 85). We want to argue that, in cultural studies, this in-betweenness is, and should be, very common.

There is another twist in this redescription. The auto/ethno continuum, even when it focuses on persons, does not always involve face-to-face relationships with a living person (although mostly we assume it does in what follows). It is difficult to draw a clear line between interview-based life history, for example, and archive-based biography. The latter may involve a very intense engagement with the life of the subject, even though it is always mediated by the archive or third-person testimony. Because historians and biographers (especially of the famous) may have access to diaries, writings and private letters and the subject may appear from many points of view, great insight may be gained into individuals and their worlds. As biographies may also be collective, the distinction between this and group ethnography starts to erode. This is why, in our preliminary mapping of methods on the circuit of cultural research at the end of Chapter 2, we placed ethnography, auto/biography and social history quite close together.

Ethnography as distinctive, indispensable, but limited

The chapters that follow complete our discussion of the range of methods in cultural studies, but they also fill out further our general arguments about method. Like all methods, the auto/ethno continuum has affinities with particular theoretical paradigms and constructs the cultural in a particular way. It enables some kinds of productive (and direct) questioning, but also disables other kinds of enquiry. In very general terms, such approaches arose initially from a conception of social relations in which individuals and social groups (rather than language or discourses, for instance) were seen as the productive authors of meaning, sense and self-identity. In cultural studies, influences from phenomenological sociologies and humanist Marxisms were especially important. As we have seen, these frameworks and practices of research have had to face the challenge of various critiques, including structuralism and poststructuralism, as well as the cumulative pressures of different political claims. This has revealed limits, complexities and complicities.

Our own argument is that methods focusing on the lives of individuals and social groups allow distinctive entries into cultural circuits and remain indispensable in cultural studies. However, like disciplines organized around the textual, they require combination – combination that also involves recasting. Sustained ethnographic fieldwork, in fact, is rare in cultural studies and all the methods within the cluster are also associated with other transdisciplinary combinations. Auto/biography, for example, can also be associated with narratology and linguistics, discursive psychology, qualitative sociology and historical and historical-literary studies. Ethnography – especially if we add the ethnological traditions – not only touches on this first cluster, but also extends to folklore studies, sociology, anthropology and certain kinds of anthropological or ethnographic history-writing. Sometimes these affinities have been actualized in the transdisciplinary dialogues, but there are also silences across disciplines, even where similar topics are discussed (Henkes and Johnson, 2002). There are separations between literary biography and sociologically-orientated auto/biography, for instance, between folklore studies and cultural studies and between anthropological and cultural-studies versions of ethnography, despite the shared interests in such issues as authenticity and the fictional or metaphorical character of ethnographic writing (compare Clifford and Marcus, 1986, and Willis, 2000). One of our aims in the chapters that follow is to try to broach some of these silences and stimulate further dialogues.

Plan of Part IV

Chapter 12 focuses on the indispensability in cultural studies of researching with people and groups. The most distinctive feature of our approach to such meetings is to insist on the interconnections between auto/biography and ethnography. While not attempting a full guide to practice in so varied an area, we offer, as elsewhere in this book, checklists of questions and issues that may be of help in the different moments of practice. We end the chapter by noting some limits of the combination of 'auto' and 'ethno' methods and the need for larger methodological combinations.

In Chapter 13, we consider the processes of analysis that follow the transcription of interviews, review of research diaries and notes or writing of memory work fragments. Here again, we argue for methods of analysis that are not only plural or multiperspectival but combined. In particular, we argue for a triple reading of auto/ethno sources. We review the moments of analytical work in the form of a checklist and suggest some further implications of this cluster of methods for our arguments regarding method more generally.

In Chapter 14, we draw many of our arguments together by considering two related agendas in cultural studies – the study of the audience and the study of identity or subjectivity as key sites of methodological combination. The latter concerns also bring into play another set of interdisciplinary relationships – that between cultural studies and psychology and psychoanalysis. Chapter 14 is also the place where the importance of the self as a resource in cultural enquiry can be returned to – one last time.

Finally, the conclusion that follows Part IV is an invitation to further dialogue.

12 Researching others: from auto/biography to ethnography

The auto/ethno continuum as a process 206
The auto/ethno continuum as a range of methods 208
The indispensability of meetings in cultural research 209
Pathways in ethnographic and auto/biographical research: two checklists 216
Checklist 1: Interviews 217
Checklist 2: Memory work 220
Conclusion and some limits of the auto/ethno continuum 222

In this chapter, we discuss methods in which our sources are people we encounter directly in live situations. Of course, there is always a textual, readable dimension in such methods (as discussed in Chapter 13) but, in face-to-face situations, researchers and researched can make mutual adjustments to each others' questions, answers, bodily performance and gestures. These forms of participation and dialogue, in which the other can be more active, extend the possibilities of research in two important ways. First, they give access to embodied meanings, the combination of meaning-making with other material practices and oral forms of everyday language use – symbolic, metaphorical or poetic. These are often unrepresented in more public circuits or else only represented in diminished ways. Such methods are especially valuable for studying 'material culture' – meaning-making, that is, via the use of objects. All sorts of objects-in-use, including clothes and domestic appliances, and their social and symbolic functions have been analysed in the context of consumer cultures and social identity (see also Chapter 10). A second feature of what we might term 'person research' is that political and ethical issues are brought out particularly clearly. As the possibilities for fuller dialogue are realized, personal responsibilities are sharpened. We might feel responsible to a dead novelist or theorist for reading their work with care, but we will not have to face this person tomorrow. It is not surprising, then, that ethnographic literature is especially sensitive to these issues.

In this chapter we explore these particular features of person research, but also how they relate to our continuing arguments about method. First, we reconceptualize auto/biography and ethnography as two poles of a continuum of methods that chart the movement from self to other in research. Second, we argue for the indispensability of these methods, elaborating the reasons sketched above. Third, we offer some pathways into ethnographic and auto/biographical research in the form of a checklist of stages or moments. Finally, we return to the topic of combining methods, the key theme of Chapter 14.

The auto/ethno continuum as a process

What we are calling the auto/ethno continuum is more than a package of methods – it describes an aspect of the *movement* of research. Ethnography depends on auto/biography and vice versa. In what follows, we describe this movement as it presents itself to the self-reflexive researcher and consider how to use the resources offered by the continuum in a systematic way.

When we start out on a project of cultural research, our first resource is our own lived relationship with our topic area. Where we choose to work on topics close to home ('close' can be meant in many very different ways), an explicit dialogue can begin between past experiences and new knowledge. This may involve recognizing experiences and selves that have been marginalized in the past by dominant definitions and our own strategies of defiance or defence. Researching such a topic may sometimes confirm or validate our previous experience, sometimes challenge and extend it. Charlotte Brunsdon's account of research on soap opera shows 'how complex are the positions from which the soap opera work emerged' (2000: 164), and how individually variable the interaction of personal experience, educational encounters and academic work can be. The women scholars she interviews were engaged in soap opera as regular viewers before they came to study it and its audiences more formally or critically. When Ien Ang, for example, read the letters from her correspondents about their responses to *Dallas*, 'none of the letters was quite surprising to me'. Instead, she was reassured by the personal recognition she found, because the responses confirmed her intuition about the programme (Ang, quoted in Brunsdon, 2000: 163). As Brunsdon argues, in recognizing that soap opera viewing involves both pleasure and displeasure, Ang 'extrapolates from her own experience in combination with what she learnt from other viewers' (164).

The value of self-reflection as a resource is not limited to the beginning of a project. As we encounter new situations in the process of research, our own fore-knowledge and horizons will be changed and challenged and this process will have to be 'digested' internally. Learning always has this aspect of personal rearrangement. In a retrospective consideration of her research for *Reading the Romance* (discussed in Chapter 9), Janice Radway presents it as a process of 'my own growing politicization', which owed much to 'the romance readers' eloquence about their own lives' (1997: 66). The reconfiguration of the self is both an effect of research and, if reflected on, a continuing resource within it. Moreover, as both Ang's and Radway's accounts suggest, and we shall see in more detail, dialoguing with others is integral to self-reflection in some way.

Another way in which to see this process is to view research as constructing relationships between our present and future selves and our past selves – as children, for instance – a process that involves a whole politics of remembering (and forgetting). Perhaps it is always true that dramatic personal change both prompts and requires cultural reflection. There are certainly examples within the history of British cultural studies of authors entering into a risky or troubling topic via such an autobiographical route. Class mobility, for example, may involve particularly dramatic changes within one or two generations that have a direct bearing on our own cultural histories. The collection *Cultural Studies and the Working Class* (Munt, 2000) contains several contributions that use auto/biography or discuss it as a strategy to explore this experience (see Steedman, 1986; Walkerdine, 1990). Similarly, there are now large and growing bodies of literature across many genres that refer to or draw on personal experiences of migration, cultural 'translation' or ethnic ambivalence (Brah, 1996; Brah and Coombes, 2000). Other kinds of past–present negotiations, around a sense of relative privilege, in class, ethnic or gender terms, are rarer, but have played a more or less explicit role in cultural research and writing (see, for example, Johnson, 1997; Ware, 1992).

Yet, although our cultural experiences may be intense, they remain partial, so that reaching out to others' worlds is always also necessary. Indeed, such worlds will impinge, often forcibly, on our own. Research becomes a way of *extending* our horizon even when a cultural practice is very close to us. Being a fan or a practitioner of a particular kind of music or dance and remembering particular episodes of collective enjoyment or exclusion, for instance, will itself yield many clues to the nature of such fascinations and pleasures. Our experience, systematically recollected and represented, can be a primary source, but it will still be necessary to check out these insights with new others who are similarly or differently placed to ourselves. As feminist work on women's genres such as Brunsdon's and Ang's has shown, researching others who are close to us in social experience can both reassure and surprise.

Although relations of difference and power are also present in self-reflection, such relations become more clearly those of self and other as we move towards the ethnographic pole. There is a clearer division, in terms of people and actual bodies, between the researcher and the researched. Research itself becomes an intersubjective process connected to pre-existing social relationships and forms of power. All the issues of objectification, 'othering' or the instrumental use of others for our own purposes now arise in ways that are hard to evade.

The nature of relationships in research may be clarified by returning to the philosophy of hermeneutics in which questions of self and other loom so large. In his major discussion of self and identity, *Oneself as Another* (1992), Paul Ricoeur considers three possible approaches to the relationship of self and other: as a theory that stresses a reaching out by the self towards the other's reality and world (Husserl); as a theory that stresses the challenge of the other to the self's conscience or responsibility (Lévinas); and as a theory (his own) that stresses the *dialectical* relationship between the inward and outward movements. Although he is here primarily addressing questions of ethics rather than the closely entwined issue of 'understanding' that dominates Gadamer's hermeneutics, his arguments fit our own case of auto/biography and ethnography, too. Interpreting Husserl, Ricoeur argues that we recognize the reality of other people's bodies and worlds by means of analogy with our own. Analogy is not the same as comparison and it does not posit sameness or difference. Rather, it admits the other as '*my counterpart*, that is, someone who, *like* me, says "I"' (335, emphasis in original). Such relations, moreover, are mutual or two-way in the fullest sense:

> It is here that the analogical transfer from myself to the other intersects with the inverse movement of the other towards me. It intersects with the latter but does not abolish it. even if it does not presuppose it. (335)

It follows that adequate ethics must attend both to questions of self-care and calls to justice from others. Indeed, these two moments are integrally related, as his example of 'the promise' shows:

> Was not this intersecting dialectic of oneself and the other than self anticipated in the analysis of the promise? If another were not counting on me, would I be capable of keeping my word, of maintaining myself. (341)

Ricoeur's account deepens our understanding of the self–other relations of research and the movement between its 'auto' and 'ethno' moments. The move from auto/biography to ethnography is a specialized and, in some ways, heightened instance of a more general process: the analogical recognition of the equal reality of another's body, identity and cultural world. It is this 'analogical transfer' that founds ethnography morally in what Ricoeur would call 'an ontology of the self'. Ethnography is, in many ways, an attempt to fill in the gap or abstraction that the rather agnostic idea of an analogy suggests. The sense of self is, therefore, necessarily involved in understanding the other; ethnography presupposes auto/biography. Self-possession or self-knowledge and openness to other worlds are integrally related, just as developing a knowledge of self depends, in large part, on a willingness to attend to alterity or difference. This is not the end of the story, however, because, as Ricoeur argues, the 'other than self' is also to be reckoned with in this dialectic. 'Openness to the other' involves taking the impacts of another very concrete person who is making the same kind of analogical transfers. As Ricoeur makes clear, this is a reality imposed not only by thinking or imagination, but also by actions and practices, including, we might add, the practices of research. Ethnography may depend on auto/biography, but the auto/biography of the researcher also gets hitched up to the ethnographic process with results that must be uncertain.

The auto/ethno continuum as a range of methods

Given this complexity, it is not surprising that the auto/ethno continuum embraces a wide repertoire of methods, with quite subtle distinctions. These can be more or less tailored to our own forms of positionality and partiality (who we are), the process of questioning (what we want to know) and our relationships to our subjects (whom we wish to dialogue with or observe and the differences and similarities of our situations). The choice of method can make a significant difference to 'results'. We might list these methods as follows.

- **Auto/biography** studying our own life and others, writing a relatively extended account. May include use of documents, diaries and other methods.

- **Individual memory work** writing shorter pieces based on recollections of particular episodes and around a specific theme or question.
- **Group memory work** group discussion and analysis of (usually individually) written memory fragments on an agreed theme. This method is usually on a 'participative' basis (see below).
- **Video diary/diary** asking another to record their life on video or in another form (see writing, photography, tape, for example) for a set period and usually around particular themes.
- **Life history interviews** eliciting accounts, usually relatively informal and extended, from another about his or her life.
- **Oral history interviews** eliciting accounts, sometimes formal, sometimes informal, with an other who can be a source about past events (including cultural practices and forms).
- **Thematic interviews** discussions that are usually shorter, more in number and often more structured than oral histories, held with individuals or groups about particular themes of contemporary relevance.
- **Focus groups** discussion groups on a particular theme that the researcher may organize and usually participates in.
- **Biography** researching/writing the life of another person.
- **Collective biography** researching/writing the life of a group, network or circle.
- **Observation** observing and recording the life of a group, working of an institution and so on.
- **Participant observation** observing while participating in group activities.
- **Participative enquiry** a term in common academic use to indicate methods in which the researcher works with groups as co-researchers. Such research may be more or less directed towards action ('action research'), but always involves attempts to modify the relationships of researchers/researched.

We have included 'participative' (or participatory) enquiry in this list, though it is not really a 'method' but, rather, an *issue* that arises in all research. Participatory or equalizing strategies – which attempt to redistribute power in the research process – can be built into *all* the methods listed above and may take many forms. Including the subjects of research in what are usually taken to be the 'core activities' of the researcher is only one way of countering the objectification, or 'othering', or unequal exchanges that occur while researching.

The indispensability of meetings in cultural research

Meetings – in the ways that we have defined them – are as essential in cultural research as is the careful reading of texts. Indeed, these two methodological clusters – which are so often polemically opposed as 'social' versus 'textual' – cannot, in the end, be so clearly distinguished. As hermeneutic frameworks suggest, careful textual practice is also an encounter with an other's world, while grasping another's world always involves reading. Person research is important, however, for a number of particular reasons.

First, there are some aspects of cultural processes that cannot be grasped in any other way. We can call these *ontological* reasons for person research. They include:

- the importance of a 'concrete' moment in cultural analysis
- the need to use the full sensuous range in grasping cultural activity, which itself is multisensual and embodied
- the irreducibility of issues of agency.

Second, the necessity of meetings is related to questions of social difference and power. These are *political* reasons for person research – in the larger sense of the politics of culture. They include:

- the need to grasp discrepancies in the ways in which different social groups relate to public knowledge and develop distinctive forms of cultural production
- the need for researchers themselves to work out their relation to these differences in the ways they research and write.

Third, there is what we may term the *educational* value of meetings. Meetings *may* have educational value for those who are researched, but we are thinking here of the educational value for researchers themselves. This includes:

- the fuller realization and understanding of dialogue, reflexivity and accountability as features of method
- the sharpening of the encounter with the issues of power and ethics, which are involved in all research.

We discuss below each of these clusters of reasons in turn.

Ontological reasonings: the concrete, the sensuous and agency

Methods in the ethno/auto range enable us to explore the processes of meaning-making, including the creation of social identities in the context of other practices, most generally of 'living'. They are a prime route into 'lived culture'. As we have argued, the analysis of publicly available texts depends on their temporary removal from the contexts of production and social use, though fuller analysis may attempt to repair these divisions. Methods of the auto/ethno range seek to grasp the cultural and social logics of a life, group, place or site or particular interaction. Like much historical and geographical work, they are concerned with 'the concrete' – in the sense of the sum or product of many different intersecting processes.

'Way of life' – a founding category in cultural studies – is an attempt to express these intersections. It includes the meaning-making agency of a social group or an individual, its self-production. It also includes the cultural forms – discourses, narratives, styles, values – by which a group makes itself culturally, including its ethical preferences. It includes the group's work around self and others – its psycho-social identifications, disidentifications, aspirations and fantasies. 'Way of life' also includes the means of subsistence, the world of objects and the everyday practices that reproduce material life. As 'life' also suggests, way of life includes the 'footprints' made on the Earth and biosphere by particular ways of living – modern consumerism, for instance. Because it *is* only one of many possible ways after all, 'way of life' offers such patterns up for complex evaluation, especially in their relations to other ways, both actual and imagined.

So, methods that involve meetings start by being open to the many-levelled chaos of a way of living and try to discern its patterns or logic. They tease out or 'unpack' cultural practices and their contextualized meanings. They are especially important in relation to what Paul Willis – perhaps the most consistent advocate of an ethnographic version of cultural studies – calls 'informal traditions of meaning making':

> They are often sedimented in their own ways, long-running and semi-ritualized, so producing their own long durees and slow-motion logics with respect to how quickly they can change and react to changed circumstances. The motives, meanings and lived dynamics of everyday culture are also manifold and organized for different questions and situation, with time scale enforced by different immediacies: getting to work, holding a family together, 'getting a life' through and on top of it all. All these are unconsciously, chaotically, and eccentrically organized with reference to each other, not rationally spoken so requiring further interpretation. (2000: xii)

This is not to say that no abstractions are made in ethnographic description. Rather, particular *forms* of thinking are involved. It is possible to make a 'thin' abstraction from ethnographic or auto/biographical representations, by chasing a narrow theme or foregrounding a particular form – narrative, for instance – and this is perfectly legitimate and can be powerful. Linguistic analysis of conversations or stories is a case in point. It is a virtue of these methods, however, that description and analysis can be 'thicker' than this, allowing us to disassemble the 'chaotic abstractions' into their many 'determinations'. Willis writes of 'throwing concepts at things'. A better metaphor, perhaps, is of pulling particular threads from a dense weave in order to understand what the pattern is.

The rich texture includes, as Willis argues, the relation to objects, the sensuous nature of these relations, and popular forms of art, creativity or agency. It is only when we keep cultural practices in their context that we can gauge the kinds of agency involved in relation to actual outcomes.

Willis' *Learning to Labour* (1977) develops a particularly complex argument about the agency of a group of working-class 'lads' in the industrial midlands of the UK. The lads' culture centred on a non-conformist and anti-academic relationship to school, an ethic of enjoyment and 'resistance' and a distinctive appropriation of working-class forms of masculinity. Willis argues that the lads' strategies combined both a cultural preparation for survival in the rough relations of manual labour and a foreclosure around other possibilities and aspirations. They produced a real knowledge certainly, but it was a knowledge of how things *are* rather than of how they *might* be or might *come* to be. This is, perhaps, the characteristic limit of a 'common sense', however resistant, that cannot place itself within a larger geography or history – in this case, as Willis later notes, the impact of a global economy on a region, decline of manufacturing industry and cultural feminization of much working-class work (Willis, 2000: 85–105).

Power, access and subordinated knowledge

The concrete, sensuous, popular and a certain kind of working-classness are, in Willis' thinking, closely related. It is by means of the manipulation of the expressive possibilities and the use value of objects and via 'the five-sensed . . . living cultural body' that subordinated groups create their own worlds, both instrumentally and symbolically. In Willis' version, the need for ethnographic practice is related to the limits of public texts that stay within the terms of formal language. He argues that working-class and perhaps other subordinated cultural practices signify in other than explicit linguistically based ways (though they involve language). This may even be a form of defence against 'linguistically borne ideological meanings':

> Generally, oppressed or subordinate groups are more likely than other groups to find meaning in hidden, unexplored or newly stressed 'objective possibilities', or meaning in new, as yet uncolonized or meaning-sedimented items, or meaning in jarring, dynamic use-functions, interrupting the cultural stillness of received forms. (2000: 26)

The heavily metaphorical language is deliberate, part of a struggle to translate 'sedimented' meanings into more articulated written forms that can be consumed by an academic readership. In terms of our own argument, Willis is insisting that there are social differences of linguistic usage and symbolic action that mean much popular expression – especially creativity – is marginalized or devalued, particularly within the public spheres where middle-class criteria tend to dominate, as in discourses around taste or art. In *Common Culture* (1990) he argues for a whole alternative 'grounded aesthetic', based in popular and especially youthful use of cultural commodities, a reception that is always a production.

Though the terms and outcomes of the struggle are rather different, it is perhaps for similar reasons that many authors from a working-class background and/or loyalty have chosen to write cultural studies in an auto/biographical form, handling the translations and transitions from embedded everyday meaning to academic language even more directly. This adds further dimensions to the argument for methods in the auto/ethno range. Autobiography and ethnography are among the few available ways to gain fresh access to popular symbolic practices and two of the best ways to represent them in something of their complexity. This complexity is formal, as we have seen, but it is also a matter of internal differences, hierarchies and exclusions. Much recent work on youth, for example, insists that consumption is also an important way in which *distinctions* are made and lived, as in those within club or music culture (see, for example, Thornton, 1995). Complexity, it seems, has to be constantly reclaimed and re-established against the pressures of dominant beliefs, whether those are the romanticization of cultural authenticity or the fear of mass deception.

Educating the researcher

Reflexivity and power

Engagement with the complexity of the popular is not, however, always accompanied by reflexivity about the relationships of meetings themselves. A key strand of criticism of the early subcultures work, including *Learning to Labour* itself, combined feminist criticism of the unthinking emphasis on masculinity in the studies and an emergent critique of the method used as insufficiently self-reflexive while being only clandestinely autobiographical (see, for example, Angela McRobbie, 1991; Walkerdine, 1990: especially 196).

Being conscious of the power relations within research is a condition for developing countervailing practices. These can, in turn, extend what can be told or heard. Indeed, the cultural studies tradition is ripe for some close examination in this regard. As Nick Couldry points out, the bias towards studies of youth cultures and the insistence on researching the contemporary in much cultural research has effectively managed to suggest that 'the experiences of the old are just not worth studying' (2000: 59). In the context of increasingly globalized and pervasive forms of contemporary youth cultures, together with the celebratory emphasis on youth as a defining moment in life, cultural studies' focus begins to look rather less democratic than we might hope. That is why critical self-reflection at the level of disciplinary or epistemological pressures is also important.

Power flows not only via the ways in which knowledge is constructed and evaluated, but also via the organization of research. It flows via the relations between researcher and researched, between the researcher and the academic community, within the researched group itself and, in bigger projects, within a hierarchy of researchers. Researchers usually retain the power to define the topic, choose and employ research methods and analyse, write and publish. Research has historically been the purview of those who are already relatively powerful, either due to their gender, perceived ability, class, age or their position within global inequities. It also offers a way of *becoming* powerful, taking on social or cultural capital (L.T. Smith, 1999) or intervening in a problem of politics, ethics or personal commitment. Research can, however, also be a way in which those with power, especially institutional power, manage the knowledge process, resisting their own objectification by foreclosing research on their own group, while encouraging inspection of subordinated others. Here, we focus on the direct relations of researchers and researched because it is these that are highlighted in ethnographic practices.

Retrospective accounts of research projects can be a helpful way of reflecting on past practice from a distance. The narrative researcher Catherine Riessman reanalysed her interactions with a working-class woman, 'Tessa', whom she had originally interviewed in 1990 (see Rosaldo, 1989). In her first account, Riessman presented Tessa primarily as a heroic survivor of marital brutality and rape. Yet, this interpretation was produced partly as a result of her own interventions in the interviews as they took place and partly by Riessman 'looking away', as she puts it, from some of the material involved, including parts of the transcript and autobiographical writings and drawings that Tessa showed her.

Riessman makes sense of her first interpretation in terms of her own biography, her similarities to and differences from Tessa, including the experience of divorce, as well as the historical circumstances of the project, conducted at a time when narratives of rape were becoming tellable, perhaps for the first time, but only in terms of victimization. Tessa appeared, in Riessman's words, 'as an exemplar of an analytic category' (2002: 203). Our own reading of the episode would lay weight on the different relations of the two women to academic knowledge and legitimation: Riessman as a sociologist constructing 'a scholarly text for professional colleagues' (200); Tessa as a student for one year at a community college with a 'talent for art and for writing' who had 'written through times of hardship' (201–2). Subsequent debates around narrative and method – especially the stress on the strategic choices made by narrators in relation to the addressee and the possibility of multiple tellings and readings of identity – have allowed a retelling of Tessa's story. However, important in both the telling and retelling are the power discrepancies of the exchange, affecting both what Tessa could say and Riessman could hear. The initial laying aside of Tessa's auto/biographical offerings is a striking example of how methodological conventions can police the forms of self-representations that are acceptable from the researched. As Riessman puts it, looking to the future, 'doing justice, in the final analysis, requires more than one voice' (210).

It is not the case, however, that the researcher is always already in a more powerful or privileged position than the researched, so strategies for qualifying the power of researchers may not always be appropriate. It is difficult to win access to people in high places. To try to empower a powerful speaker by allowing them to determine the interview agenda may also be to ensure that your questions remain unanswered and the lived contradictions are tucked away. The crux is not how to give a voice (as though this could ever be 'given'), but how to punctuate a smooth and practised self-presentation so as to avoid becoming either complicit or visibly angry, thereby terminating the interview! Such situations should be distinguished from the commoner feeling of disempowerment that researchers feel when encountering unfamiliar situations that can lead to excessive dependence on the researched. As interpersonal relations are built and our familiarity increases, researchers will often regain the upper hand. However, in all circumstances, *acknowledging* the power dynamics of research – including the part played by our own emotions and fantasies – is a condition for both using these experiences productively and changing the relationships. This may mean experimenting with the sharing of power by adopting more participatory methods.

Dialogue as participation

An explicit ethics of participation should be embedded in ethnographic research because all ethnography involves some participation by those whom we study. Research that is more fully participatory will aim to use the research process itself to empower those who are being researched. Strategies include researching a problem identified by the researched as significant, involving the researched in core activities of design, researching and writing and disseminating findings back to the researched group for comment and action. Participatory approaches, though always contradictory, help to challenge power relations during the research process and can offer some form of (qualified) enfranchizement once it is over.

While it is difficult to use fully participatory methods in a thesis or dissertation because of the individualization built into academic assessment, it *is* possible to take significant steps towards more participation in research. For example, good ethnographic research requires research questions to be sequentially adjusted as the project evolves, in order to take on board the viewpoints of participants. Cultural research in particular must take account of the complexity, layering and contradictoriness of all lived cultural forms. This entails the careful hearing of extended narratives and a relatively intensive participation in the social world of the researched. Relatively unstructured and open-ended methods are thus favoured such as semi-structured interviews, life histories, group auto/biography and focus group discussions, as well as, where possible, participant observation. Apart from some initial fact-finding, questions are rarely standardized in such interviews and some questions should always be open-ended to allow for the specificity of each interaction. This means that interviewees can control the agenda at some points, while the researcher may reclaim control at others. Ceding control temporarily in this way allows the interviewee's responses to shift the focus of the research, identifying new issues or reconfiguring existing ones.

Yet, this is some way from completely sharing the researcher's power in a productive, educative relationship between intellectuals and popular social groups. For Gramsci, such 'organicity' had primarily to do with 'the source of the problems which it [an intellectual movement] sets out to study and resolve' (1971: 330). In our own terms, it depends where the agenda of research come from: an academic discipline or, more organically, the life of a social group.

What, then, are the organizational forms that might secure the active participation, not only of the researched in the research, but also of the researcher in the world of the researched? Gramsci's answer was a political one – the formation of a political 'party' in the loosest sense, which might mean a social movement or even a newspaper. Although organic relations in research are clearly hard to secure from an academic base, researchers can take the initiative in setting up support groups from within the constituencies they are researching. Such groups may confine themselves to improving access and feedback, but they may also break through the knowledge barriers by becoming involved in the research activity itself. One way to enable this is by means of group memory work or a collective auto/biography project – a method used in adult and further education, community history groups, worker-writer circles, women's groups and men's groups, as well as in university departments of cultural studies (Clare and Johnson, 2000; Morley and Worpole, 1982). Indeed, because of its possibilities for participation, we have chosen memory work as an exemplary pathway later in this chapter.

Accountabilities

We have already posed the general question: 'To whom and in what ways are we accountable as researchers?' This question is sharpened in ethnographic work not only because of the impulse to democratize research and make space for marginalized voices but also because ethnographic practice shows up contradictions in different accountabilities 'on the ground'. We have to reckon with the usual demands linked to funding and disciplinary prestige, but the basic ethnographic ethic of 'doing justice' to our subjects is also made more complicated.

In a study of domestic workers in India originally developed for a doctoral dissertation, the question of accountability was posed very sharply (Raghuram, 1993). First of all, it was difficult to translate the idea and usefulness of a thesis into a form of words that would have some meaning in the lives of the domestic workers. Instead the author represented the work as 'a book'. Even this raised ethical dilemmas. Did such a representation involve a degree of deception? Those workers who had some interest in the topic linked the idea of 'research' to policy changes that would directly improve their lives, yet this could not be delivered by a thesis (or even 'a book') alone. During the research itself, a property dealer who employed the domestic workers was also interviewed. As the meeting progressed, the dealer, on advice from his colleagues, said that the researcher would only be allowed to proceed if assurance could be given that he first vetted everything that was written. Although some assurances *were* given, the interviews were conducted without letting him know, thus putting at risk both the researcher and the workers, who were already being abused and threatened.

Would it have been better to have agreed to have the writing vetted or was the more ethical course the one adopted – to undertake the research covertly and report the findings? If accountability is coupled with the desire to challenge exploitative power relations we are faced with difficult – but necessary – decisions such as this. In these situations an even-handed openness towards all participants may neither be possible nor desirable.

Pathways in ethnographic and auto/biographical research: two checklists

So far, we have argued for the indispensability of person research in cultural study for ontological, political and educational reasons – the latter associated with the general criteria of method that we developed in Chapter 3 – reflexivity, dialogue and social accountability. We now want to further concretize some of the issues by suggesting a sequence of research acts and decisions in two types of research, chosen for their illustrative value: the conduct of a set of interviews and the organization of a memory work group.

We start by positing a moment when there is an open choice of methods from the whole auto/ethno range – A: Choosing methods in Checklist 1, below. Thereafter, we follow a route on the ethno side of the continuum – Moments B–D – by imagining a project that involves both observation and interviews. This is followed by a further list – B1–D1 – based on the choice of a memory work project. Our aim throughout is to pose questions for reflection, suggesting *procedures* rather than *answers*.

Checklist 1: Interviews

A: Choosing methods

This moment continues the work of research design (see Chapter 4), but under the more immediate demands of practice.

1: Auto/biographical resources

What do I know about my topic from my personal experience? What research possibilities are offered by my ordinary participation in the world, such as jobs – past and present – family, friends, community and religious links, education, leisure activities? How far might these provide contacts to others? What are the limits of my world, my circles? How do these structure my fore-knowledge in, for example, class, ethnic or generational terms? Would a more extended auto/biographical project be useful? (See individual memory work at B1 below).

2: Public sources

How far can the limits be extended via publicly available sources? What can they show and hide? What are their forms of partiality/ideology? If I am interested in a group, what public forms do *they* use?

3: Profiling person research

Who do I need to talk to, where and when? Are there privileged points of view in relation to my topic that are likely to produce strong insights? If I am interested in a group, would the perspective of other groups be interesting? What power relations exist within or between such groups and how am I likely to be implicated within them?

4: Selecting and combining methods

Do I seek to learn about the everyday practices of a group or an institutional site or the shared 'common sense' or 'public' of a group or individual subjectivities and personal contradictions? The first might point to forms of (more or less participant) observation, the second to group discussions and the third to individual interviews.

5: Practicalities

Person research is time-consuming and, with travel, can be costly. It takes time to become familiar with a place, make contacts, clear permissions, organize meetings and so on.

How long do I have? Does the research design need to be scaled down?

What political and ethical issues does ethnographic entry raise? What are the implications for my own health and safety? (Most academic institutions will have procedures alerting researchers to these aspects in advance).

B: Setting up meetings

Our project involves both observation and interviews. We have chosen the locations and the profiles of people to meet.

1: Contacts and permissions

Do I need permissions from an institution or is individual agreement enough? What can I offer people or institutions – for example, in terms of participation?

Seeking permissions usually means negotiating terms of entry and the subsequent use of material – such as the anonymity of people and places, the right of subjects to review transcripts and so on. Bear in mind power relations here, but persevere!

If permissions are informal only, how will I seek acceptance? How will I present myself? Usually, there are pre-existing identifications here that will affect how we are positioned, so adults in a school are 'teachers' or 'assistants', adults in a youth club are 'youth workers' and so on. Some contexts may be especially difficult, such as all-male contexts for women. How will this affect the terms of observation and conversation?

2: Questions

Questions can be given in advance to interviewees or used only to guide the interviewer.

How can I adjust my general research questions to the particular addressee and context, make them concrete in this sense? How do I build in some open-ended questions and relatively goalless observation to gather participants' agendas? Do I also need more precise questions to focus my enquiry?

C: Conducting dialogues

This is the most context-specific moment in researching, so best practice will differ, but a few points or dilemmas may fit most cases.

1: Piloting

It is often useful to try out questions (on friends or acquaintances, perhaps, with relevant knowledge).

What mistakes have I made? What can I learn from them? Have I time for more elaborate pilots. If not, where shall I start?

2: Sequencing

A common sequence is general observation or hanging around, group discussion, then individual interviews. This allows familiarization with the milieu and its social relations and the choice of groups and individuals for more intense interaction.

How am I disturbing the situation? Do I disturb it more or less? What can I learn from reactions to my presence?

3: Together or apart?

How does each group see the other? To find out, should I interact with groups together or apart or both in turn?

4: Losing control and time for reflection

All person research risks losing control of the process for the reasons we explored above. Risking this and learning from it is part of the method. Reflection and rest between interviews or rounds of observation is essential to recognize and digest surprises and refine strategies and questions.

5: Reflecting with others

Experienced advice and support is essential – if only via e-mail. How can I formulate my problems and confusions for a supervisor?

6: Questions for reflection during research

How am I affecting the situation of the researched? How do they see me? How does this affect what they say or do? What are my feelings about them? To what does this relate in my own biography? When am I learning most and why? What kind of power do I wield in this situation and over whom? Where am I subject to power? How can I change strategies to get better material or change a situation?

D: Recording as text

Analysis – the next stage – depends on the adequacy of records and recall.

How am I constructing by own future ethnographic resources? Is my every decoding (witnessing, reading) another encoding (noting, writing)?

1. Choice of technologies

Audio-recording (for interviews) plus field notes and diaries (for observations) are the technologies of choice for most ethnographers.

How are my chosen technologies affecting the situation? What are their culturally familiar uses (such as family videos)? Does a running tape recorder draw less attention to me as recorder than writing notes?

2: Dairies and notes

These are essential and may best be compiled from memory as soon as possible after the events they record.

Am I recording feelings (my own and evidence of others') as well as doings and sayings? Am I covering what cannot be heard on tape?

3: Transcription

Transcription is treated here as a first step in analysis (see Chapter 13).

Checklist 2: Memory work

B1: Constituting a memory work group or circle

Memory work can be practised in a face-to-face group or organized via a looser circle of people who do not meet each other. It can also be done by the researcher alone.

1: Profiling a group

Who do I want to include in the group/circle and how should they be chosen? What are the different points of view/social positions/power relations? Am I trying to represent a community or social group, including its internal differences?

2: Contacting members

How far can I use existing contacts – friends and acquaintances, friends of friends, fellow students, relatives, members of a community group or circle? What are the effects of this in terms of social horizons and power relations? Are there places where groups might be found or formed: study or book groups, adult or further education classes, circles around parenting childcare and so on? What are the limits of this? Are there media in which I can advertise for members? What can I offer? What is the nature of the commitment being asked for?

C1: Conducting memory work

1: Deciding where to meet

Where would be the most appropriate place to meet, in terms of facilitating the interaction?

2: Negotiating ground rules

These should cover the use and possession of material and issues of confidentiality and anonymity.

Am I being clear about group purposes – for example when is a supportive study group not a therapy group nor a literary-critical circle?

3: Explaining procedures

It is important to go through procedures involved in advance so people know what to expect and can negotiate exit and conditions. It should be stressed that writers can, to some extent, control the risks they take by their choice of theme or episode.

Am I making the procedure explicit? Do they all agree?

4: Negotiating a theme

What themes bear on my research and the interests of group members? (Themes may be widely or narrowly drawn to take on the interests of the group or pursue a research argument.)

How does the chosen theme position members of the group differently? Are people being excluded? Is there an implicit social agenda? Is everyone heterosexual in this group? Is everyone vocally participating in choosing themes?

5: Choosing an episode

Each participant chooses an episode from their own life that relates to the theme with a real effort to remember.

6: Rules for writing about it

The ideal piece is short – not more than two handwritten A4 pages and not taking longer than 30 minutes to write, without editing or redrafting. The method works best if details and feelings do not disappear under analysis.

Are group members representing feelings and episodic details?
Are you giving time for remembering?

7: Reading and discussing stories

The method works best if pieces are written on the spot, read out loud and discussed, circulating them as text afterwards. Discussion is essential – it shades into analysis – because it may reframe a story in relation to others' experiences.

Am I (and the group) taking account of emotional dynamics, power relationships within the group and different skills and aptitudes in writing, remembering and valuing a life?

It may be best if the authors frame their stories first before discussion, providing contexts and so on.

D1: Recording and text

1: Recording

Written stories can be circulated and collected. Discussions or oral accounts can be taped or minutes written up.

2: Ownership, use and the researcher's role

The researcher must also be a participant, writing down stories and having them discussed. The researcher may facilitate, depending on group skills. The process will take on its own dynamic. It may push towards a more participatory project. It may lead to conflict.

How can we negotiate different uses of the material, both for thesis and the group or community?

Even if the researcher/ thesis writer does not formally use the materials, such group work can be a major support and learning experience. It provides material for a study in cultural self-narration and identity construction and many other themes. It provides object lessons in the relations of self to other in research. Yet, it also raises an interesting question: when we discuss our own and others' auto/biographical writings in a group of participants are we doing ethnography or auto/biography?

Conclusion and some limits of the auto/ethno continuum

We have argued that auto/biography and ethnography, in different combinations, are essential in cultural studies. They give access to cultural phenomena that are not visible in public texts. They pose, with a particular sharpness and intimacy, issues of difference and power. They sharpen the education of the researcher in these realities, which aids a fully reflexive practice –

examples of which, in the shape of interviews and memory work, we have sketched in outline.

Together and apart, however, these methods have their limits. Even a (self-)critical auto/biography is in danger of being read as a unique life or utterly typical of a place, time or social collectivity. Ethnographies, meanwhile, powerfully pressure both author and the reader towards a work of identity in which the other is used to define the self, but the self is hidden. In ethnographies that are written across major differences of power (such as those of gender, class or ethnicity), the recorded group can come to carry the burden of representation as 'out of the ordinary', just as in general discourse women have so often been 'the sex', working-class people have been the bearers of class and 'race' has meant 'black'. Putting the researcher into the picture is an important counterpoint to this, though it also matters how the researcher appears. Whatever the author's social positionalities, his or her presence in the text will be a significant intervention. Perhaps this is why ethnography plus auto/biography, or memory work plus socio-historical contextualization are such common combinations in cultural studies and adjacent approaches (see, for example, Redman and Mac An Ghaill, 1997; Steedman, 1986; Walkerdine, 1990; Ware, 1992).

Yet, both methods attend especially to meanings that seem to arise from local experiences. There is an historical, though not a necessary association, between these representational practices and 'a local habitation' – a circumscribed place or home, wherever it may be (Hoggart, 1988). Post-colonial genres of all kinds and what John Tomlinson calls the 'complex connectivity' of late modernity (1999), are breaking this association down. However, both the strength and weakness of research that is focused on people or lives is that it is limited in spatial, temporal and social terms. Even accounts of migrancy or nomad lives involve selected trajectories and routes. Yet, there is much that bears on the life of an individual or group or is of more general concern that does not appear in immediate record or remembrance. As these methods are stretched to make public and global connections, they must needs borrow from other traditions – media studies, political economy or the larger, longer, history of cultural formations.

The importance of commercial popular culture – with its connection to global, especially US-based, media industries – in the cultures of young people across the world is an obvious case in point (Massey, 1998; Pilkington and Johnson, 2003; Skelton and Valentine, 1998). In a study of white youth in the North-east of the UK, Anoop Nayak has described a group who are 'black wannabes', aspiring, in a rather 'white' part of the UK, to blackness in terms of style and cultural self-positioning. This group is opposed – in the course of the research and in social life – to those young people who see themselves as 'true Geordies' – inheritors of a respectable local working-class identity and laddish cultural repertoire (Nayak, 2003). Similar polarities between the globally oriented and the local, between ethnically hybrid and insistently (and impossibly) pure, can be found in many youth studies in different parts of the world. Methods in the ethno/auto range provide ways into the circuits, but cultural forms have longer histories and distant origins that are often hidden from immediate users who have, as Gramsci puts it, 'no inventory'.

Our argument in this chapter points, once more, to the principle of methodological combination. It suggests not only crossing the boundary between ethnography and auto/biography but also meeting up with other cultural methods and questioning the larger methodological divides – those between text and person-based research, for example. These suggestions are developed by means of questions of textuality in ethnography in Chapter 13 and the examples of audience research and the study of identity in Chapter 14.

13 Representing the other: interpretation and cultural readings

Analysis as dialogue 225
Multiple readings, multiple theories 226
Reading for actors' meanings 227
Reading for cultural structures and processes 229
Working the other way: individualizing conventional forms 230
Making yourself in and against the school 231
Reading for structure and context 233
The four dialogues of analysis: a checklist 234
Representing the other: dialogic implications 237
Representing across power: particular strategies 239
Conclusion 241

In this chapter we continue many of the themes of Chapter 12, but focus, not on the practices of autobiography, interviewing or fieldwork, but on *analysing* their traces in transcriptions, field notes, writings and memories. In the first part of the chapter, we explore analysis as a form of dialogue that raises similar questions about reflexivity and power as the interrogative activity of researching itself. Then, continuing some of the themes of Part III, we explore the different forms of *reading* – typically of interview transcripts – that can be adopted when cultural questions are allied to issues of power. In the third part of the chapter we offer a practical checklist to guide the analysis – especially, of fieldwork texts. Finally, returning to some of the themes of Chapter 4, we discuss dilemmas and strategies in representing others in writing.

Analysis as dialogue

We have already argued in Chapter 12 that person research provides the most overt examples of dialogic processes in cultural study. The issues of accountability that arise in direct dialogue extend also to the moments of analysis and representation. Indeed, analysis involves a second layer of dialogic process that is superimposed on and interacts with the first, more direct encounter.

'Research' and 'analysis' are not separated moments but part of the same process. Research (in the sense of a set of interrogative tasks) involves instant practical assessments and a replaying of events in our heads immediately afterwards. The best thoughts often come in this mulling over and 'sleeping on it' time. Yet fuller analysis is usually removed from the researching context – the dynamics of a group, the pressures of a situation. This removal from 'the action' allows more intense reflection and 'standing back' or contextualization. Reflection is now mediated by texts: tapes, transcripts, diaries, field notes, video diaries, memory work pieces or diary entries. The distancing that textualization allows is very important in cultural research. Having a text (which may be a written memory) means that we can consider language or accounts of symbolic actions much more closely and specify our more intuitive understandings. We can identify what Paul Willis, an ethnographer deeply influenced by literary work, calls 'the form' or even 'the art' of a cultural practice. Willis recalls transposing techniques of 'close reading' from analysing a poem by William Blake (The Tiger, Tiger) to studying the details of a Birmingham motorbike subculture – cattle horn handlebars, chrome exhausts, no helmets (2000: ix; and Willis, 1978). Thus, ethnographic material *can* be treated as a text, though it is particularly multivocal and multilayered. The speaker may be recorded as saying one thing on the transcript, for example, but the field notes on his bodily appearance, gesture and actions can 'say' quite another.

So, in a way, there are two researching selves or a split self in ethnographic and similar work: the self who participates and makes sense under the immediate pressures of social action and the self who can stand away from this process and be reflexive and, if need be, self-critical. The double dialogue – face-to-face and with the record of a person's 'sayings' – has important consequences for method. Unlike purely text-based work, we can check out memory against text and vice versa. We can 'pin down' interactions and meanings we grasped more intuitively at the time by referring to the record. There is a tendency, however, even in contemporary debates about ethnography, to overvalue the 'graphos' – the written part. Yet, to rely only on documentation is to reduce the specific power of 'autoethnography'. Memory exceeds formal documentation and can be productive of fresh textualization. The validation of auto/biography and written memory work in cultural research offers ways to supply gaps or provide additions to initial ethnographic documentation. They may offer vital insights and observations that were not formally recorded at the time. Student-researchers who are relatively new to field research will often gain informal knowledge that has not been formally recorded, yet can transform the meaning of the data already presented. This is especially the case in relation to those forms of embodied performance or symbolic action that can be observed, but, without the video camera, are hard to record even in what has been called a 'thick' record (Carspecken, 1996: 44–54). In person research, it is always important to keep all the channels of dialogue open. It is the *interaction* between the memory of multisensual interactions (which can be further textualized) and the textual record that makes the method so uniquely productive.

Multiple readings, multiple theories

What, then, is the nature of the dialogue between the researcher as analyst and the textual record of the research activities, with its supplements of initial hunches and memory? As we have argued, dialogue depends on the researchers' questions, theories, psychological investments and, ultimately, social and cultural positionings. In person research, the pressure from 'the source' is also personal, dynamic and may be decisive in shifting the agenda. However, there are also more general pressures on method that arise from the broad object of our research, the concern with culture and power. Whatever the particular aim of the cultural researcher or the nature of the text and its coproducer(s), multiple forms of reading – an extensive reading repertoire – will be necessary to do justice to the complexity or 'richness' of the objects (see Popular Memory Group, 1982).

This reading repertoire includes at least four ways of reading – no doubt there are more. These are not alternatives between which we must choose, but methods that should be combined. The first reading focuses on an interpretation of the meanings of actors. A second mode of reading involves an analysis of the cultural forms that actors use – or that use them – as the means of organizing meanings and practice in their lives. The third reading involves a fuller analysis, less site- or text-specific, of the contexts and relations of power and difference and how they delimit the actions and meanings of actors. Finally, there is a reading that focuses on self-production or self-representation or on the construction of identity.

These four forms of reading move from a concern with 'agency' to a concern with its conditions and back again. The first reading stresses the *agency or cultural creativity* of individuals and groups. The second explores the *cultural means* that are used in cultural exchanges, whether they stem from the interactions of a group or locality or have a larger, more global circulation. The formal analysis of specifically cultural conditions is important here: forms of language, embodied styles, narrative genres and so on. The third seeks the *social conditions* of this cultural production, especially the distributions of power that are not primarily cultural. Yet, after the detour through means and conditions, we need a fourth reading that comes back to issues of agency, authorship or identity, not as a starting point, but as a problem to be explored. How can we understand cultural self-production under the particular pressures of social and cultural conditions and cultural means? The first three forms of reading will concern us in this chapter; the final (and most integrative) form of reading will be discussed in Chapter 14.

All four forms of the questioning of cultural texts have their own theoretical anchorages or affinities, which we have already explored earlier in this book (especially Part III and Chapter 2). Here, we argue that there is nothing about ethnographic analysis that exempts it from the importance of the research question and, therefore, of theory. All ethnographies start out with some purpose that informs how the researcher 'sees and hears' (Turner, 1990: 174).

Reading for actors' meanings

Understanding the meanings of actors – as individuals or as collectivities in the making – remains the central project of ethnographic work. In an influential account of the development of ethnography in the twentieth century, Norman Denzin and Yvonne Lincoln have distinguished five moments of challenge and change and a range of possible contemporary strategies (1994: 1–17). These coincide in many ways with our own arguments and include the ethnographer as 'co-author with the other', writing 'the auto-ethnographic text' and movements towards some of the features of journalism, fictional writing and 'the performance text'. Even so, for Denzin:

> Although the field of qualitative research is defined by constant breaks and ruptures, there is a shifting centre to the project: the avowed humanistic commitment to study the social world from the perspective of the interacting individual. (1997: xv)

Such a reading is concerned to tease out and make more explicit the key features of a lived culture or an individual's or group's point of view. It highlights the meaning-making practices of the agents themselves: their habitation and construction of a world, a situation, a happening, their everyday creative and interpretative work. It is important to enter this world, understand its logic and pressures, grasp the rationales of actions and beliefs that at first surprise and may even offend. In cultural studies, such readings have typically focused on the making of a collective consciousness or the recovery of subordinated or denied pleasures or the validation of a set of tastes that have been deemed trivial or passive or the everyday cultural inventiveness that crosses over ethnic or other boundaries and challenges dominant forms of cultural nationality or ethnicity. The aim of such readings is to produce a more or less rich description that does full justice to lived responses, however limited or fixed they may prove to be. As we have argued, the best work of this kind is also about questioning or extending the researcher-activist's own point of view – an outcome most evident, perhaps, in feminist work and theory.

Denzin and Lincoln argue that there is always a link between this intellectual commitment or 'centre' and what they call 'the liberal and radical politics of qualitative research':

> Action, feminist, clinical, constructivist, ethnic, critical, and cultural studies researchers are all united on this point. They all share the belief that a politics of liberation must always begin with the perspectives, desires, and dreams of those individuals and groups who have been oppressed by the larger ideological, economic, and political forces of a society, or a historical moment. (1994: 575)

As we have seen, these kinds of popular identification have indeed been a strand in cultural studies and allied approaches. It may even be, as Denzin and Lincoln imply, that some 'qualitative' or 'interpretative' forms of sociology or anthropology have become almost indistinguishable from cultural studies. Yet, the affinities implied in what seems a rather arbitrary list can provoke unease. Perhaps we should try to distinguish cultural studies approaches more clearly.

The differences are partly theoretical. Even though rescuing and understanding ways of life is an aim in humanist Marxist and cultural materialist approaches, cultural studies ethnography (like social history) inherited a stronger sense of structure or conditions than that found in the classical phenomenological and Weberian lineage of interpretative sociologies. This is related no doubt to the greater currency of Marxism in European critical sociologies (and social movements) compared with those of the United States. This interest in structure includes a fascination with cultural form, whether this is understood in structuralist, Marxist or more dialogic ways. Cultural studies, in its formative debates, refused to privilege 'the interacting individual'. It sought instead to explain *why* actors (usually collective) see the world in the way they do or *why* they invest in particular discourses. It is, therefore, misleading to equate cultural studies only with interpretation, whether this refers us to classical hermeneutic models of 'I–thou relations', or the more culture-rich accounts found in qualitative sociologies. One of the formative early debates in cultural studies concerned the inadequacy of radically phenomenological approaches to people and culture, which put too little stress on the pressures of hegemonic meanings and the wider and systemic social conditions in which meaning is produced.

This refusal to stop with interpretation is a further reason why cultural studies – at its best – is not at all the simple 'populism' of recent critics. Perhaps such critics have read cultural studies texts through the lens of interpretative sociology and missed the quite pessimistic structural undertow of work such as Willis' *Learning to Labour* (1977) or Christine Griffin's *Typical Girls?* (1985). As we have argued before, especially in Chapter 11, the most complex cultural studies work has held in balance an interest in popular creativity or resistance and a concern with hegemony or structural reproduction. Similarly, if ethnography, in Lincoln and Denzin's traditions, has mainly focused on oppressed or marginal groups, cultural studies has included the cultural forms by means of which hegemony is secured. In its explicitly ethnographic work, however, it has often shared the horizon of qualitative sociologies, being too little concerned with ethnographies of powerful and privileged people. Yet, it is vital to understand, say, ruling masculinities or the lived cultures of the global 'super-class' if we are to grasp the power questions effectively – not least in order to chart the academy's own complicities with these ways of life.

In cultural studies, then, reading for actor's meanings has almost always been attended by other readings. 'Attended' because the aim should not be to reduce or cancel out actors' meanings, but to qualify or extend them. Again, we insist on combination and not substitution or pluralism. Also, readings that *ignore* or *cancel* actor's meanings as ideology only or *replace* them with those of the analyst (as some psychoanalytic readings do) are as insufficient as readings that limit themselves to the interpretative.

Reading for cultural structures and processes

This second way of reading directs the focus away from individual and group agency and towards the pressures that the cultural forms themselves exercise on identity and culture. We can ask, for example, what discourses or narratives actors use to position themselves in making their claim for cultural space or recognition from powerful others. The actor's own words, gestures and performances are always part of larger cultural formations that have their own histories. This may be understood as a group or national language, style or dialect or as an ideological formation, serving very particular political ends or as a constructed alliance or social negotiation of some kind or as a partially transformed reproduction of some very familiar storyline or genre – a snippet of romantic narrative, for instance. Always, however, the significance of meanings and means deployed by social actors exceeds the terms of the immediate context and refers to other contexts, both social and formal. It is in the nature of language and, in fact, all cultural forms to exceed any local situation in this way. In the 1920s and 1930s, Mikhail Bakhtin and the Leningrad circle were especially interested in this deeply social character of language/culture:

> As a living, socio-ideological concrete thing, as heteroglot [many-voiced] opinion, language, for the individual consciousness, lies on the borderline between oneself and the other. The word in language is half someone else's. It becomes 'one's own' only when the speaker populates it with his own intention, his own accent, when he appropriates the word, adapting it to his own semantic and expressive intention . . . Language is not a neutral medium that passes freely and easily into the private property of the speaker's intentions; it is populated – overpopulated – with the intentions of others. Expropriating it, forcing it to submit to one's own intentions and accents, is a difficult and complicated process. (Bakhtin, 1981b: 293–4)

What is striking in these and similar arguments is the combined recognition of both authorship – 'his own intention' – and of the socially or dialogically produced – 'overpopulated' – nature of the forms used. Bakhtin sees language as both constraining – it is a struggle to bend it to the speaker's intentions – and productive, not only in the ways a speaker intends. Language and other cultural forms should not be understood as a realm of freedom and creativity only; they also carry their own pressures, limits or 'determinations'. This is especially clear if we link the forms of language to their key point of articulation or production – in forms of media production or commodity forms or political discourses, for instance. There are now few local cultural processes that are exempt from global pressures of this kind. In terms of our circuit model, 'lived cultures' are not only a group's own production, they bear the signs of past hegemonies and emerging public forms.

Working the other way: individualizing conventional forms

We can see why this second reading must not cancel the first by exploring how productive the *interaction* of the two readings can be. Sometimes everyday cultural practices are made more meaningful by being understood in terms of their conventions and larger cultural contexts. In cultural research, however, it is also common to work the other way – that is, use individual or group meanings to throw new light on some very familiar public convention. Refreshing the narrative in this way has been a major motive of audience studies – especially where the public forms are seen as trashy, trivial or demeaning. Such readings have often radically reframed genres as apparently familiar as popular romantic fiction, the action movie and the talk show. As dialogic theories suggest, we need to repeat, in analysis, the processes by which these public forms became popular in the first place – even when they are at their most ideological. As it is put in *Marxism and the Philosophy of Language*:

> The ideological sign must immerse itself in the element of inner, subjective signs; it must ring with subjective tones in order to remain a living sign, and not be relegated to the honorary status of an incomprehensible museum piece. (Volosinov, 1973: 39)

A striking example of 'ringing with subjective tones' is provided by a study of family photograph albums in Australia (Chambers, 2003).[1] The study was concerned with the meanings such family albums offered to women who had compiled them during the 1950s, a period of rapid social change within Sydney's expanding western suburbs. Ten white women in their sixties and seventies were interviewed about their own family albums. What initially struck the researchers most was an overwhelming sense of sameness and predictability about the albums, both in terms of content and presentation. They were characterized by rigidly formalized and repetitive sequences of snapshots and visual narratives. These included amateur and studio photographs of weddings and christenings, posed pictures of babies and 'candid' and 'action' snaps of children growing up, especially outdoors and on holiday. Yet, what seemed at first to be crushingly familiar turned out 'strange' and interesting as the project – and especially the interviews – proceeded. By clustering images and interviews by theme, the researchers pieced together stories that were distinctive and uses of the family albums that were quite specific. As cultural products that seemed, at first glance, familiar, mundane and highly formulaic, the albums proved to offer invaluable access into rich and complex familial narratives.

Making yourself in and against the school

Another example may make our (so far) double reading clearer and introduce our third. The following exchange is drawn from an interview between an ethnographic researcher (Mairtin Mac an Ghaill) and 'two young working-class women':

> *Nihla:* It's funny the teachers think, oh you're a typical oppressed Asian girl and all that. But at home, I'm a real tomboy. I wear jeans most of the time, play football with my brother and cousins and go around in cars.
>
> *MM:* And at school?
>
> *Nihla:* At school they try and make you act like their stereotype of a girl and for us they have a stereotype of an Asian girl, all quiet and passive. I don't know why they feel threatened if girls act differently. It's like they blame us for not acting like Asian girls. But it's not us that's the problem. We're just not living up to their stereotypes because it doesn't mean anything to us.
>
> *Niamh:* It's been the same for me. I was brought up on a farm in Ireland and in a lot of ways the differences in school between boys and girls was less than in England.

> *MM:* Like what things are different?
> *Niamh:* At home it's just normal for me to go round with my brothers but at school the teachers say, 'you're acting more like a boy, no one will respect you'. They say I'm rough and run around the playground too much shouting. In Ireland you had more freedom in school. My ma says the English are funny about these things. I don't know. (1994: 126)

Our first reading would pay close attention to how these young people construct their world, especially in the immediate context of talking to a white, adult, male researcher (of Irish heritage) who has clearly won their trust. Such an analysis might focus, for instance, on the positive figures of tomboy, playing football, going around with brothers and acting rough, and the negative scripts of Asian girls and quietness and passivity as key points of self-construction. There is no difficulty in recognizing the perceptiveness of the girls' analysis, their acuteness, for instance, about social and cultural differences in the school and about their teachers' dominant versions.

What is so interesting about this extract, however, is that the girls themselves undertake elements of our second reading. They have made a keen analysis of school-based femininities in gendered and ethnicized terms and of the ways in which they themselves are seen as not conforming. Nihla has a wide understanding of the cultural forms that are used to represent young Asian women in white English culture. Niamh understands very well that national cultures – here Irish and English – differ in the ways in which specificities of gender are handled. Both the girls are extremely shrewd about gender interactions within the school, especially their own interactions with boys and teachers. Both use quite analytical language to describe the pressure of these dominant forms – language sharpened, perhaps, by their interactions with the researcher, evident from the use of 'stereotype', 'living up to their stereotypes', 'feel threatened if girls act differently' and so on. Like many ethnographic subjects today, they do their own cultural studies. It is no surprise to find, later in the book, that they were 'key individuals', classic enablers in the research, 'helping me to become familiar with the located meanings embedded in the cultural map that constituted the young women's lives at Parnell School' (176; citing also Whyte, 1943).

At the same time, the girls have less awareness (in this exchange at least) of the modes they are visiting to define themselves positively, as resisting subjects. It is hard to work out whether the girls are referring to a less gender-segregated pattern of growing up in their respective home communities or individual households, for example, or if, rather, they – Nihla as a self-designated tomboy, Niambh as identifying with a teacher who is a grown-up tomboy – are also drawing on current post-feminist discourses of 'girl power' also available in white/anglo youth cultures. Mac An Ghaill's own main focus is on the self-production of heterosexual boys and male teachers. He draws on the sideways, critical vision of the girls and gay pupils who interacted with them in order to achieve a critical, multidimensional perspective on conventional masculinities. His analysis is mainly confined to the school, so that the wider connections and limits of these resistant girl identities are not made available to the reader.

Reading for structure and context

This example shows how the third kind of reading – for context or structure – is also needed. Such a reading looks for the structural and historical determinants of particular ethnographic interactions. Again, it is in the spirit of the first reading to take the clues for this from the actor's own understandings, but our argument here also connects with our stress on spatial, temporal and social contexts in Part II and, similarly, points to combined or supplementary methods and research. The tendency to formalism in literary or linguistic studies is paralleled by another kind of abstraction in ethnographic work – that of isolating a little local world explored in research from its larger, even global, contexts. Mac An Ghaill's analysis of the making of men in the school does, however, operate on this national or global level, too. He shows how the formation of masculinities in the school is articulated to wider processes, including differentiation in terms of class, alignments to educational reform and neo-liberal policies and the effects of a resurgent, ethnicized English nationalism.

Whereas the second reading stays, as it were, on the surface of language and with the cultural forms themselves, the third reading treats language and gesture as representing something else. This may be 'levels' or social practices other than those that are directly present in the text. A typical focus is on the systematic relations of power that shape gender, class, ethnic, racialized and generational relations and hierarchies. Speech and gesture are thus read as evidence for something else, perhaps a state of powerful relationships or a set of past and present happenings and situations. At the same time, however, ethnographers (and critical auto/biographers) expect to learn something new about such structures from the very particular interactions they have in view.

The oral history study of family albums that we discussed earlier in this chapter provides a final example of the value of triple readings (Chambers, 2003). We have seen how the personal stories brought the albums alive. Patterns and differences were then sought by categorizing the themes thrown up by the photos and the interviews. Among the themes that emerged, the handling of space was prominent.

The album owners could be divided into two groups, distinguished by their understanding of their spatial surroundings and histories. The first group were women whose families had lived in the country towns of Australia before suburbanization. They chose to ignore or deny the spatial changes around them. Country backdrops were selected when they were photographing families and friends so as to avoid images of the encroaching new suburbs. They identified themselves as proud country town folk and did not claim the suburban dream as a positive part of their family's experience – indeed, the opposite was the case, they saw it as an intrusion.

The second group consisted of families who had moved to the region during the crucial period of suburban expansion. By contrast, they produced visual celebrations of their arrival in the promised land of suburbia with shots of cars, their homes and next door neighbour's homes in full view. The move to the suburbs appeared as a progressive gesture in which the poor conditions of the inner city were forsaken for the Australian dream of fresh air, wide open spaces and home and car ownership.

This insight relied on relating all three readings – an interpretation of the stories of album owners, a reading of the conventions of the photo album and a more structural or historical rereading focused by means of representational differences.

The four dialogues of analysis: a checklist

If such readings are central to understanding and explanation in cultural studies, they must play a part in a larger process of analysis. The following checklist – like the other checklists in this book – does not specify necessary or invariable procedures. It offers prompts, not rules and illustrates our general arguments on method.

We can chart analysis in terms of *four* dialogic moments or aspects described below.

A: Recalling

The process of analysis began in research itself – impressions were accumulated, hunches were crystallized into theories or rethought. There were moments of insight, epiphanies. Analysis can begin by recalling this learning process.

This is the *first dialogue*, mediated, initially, via memory. Memory *is* selective, but picks out what was *significant*.

1: Clarifying hunches

What hunches did I start with? How and when did my questions shift? What are my best guesses today?

2: Salient episodes

Who and what stays powerfully in the memory from the research? When did I learn most, change most? From whom or what? When was researching most strange, most surprising (Goffman, 1961; Turnbull, 1973)? When did the familiar become strange ? (Garfinkel, 1967).

3: Recordings

Which of these instances are recorded? From the record, now, why was this episode so productive? What was I learning?

4: Headnotes

Write a version of these episodes now. Are they key moments in method? What theses or themes were generated?

Sanjek (1990) calls these memories, consolidated as we read our field notes, 'headnotes'. They help us to recall our feelings, our moods and the nuances that may have escaped reportage in the formal documentation. Headnotes can often provide the tone and the feel to our analysis.

Research is an embodied experience involving pain, pleasure, excitement, fear, boredom and even anxiety, and all these influence what we remember and how we remember. Constructed in this way, our headnotes bind together our field notes, our diary, our transcripts and all the other sources that we use in constructing a story.

B: Listening around

We focus now on the materials, texts. We review their extent and adequacies extensively, as a whole. We transcribe in full or more selectively. We index what we have. We consider possible uses. We review clusters and concentrations, notice gaps. This moment, in larger projects, may sometimes lead to 'research within analysis', which is further research that, however, at this stage, can be very focused.

This is the *second dialogue* with the material, with the text, *in extenso.*

1: Developing a strategy for extensive review

What kind of extensive review is appropriate? For example, with what forms, discourses, genres does this group typically make meanings? What themes do they foreground – meanings about what? What typical agenda or priorities?

If the material is extensive, we may need relatively standardized and limited categories that, nonetheless, can pick up key differences.

2: Transcription

What are the implications of our method of extensive analysis for transcription? Do we need to transcribe everything in full or more selectively?

The advantage of full transcription, if we do it ourselves, is a thorough familiarity with the material and its full availability for processing further. However, full indexing, based on note-taking while listening to tapes, with partial transcription, also gives access to the materials as a whole.

Transcription should preserve and indicate as many of the markers of meaning – pauses, silences, laughter, sighs, emphatic words or phrase – as possible. It should also include the researcher's own voice in full.

3: Extensive review and analysis

This is often described as 'coding', which is a kind of elaborated indexing or sorting, involving reading through all the material according to certain fixed categories. As any typology means that certain specificities are dropped in the interests of abstraction, it is important not to *substitute* such types for more open devices, such as direct quotation, that have a closer relation to field notes, transcripts and diaries. Cultural analysis will often be content with annotating transcriptions or diaries with more or less elaborately coloured underlinings or other markings, noting quotations that are exemplary or puzzling so that they can be recovered.

Some researchers take the thematic categorization of material a stage further and enlist the help of computer packages to speed up the process of identifying categories and analysing their significance. There are several computer packages available, such as NUDIST (Non-numerical Unstructured Data Indexing, Searching and Theorizing) and Ethnograph (for some uses, see, for example, Richards and Richards, 1987a, 1987b and 1988 and Richards, 1990).

However, cultural first readings are often more intuitive and, as we have argued, use smaller samples than such methods imply. Cultural analysis, even when it is extensive, is more likely to look for patterns of meaning or structures of feeling than keywords. It will be alive to oddities, contradictions, marginalia, unexpected remarks, anything that might alter our preconceptions about the material – but also, of course, repetitions – asking why is this coming up, over and over again?

In this moment of dialogue, reading must be open to the strangeness and specificity – or alterity – of the other's reality and truths. Strongly empirical or inductive methodologies in the qualitative social sciences – the approach termed 'grounded theory', for example – are especially aware of this aspect (Glasser and Strauss, 1967). It is argued that the researcher's generalizations should emerge from the social actions of members of the lived culture that is being studied, which may then be classified, compared and contextualized. A limit of this approach may be that, in Gadamer's language, the researcher's own 'prejudices' (or starting theories) need to be more visible.

4: Yet others?

We need to ask a painful question: is the material adequate to my question? Are there critical absences (for my purposes, arguments)?

5: Supplements?

Can gaps be covered by reference to secondary literature or by means of memory work? Do I need to do more research?

Research or reading can be very focused at this stage, therefore making it economical.

6: Reformulating key theses

What does extensive analysis, the second dialogue, suggest for the key theses and arguments – revised hunches – derived from the first dialogue?

C: Close reading

Knowing my material now, having a sense of possible arguments, what case studies will develop them or ground them more thoroughly in ways that will convince? These may become examples in the writing.

They will often overlap with instances that figure in the first dialogue, but should include additions.

This is the *third* dialogue.

1: Selecting key instances

These are 'keys' to developing my understandings and explanations. They can be argument-led at this stage.

Are there typical cases for my argument? Are there apparent exceptions? Are there rich and problematic examples that might extend my argument?

2: Three or more readings?

So how is meaning or identity produced? From what resources? Under what circumstances?

3: Comparing key cases

What is common across these instances? What is different? How are my general arguments qualified or extended? Are these different routes or strategies? Are the conditions different?

4: Contextualization again

Are there contexts not addressed in the cases used? Are there absence or silences? What rereadings do they suggest?

D: Representing self and others

Thus, we come to writing again – representing the self and other in their relations – for other others, the readers.

Writing as *representation* is the *fourth* dialogue.

Representing the other: dialogic implications

We have already discussed issues involved in representing the other under the heading Accountabilities (Chapter 12) and concerning writing (at the end of Chapter 4). In what follows, we seek to state some principles for a fully dialogic approach to representation that is followable in practice. This, and the final section of this chapter, should be read in relation to the sections on writing towards the end of Chapter 4. In stating some principles, we risk a certain didacticism, but trust that you know us well enough by now not to treat our *arguments* as finished rules to follow!

Dialogue is not leaving the self aside

We are sceptical about representational strategies that try to step aside and 'let the other speak' or act as 'scribes for the other' (Denzin, 1997). Relationships and dialogue cannot be represented if the researcher tries to vanish. Moreover, this strategy presupposes that the researcher is, in most respects, in a position of power over the researched and this is not always the case. We have argued that cultural research should include the most powerful groups, but even where they don't figure, power relations are complex and mixed. Where researchers *are* powerful, their complicity in power relations needs to be acknowledged and worked on textually and in other ways. It is hard to imagine good critical work on forms of racism by a white researcher who is not alive to the ways in which whiteness is constructed in relation to histories of white supremacy. To 'represent otherwise' requires a knowledge of the history of disciplinary complicities in racialization, too – of the ethnological and anthropological disciplines, for example.

Dialogue is not monologue

Well, obviously! However, there are many ways in which to make a self so big that there is no space for others – that it ends up 'eating the other', as bell hooks puts it (1989). The other's experience and best truths can be appropriated. Authors can appear as the one who knows the others and shows them off to the reader. Authors can imagine that they know what it is like for the other. They can believe that bridging alterity is easy. They can believe that underneath it all ('the skin'?) 'we' are all really the same. However, this is to disempower the person who is being 'understood'. As Gadamer puts it:

> By understanding the other, by claiming to know him, one robs his claims of their legitimacy. In particular, the dialectic of charitable or welfare work operates in this way, penetrating all relationships between men as a reflective form of the effort to dominate. The claim to understand the other person in advance functions to keep the other person's claim at a distance. (1989: 360)

Dialogue is relational

So, both self and others should be represented, in dialogue. This includes the other's claims and truths.

This involves the reflexive self

This means a voice that represents the layered dialogues of which we have spoken so often – dialogues in research, dialogues in different moments of analysis, dialogues in writing itself. This is the observing, listening, remembering self, the self moved by alterity or power in or behind the writing. This self struggles also to define a position in relation to the other or the other's truths, morally, politically or aesthetically.

Listening to the other

It is not only the researcher who listens. The readers of our texts need to be enabled to listen, too. The researched others should therefore appear as much as possible in their own terms and in their own words. So, in quoting the other (can we quote gesture or style?) the dialogic text will be relatively extended, superfluous even, because surplus quotation makes room for other interpretations, as well as giving space to the interpreted to interpret themselves.

Listening also has to do with the modes and qualities of the author's interpretations. These can dismiss or replace the other's own interpretations or they can argue with them explicitly, trying to identify their truths and the limits of these truths. Authors can try out various hunches and hypotheses against the pressure of the texts or sayings or doings they seek to interpret. They can record moments of conviction or rejection.

Such dialogue risks the self

Person research is implicitly comparative. It is by means of comparison or difference that we position ourselves. Is this inevitable as a psychological, social and ethical process? Perhaps. If so, reflexive writers can only be aware of this process – not cancelling it out, but reflecting on it. As Catherine Riessman has noted, some of the most interesting writing in cultural studies has involved a 'double take' of this kind. Valerie Walkerdine rereads her relation to the film, *Rocky II* and the family that watches it by becoming aware of the dynamics of her own familial involvements. Kobena Mercer rereads his first reactions to Robert Mapplethorpe's fetishistic black nudes by recognizing the shock value produced by their juxtaposition with dominant codes of Western (white) aesthetics. As we have seen, Riessman herself revisits testimony about a rape to see how she defended herself against her own pain in hearing the story and how this affected her interpretation (Mercer, 1994; Reissman, 2002: 193–214; Walkerdine, 1990). The dialogic self is a vulnerable self capable of second thoughts, not a self that is anchored firmly by comparison with its others.

One of the reasons specifications of these kinds are tricky is that so much depends on context – especially the context of power. In the final section of this chapter – which considers specific representational strategies – we want to foreground this problem.

Representing across power: particular strategies

Clifford (1986) claims that all ethnographic accounts are inevitably partial. He recommends ways of moving away from the traditional unified ethnographic gaze towards texts in which a multiplicity of voices can be heard and the ethnographer's is just one among many, all of whose underpinnings are made equally explicit. Clifford's perspective has led to a shift from the idea of authorship to that of orchestration, so that more space is allocated to ethnographic participants in which they can speak for themselves. The argument for the 'multivoiced' or 'messy' text is attractive, but we have noted already (Chapter 4) how orchestration underestimates and may hide the power of the authorial function.

An alternative is what might be called 'multisi(gh)ted texts'. By this we mean texts that do not simply record a multiplicity of viewpoints, but those where dominant versions are challenged, extended or repositioned. The new voices may be aligned with the researcher's own voice and point of view or they may not. Indeed, conflicts may be staged as interruptions to the researcher's own perspective.

The history of cultural studies is full of such interventions. Sometimes change has come about by including a new social space in the analysis ('multisited'). Much contemporary critical writing about culture seeks to go beyond the emphasis on limited local (especially national) cultures and bounded identities by siting them globally, stressing boundary crossing or encompassing the economy and other spheres of life that have not usually figured in cultural analysis (see, for example, Saukko, 1998).

Sometimes interventions have been 'multisighted', in that they have brought a new social perspective to bear, changing the horizon of the research. This process has often been driven by new political agenda. When it has worked most productively, it has extended existing knowledge, just as, politically, it has extended notions of the popular or democratic politics. Feminist critiques of early cultural studies research is a generative example here, both in the criticisms made of youth subcultural studies (see, for example, Angela McRobbie, 1981; Women's Study Group, 1978) and in interventions in media studies. Though such critiques started by noting the absence of women in such studies, they extended to analyses of male researchers' complicities with masculine cultures, the romanticization of spectacular forms of youth culture and the absence of concern with issues of intimacy, sexual relationships and the domestic or familial environment (Roman, Christian-Smith and Ellsworth, 1988).

Another difficulty with the multivoiced text is that the world being represented does not itself ensure all voices are equal. It is one thing to represent the underrepresented, quite another to give space to voices that are a means of oppression for others. What do we do when the people we interview and interact with as part of our ethnographic study seem to tell us contradictory things? What do we do if we find it difficult to sympathize with their version of the world? Ethnographic research is bound to privilege some voices and eclipse others as it involves interpersonal relationships that vary in understanding, empathy, trust, liking and loving. Such relations lay the basis for the micropolitics of research (Bhavnani, 1994).

An example of this problem was experienced in a PhD project on domestic workers in Delhi that we discussed earlier (Raghuram, 1993). The author analysed the division of labour within households by conducting interviews with both women domestic workers and their husbands. Many of the latter claimed that the housework was equally shared between themselves and their wives. However, the researcher found that, in her analysis, she tended to treat such claims sceptically. There may have been many reasons for making this analytical choice – personal experience of the division of domestic labour in this part of India; a feminist commitment to privileging women's voices; a lack of close rapport with the men that showed itself in shorter interviews and, perhaps, a certain flippancy about the topic displayed by the men when talking to her. It seems to us that to try to be balanced here would not have helped the research. The better strategy was to include, not suppress the men's accounts, discuss the reasons for the discrepancies directly, but also privilege the women's versions as the participants most involved in and most insightful on the topic.

Though value positions and side-taking are always present in research, they should be open to questioning and change. Making them explicit, for both researchers themselves and readers, is a fundamental condition of an adequate practice. By the same rule, as researchers, we have to make a commitment to interpret accounts with as much sensitivity as we can muster to the value systems of those being researched. We do not have to be in agreement with them in order to understand the reasons for such values. As Amadiume urges, researchers should try to 'let themselves go' (1993), even if this is not very easy.

Indeed, it may sometimes be important to depersonalize or de-moralize ethnographic material, at least as one analytic moment. In an engaging discussion of femininity as discourse, Dorothy Smith (1988) argues that textually mediated discourses organize local practices and relationships in multiple sites, stressing the active roles and knowledge of women in acting out discourses of the feminine. Smith's analysis ranges across a whole variety of cultural forms and practices, from nineteenth century fiction (Mrs Gaskell) and Victorian conduct books to contemporary fashion and make-up for black women and discourses of anorexia. For her, women produce themselves as feminine in very many ways, but under conditions not within their own control. In effect, Smith is prioritizing here a version of our second and third readings. In producing their views and actions, social actors – women here – enter social relations via their negotiation with already existing systems of meanings, such as 'femininity', 'masculinity' and ethnicity. When we interview men and women, we are tapping into such discourses – not primarily in order to make judgements on the people involved or on the truthfulness of what they say, but to work out the ways in which they are discursively positioned and how they get to be where they are.

Conclusion

We have suggested throughout this chapter that analysis can best be understood as a second set of dialogues – themselves layered and repeated – on the basis of the first face-to-face encounters. Similarly, we have suggested that interviews and similar transcripts or other forms of representation, such as family photo albums, can be read in multiple ways. These ways of reading rest on rather different theoretical premises, from a humanist commitment to listening closely to another's sayings, to a fascination with the work that language and other codes do in producing both the accounts and their subjects. We have argued, however, that these readings, in sequence, are complementary. They add explanation to interpretation and give access to different aspects of the construction of meaning within space, time and relations of power. We hope we have already made the case for working across theoretical and methodological traditions, but it is in relation to a fourth way of reading, only hinted at here, where the logic of combination becomes most pressing. This is the main theme of our final chapter.

Note

1 The family photograph album research project was conducted with Carol Liston, Summer Research Scholar of the University of Western Sydney Nepean, Louise Denoon and research assistant Robyn Arrowsmith at the Women's Research Centre, University of Western Sydney, Nepean. The project was funded by a seed grant from the University of Western Sydney, Nepean 1992. The research findings have been discussed in Chambers (2003).

14 Remaking methods: from audience research to studying subjectivities

'Indiscipline' and combination **243**
Studying media audiences: promises unfulfilled? **245**
Researching subjectivities: reflexive selves, discursive subjects **255**
Conclusion: remaking methods **266**

In this chapter we develop our arguments about combining methods by exploring two particular programmes of research: the study of media audiences and of subjectivity or cultural identity. We choose these examples because they show the need not only to combine methods but also remake and invent them.

The logic of enquiry in audience research puts particular pressures on the conventional separation of methods and their underpinning theories. 'Reading', we will argue, is the most integrative moment on the cultural circuit. In this case, however, while the integration of methods is promised, it has, in practice, been rarely achieved. Instead, the analysis of media texts or programmes has been split off from engagement with media audiences and vice versa. Overcoming this split requires not only changes in methods but also some movement in the objects of study. One such shift is towards researching the production of cultural identities and subjectivities – the most lively area of new work in and around cultural studies.

In what follows, we first remind our readers of the possibilities of combination by revisiting some well-known and rather 'indisciplined' studies. Second, we consider, once more, the ontological basis of combination, paying attention this time to the moment of audience or reading. Finally, we address contemporary concerns with the production of identity or subjectivity. As well as holding the promise of new transdisciplinary dialogues – now with the psychological disciplines – identity theory and research show how new lines of enquiry require the remaking of methods.

'Indiscipline' and combination

In editing Richard Hoggart's *The Uses of Literacy* (1956) for an American readership (1992), Andrew Goodwin notes that 'its author seemed unembarrassed by its mixture of personal memoir, social history and cultural critique'. By the academic standards of the time, 'Richard Hoggart was . . . dangerously indisciplined' (1992: xiii). Today, Goodwin argues, a more systematic cultural studies can avoid Hoggart's 'mistakes', but risks a specialist narrowing of its own. Hoggart's 'indisciplined' interdisciplinarity, by contrast, derived from the urgency of his personal and social project – the desire to understand 'changes in working-class culture during the last 30 or 40 years' (Goodwin, 1992: xxxiii–iv). Goodwin's preferences – in particular the *combination* of personal reference, interpretation of lived cultural forms, historical and spatial positioning and a critical awareness of dominant discourses and narratives – have also been emphasized in this book.

Carolyn Steedman's *Landscape for a Good Woman* (1986), though written by a social historian, is unclassifiable in terms of academic genre and discipline. It is a kind of answer to Hoggart, transforming a favourite image from *The Uses of Literacy* – a 'landscape (with figures)'. Like Hoggart, Steedman focuses on the emotional and material particularity of working-class lives. Unlike Hoggart, she avoids generalizing from an autobiography that is partially concealed. Instead, she insists that understanding her mother's (and her father's) life is a challenge to 'the tradition of cultural criticism in this country, which has celebrated a kind of psychological simplicity in the lives lived out in Hoggart's endless streets of little houses' (1986: 7). In this way, historical auto/biography functions as a critique of the 'othering' tendencies of ethnography, not as an undercriticized substitute for it. Though Steedman's book is about many things – including the processes of memory and storytelling and the careful, painful honouring of a woman's hard, unclassifiable life – it problematizes cultural criticism more generally, including much cultural and feminist theory. In its piecing together of story fragments, it resembles critical memory work or life history. Interestingly for our later argument, Steedman likens parts of her text to the narrative forms of a written psychoanalytical case study (1986: 20–1).

Valerie Walkerdine's work is more explicitly 'critical psychology'. In a much-discussed essay 'Video Replay' (1990, but first published in 1985) and in a subsequent book, *Daddy's Girl* (1997), tensions between ethnography and autobiography, but also complimentarities, are explored. Though this essay is a kind of audience study, the cultural themes of popular narrative are viewed as components in everyday subjectivity. Walkerdine begins by describing her experience of sharing the viewing of the boxing film *Rocky II* with a working-class family she calls 'the Coles' in their living room. She explores her realization of the significance of the film's representation of fighting for Mr Cole as a theme that threads through his life, too, but she is also riveted by Mr Cole's relationship with his daughter, whom he calls 'Dodo'. It is here that the writing, which has already made a problem of Walkerdine's own voyeurism as a researcher, swoops into auto/biographical mode, drawing on the fantasy elements in her own parents' representations of her as a child. *Daddy's Girl* continues and extends these themes, criticizing much cultural studies for its romantic (and regulative) misrecognition of 'survival' for 'resistance'. Walkerdine insists that researchers' own subjectivities are resources. Making them explicit extends the data available and exposes the power-laden identifications and fantasies in play between *all* the participants, including the researcher as the 'Surveillant Other' (1990: 195; 1997: 63–77).

Different combinations of ethnography with autobiography and of both with analysing public texts and discourses are now common in cultural research (see, for example, Brunsdon, 2000; 1994; Epstein and Johnson, 1998; Hall, 1990; Redman and Mac An Ghaill, 1997; Steinberg, Epstein and Johnson, 1997; Ware, 1992). Such work is both risky and productive. Some examiners are still disconcerted by autobiographical explicitness and may be opposed to the underlying epistemologies. Interdisciplinary research may not be historical enough for historians, nor ethnographic enough for anthropologists, nor concerned enough with literary or linguistic form for literary critics. Yet, student-researchers can increasingly refer their assessors to work that, like *Landscape* and 'Video Replay', have innovated methodologically and shown us new truths. The combination of auto/biography with social history (Steedman) or with a psychologically informed style of ethnography (Walkerdine) drew attention to the subjective aspects of class–gender relations. After these interventions, class has to be seen as an emotional or psychic relation, not just a socio-economic one. While there was a handling of emotion in Hoggart's study, too, the emotional register is narrower – Steedman's 'psychological simplicity' – centring perhaps on a certain nostalgia. Steedman and Walkerdine bring out the pain and ambivalence of class subordination by drawing more explicitly on the auto/biographical.

Studying media audiences: promises unfulfilled?

There are several excellent critical reviews of the history of audience research (Ang, 1996; Brunsdon, 2000; Hay, Grossberg and Wartella, 1996; Morley, 1992; van Zoonen, 1994). We do not need to tell this story again. Rather, we want to argue three particular theses. First, studies of readership, audience or reception have the potential to transform methods of research – in relation to each other. This is one of the reasons feminist media research (in which audience has often been central) has been so generative for cultural studies as a whole (and for our arguments). Second, there are few fields of cultural research that are so criss-crossed by paradigmatic, disciplinary and methodological differences. This means that its potential for a larger understanding of cultural processes is often jeopardized and methods and approaches remain very split. Third, we want to suggest the need for both methodological innovation and a shift of object.

Integrative possibilities

The particular potential of studying the moment of reception or reading for understanding cultural processes can be seen in two main ways. The first is to return to a formative text of the cultural study of the media – Stuart Hall's *Encoding and Decoding in the TV Discourse* essay of 1973 (1973b; edited version 1980d, much reprinted thereafter; and see the closely related Hall, 1973a). Hall's argument can be extended and supplemented, however, by Paul Ricoeur's account of reading in *Time and Narrative* (1988, vols. 1–3).

Encoding and decoding

Hall argues that, like 'the skeleton of commodity production offered in Marx's *Grundrisse* and *Capital*', cultural circuits consist of 'linked but distinctive moments' that, though formally separate, are also interdependent.

> The value of this approach is that while each of the moments, in articulation, is necessary to the circuit as a whole, no one moment can fully guarantee the next moment with which it is articulated. (1980d: 128–29)

Hall's version of the circuit had the particular purpose of giving some autonomy to both encoding and reading. With television in mind, the circuit was rendered in terms of three moments: 'encoding'; the 'programme as "meaningful" discourse'; and 'decoding'. Decoding marks the 're-entry into the practices of audience reception and "use"', each with their own structures of understanding, 'social and economic relations' and characteristic products (1980d: 130). A semiological (and exclusively cognitive) treatment of 'the message', in terms of code, signification and 'preferred reading', was dovetailed with a Gramscian account of hegemonic, 'corporate' and counter-hegemonic readings. This made space (away from the logic of 'economic production') for a specifically discursive analysis, while also suggesting (in a point often overlooked) that production, too, was necessarily discursive. This explains the stress on 'the discursive form of the message' as having 'a privileged position in the communicative exchange' (1980d: 129) and on the extended notions of 'code' and 'reading position' (as inscribed in text or code). Further targets, however, were forms of structuralist analysis that derived readings wholly from closed media codes or discourses. In Hall's account, both the production and reading of media gather in many other elements from 'the wider universe of ideologies in a society' (1980d: 134).

Later versions of the circuit have been less preoccupied with 'the relative autonomy' of code and reading and more with re-embedding culture in economy and vice versa (du Gay et al.,1997; Johnson, 1983; and Chapters 2, 3 and 8 above). They also recover Marx's stress on the *interdependence* of moments and the idea (Hegelian rather than structuralist) that such moments are *internally* related to each other. Just as Marx argues that there is a consumption (of labour and raw materials) in production (see, for example, Marx, 1976: 717–18), so cultural production always involves an appropriation and consumption – or selection and interpretation – of cultural forms that are already in public circulation. Texts also select elements from a more general stock of cultural forms sedimented in language and ways of life and rework them. Similarly, cultural *consumption* is a process of the *production* of new meanings and identities, though this does not mean that it is *freely* productive. Finally, 'textuality', or what Hall calls 'the discursive form', is present at every moment – in production, everyday life and, most obviously, reading – as well as constituting a point of relative abstraction and fixity, as in a book, photograph album or video.

Methodologically, this suggests that it is crucial to hold on to the *two-fold* nature of the moments in the circuit – *both* their specificity *and* their interdependence. As argued in Chapters 2 and 3, specificity points to the need for *different methods,* while interdependence points to the need to *integrate and rework* them.

Ricoeur on reading

Paul Ricoeur's arc of mimesis or representation helps to fill out the nature of the reading moment (1984: 52–87; 1988: 157–79 and Chapter 2 above). For Ricoeur, too, reading, or 'mimesis 3', is a point of integration. Drawing on different theories of reception, he shows how reading also involves production and authorship (1988: 160–4). He starts out from the persuasive strategies of the implied author – a textual category close to Hall's 'preferred reading'. However, Ricoeur rejects any version of reading that stays within the terms of the text itself, whether this is expressed as authorial intention or as a textual structure. Textualization or 'configuration' is only one moment in the 'arc' of representations. It is rooted in 'mimesis 1' – in prefigurative or half-articulated forms of representation or experience that may already be symbolized, which is an idea close to Willis' 'grounded aesthetic' (see Chapter 12). It is only on the basis of this prefigurative moment that Ricoeur sees mimesis 2 – or 'configuration' – as a process of 'schematization' and 'traditionality' (1984: 64–8).

'Schematization' is the representation of actions in a schema or plot. The term 'traditionality' draws attention to the historical nature of this process: configuration is a fresh production that uses and may change existing genres and conventions. Reading, or mimesis 3, however, is also necessary to complete the circuit: 'schematization and traditionality are thus *from the start* categories of the *interaction* [our emphasis] between the operations of writing and reading'. Further:

> On the one hand, the received paradigms structure readers' expectations and aid them in recognizing the formal rule, the genre, or the type exemplified by the narrated story. They furnish guidelines for the encounter between a text and its readers. In short, they govern the story's capacity to be followed. On the other hand, it is the act of reading that accompanies the narrative's configuration and actualizes its capacity to be followed. To follow a story is to actualize it by reading it. (1984: 76)

So there are therefore 'three [or really four?] moments' within the process of reading and also 'three [or really four?] neighbouring, yet distinct, disciplines' that help us to grasp them. In Ricoeur's words, but with our own glosses:

1 the strategy as concocted by the author and directed toward the reader [for example, making the reader laugh or cry]
2 the inscription of this strategy within a literary configuration [via genre, schematization, plot, tradition and so on]
3 the response of the reader considered either as a reading subject [an individual reader] or [4] as the receiving public. (1988: 160)

The full study of reading, therefore, requires:

1 a *rhetorics*, which analyses authorial strategies
2 a *poetics* centred on features of strategy embodied in texts
3 an account of the production of reading publics – the work of *literary history*
4 an account of the actual act of reading, which Ricoeur assigns to a '*phenomenological psychology*'. (1988: 167)

Three further features are important for cultural studies debates (1988: 157–79). First, Ricoeur views reading as both active *and* passive. The reader's activity is based on the nature of the text in several different ways. In one sense, texts are always incomplete, inadequately concrete, needing fresh realizations. Though fictional characters may be described psychologically, for example, their physical 'presence' may not be, so can be imagined by the reader. Moreover, a text is never perceived all at once – the reader casts a kind of wandering or provisional eye on it, looking for clues or meanings. As Ricoeur puts it, 'there is a continual interplay between modified expectations and transformed memories' (1988: 168, summarizing Iser, 1978). Reading may also involve a response to 'deception' or 'difficulty', as in James Joyce's *Ulysses*, where the reader has to work hard to create coherence. Moreover, every text also presents an excess of *possible* meanings not easily contained within one (preferred?) version, so that readers have to make their own inventions. For Ricoeur, 'it is the prerogative of reading to strive to provide a figure for this unwritten side of the text'. These forms of dialectic or dialogue 'make reading a truly vital experience' (1988: 169).

The second key point is that reading is a relation between the world of the work and the world of the reader. Ricoeur insists on the referential or representational nature of fiction as well as the rootedness of all figuration in everyday suffering and acting. So, reading is always 'about' something more than the text or genre; it is about a world in relation to another world however metaphorical or poetic the language may be:

> What a reader receives is not just the sense of the work, but, through its sense, its reference, that is, the experience it brings to language and, in the last analysis, the world and the temporality it unfolds in the face of this experience. (1984: 78–9)

Finally, Ricoeur follows Gadamer in insisting that reading is also about 'application' to acting and living. Narrative makes explicit a world of *actions*, a 'story' in this technical sense. Narration adds meaning to actions, grasping them as a whole. As Gadamer puts it, 'understanding always involves something like applying the text to be understood to the interpreter's present situation' (1989: 308). 'World' is not just a matter of mental horizon; it is also a question of 'being.' For Ricoeur, 'the more readers become unreal in their reading, the more profound and far-reaching will be the work's influence on social reality' (1988: 179).

Ricoeur's account redescribes elements familiar from the encoding/decoding model, but underlines the importance of *grasping them together*. Adding 'the audience' to text-based studies is insufficiently integrative. 'The audience' is always a *relation* rather than a fixed site of consumption, a relation that reaches back into text and its rhetoric of persuasion and, thence, to conditions of production as well as forward into various already constituted reading publics and their social and cultural conditions. Deciding where to cut into the reading circuit is less important than recognizing that the different moments interlink: the link between intentions or needs of producers, for instance, and rhetorical strategies of text or genre; the link between these strategies and the reader's world (which make the work popular or not), which concerns, centrally, the reader's own reading. In a strong and palpable sense, but hidden by deficiencies in method, each moment is present in the other.

Disappointments of media research

Despite these possibilities, the separation of text- and audience-based approaches is a striking feature of media research. It has been unusual to combine, in anything like equal weight, attention to the textuality of encoding, the social conditions of readership and that vital bridge – the 'phenomenological psychology' of a reading, in Ricoeur's sense. This split was foreshadowed in the first uses of the (notably integrative) encoding/decoding model – the *Nationwide* studies. These were divided between an analysis of this popular British news programme and a separate audience study (Brunsdon and Morley, 1978; Morley, 1980 and see also Brunsdon and Morley, 1999).

Texts without audiences

On one side of this division, a text analysis can centre on a single film or television programme, a particular genre (see, for example, Caughie, 2000) or authorial *oeuvre*, a set of intertextual relations, attached to a star (see, for example, Dyer, 1979, 1986) or a fictional character (Bennett and Woolacott, 1987) or even a whole 'apparatus' or industry – cinema or television, for instance (Ellis, 1992; Metz, 1974). Such studies have been more or less modest in the claims that they make about the audience and some text-based analysts are critical of audience studies as such (see, for example, Bennett and Woollacott, 1987; Modleski, 1986). It is commoner now, however, to leave a conceptual space in such studies for audience research.

One example of rigorous text analysis is the tradition of feminist film theory, which has centred on the way in which the viewer is pressured to take up a particular social-psychic position by the functioning of the cinematographic apparatus – the darkened room, screen, narrative form used and heavily gendered pleasures of spectatorship and 'the gaze' (Doanne 1982; Mulvey, 1975). Theoretically, this work developed the close associations between structuralist analysis (already central to much film theory) and Lacanian psychoanalysis – itself a structuralist appropriation of aspects of Freud's work. According to Lacan, the acquisition of language is part of the same process by which the unconscious is formed and human subjects are gendered within patriarchal power regimes. Adapted to the analysis of the viewing pleasures of film texts, this suggested that the spectator was an 'effect' of the cinema apparatus rather than a concrete person watching the film with particular responses and feelings. This work produced intense debate on the gendered aspects of film spectatorship, a debate that has helped to provoke a movement towards concrete audience research (Branston, 2000; de Lauretis, 1984; Doanne, Mellencamp and Williams, 1984; Gledhill, 1984; Kaplan, 1983; Modleski, 1988; Stacey, 1987, 1994; for a summary, see van Zoonen, 1994: 87–104). Analysing spectatorship in this textually-encoded sense is a productive way into the rhetorics and immediate setting of a particular medium. Similar ideas have been extended to television, where uses of domestic space, intimate social relations and forms of media address situated audiences rather differently (Ellis, 1992; compare Ang, 1996: 19–52).

Another text-based strategy has been to explore a whole field of discourses and 'reading formations', as in Bennett and Woollacot's (1987) study of the James Bond phenomenon. 'Reading formations' reminds us that readers of a particular genre at a particular historical time have to learn *how* to read it – as gendered and class subjects, for example (see, for example, Batsleer et al., 1985). Exploring such relationships involves combining text reading and historical contextualization – it is not always necessary or possible to talk to members of such a reading public. In summing up these forms of cultural study, Brunsdon makes a good case for 'the textual analysis of programmes', including the very close analysis of particular televisual features in a longer historical perspective (Brunsdon et al., 2001).

Difficulties arise, however, when analysts infer from their own reading the significance of the texts for other readers, today or in the past. The move from 'spectatorship' to 'social audiences' (Kuhn, 1984) cannot be so straightforward as too many additional determinations are involved. Another issue arises from our own stress on auto/biography. Analysts themselves always read from a certain position, within their own worlds, and/or from other worlds that they can imagine or fantasize about – that of 'the ordinary reader', for instance. Extending text-based approaches requires, therefore, two moves: first, a more self-conscious recognition of the analyst's own positionings and fantasies, and, second, systematic dialogue with other readers.

Referring readings to universal psychoanalytical mechanisms (that may have force in the analyst's own experience) is also quite a limited strategy. While there must be *some* common features in the viewing of any cultural form, adequate cultural analysis only really begins when we build variance into the ways in which individuals and groups react to the same text on the basis of their own social, cultural and psychic formation. As our knowledge of cultural–psychic processes advances – not least via therapeutic practices and writings – it becomes obvious that no one model of psychic processes applies to all texts, persons, times and places. Growing interest in the *range* of psychoanalytic theories – not only Freudian and Lacanian but also Kleinian, Object Relations, Jungian and so on – is an indication of the pursuit of psychic variance and complexity (for a useful introduction to different schools, see Frosch, 1987; for uses in cultural studies, see du Gay, Evans and Redman, 2000).

Audiences without texts

On the other side, 'concrete' research on audiences has focused on the social relations and conditions of reading and readers. In the case of television (the dominant medium among researchers), this has meant focusing on the gendered power relations of domestic spaces, the gendering of viewing preferences, ways in which television watching is either fitted into a routine or perceived as an 'event', temporal rhythms and 'levels of attention' involved in viewing, diversity of technologies and their patterns of use and, on ethnically specific readings, a still underdeveloped area (see, for example, Bausinger, 1984; Gillespie, 1989; Gray, 1992; Hermes, 1995; Hobson, 1980; 1982; Jhally and Lewis, 1992; Morley, 1980; 1986; 1992; Morley and Silverstone, 1990). Often lost in this 'radical contextualism' (Ang, 1996: 66–81) is detailed engagement with cultural forms by means of their textuality.

We have already suggested that feminist analysis of the audience is a partial exception to this splitting. The commitment to revaluing media texts watched by women in terms of the pleasures, resources, forms of support or escape that they provide has encouraged a closer engagement with the actual meanings of texts for readers. The text provides clues to (some) women's lives – especially their pleasures or identifications. Even the most integrative of feminist audience studies, however, do not altogether escape the splits we are describing. Ien Ang's study (1985) of the audience for the US primetime television drama *Dallas* in the Netherlands has something of the combinatory scope of Radway's *Reading the Romance*, discussed at the end of Chapter 9. As Brunsdon says of *Watching Dallas*:

> So Ang brings together work from many fields. She uses ideas from film and literary studies – pleasure and the melodramatic imagination – which are historically associated with a textual, rather than an empirical, audience, to investigate the television audience, normally conceptualized within mass communications and 'effects' paradigms. (2000: 149)

Ang's study drew on the material provided by a self-selected group of readers – primarily women – who responded to an advertisement she placed in a women's magazine, *Viva*, asking about the pleasures and ambivalences the programme elicited. Ang's work was pioneering in its use of the researcher's own responses (see Brunsdon, 2000: 150–1), but also in drawing together respondents' reasons for liking or hating the programme with a detailed account of the series as a melodrama. A connecting link of Ang's study is 'the tragic structure of feeling' that is central to the programme and active in the fantasy lives of its viewers. She holds back from considering the fuller significance of this structure in women's lives, regarding questions of pleasure and political evaluation as separate issues. This might be thought a limitation of the study and it follows, perhaps, both from the constraints of media studies as a research genre and from her indirect method of contact with respondents. Ang's account has also been criticized as too text-dependent, in the sense that the text of *Dallas* is taken as the primary determinant of meaning, which ultimately leads to the privileging of the interpretative claims of the theorist herself (Nightingale, 1993). The more anthropological critics see

Ang's work, perhaps misleadingly, as continuing to occupy the more literary, text-based side of media methodologies. This misses, however, the subtle shift of object in Ang's work – from the study of a text and its audience to an understanding of particular 'structures of feeling' that appear in one form in the media and another in women's everyday lives.

Recomposing media research

So why do these splits arise and why do they persist? How can they be deconstructed or recomposed? Are there some intrinsic limits to media studies that suggest a need to shift the object of study, to change the frame?

Splits and neglects

The splits persist in part because they correspond to disciplines and their core identities. Some version of the split between text and audience and text and production is likely to persist while social science students lack skills of text analysis and humanities students do not study social institutions or encounter debates in social theory and methodology.

Splitting also derives from traces of the politically inspired agendas of critical media studies. Here, too, a sharp division was made between media texts and audiences, with the first (often without much analysis) identified with dominant ideologies and the second with forms of 'resistance'. A fuller sense of the ambiguous relationship between the rhetoric of texts and the detailed subjective *work* of consumption is often lost in these confrontations.

The commonest absence in media studies is perhaps the phenomenological psychology of the reading itself. By this we mean, following Ricoeur in the main but also the work of Ang and Radway, some account of the significance of the world of the text in the world of the reader and also the reader's own applications of these features to their own lives. Media studies (as the study of culture) really clicks, in our view, when researchers define a feature of a text that resonates powerfully in the lives of readers and tell us why. Of course, there is a psychology in psychoanalytical accounts of spectatorship, but the psychology is first *described in the text* or the apparatus and then merely *ascribed to the reader*. The text 'writes' the reader; the reader is 'inscribed' in the text. There is no enquiry into the life and subjectivity of the reader prior to, or aside from, the mechanisms of the text.

Curiously, there is often a similar absence in audience studies, especially in its more sociological modes. Here, both the reading of the media text and the reading that the reader makes of it is often very abbreviated. It disappears into concern with the reader's social position and the immediate conditions of readership. Yet, though readings are always positional, they cannot be ascribed to a *social* position any more than they can be ascribed to the text that is read. Individual and psychic dynamics are always involved. Social positions, moreover, with their psychic accompaniments, are not simply given; they are always in the process of being made or remade. Interactions with media forms are part of this production of difference.

The more closely we look at readings, the better we understand the cultural work that media does, but, paradoxically, the further we move away from media studies. Much of the feminist work we have cited is only secondarily addressed to understanding media or even media audiences. Primarily, it has concerned women's subjective strategies – pleasures, desires, defences, compensations – in an oppressively gendered world. Studies such as *Reading the Romance* and *Watching Dallas* lead on to a different topic, which we could call 'identity research'. They are interested in understanding how individual and collective identities are constituted via readings, discourses, memories, narratives and material ways of life. As Ien Ang puts it:

> What matters is not the certainty of knowledge about audiences, but an ongoing critical and intellectual engagement with the multifarious ways we constitute ourselves through media consumption. (1996: 52)

To this we would add that it is not only via 'media consumption' that 'we constitute ourselves'. Studying the constitution, or self-production, of identities repositions media studies, altogether.

Recompositions in the media

The blurring of the text/audience boundary is especially evident in the new interactive media of the twenty-first century and in the reality TV formats that have emerged (Tincknell and Raghuram, 2002). Perhaps the most notable example, *Big Brother*, first appeared in The Netherlands in 1999 and was subsequently formatted throughout Europe, as well as the USA, Australia and Argentina during 2000. In the UK, it was the most successful of a cluster of programmes, including *Survivor* and *Castaway 2000*, which combined reality footage with a competitive element. Featuring a group of strangers living together for a period of nine weeks in a purpose-built house under the constant scrutiny of hidden television cameras, *Big Brother* offered a money prize for the contestant who stayed longest in the house. While the inhabitants volunteered two of their fellow inmates for eviction every week, it was the audience's vote for one of the two nominees that decided the outcome. Furthermore, in addition to the primary text – the television show with its edited highlights from daily video footage – viewers were offered continuous visual access to the house inhabitants via Internet webcams.

Big Brother is of special interest here because it made concrete what is true about *all* cultural production – that is, *the audience is always part of the production of textual meaning*. *Big Brother* compels us to recognize the artificiality of the academic distinction between 'text' and 'audience' and supports a closer relation between textual and ethnographic approaches. The blurring of the text/audience boundary occurs in two main ways.

First, unsuccessful contestants, expelled from the house, stepped out of 'the text' into the wider, intertextually mediated world. They gave interviews, wrote autobiographies and books of personal philosophy; they intervened in the production of meanings about themselves and each other. In effect, they redefined *Big Brother* itself. All this affected the audience, which was both extended and dislocated. The availability of the programme across multiple websites, together with the take-up of the show by more traditional media meant that who and where the audience might be at any given time became difficult to ascertain.

Second, however, the format made the participation of viewers in a weekly vote a central component of the programme, their preferences directly influencing the development of the 'plot'. So, not only was the *Big Brother* audience not defined by clear social and spatial locations, it actively participated in the 'events' it viewed (which themselves referenced everyday life). The narrative was explicitly shaped by audience preferences, expressed by means of the voting process but undoubtedly negotiated – and perhaps struggled over – on the website chat pages. The idea that the programme carried a set of 'preferred meanings' driven by institutional structures alone that produced and organized ideology was thus problematized when the audience became the 'author' of the text.

We are not arguing a romantic populist case for *Big Brother* any more than for the host of programmes where viewers vote or choose. Bazal, *Big Brother*'s production company, retained editorial control throughout, just as it constituted the rules and conventions of the new genre. However, we can say that interactive media encourage us to reform our divided methods. Just as the ideological cannot be ascribed simply to the media text and also inheres in popular choices, so methods of close reading that centre on textuality should not be reserved for the words and images that appear on the television set alone, but must also be applied to popular readings. To oppose reading media texts to studying media audiences and institutions is to keep running down a cul de sac. What is at issue, rather, is the place of textuality within the study of cultural processes as a whole and the forms of reading that are involved.

Remaking methods, shifting objects

Close reading in media studies developed in relation to the analysis of the media product as a text. However, as we have argued throughout this book, treating cultural practices as text is a *general* resource, to be applied to domestic discussions, chatroom interactions, interview transcripts and ways of riding motorbikes, too. Close textual analysis is also needed when it comes to studying readers' readings. This has implications for *research* as well as for *analysis*, and for sources as well as methods. We need *extended textual material that is produced by readers themselves* – life histories, extensive interviews or written or spoken memory work, for example. We need intensive work with respondents and coworkers that throws up associations and other half-conscious material and can work with transferences, resistances or defences. These could be workshops on particular media texts, for example, but equally on participants' lives. Such methods are more common in life and oral history, narrative inquiry, or, most recently, psycho-social research (see, for example, Hollway and Jefferson, 2000) than media studies. They connect with some kinds of cultural studies pedagogy (see, for example, workshops on particular media texts) and, indeed, with therapeutic practices. It is only by remaking methods in this way that the long-standing commitment to taking popular culture seriously can be fully realized.[1]

A similar argument applies to modes of analysis. We have already argued for combined and multiple readings in relation to ethnographic texts. There are always many coexisting but divergent processes going on in any cultural transaction, not all them available on first reading, only yielded up in further dialogue. This points to methods and styles of research that resemble group work and is where distinctions between research and analysis and researcher and researched are negotiated. Groupwork provides a space, also, to deal with the major ethical and political issues that arise where half-conscious material is sought and analysed. Such research may be difficult to conduct when the researcher's own subjective material is not also, in some way, on the line (see the discussion of the ethics of researching psycho-social subjects in Hollway and Jefferson, 2000: 83–103).

From this point of view, there are pros and cons of starting from a media text, a particular book, film or television programme or some specific genre. Such texts provide provocative or suggestive material with themes and generic forms that can be made very explicit. On the other hand, as agents produce themselves culturally in many different ways, we may sometimes need to start somewhere else.

Researching subjectivities: reflexive selves, discursive subjects

The shift from audiences to cultural identities is not a simple one. The study of identity itself has a long and complex cross-disciplinary history, with all terms strongly contested. In this chapter we can only sketch some involvements of cultural researchers and theorists in these themes, with an eye to the relations with psychological disciplines. In the rest of this chapter we argue, first, for a particular approach to cultural identity that has been termed 'psycho-social' and, second, for the adoption of particular methods of enquiry.

The limits of 'experience'

Many of the concerns suggested today by terms such as 'identity' or 'subjectivity' have been carried in cultural material traditions (and in much everyday language) by the term 'experience'. In *The Making of the English Working Class* (1963) E. P. Thompson drew on Marx's idea of 'class consciousness', but argued, with a distinctively New Left inflection, that the class created itself by coming to consciousness via experience. 'Experience', then, is a term that links conscious self-making, in practices as well as ideas, to social processes that forcibly reorder people's lives. In Thompson's book, the working class is 'made' as a result of collective responses to industrialization, proletarianization and the loss of common rights.

Difficult to clarify as a systematic idea, 'experience' was a keynote in all the social movements of the 1960s and 1970s. A new consciousness about the experiential self, for example, was central to early second-wave feminism. Betty Friedan (1963) set out to identify the experience of suburban alienation – 'the problem which has no name'- as the reason for (white) middle-class women's chronic discontent in the United States during the affluent post-war period. By identifying and analysing experiences specific to (some) women, she also helped to change what could be publicly spoken of and in what ways.

Twenty years later, Doris Sommer applied a similar approach to understanding women's memories and subjectivities in her work on Latin American women's 'testimonios', or accounts of the self. Sommer describes the witness given by Bolivian women, who were involved in a political struggle against the fascist dictator Somoza, of rape and torture while they were imprisoned.

Crucially, the women's articulations of the issues are based on a collectively produced sense of self, where 'the singular represents the plural not because it replaces or subsumes the group but because the speaker is a distinguishable part of the whole' (1988: 108). The testimonial becomes a way of producing change, offering 'the possibility to get beyond the gap between private and public spheres' (Sommer, 1988: 110). Feminist interventions have always sought to redefine experience to include the private as well as public spheres. The critical deconstruction of the relationship between the personal and the political helped to open up aspects of both 'private' and 'public' life for analysis and questioned this division itself, helping to make the problem of the cultural production of gender roles and identities more visible. This stress on socially situated experiences and knowledge, of the kind produced by feminist 'consciousness-raising', underlay, as we have seen, many of the epistemological and methodological changes of the later twentieth century, from standpoint epistemologies to the validating of subjectivity and auto/biography in research to specific methods such as memory work and some kinds of action research.

Rosalind Coward's *Female Desire* (1984) is an interesting 'transitional' text in this context. A kind of feminist *Mythologies* (Barthes, 1972), it ranged wider than the media, addressing questions of desire, sexuality, subjectivity and identity in women's everyday lives. Coward used psychoanalytically informed theories to explore the unconscious dimensions to women's relationships to eating, cooking, dressing, bodily ideals and photographs, reading novels, loving, kissing and keeping house. Her aims were to understand 'how the representations directed at women enmesh with our actual lives' and how '[f]eminine positions are produced as responses to the pleasures offered to us', often making change 'a difficult and daunting task' (1984: 15 and 16). Like Janice Radway (see Chapter 9), Coward uses theories of the unconscious to explore the continuing appeal of narratives that speak to women yet seem to reconfirm their subordination.

Both the general category of experience and the methodological inventions of feminism were subjected to the pressure of three sets of developments in the later 1980s. First, there was a move away from the kind of generalizing versions of psychic dynamics, mainly based on Lacanian theory, that had accompanied structuralist accounts of texts. Second, as we have seen, the main tendency in cultural theory was away from the big categories – such as 'women' and 'experience' – and towards a finer analysis in which difference and diversity played a central role. Finally, unified *political* categories were also challenged. The women's movement, for example, was charged with being exclusive, heterosexual, white and of the First World. 'Experience' could no longer be an unproblematical basis for epistemological or political claims. While Coward could draw relatively unproblematically on the experiences of 'herself and her friends and family' (1984: 14–15) as the source for her fieldwork, the question of auto/biography, along with the issues of self, other and identity, became major areas of contestation and debate (for a thoughtful overview, see Probyn, 1993).

One way in which to understand the subsequent work on subjectivity and identity is as an attempt to specify what is actually involved in the very chaotic term 'experience'. 'Experience' was unpacked: it included multiple differences in social positionalities; it included linguistic and psychic processes; it involved the discursive practices by means of which 'subjects' are made. It was a product, not an explanation. As Foucault put it, describing his work on sexuality:

> In short, it was a matter of seeing how an 'experience' came to be constituted in modern Western societies, an experience that caused individuals to recognize themselves as subjects of a 'sexuality', which was accessible to very diverse fields of knowledge and linked to a system of rules and constraints. (1987: 4).

Poststructuralist Interventions

From the mid-1980s, the problem of subjectivity or identity as discussed in cultural research started to take its contemporary shape. Much work in cultural studies (and cultural sociology and geography) focused on the complex intersections between social identities as foci of power and the production of complex selves – those between national identity and gender, race, ethnicity and sexuality, for example (see, for instance, Anthias and Yuval-Davis, 1989, 1992; Bhabha, 1990, 1994; Brah, 1996; Gilroy, 1986). Under the pressure both of new ways of thinking (especially poststructuralist theory) and new forms of political organization (the recognition of differences and the need for alliances or coalition politics), there was a strong interest in pluralizing identities – different masculinities and femininities, differently 'queer' sexualities (gay and straight), new ethnicities, which were the product of migration, multicultural association and cultural hybridity (on masculinities, see, for example, Chapman and Rutherford, 1988; Connell, 1995; Haywood and Mac An Ghaill, 2003; Mercer and Julien, 1988). At the same time, there were new disciplinary convergences, especially between cultural approaches to identity and critical strands in the psychological disciplines.

Postmodern redefinitions

These convergences happened within the broader context of postmodernism (as a shift in ways of thinking) or postmodernity (as a moment in historical change). Postmodern approaches have had an influence right across the humanities and social sciences, creating a common vocabulary with which to talk about issues of identity and subjectivity. These intellectual shifts, much broader than what is sometimes called 'the linguistic turn', have produced major changes in the ways in which personhood, the self and experience can be conceptualized (for a broad historical account of shifts in identity theory, see Hall, 1990).

If, as is often argued, the ontological self only comes into being via language, experience is itself produced by processes that are predominantly linguistic or discursive. To this we would add our own, more materialist stress on the importance of social practices of all kinds, including prefigurative symbolic action. However, the seemingly simple recognition that the category of 'experience' is actively constituted by cultural forms and social practices has far-reaching implications.

Important, too, has been the (still much contested) reintroduction of psychoanalytical ways of thinking about the self. This reintroduction has come from different sources – from the embedding of Lacanian psychoanalytical ideas within structuralist/poststructuralist theory, from independent feminist rereadings of Freud and his successors (Jessica Benjamin, 1990; Chodorow, 1978; Kristeva, 1984; Mitchell, 1974) and from a concern within literature and culture, with us–other relations of power and the subjectivities of racism in colonial and post-colonial contexts (Ashcroft, Griffiths and Tiffin, 1989; Bhabha, 1994; Chambers and Curti, 1996; Fanon, 1986; Said, 1978; Spivak, 1990) The older theoretical vocabularies – experience, the self, the individual, identity, consciousness – have therefore been questioned and often replaced by newer keywords – interpellation, the subject, subjectivity, identification, self–other relations.

As *processes* of the *constitution* of the self and social identities become important objects of study, a new series of questions emerge for cultural analysis. In particular, the ontological and epistemological relationships between what is unconscious or not conscious (defined psychoanalytically or otherwise) and what we categorize as our 'consciousness of experience' cannot be taken for granted, but must be explored as part of the enquiry.

Changing the subject: cultural studies and psychology

Changing the Subject was a key book for these questions in the mid-1980s (Henriques et al., 1984). It is significant for our argument, too, because it was read closely by two rather different readerships. It was put together by a group of close friends, all of whom had studied psychology or had professional engagements with the discipline, especially via educational studies. Dissatisfied with a first wave of critical humanistic psychologies, they were attracted, in differing degrees, to Foucauldian and psychoanalytical theory – strands of thinking often mutually opposed. *Changing the Subject* also connected with an existing cultural and linguistic turn within the psychological disciplines, the contested history of which over this period can be traced in attempts of vigorous minorities to reconstruct and deconstruct its theories and practices. In the 1990s, new psychologies – 'discursive' or 'critical' – developed in a complex relation to cultural studies and other cultural approaches, sometimes critiquing them quite harshly (see, for example, Billig, 1997), sometimes borrowing elements of theory and research to repair the 'lack in psychology's own methods – a theory of how meaning is achieved' (Hollway, 1989: 4).

Changing the Subject also became a standard text on many cultural studies reading lists, influencing many thesis writers and MA students. Cultural studies readers liked its concern with subjectivity and identity and the way in which the authors drew from familiar sources but put them together in new ways – Foucauldian discourse theory with elements of psychoanalysis, for instance. Moreover, the authors were addressing particular social identities as loci of complex forms of power. They used psychoanalytical notions mainly to show how subjects 'invested' in particular discourses, not as an all-embracing scheme. That cultural studies needed a psychology was widely recognized in the mid-1980s; it took longer to listen properly to what radical psychologists – with notable exceptions – were saying, even when themes or theories overlapped, as in Billig's work on fascism, ideology, monarchy, national identity and his interest in Bakhtin (Billig, 1978, 1982, 1992, 1995, 1997). Most commonly, perhaps, *Changing the Subject* was itself seen as a cultural studies book.

Approaching subjectivity

In a useful mapping of contemporary work on identity, du Gay, Evans and Redman distinguish three approaches that they call 'the subject in language', 'genealogies of subjectification' and 'psycho-social relations' (2000: 1–5). The first is familiar from our own discussions of structuralist theory (see Chapter 9), especially in its connections with psychoanalysis. As we have argued above, insufficient attention is paid to the world of the reader in its social, spatial, temporal and cultural aspects – hence the tendency to produce a flattened account of the reading process itself.

The limits of genealogy

The second approach identified by du Gay, Evans and Redman puts together two theoretical traditions that we have tended ourselves to separate: a Foucauldian genealogy or archaeology on the one side (see Chapter 7) and macro social theories of a broadly sociological kind on the other (see Chapter 8, and compare the sharper distinction made by Rose, 2000: 312). Central to both these socio-historical approaches, however, is a kind of determinism of social forms. It is, apparently, enough to describe the discourses (or the main social dynamics) to discern the forms of subjectivity. As du Gay puts it:

> Categories of persons, we discover, are only intelligible with reference to a definite substratum of discourses and practices which together give them their – complex and differentiated – forms . . . [L]egal, governmental and aesthetic forms of person, for example, stand in no general relationship to one another. No claim can be made that one of them is, in fact, *the* person itself. Each is a definite but limited form of personhood. (2000: 280)

One of the most consistent applications of this approach is Nikolas Rose's genealogies of the development of the psychological disciplines and the therapeutic practices that they founded (1990). In Rose's account, issues of context and reading – in the more phenomenological or psychological sense – dwindle to the point of disappearance:

> Such a genealogy, I suggest, requires only a minimal, weak or thin conception of the human material on which history writes . . . The human being, here, is not an entity with a history, but the target of a multiplicity of types of work, more like a latitude or a longitude at which different vectors of different speeds intersect. (2000: 321)

At most, for Rose, there is a kind of 'infolding' of 'anything that can acquire authority' or be discursively and spatially organized and institutionalized.

If we view this way of looking at identity and subjectivity methodologically, it presents familiar aspects. It reads particular kinds of texts in particular ways. There is the relatively abstracted text – typically, texts of 'the good life', manners or conduct or governmental regulation (see, for example, Rose, 1990). These texts are read not for what they represent, nor for the experiences they encode, but, rather, for the forms – usually the discourses – that can be abstracted from them. These are then taken as powerfully determining the forms of subjectivity. This method resembles, in short, our 'second reading' of Chapter 12.

We have argued already that, duly qualified, this is an essential mode of reading for any adequate cultural study. It enables the identification of the forms in relation to which human beings live subjectively as they are carried in the more public narratives and discourses. Staying with such a reading, however, restricts the questions we can ask about cultural processes and can circumscribe our forms of social participation in research. There are many questions without an answer within these frameworks – we can only indicate a few here.

- How do concrete persons or social groups negotiate the relationships of *different* discourses, 'infoldings' or subject positions, contemporaneously or historically?
- How can we speak about the different degrees and kinds of subjective involvement with which concrete persons take up, actively reject or are passively complicit in forms of identity and subjectivity? How can we distinguish instrumental attachment or occasional conformity from conviction or commitment?
- How can we explore forms of living that do not, on the whole, appear in the public records such methods usually use?
- From what position does the analyst speak when undertaking a work of genealogy or archaeology?
- What are the principles of historical continuity or 'tradition' in identities or discursive formations? What part do memory and anticipation and other representations of the past and the future play in the process of producing individual and collective identities?
- What does radical discourse analysis imply for self–other relations in research – or, indeed, for intersubjective social practices more generally?

Althusser's and Macherey's question (see Chapter 11). – about 'answers which have no question' – is also relevant here. Radical Foucauldian accounts, such as Rose's, continue to invoke features of human individuals and social groups that, in theory, they have bracketed out or erased: 'the soul' (governable, it seems, but with no substance of its own), 'human material' ('thin' but there?), 'human being' (which is 'enacted' or performed, but has no features), 'memory' (organized by rituals and practices but not remembering anything in particular?) or passion or the 'affective' (only describable in terms of its 'secluded spaces' and 'sensualized equipment') (Rose, 2000; 1990). Specifically human activities, such as memory, emotion, imagination or thinking, are ascribed to 'apparatuses' or 'technologies'. As a form of understanding, it often seems as though applied genealogy, though fascinating, is also itself quite 'thin', insensitive to ambiguities, silences and the irrational nature of investments in power, knowledge and identities and, therefore, curiously un-self-aware.

As we have stressed throughout, theoretical and methodological choices are closely related to practical agendas. The form of genealogical analysis developed by Rose, for instance, provides an incisive way of identifying and describing regulative practices – the particular governmental regimes associated with neo-liberalism or with Third Way politics, for example (Rose, 1996, 1999a). These can be read as forms of regulation of the self in which subjects, including professional subjects, are incited to reinvent themselves continuously according to the requirements of constantly shifting occupational structures in a globalized economy. It is not surprising that genealogical approaches to governmentality are of interest to those who see cultural studies as a reformer's science (see, for example, Bennett, 1998).

The fostering of popular agency and making a different kind of world is less well served by this approach. So are professional practices that centre on interpersonal or intersubjective exchanges and recognition, such as educational and therapeutic practices. Though such practices may officially conform to overarching forms of regulation, they are often also about finding spaces in between. Where face-to-face or intersubjective relationships are important, issues about biography, personal histories and feelings necessarily arise. They arise, too, in a different form, in practices of political organization, the building of coalitions or development of social movements. Such political practices can never be only a matter of rearticulating discourses – they involve solidarities, passion and forms of imagination that go beyond current realities. These concerns point towards a 'thicker' or 'stickier' notion of 'the human material on which history writes' than is thinkable within a Foucauldian framework.

Psycho-social relations – or the case of the 'sticky' subject

We recognize – along with most contemporary writers on identity – that there is no going back to the idea of individuals simply as authors of their lives, in charge of their own identity. The (de)constructivist rereading of identity as in some sense impossible or a fiction is especially important today, given the dominance of neo-liberal, or consumerist conceptions of the subject that centre on an individualized self-making characterized in terms of 'lifestyle' or 'choice'. By stressing individual autonomy, neo-liberal ideologies also fail to grasp the nature and sources of social and psychic dependence or interdependence at every level of the social scale – between people, in and between groups and collectivities, and at the level of the global. We are, therefore, particularly attracted to those forms of postmodern theory – broadly dialectical or dialogic – that restore a sense of the *relational* nature of identity or subjectivity, while recognizing that, unlike the 'community' of Third Way politics, the forms of the social are often unfair and antagonistic and subject to contestation. The challenge, then, is to rethink our ideas of individual and collective identity in the face of an understanding of emotional life and the social-cultural construction of identities as forms of *difference* and *relationship* on a worldwide scale.

Social identities are an aspect of social relations, which always involve meaning, power and psychic or emotional dimensions. Collective identities and individual subjectivities are the outcome of socio-cultural processes. As psychoanalytical and neurological insights make clear, our bodily capacities are activated by means of sensual, cognitive, emotional and practical interactions that join us to the natural and social world. In a properly concrete analysis, however, these interactions always exceed the terms of any one discursive construction. Certainly, new interpellations or emergent discourses carry their own constructive force, produce 'new subjects' in this 'thin' or limited sense, but the *material* on which they work is not thin at all. Rather, it consists of what is already constituted in history, space and social relations and embedded in ongoing cultural formations. These pre-existing forms of life, with their emotional identifications and animosities, often peculiar and personal, act as a viscous medium, sometimes attracting new additions, sometimes repelling them. This is true for individual biography and memory, but also for more collective histories of local or institutional sedimentation and change. It is in this sense that the human material of self-making is always 'sticky' – it always carries with it elements from past encounters, both consciously present as emotionally invested stories of the past and as less conscious effects of a past history. From a political point of view, contemporary identities and possibilities of change are formed in a history of hegemonies, failed settlements, partial victories, oppositions and alternatives, unfinished business and remaining hopes. This is why the first and final moment of the circuit is so important in any account of method – the sedimented forms of everyday ways of living are both the starting point *and* the complex *product* of the cultural circuit as a whole.

The other postmodernisms

While some strands in identity theory stress the flux, indeterminacy and 'impossibility' of identity in post- or late-modern conditions, others extend and deepen notions of social relations derived from Marxist theory and emancipatory forms of politics. We include some, but not all, forms of psychoanalysis, especially those that focus on intersubjective relations and can handle, centrally, issues of power discrepancy and misrecognition (Jessica Benjamin, 1990; du Gay,

Evans and Redman, 2000: 121–276). Psychoanalysis is important for cultural analysis not so much for its ready-made stories of the making of gendered and sexed subjects, but for its repertoire of ideas for understanding the unconscious, partly conscious, non-rational and emotional aspects of social relationships and meaning production. This form of postmodern sensitivity draws together its own selective dialectical and dialogic 'tradition' (see, for example, du Bois, 1989; Bakhtin, 1981b; Fanon, 1986; Hegel, 1977; Marx, for example, 1973; Volosinov, 1973). The strongest applications are around colonial histories, post-colonial interactions and issues relating to the sexual, though class, too, can be (re)understood in these terms – as an emotionally laden social relationship of a particular kind, as much a 'subjective' as an 'objective' one (see, for example, Stallybrass and White, 1986).

'Queer theory' is especially interesting here because it brings together rereadings of Foucault's extensive work on the sexual with borrowings from different psychoanalytic schools. Where Foucault rejected psychoanalysis as just another disciplinary apparatus, Judith Butler (1993) attempts to bring Foucauldian models of discourse together with a reading of Freud. For Butler, sexuality is also central to discourse, but she argues that the materiality of bodies is as important as discursive structures in the production of subjectivities. Butler aims to free feminist theory from the necessity of having to construct a single or abiding ground from which to argue as this will always be contested by those whose identity positions it excludes. However, she also posits that the construction of 'woman' as a coherent and stable category is the result of the regulation and reification of gender relations, especially in the practice of naming or citing sexual difference – something that has created the appearance of a natural division. Butler calls this the 'performativity' of sex and gender, a system whereby the iteration of sexual norms or practices by legal, medical or educational citation produces a hegemonic version of subjectivities. The performance of femininity or masculinity thus involves the reiteration of a set of norms that are themselves compelled by the regulatory discursive regimes of heterosexuality, gender and normativity and, therefore, involve forgettings or forms of 'melancholia', especially around same sex desire.

It is from this perspective that developments in contemporary psychology – 'critical', 'rhetorical' or 'discursive' (with their own controversies) – are of great interest (see, for example, Billig, 1996; Hollway, 1989; Sampson, 1993; Walkerdine, 1990).[2] These tend to focus on smaller-scale intersubjective interactions rather than the institutionalized social narratives that interest the genealogists. Like ethnographic forms of cultural studies, they are close to, but also critical of, phenomenological traditions in sociology and philosophy. A common empirical focus is conversational analysis, where identities are seen as being constructed, via discursive means, in intersubjective relations. Like some main strands of cultural studies, critical psychologies are attracted to dialogic theories of language and are often critical of structuralism. Here, too, however, familiar debates take place between those attracted to psychoanalytical theory (long scorned by psychological 'science') and those who are closer to the genealogists in seeing discourse or performative practices as sufficient to found the subject

(Wetherell, 2003). The key issue here is whether or not an internal domain of the human subject, with its own distinctive world of objects – images, emotions, the unconscious – exists at all.

Method again: sources, analysis

The cultural study of identity and subjectivity involves innovations in the production of materials (research) and ways of reading (analysis). We end this chapter by returning to two earlier arguments about methods – that of the importance of auto/ethnography, including group memory work discussed in Chapter 12, and the necessity of a fourth reading of such materials, covered in Chapter 13. We conclude by emphasizing the integrative nature of this kind of research.

Cultural psychology and auto/biographical representation

A persistent difficulty of cultural approaches to subjectivity concerns their empirical basis. Psychoanalysis has depended on clinical case work and, in the case of the Kleinian tradition especially, on the observation of children's play, though self-analysis has also played a part. Cultural approaches to subjectivity, however, presuppose that subjectivities are constituted via particular cultural forms. How, then, are these to be accessed? They almost always have some 'external' presence in word or performance, but they also operate, as our experience of everyday self-narration suggests, in an inner domain as well. As Volosinov in *Marxism and the Philosophy of Language* asks, 'What, then, is the sign material of the psyche?' (1973: 28) or what are the types of inner speech and mental image-making?

Although inner process accompanies and is often incited by social performance, it is often hard to gain access to inner meanings except very indirectly. There are, however, many different ways in which – in everyday life and specialist practices – these inner processes are 'quoted' and externalized. Inner speech, feelings or thinking are, for example, frequently represented in fictional writing and other imaginative forms, such as film. Diary-writing and self-analysis are used in psycho-dynamic theory and training. Auto/biographical writings are especially important here – they may mimic, though they cannot quite reproduce, inner dialogue and narrative. The translation between inner process and its external representation is itself a social realization of inner expressions that are inchoate, half-formed and often highly condensed – we may only know what we are thinking or feeling when we express it to others, give it definite cultural form. However, it is a common experience to feel a sense of loss or diminution when some private desire is articulated. Either way, there is material enough for self-understanding and communicating to others something of an inner world. There is also the possibility of textualization and, therefore, a closer cultural analysis.

Group auto/biography provides opportunities for the close and comparative production of such materials. It is also possible to tell stories in such a group and transcribe and analyse them, paying particular attention to intonation, hesitations and markers of emotional significance. There is much scope here for linking cultural, linguistic and psychologically informed analysis. Moreover, as subjects are participating, longer-term, in group work, it is possible for stories to be contextualized by further memory narratives and scene-setting. Indeed, it can be a rule of procedure that the first contextualizing comments always come from authors themselves. In this way, a group of relative equals, working auto/biographically, can lessen, though they cannot altogether avoid, the intractable issues of power and ethics that arise in analysing, with no therapeutic intention or safeguards, someone else's psychic processes.

Auto/biography, self-production and the fourth reading

Auto/biographical texts can, in principle, be analysed in all the ways we recommend for ethnographic transcriptions – that is, aiming to understand the author's situated production of meaning, the cultural forms (such as forms of narrative) that are used in such self-production and engage with the conditions of a life, a world and a horizon. These different readings, however, are given an integrative focus if we treat such narratives as examples of self-production, as they often are. This self-production occurs under material and cultural conditions that authors cannot control, though they give their stories their own intonation and individual symbolic value. The researcher (who may also be the storyteller) can ask the following questions.

- What are the cultural forms that are drawn on to narrate this self?
- How are public/social versions of this narrative being used or transformed?
- What is the character of the subject so produced?

From a more dialogic perspective, questions can centre on how a story is shaped and constrained by the conditions of its production and reception. This involves paying as much attention to the process by which a story is selected, written and/or read as to the form and content of the story itself.

Identity work and integration

The whole circuit of cultural production is manifestly present in such forms of researching, with a corresponding necessity to integrate a wide range of methods and readings. As a micro social interaction, speaking or writing about your life for particular others and according to certain conventions mimics the larger social processes by which individuals or particular communities make their bids for social recognition and are linked to wider public practices (see, for example, Plummer, 1995; also the account of memory work in Chapter 12 above). Depending on the power relations of the wider cultural field, which are themselves configured by economic, coercive and other structures, such bids may be recognized and enabled to develop, refused or denied or recognized only under certain conditions of conformity. Following such pressures to remodel an identity – cutting or stretching a self to fit some dominant template – is perhaps the commonest experience of identity in unequal societies. Moreover, it is as a result of these relations of social (mis)recognition, that inner/outer boundaries – what can and can't be represented within a situation – are themselves constituted. The production of a self is always contingent on conditions that operate right round the cultural circuit and enter into the psyche itself. Self-production is also intimately a coproduction – that of a self in relation to other selves and in relation to larger social conditions. Researching the self in cultural studies is not *only* a way of finding out about the relations of self and others or even, as it undoubtedly is, a way of exploring larger socio-cultural circumstances. It is also a way of producing ourselves in our relations to others anew and coming up with some new possibilities. As Elspeth Probyn puts it, in a book that parallels many of our own concerns, 'Speaking the self does not necessarily imply any triumphant move; rather . . . the self may simply and quietly enable yet more questions . . .' (1993: 106).

Conclusion: remaking methods

We have argued in this chapter for approaches to the study of culture that move beyond the splitting of methodological traditions characteristic of much media studies. Here, textuality tends to be assigned to the media text itself, while audiences are looked at more sociologically, with an eye to the conditions of reception. One key integrative move, which is found only in a few studies (see, for example, Ang, 1985; Radway, 1984), is to evoke and then analyse a relatively elaborate account of the *readers' reading of a text or genre* – the readers' own quoting, framing and interpretation, for instance, of a text that has moved them emotionally. Such an approach is methodologically integrative. It must deal with the reader's life and circumstances (in its social, spatial and temporal aspects for example), but must also engage textually not only with the text that the reader reads but also the reading that the reader makes of it. In an extension of the approach well beyond the current limits of media studies, it can also explore the consequences or applications of such a reading in the reader's life – its resonances in memory and practice, for example, in later life stages.

As Ang herself makes clear, the logic of *developing* the problematic of media audience studies leads us out of media studies into a different programme of research. This takes subjectivities or identities as the main topic. It explores the relationships between the most powerful discourses that circulate in small and extended public spaces and the narratives, fantasies, symbols and personal myths by which individuals and groups live their lives in relation to others. At this point, cultural analysis – with or without a psychoanalytical inflection – converges with the new discursive and critical psychologies, which are also interested in how subjects position themselves within a cultural field or set of discourses.

Two issues then arise for cultural studies. The first concerns the sources for such a study; the second the forms of analysis to be pursued.

We have argued that the auto/biographical turn in cultural studies, sociology and literary studies (which includes group memory work) provides materials for this kind of analysis, though, in truth, these lie everywhere to hand. It also suggests ways in which to organize research in small collectives that lessen or make more explicit and more manageable the problematic ethical–political issues that are involved.

In analysing auto/biographical texts of this kind, it is possible to learn both from the text and the experience of its production. The text can tell us about the forms of subjective life, the larger contexts and personal meanings of which can be explicated by the author and critically read by researchers. The process of production for group consumption can itself tell us much about the dialogic aspects of identity especially the shaping of self-representation by the conditions of reception.

In such studies, text- and person-based research is integrated rather than split off. The person is a bearer of many texts, texts that signify, most fully, according to personal repertoires of meaning and feeling, conscious and unconscious, that are related to biography. These repertoires can themselves be textualized in different practices and therefore investigated by critical auto/ethnographic means. Similarly, from this point of view, it makes much less sense to split methods for dealing with relatively abstracted public forms from those that explore the local and the concrete. The publicly circulating cultural forms, discourses or hegemonic philosophies are conditions of production for local meanings and vice versa. These exchanges and interpenetrations become more and more complex with the new cultural propinquities that are typical of a globalized world. At the same time, although this world is, in one sense, compressed in space and time, the social production of differences in space and time is by no means abolished, so a critical sense of space and time is integral to such methods. One typical deficiency of contemporary cultural theorizing is precisely this failure of time/space placement and the recognition of continuing differences and power relations.

The combination and integration of methods is not, however, the same as reducing all methods to one, nor should it be a reason to abolish specialisms. We are assuming a transdisciplinary academic world, not a post-disciplinary one. Students of the cultural-in-context do need perspectives and methods drawn initially from literary, linguistic and visual disciplines – even at their most elaborate and formal – as well as those from the disciplines of context. They need to engage with the findings and main theoretical frameworks of sociologists and those who make a specialism of different ways of studying power.

Cultural studies might then be thought of as a kind of specialism of non-speciality. Its interest is in interpreting and explaining cultural processes as a whole, as they operate in time, space and social relations. Above all, perhaps, it stays alive to what is happening in (and to) the world as a special kind of responsibility.

Notes

1 We are grateful to Joanne Whitehouse for discussions on these themes in relation to her own innovative project, which in many ways, takes off where this chapter ends.
2 We are especially grateful to Nigel Edley, Peter Redman, Valerie Walkerdine and Margaret Wetherell for discussions concerning the relationships of discursive and critical psychologies and cultural studies approaches to identity and to The Changing Men and Memory Work Group, the Narrative Group and Popular Memory Group (1982–1986) for their different roles in developing memory work methods.

In conclusion

The moment of writing in research is often understood and treated as a moment of closure, a 'happy ending', perhaps, to the project. In particular, the conclusion to a book offers a device, a textual strategy, for this closure. Conclusions are expected to draw strands and ideas together, establish finishing points and summarize arguments – even where this is explicitly recognized as a convention rather than an expression of the finiteness of the work. Yet writing, particularly writing conclusions, also always involves a reader or readers, reading constituencies and communities. If we return briefly to Gadamer, we can see that, rather than being a point of absolute closure, writing becomes a point in the process of dialogue with 'thou', the other. The text is opened out to others, different readings and alterity. Rather than offering this conclusion as closure for this book, then, we want to emphasize the potential here for opening ourselves up to further conversations. The best learning is always a form of dialogue and involves exposing ourselves to (self-)assessment rather than uncritical tradition-building.

Throughout this book, we have emphasized the need to create our own methods to fit our research questions. We have argued that we can only offer positional readings and arguments, grounded in our own (social and political) contexts. However, it is equally important to open these up, have our methods reframed within other contexts. Engagements in questions of culture-as-power have involved a set of shifting concerns and positions, from class and nationality to gender, race, ethnicity, sexuality and ability – all of which entail moves in ontological and epistemological discourse.

Openness to difference and especially differences that make a difference, have therefore been central to the project of cultural research. We expect that the emergence of new cultural formations and identities – perhaps of a character that we cannot currently conceptualize – will bring with them new concerns and critical interventions. Most importantly for us, we recognize that the nature of cultural research is likely to be transformed by the increasingly globalized and international focus of all kinds of contemporary culture. These concerns will perhaps be framed in other ontological and epistemological contexts, requiring other methods or combinations of methods.

Thus, in this conclusion that is not a conclusion, we would like to argue for some continuities with the past, but also want to encourage critical contestations. Struggles over meaning and knowledge are ultimately productive, even if they are sometimes painful. Writing this book has made us aware of our own attachments to positions and disciplinary frameworks. However, we would argue that cultural studies has always made space for awkward people. This is a good tradition. Our reading of method, we hope, enables this awkwardness. Being critical about methodology as well as theory – especially the institutionalization of methods and their defence in relation to disciplinary power – is and will be crucial to future academic and political practice.

References

Adorno, T.W. and Horkheimer, M. (1972) 'The culture industry – enlightenment as mass deception', in J. Cumming (tr.), *Dialectic of Enlightenment*. New York: Herder and Herder.

Alasuutari, Pertti (1995) *Researching Culture: Qualitative Method and Cultural Studies*. London: Sage.

Althusser, Louis (1969) *For Marx*. Tr. from the French by Ben Brewster. London: Allen Lane.

Althusser, Louis (1971) *Lenin and Philosophy and Other Essays*. Tr. from the French by Ben Brewster. London: NLB.

Althusser, Louis (1971) *Lenin and Philosophy*. New York: Monthly Review Press.

Althusser, Louis and Balibar, Etienne (1970) *Reading Capital*. Tr. from the French by Ben Brewster. London: NLB.

Altman, Rick (1989) *The American Film Musical*. Bloomington: Indiana University Press.

Amadiume, I. (1993) 'The mouth that spoke the falsehood will later speak the truth: going home to the field in Eastern Nigeria', in Diana Bell, Pata Caplan, and Wazier Jahan Karim (eds), *Gendered Fields: Women, Men and Ethnography*. London: Routledge. pp. 182–98.

Anderson, B. (1991) *Imagined Communities: Reflections on the Origins and Spread of Nationalism*. Revised edition. London: Verso.

Ang, Ien (1985) *Watching Dallas: Soap Opera and the Melodramatic Imagination*. London: Methuen.

Ang, Ien (1996) *Living Room Wars: Rethinking Media Audiences for a Postmodern World*. London: Routledge.

Ang, Ien (1998) 'Doing cultural studies at the crossroads: local/global negotiations', *European Journal of Cultural Studies*, 1 (1): 13–32.

Anthias, Floya and Yuval-Davis, Nira (1989) *Woman-Nation-State*. London: Macmillan.

Anthias, Floya and Yuval-Davis, Nira (1992) *Racialized Boundaries: Race, Nation, Gender, Colour and Class and the Anti-racist Struggle*. London: Routledge.

Appadurai, A. (1990) 'Disjuncture and difference in the global cultural', in M. Featherstone (ed.), *Global Culture: Nationalism, Globalization and Modernity*. London: Sage.

Armistead, N. (ed.) (1974) *Reconstructing Social Psychology*. Harmondsworth: Penguin.

Ashcroft, Bill, Griffiths, Gareth and Tiffin, Helen (1989) *The Empire Writes Back: Theory and Practice in Post-colonial Literatures*. London and New York: Routledge.

Back, Les (1994) *New Ethnicities and Urban Culture: Racisms and Multi-culture in Young Lives*. London: UCL Press.

Back, Les (1998) 'Reading and writing research', in C. Seale (ed.), *Researching Society and Culture*. London: Sage.

Bakhtin, M.M. (1981a) *The Dialogic Imagination*. Michael Holquist (ed.) and Caryl Emerson and Michael Holquist (tr.). Austin: The University of Texas Press.

Bakhtin, Mikhail (1981b) 'Discourse and the novel', in Michael Hollquist (ed.) and Caryl Emerson and Michael Holquist (tr.), *The Dialogic Imagination*. Austin: University of Texas Press. pp. 259–422.

Barker, Chris (2000) *Cultural Studies: Theory and Practice*. Foreword by Paul Willis. London: Sage.

Barker, M. (1981) *The New Racism: Conservatives and the Ideology of the Tribe*. London: Junction Books.

Barrett, Michelle (1991) *The Politics of Truth: From Marx to Foucault*. Cambridge: Polity Press.
Barthes, Roland (1967) *Elements of Semiology*. London: Jonathan Cape.
Barthes, Roland (1971) 'The rhetoric of the image', *Working Papers in Cultural Studies*, 1: 37–50.
Barthes, Roland (1972) *Mythologies*. Selected and tr. from the French by Anette Havers. London: Cape.
Barthes, Roland (1977) *Music-Image-Text*. Essays selected and tr. from the French by Stephen Heath. London: Fontana.
Batsleer, Janet, Davis, Tony, O'Rourke, Rebecca and Weedon, Chris (1985) *Rewriting English: Cultural Politics of Gender and Class*. London: Methuen.
Bausinger, H. (1984) 'Media, technology and daily life', *Media, Culture and Society*, 6 (4): 343–51.
Beck, Ulrich (1992) *The Risk Society: Towards a New Modernity*. London: Sage.
Beck, U., Giddens, A. and Lash, S. (1994) *Reflexive Modernisation*. Cambridge: Polity Press.
Belsey, Catherine (1980) *Critical Practice*. London: Routledge.
Bendix, Regina (1997) *In Search of Authenticity: The Formation of Folklore Studies*. Wisconsin: University of Wisconsin Press.
Benjamin, Jessica (1990) *The Bonds of Love: Psychoanalysis, Feminism and the Problem of Domination*. London: Virago.
Benjamin, Walter (1992) *Illuminations*. London: Fontana.
Bennett, Tony (1998) *Culture: A Reformer's Science*. London: Sage.
Bennett, Tony and Woollacott, Janet (1987) *Bond and Beyond: The Political Career of a Popular Hero*. Basingstoke: Macmillan.
Bernstein, Basil (1973) *Class Codes and Control*, Vol 1. St Albans: Paladin.
Bhabha, Homi K. (ed.) (1990) *Nation and Narration*. London: Routledge.
Bhabha, Homi K. (1994) *The Location of Culture*. London: Routledge.
Bhavnani, K. (1994) 'Tracing the contours: feminist research and feminist objectivity', in Haleh Afshar and Mary Maynard (eds), *The Dynamics of 'Race' and Gender: Some Feminist Interventions*. Bristol, Pennsylvania: Taylor and Francis. pp. 26–40.
Billig, Michael (1978) *Fascists: A Social-psychological Analysis of the National Front*. London: Academic Press.
Billig, Michael (1982) *Ideology and Social Psychology: Extension, Moderation and Contradiction*. Oxford: Basil Blackwell.
Billig, Michael (1992) *Talking of the Royal Family*. London: Routledge.
Billig, Michael (1995) *Banal Nationalism*. London: Sage.
Billig, Michael (1996) *Arguing and Thinking: A Rhetorical Approach to Social Psychology*. London: Sage.
Billig, Michael (1997) 'From codes to utterances: cultural studies, discourse and psychology', in Marjorie Ferguson and Peter Golding (eds), *Cultural Studies in Question*. London: Sage. pp. 205–26.
Blair, Tony, speeches – see end of References section.
Bloom, Allan (1987) *The Closing of the American Mind*. New York: Simon and Schuster.
Blunt, A. (1994) 'Reading Mary Kingsley's landscape descriptions', in A. Blunt and G. Rose (eds), *Writing Women and Space: Colonial and Post-colonial Geographies*. London: Guildford University Press.
Bordwell, David (1985) *Narration in the Fiction Film*. Madison, Wisconsin: University of Wisconsin Press.
Bourdieu, Pierre (1986) *Distinction: A Social Critique of the Judgement of Taste*. London: Routledge and Kegan Paul.
Brah, Avtar (1996) *Cartographies of Diaspora: Contesting Identities*. London: Routledge.

Brah, Avtar and Coombes, Annie (eds) (2000) *Hybridity and its Discontents: Politics, Science, Culture*. London: Routledge.

Brannigan, John (1998) *New Historicism and Cultural Materialism*. Basingstoke: Macmillan.

Branston, Gill (2000) *Cinema and Cultural Modernity*. Buckingham: Open University Press.

Bromley, Roger (1986) 'The gentry, bourgeois hegemony and popular fiction: Rebecca and Rogue Male', in Peter Humm, Paul Stigant and Peter Widdowson (eds), *Popular Fictions: Essays in Literature and History*. London: Methuen. pp. 151–72.

Brunsdon, Charlotte (2000) *The Feminist, The Housewife and the Soap Opera*. Oxford: Clarendon Press.

Brunsdon, Charlotte and Morley, David (1978) *Everyday Television: 'Nationwide'*. British Film Institute Monograph, London: BFI.

Brunsdon, Charlotte and Morley, David (1999) 'The *Nationwide* project: long ago and far away', in D. Morley and C. Brunsdon, *The Nationwide Television Studies*. London: Routledge.

Brunsdon, Charlotte, Johnson, Catherine, Moseley, Rachel and Wheatley, Helen (2001) 'Factual entertainment on British television: the Midlands TV Research Group '8–'9 Project', *European Journal of Cultural Studies*, 14 (1): 29–62.

Bush, George W., speeches – see end of References section.

Butler, Judith (1993) *Bodies that Matter: On the Discursive Limits of 'Sex'*. New York: Routledge.

Butler, Judith (1999) *Gender Trouble* (10th Anniversary edn). New York and London: Routledge.

Carr, M. (1996) *Speaking Out: Women's Economic Empowerment in South Asia*. Intermediate Technology.

Carspecken, P.F. (1996) *Critical Ethnography in Educational Research: A Theoretical and Practical Guide*. London: Routledge.

Castells, M. (1994) 'European cities, the information society, and the global economy', *New Left Review*, 204.

Castells, Manuel (2000) *The Rise of the Network Society* (2nd edn.). Oxford: Blackwell.

Caughie, John (2000) *Television Drama: Realism, Modernism and British Culture*. Oxford: Oxford University Press.

Centre for Contemporary Cultural Studies (1973) 'Literature/society: mapping the field', *Working Papers in Cultural Studies*, 4 (Spring): 21–50.

Centre for Contemporary Cultural Studies (1977) *On Ideology*. Birmingham: The Centre.

Centre for Contemporary Cultural Studies (1982) *Making Histories: Studies in History-writing and Politics*. London: Hutchinson.

Centre for Contemporary Cultural Studies Education Group (1980) *Unpopular Education: Schooling and Social Democracy Since 1944*. London: Hutchinson.

Centre for Contemporary Cultural Studies Education Group II (1991) *Education Limited: Schooling and Training and the New Right since 1979*. London: Hutchinson.

Chambers, D. (2003) 'Family as place: family photograph albums and the domestication of public and private space', in J. Schwartz and J. Ryan (eds), *Picturing Place: Photography and the Geographical Imagination*. London: I.B. Tauris. pp. 96–114.

Chambers, Iain and Curti, Lydia (eds) (1996) *The Post-colonial Question: Common Skies, Divided Horizons*. London: Routledge.

Chan, Stephen (2001) *The Zen of International Relations*. London: Palgrave.

Chandavarkar, Rajnarayan (1997) 'Histories: the making of the working class: E.P Thompson and Indian History', *History Workshop Journal*, 43 (Spring): 177–97.

Chapman, Rowena and Rutherford, Jonathan (1988) *Male Order: Unwrapping Masculinity*. London: Lawrence and Wishart.

Cheater, A. (1995) *The Anthropology of Power*. London: Routledge.

Chodorow, Nancy (1978) *The Reproduction of Mothering: Psychoanalysis and the Sociology of Gender.* Berkeley, California: University of California Press.

Clare, Mariette and Johnson, Richard (2000) 'Method in our madness? Identity and power in a memory work method', in Susannah Radstone (ed.), *Memory and Methodology.* Oxford: Berg.

Clarke, Alan (1992) '"You're nicked!": Television police series and the fictional representation of law and order', in Dominic Strinati and Stephen Wagg (eds), *Come on Down? Popular Media Culture in Post-war Britain.* London and New York: Routledge.

Clifford, J. (1986) 'Introduction: partial truths', in J. Clifford and G.E. Marcus (eds), *Writing Culture: The Poetics and Politics of Ethnography.* Berkeley, California: University of California Press

Clifford, J. (1988) *The Predicament of Culture: Twentieth-century Ethnography, Literature and Art.* Cambridge, Massachusetts: Harvard University Press.

Clifford, James and Marcus, George (eds) (1986) *Writing Culture: The Poetics and Politics of Ethnography.* Berkeley, California: University of California Press.

Cohan, S. (2000) 'Case study: interpreting *Singin' in the Rain*', in C. Gledhill and L. Williams (eds) *Reinventing Film Studies.* London and New York: Arnold and Oxford University Press.

Cohen, Phil (1972) 'Subcultural conflict and working-class community', *Working Papers in Cultural Studies* 2, and republished in S. Hall, D. Hobson, A. Lowe and P. Willis (eds) (1980) *Culture, Media, Language.* London: Hutchinson. pp. 78–87.

Cohen, Phil (1993) *Home Rules: Some Reflections on Racism and Nationalism in Everyday Life.* London: University of East London.

Collins, Patricia Hill (1990) *Black Feminist Thought: Knowledge, Consciousness and the Politics of Empowerment.* Boston, Massachusetts: Unwin Hyman.

Connell, R.W. (1995) *Masculinities.* Cambridge: Polity.

Corner, John and Harvey, Sylvia (eds) (1991) *Enterprise and Heritage: Cross currents of National Culture.* London: Routledge.

Couldry, Nick (2000) *Inside Culture: Re-imagining the Method of Cultural Studies.* London: Sage.

Coward, Rosalind (1984) *Female Desire: Women's Sexuality Today.* London: Paladin.

Cox, R.W. with Sinclair, T.J. (1996) *Approaches to World Order.* Cambridge: Cambridge University Press.

Crang, M. (2000) 'Relics, places and unwritten geographies in the work of Michel de Certeau (1925–86)', in M. Crang and N. Thrift (eds), *Thinking Space.* London: Routledge.

Crang, M. and Thrift, N. (eds) (2000) *Thinking Space.* London: Routledge.

Culler, Jonathan (1976) *Saussure.* Glasgow: Fontana/Collins.

de Certeau, M. (1984) *The Practice of Everyday Life.* S. Rendall (tr.). Berkeley, California: University of California Press.

Delamont, Sarah, Atkinson, Paul and Parry, Odette (2000) *Survival and Success in Graduate School: Discipline, Disciples and the Doctorate.* London: Falmer.

de Lauretis, Teresa (1984) *Alice Doesn't: Feminism, Semiotics, Cinema.* London: Macmillan.

Deleuze, G. and Guattari, F. (1988) *A Thousand Plateaus.* Minneapolis: University of Minneapolis.

Denzin, Norman (1997) *Interpretative Ethnography: Ethnographic Practices for the Twenty-first Century.* London: Sage.

Denzin, Norman K. and Lincoln, Yvonna S. (eds) (1994) *Handbook of Qualitative Research.* London: Sage.

des Chene, M. (1997) 'Locating the past', in Akhil Gupta and James Ferguson (eds), *Anthropological Locations: Boundaries and Grounds of a Field Science.* Berkley, California: University of California Press. pp. 66–85.

Doane, Mary Ann (1982) 'Film and the masquerade: theorizing the female spectator', *Screen*, 23 (3–4): 74–87.

Doane, Mary Ann, Mellencamp, Patricia and Williams, Linda (eds) (1984) *Re-Visions: Essays in Feminist Film Criticism*. Frederick Maryland: American Film Institute.

Dollimore, Jonathan (1984) *Radical Tragedy: Religion, Ideology and Power in the Drama of Shakespeare and his Contemporaries*. Hemel Hempstead: Harvester Wheatsheaf.

Dollimore, Jonathan (1991) *Sexual Dissidence: Augustine to Wilde, Freud to Foucault*. Oxford: Clarendon Press.

Donald, James and Rattansi, Ali (eds) (1992) *'Race', Culture and Difference*. London: Sage.

Downing, John, Mohammadi, Ali and Sreberny-Mohammadi, Annabelle (eds) (1995) *Questioning the Media: A Critical Introduction*. London and Thousand Oaks, California: Sage.

du Bois, W.E.B. (1989) *The Souls of Black Folk*. New York: Bantam.

du Gay, Paul and Pryke, Michael (eds) (2002) *Cultural Economy: Cultural Analysis and Commercial Life*. London: Sage.

du Gay, Paul, Evans, Jessica and Redman, Peter (eds) (2000) *Identity: A Reader*. London: Sage.

du Gay, Paul, Hall, Stuart, Janes, Linda, Mackay, Hugh and Negus, Keith (1997) *Doing Cultural Studies: The Story of the Sony Walkman*. London: Sage, in association with the Open University.

Durkheim, Emile (1952) *Suicide: A Study in Sociology*. London: Routledge and Kegan Paul.

Dyer, Richard (1979) *Stars*. London: BFI

Dyer, Richard (1986) *Heavenly Bodies: Film Stars and Society*. Basingstoke: Macmillan.

Eco, Umberto (1979) 'The narrative structure in Fleming', in *The Role of the Reader*. Bloomington, Indiana: Indiana University Press.

Edwards, D. (1997) *Discourse and Cognition*. London: Sage.

Edwards, D. and Potter, J. (1992) *Discursive Psychology*. London: Sage.

Eickhoff, Martyn, Henkes, Barbara and van Vree, Frank (eds) (2000) *Ras, Cultuur en wetenschap in Nederland 1900-1950*. Zutphen: Walburg Press.

Eiton, G.R. (1967) *The Practice of History*. Sydney: Sydney University Press.

Ely, Margaret, Vinz, Ruth, Downing, Mary Ann and Anzul, Margaret (1997) *On Writing Qualitative Research: Living by Words*. Lewes, Sussex: Falmer Press.

Ellis, John (1992) *Visible Fiction: Cinema, Television, Video*. London: Routledge.

Engels, Friedrich (1962) 'Letter to J. Bloch September 1890', in Karl Marx and Friedrich Engels, *Selected Works*, vol. II. Moscow: Foreign Languages Publishing House. pp. 488–90.

Epstein, Debbie and Johnson, Richard (1998) *Schooling Sexualities*. Buckingham: Open University Press.

Epstein, Debbie, Johnson, Richard and Steinberg, Deborah (2000) 'Twice told tales: transformation, recuperation and emergence in the age of consent debates 1998', *Sexualities*, 3 (1): 5–30.

Evans, Peter William and Deleyto, Celestino (eds) (1998) *Terms of Endearment: Hollywood Romantic Comedy of the 1980s and 1990s*. Edinburgh: Edinburgh University Press.

Fairclough, Norman (2000) *New Labour, New Language*. London: Routledge.

Fanon, Frantz (1986) *Black Skin, White Masks*. London: Pluto.

Ferguson, Marjorie and Golding, Peter (eds) (1997) *Cultural Studies in Question*. London: Sage.

Feuer, Jane (1992) 'Genre study and television', in Robert C. Allen (ed.), *Channels of Discourse, Reassembled*. London: Routledge.

Fine, M. (1994) 'Working with the hyphen: reinventing the self and other in qualitative

research', in N.K. Denzin and Y.S. Lincoln (eds) *Handbook of Qualitative Research*. London: Sage.
Fortmann, Louise (1996) 'Gendered knowledge: rights and space in two Zimbabwe villages', in Dianne Rocheleau, Barbara Thomas-Slayter and Esther Wangani (eds), *Feminist Political Ecology: Global Issues and Local Experiences*. London: Routledge. pp. 211–23.
Foucault, Michel (1967) *Madness and Civilisation: A History of Insanity in the Age of Reason*. London: Tavistock.
Foucault, Michel (1972) *The Archaeology of Knowledge*. London: Routledge.
Foucault, Michel (1974) *The Order of Things: An Archaeology of the Human Sciences*. London: Routledge.
Foucault, Michel (1977) *Discipline and Punish: The Birth of the Prison*. London: Allen Lane.
Foucault, Michel (1979) *History of Sexuality: An Introduction*, vol. I. London: Allen Lane.
Foucault, Michel (1980) *Power/Knowledge: Selected Interviews and Other Writings 1972–1977*. Colin Gordon (ed. and tr.). Brighton: Harvester Press.
Foucault, Michel (1986) 'Nietzsche, genealogy, history', in Paul Rabinow (ed.), *The Foucault Reader*. London: Penguin. pp. 76–100.
Foucault, Michel (1987) *The Use of Pleasure: History of Sexuality*, vol. II. London: Penguin.
Freud, Sigmund (1973 [1916–17]) *Introductory Lectures on Psychoanalysis*. Harmondsworth: Penguin.
Friedan, Betty (1963) *The Feminine Mystique*. New York: W.W. Norton.
Friedman, M. (1969) *The Optimum Quantity of Money and Other Essays*. Chicago: Aldine Publishing.
Frosch, Stephen (1987) *The Politics of Psychoanalysis*. Basingstoke: Macmillan.
Fryer, Peter (1984) *Staying Power: The History of Black People in Britain*. London: Pluto Press.
Gadamer, Hans-Georg (1989) *Truth and Method* (2nd edn.) London: Sheed and Ward.
Gadamer, Hans-Georg (1998) *Praise of Theory: Speeches and Essays*. New Haven: Yale University Press.
Gagnier, Regenia (2000) *The Insatiability of Human Wants: Economics and Aesthetics in Market Society*. Chicago: University of Chicago Press.
Garfinkel, H. (1967) *Studies in Ethnomethodology*. Englewood Cliffs, New Jersey: Prentice-Hall.
Garnham, Nicholas (1986) 'Contributions to a political economy of mass communication', in Richard Collins et al. (eds) *Media, Culture and Society: A Critical Reader*. London: Sage. pp. 9–32.
Garnham, Nicholas (1990) *Capitalism and Global Communication: Global Culture and the Politics of Information*. London: Sage.
Geertz, Clifford (1988) *Work and Lives: The Anthropologist as Author*. Cambridge: Polity Press.
Gellner, Ernest (1983) *Nations and Nationalism*. Oxford: Blackwell.
Genette, Gerard (1972) *Narrative Discourse: An Essay in Method*. Ithaca, New York: Cornell University Press.
Genovese, E.D. (1974) *Roll, Jordan Roll: The World the Slaves Made*. London: Deutsch.
Gibson, W. (1984) *Neuromancer*. London: Gollancz.
Gibson-Graham, J.K. (1996) *The End of Capitalism (As We Knew It): A Feminist Critique of Political Economy*. Oxford: Blackwell.
Giddens, Anthony (1998) *The Third Way: The Renewal of Social Democracy*. Cambridge: Polity Press.
Gillespie, M. (1989) 'Technology and tradition: audio-visual culture among south asian families in west London', *Cultural Studies*, 3 (2): 226–39.

Gilroy, Paul (1986) 'Steppin' out of Babylon – race, class and autonomy', in Centre for Contemporary Cultural Studies, *The Empire Strikes Back: Race and Racism in '70s Britain.* London: Routledge. pp. 276–314.

Gilroy, Paul (1987) *'There Ain't No Black in the Union Jack': The Cultural Politics of 'Race' and Nation*. London: Hutchinson.

Gilroy, Paul (1993a) *Small Acts: Thoughts on the Politics of Cultures*. London: Serpent's Tail.

Gilroy, Paul (1993b) 'Cultural studies and ethnic absolutism', in Lawrence Grossberg, Gary Nelson and Paula Treichler (eds), *Cultural Studies.* New York: Routledge. pp. 187–98.

Gilroy, Paul (1993c) *The Black Atlantic: Modernity and Double Consciousness.* London: Verso.

Glaser, B. and Strauss, A. (1967) *The Discovery of Grounded Theory.* Chicago: Aldine.

Glasgow Media Group (1976) *Bad News.* London: Routledge and Kegan Paul.

Glasgow Media Group (1980) *More Bad News.* London: Routledge and Kegan Paul.

Glasgow Media Group (1982) *Really Bad News.* London: Routledge and Kegan Paul.

Gledhill, Christine (1984) 'Developments in feminist film criticism', in Mary Ann Doanne, Patricia Mellencamp and Linda Williams (eds), *Re-visions: Essays in Feminist Film Criticism.* Frederick, Maryland: American Film Institute.

Gledhill, Christine and Williams, Linda (eds), (2000) *Reinventing Film Studies.* London and New York: Arnold and Oxford University Press.

Goffman, E. (1961) *Asylums: Essays on the Social Situation of Mental Patients and Other Inmates.* New York: Doubleday.

Goodwin, Andrew (ed.) (1992) 'Introduction', in Richard Hoggart, *The Uses of Literacy.* New Brunswick, New Jersey: Transaction Publishers.

Grace, H. (1991) 'Business, pleasure, narrative', in R. Diprose and R. Ferrell (eds), *Cartographies: Poststructuralism and the Mapping of Bodies and Spaces.* Sydney: Allen and Unwin.

Gramsci, Antonio (1971) *Selections from the Prison Notebooks of Antonio Gramsci.* Q. Hoare and G. Smith Nowell (ed. and tr.). London: Lawrence and Wishart.

Gramsci, Antonio (1985) *Selections from Cultural Writings.* David Forgacs and Geoffrey Nowell-Smith (eds). London: Lawrence and Wishart.

Gray, Ann (1992) *Video Playtime: The Gendering of a Leisure Technology.* London: Routledge.

Green, M. (1997) 'Working practices', in J. McGuigan (ed.), *Cultural Methodologies.* London: Sage

Greenblatt, Stephen (1981) 'Invisible bullets: Renaissance authority and its subversion', *Glyph* 8: 40–61.

Griffin, Christine (1985) *Typical Girls? Young Women from School to the Job Market.* London: Routledge and Kegan Paul.

Griffiths, J. (1999) *Pip Pip: A Sideways Look at Time.* London: Flamingo.

Griffiths, Morwenna (1998) *Educational Research for Social Justice.* Buckingham: Open University Press.

Grossberg, Lawrence (1992) *We Gotta Get Out of This Place: Popular Conservatism and Postmodern Culture.* New York and London: Routledge.

Grosz, Elizabeth (1993) *Volatile Bodies.* Bloomington, Indiana: Indiana University Press.

Guba, Egon G. and Lincoln, Yvonna S. (1994) 'Competing paradigms in qualitative research', in Norman K. Denzin and Yvonna S. Lincoln (eds), *Handbook of Qualitative Research.* London: Sage.

Hall, Catherine. (1992a) 'Missionary stories: gender and ethnicity in England in the 1830s and 1840s', in Laurence Grossberg, Cary Nelson and Paula Treicher (eds), *Cultural Studies.* London: Routledge.

Hall, Catherine (1992b) *White, Male and Middle-class: Explorations in Feminism and History.* Cambridge: Polity Press.

Hall, Catharine (1996) 'Histories, empires and the post-colonial moment', in Iain Chambers and Lidia Curti (eds), *The Post-colonial Question: Common Skies, Divided Horizons*. London: Routledge. pp. 65–77

Hall, Stuart (1973a) *A Reading of Marx's 1857 Introduction to the Grundrisse*. Centre for Contemporary Cultural Studies Stencilled Occasional Paper, No 1. Birmingham: Centre for Contemporary Cultural Studies.

Hall, Stuart (1973b) *Encoding and Decoding in the TV Discourse*. Centre for Contemporary Cultural Studies Stencilled Occasional Paper, No 7. Birmingham: Centre for Contemporary Cultural Studies.

Hall, Stuart (1977) 'Culture, media and the ideological effect', in J. Curran, M. Gurevitch and J. Woolacott (eds), *Mass Communications and Society*. London: Edward Arnold.

Hall, Stuart (1980a) 'Cultural studies and the centre: some problems and problematics', in Stuart Hall, Dorothy Hobson, Andrew Lowe and Paul Willis, (eds), *Culture, Media, Language: Working Papers in Cultural Studies 1972–79* London: Hutchinson in association with the Centre for Contemporary Cultural Studies.

Hall, Stuart (1980b) 'Introduction to media studies at the Centre', in Stuart Hall, Dorothy Hobson, Andrew Lowe and Paul Willis (eds), *Culture, Media, Language: Working Papers in Cultural Studies 1972–79*. London: Hutchinson in association with the Centre for Contemporary Cultural Studies. pp.117–21.

Hall, Stuart (1980c) 'Recent developments in theories of language and ideology: a critical note', in Stuart Hall, Dorothy Hobson, Andrew Lowe and Paul Willis (eds), *Culture, Media, Language: Working Papers in Cultural Studies 1972–79*. London: Hutchinson in association with the Centre for Contemporary Cultural Studies. pp.157–62.

Hall, Stuart (1981) 'In defence of theory', in Samuel Raphael (ed.), *People's History and Socialist Theory*. London: Routledge and Kegan Paul. pp. 378–85.

Hall, Stuart (1986) 'On postmodernism and articulation: an interview', *Journal of Communication Inquiry*, 10: 45–60.

Hall, Stuart (1988) 'The toad in the garden: Thatcherism among the theorists', in Cary Nelson and Lawrence Grossberg (eds), *Marxism and the Interpretation of Culture*. Basingstoke: Macmillan. pp. 35–74.

Hall, Stuart (1990) 'Cultural identity and diaspora', in Jonathan Rutherford (ed.), *Identity, Community, Culture, Difference*. London: Lawrence and Wishart. pp. 222–37.

Hall, Stuart (1992) 'Cultural studies and its theoretical legacies', in Laurence Grossberg, Gary Nelson and Paula Treichler (eds), *Cultural Studies*, London: Routledge. pp. 277–94.

Hall, Stuart (1996a) 'New ethnicities', in David Morley and Kuan-Hsing Chen (eds), *Stuart Hall: Critical Dialogues*. London: Routledge. pp. 411–40.

Hall Stuart (1996b) 'What is this "black" in black popular culture', in David Morley and Kuan-Hsing Chen (eds), *Stuart Hall: Critical Dialogues*. London: Routledge. pp. 465– 75.

Hall, Stuart (1996c) 'When was the post-colonial?', in Iain Chambers and Lidia Curti (eds), *The Post-colonial Question: Common Skies, Divided Horizons*. London: Routledge.

Hall, Stuart (1996d) 'Cultural studies and the politics of internationalization: an interview with Kuan-Hsing Chen', in David Morley and Kuan-Hsing Chen (eds), *Stuart Hall: Critical Dialogues*. London: Routledge.

Hall, Stuart (ed.) (1997) *Representation: Cultural Representations and Signifying Practices*. London: Sage, in association with the Open University.

Hall, Stuart (1998) 'Breaking bread with history: C.L.R. James and the Black Jacobins: interview with Bill Schwarz', *History Workshop Journal*, 46 (Autumn): 17–32.

Hall, Stuart (1999–2000) 'Whose heritage? Un-settling "the heritage": re-imagining the post-nation', *Third Text*, 49 (Winter) 3–13.

Hall, Stuart and du Gay, Paul (eds) (1996) *Questions of Cultural Identity*. London: Sage.
Hall, Stuart and Jacques, Martin (eds) (1983) *The Politics of Thatcherism*. London: Lawrence and Wishart.
Hall, Stuart and Jefferson, Tony (eds) (1976) *Resistance Through Rituals: Youth Subcultures in Post-war Britain*. London: Hutchinson, in association with the Centre for Contemporary Cultural Studies.
Hall, Stuart, Lumley, Robert and McLennan, Gregor (1978) 'Politics and ideology: Gramsci', in Centre for Contemporary Cultural Studies, *On Ideology*. London: Hutchinson.
Hall, Stuart, Held, David and McGrew, Tony (1992) *Modernity and Its Futures*. Cambridge: Polity Press.
Hall, Stuart, Critcher, Chas, Jefferson, Tony, Clarke, John and Roberts, Brian (1978) *Policing the Crisis: Mugging the State and Law and Order*. London: Macmillan.
Hammersley, M. and Atkinson, P. (1995) *Ethnography: Principles in Practice* (2nd edn). London: Routledge.
Hansen, A., Cottle, S., Negrine, R. and Newbold, C. (1998) *Mass Communication Research Methods*. London: Macmillan.
Haraway, Donna J. (1991a) *Simians, Cyborgs, and Women: The Reinvention of Nature*. London: Free Association Books.
Haraway, D. J. (1991b) 'Situated knowledges: the science question in feminism and the privilege of partial perspective', in D. Haraway *Simians, Cyborgs and Women: The Reinvention of Nature*. London: Free Association Books. pp. 183–201.
Haraway, Donna J. (1997) *Modest_Witness@Second_Millenium.FemaleMan©Meets_OncoMouse™* New York: Routledge.
Harding, Sandra (1987) 'Introduction: is there a feminist method', and 'Conclusion: epistemological questions', in Sandra Harding (ed.), *Feminism and Methodology*. Bloomington, Indiana: Indiana University Press.
Hardt, Michael and Negri, Antonio (2000) *Empire*. Cambridge, Massachusetts: Harvard University Press.
Hartsock, Nancy (1985) *Money, Sex and Power: Towards a Feminist Historical Materialism*. Boston, Massachusetts: Northeastern University Press.
Hartsock, Nancy (1987) 'The feminist standpoint: developing the ground for a specifically feminist historical materialism', in Sandra Harding (ed.), *Feminism and Methodology*. Bloomington, Indiana: Indiana University Press. pp. 157–80.
Harvey, David (1989) *The Condition of Postmodernity*. Oxford: Blackwell.
Haug, Frigga (ed.) (1987) *Female Sexualization: A Collective Work of Memory*. London: Virago.
Hay, J., Grossberg, L. and Wartella, E. (eds) (1996) *The Audience and Its Landscape*. Boulder Colorado: Westview Press.
Haywood, Chris and Mac An Ghaill, Mairtin (2003) *Men and Masculinities: Theory, Research and Social Practice*. Buckingham: Open University Press.
Hebdige, Dick (1979) *Subculture: The Meaning of Style*. London: Methuen.
Hegel, G.W. (1977) *Phenomenology of Spirit*. Oxford: Oxford University Press.
Held, David (1980) *Introduction to Critical Theory: Horkheimer to Habermas*.
London: Hutchinson.
Henkes, Barbara and Johnson, Richard (2002) 'Silences across disciplines: folklore studies, cultural studies and social history', *Journal of Folklore Research*, 39 (2–3): 125–46.
Hennesey, Rosemary (1995) 'Queer visibility in commodity culture', in Linda Nicholson and Steven Seidman (eds), *Social Postmodernism: Beyond Identity Politics*. Cambridge: Cambride University Press. pp. 142–86.
Henriques, Julian, Hollway, Wendy, Urwin, Cathy, Venn, Couze and Walkerdine, Valerie

(1984) *Changing the Subject: Psychology, Social Regulation and Subjectivity.* London: Methuen.

Hermes, Joke (1995) *Reading Women's Magazines.* Cambridge: Polity Press.

Hobsbawm, Eric (1959) *Primitive Rebels: Studies in Archaic Forms of Social Movement in the Nineteenth and Twentieth Centuries.* Manchester: Manchester University Press.

Hobsbawm, Eric (1997) 'Identity history is not enough', in Eric Hobsbawm, *On History.* London: Wiedenfeld and Nicholson. pp. 266– 77.

Hobson, Dorothy (1980) 'Housewives and the mass media', in S. Hall, D. Hobson, A. Lowe and P. Willis (eds), *Culture, Media, Language.* London: Hutchinson.

Hobson, Dorothy (1982) *Crossroads: The Drama of a Soap Opera.* London: Methuen.

Hoggart, Richard (1957) *The Uses of Literacy.* London: Penguin.

Hoggart, Richard (1988) *A Local Habitation: Life and Times 1918–1940.* Oxford: Oxford University Press.

Hoggart, Richard (1992) *The Uses of Literacy.* Andrew Goodwill (ed. and Introduction). New Brunswick, New Jersey: Transaction Publishers.

Hollway, Wendy (1989) *Subjectivity and Method in Psychology: Gender, Meaning and Science.* London: Sage.

Hollway, Wendy and Jefferson, Tony (2000) *Doing Qualitative Research Differently.* London: Sage.

hooks, bell (1981) *Ain't I a Woman: Black Women and Feminism.* Boston, Massachusetts: South End Press.

hooks, bell (1984) *Feminist Theory: From Margin to Center.* Boston, Massachusetts: South End Press.

hooks, bell (1989) *Feminist Thinking Black.* London: Sheba Feminist Publishers.

hooks, bell (1991) *Yearning: Race, Gender and Cultural Politics.* London: Turnaround.

hooks, bell (1992) *Black Looks: Race and Representation.* London: Turnaround.

Horkheimer, Max and Adorno, Theodor (1972) *The Dialectics of Enlightenment.* John Cumming (tr.). New York: Herder and Herder.

Huntingdon, Samuel, P. (1993) 'The Clash of Civilizations', *Foreign Affairs* 72 (3) (Summer): 22–49.

Iser, Wolfgang (1978) *The Act of Reading: A Theory of Aesthetic Response.* Baltimore, Maryland: Johns Hopkins University Press.

Jabbour, Alan (1983) 'American folklore studies: the tradition and the future', *Folklore Forum* 16: 235–47.

Jackson, David (1990) *Unmaking Masculinity: A Critical Autobiography.* London: Unwin Hyman.

Jackson, P. (1989) *Maps of Meaning: An Introduction to Cultural Geography.* London: Routledge.

Jameson, F. (1981) *The Political Unconscious: Narrative as a Socially Symbolic Act.* London: Methuen.

Jenkins, H. (1995) *Science Fiction Audiences: Dr Who, Star Trek and their Followers.* London and New York: Routledge.

Jenson, Joli and Pauly, John (1997) 'Imagining the audience: losses and gains in cultural studies', in Marjorie Ferguson and Paul Golding (eds), *Cultural Studies in Question.* London: Sage. pp. 155–69.

Jhally, SUT and Lewis, Justin (1992) *Enlightened Racism: The Cosby Show, Audiences and the Myth of the American Dream.* Janice Radway, Foreword. Boulder Colorado: Westview Press.

Johnson, Richard (1978) 'Edward Thompson, Eugene Genovese and Socialist – Humanist History', *History Workshop Journal*, 6 (Autumn): 79–100.

Johnson, Richard (1979a) 'Histories of culture/theories of ideology: notes on an impasse', in Michele Barrett, Phillip Corrigan, Annette Kuhn and Janet Wolff (eds), *Ideology and Cultural Production*. London: Routledge and Kegan Paul, and New York: St Martin's Press.

Johnson, Richard (1979b) 'Socialist history', *History Workshop Journal*, 8 (Autumn): 196–98.

Johnson, Richard (1981) 'Against absolutism', in Raphael Samuel, *People's History and Socialist Theory*. London: Routledge and Kegan Paul. pp. 386–95.

Johnson, Richard (1982) 'Reading for the best Marx: history-writing and historical abstraction', in Centre for Contemporary Cultural Studies, *Making History: Studies in History-writing and Politics*. London: Hutchinson.

Johnson, Richard (1983) 'What is cultural studies anyway?' *Anglistica* XXVI, 1–2: 1–75.

Johnson, Richard (1991) 'Two ways to remember: exploring memory as identity', *Nothing Blood Stands Still: Magazine of the European Network for Cultural and Media Studies*, 1, 26–30.

Johnson, Richard (1996) 'What is cultural studies anyway?', in John Storey (ed.), *What is Cultural Studies? A Reader*. London: Arnold. pp. 75–114.

Johnson, Richard (1997) 'Teaching without guarantees: cultural studies, pedagogy and identity', in Joyce E. Canaan and Debbie Epstein (eds), *A Question of Discipline: Pedagogy, Power and the Teaching of Cultural Studies*. Boulder, Colorado: Westview Press.

Johnson, Richard (1997a) 'Grievous recognitions', in Deborah Lynn Steinberg, Debbie Epstein and Richard Johnson (eds), *Border Patrols: Policing the Boundaries of Heterosexuality*. London: Cassell. pp. 204–52.

Johnson, Richard (1998) 'Complex authorships: intellectual coproduction as a strategy for the times', *Anglistica: Journal of Theoretical Humanities*, 3 (3): 189–204.

Johnson, Richard (1999) '"Politics by other means?" Or, teaching cultural studies in the academy is a political practice', in Nannette Aldred and Martin Ryle (eds), *Teaching Culture: The Long Revolution in Cultural Studies*. Leicester: National Institute of Adult Continuing Education. pp. 22–38.

Johnson, Richard (2000a) 'Exemplary differences: mourning (and not mourning) a princess', in Adrian Kear and Deborah Lynn Steinberg (eds), *Mourning Diana*. London: Routledge.

Johnson, Richard (2000b) 'Academic under pressure: power and paradigm in two historical periods', in Martyn Eickhoff, Barbara Henkes and Frank van Vree, (eds), *Ras, Cultuur en wetenschap in Nederland 1900–1950*. Zutphen: Walburg Press.

Johnson, Richard (2001) 'Historical returns: transdisciplinarity, cultural studies and history', *European Journal of Cultural Studies*, 4 (3) (August): 261–88.

Johnson, Richard (2002) 'Defending ways of life: the (anti-)terrorist rhetorics of Bush and Blair', *Theory Culture and Society*, 19 (4): 213–33.

Johnson, Richard and Steinberg, Deborah (eds) (2004) *Blairism and the War of Persuasion: Labour's Passive Revolution*. London: Lawrence and Wishart.

Johnston, L. and Valentine, Gill (1995) 'Wherever I lay my girlfriend that's my home: performance and surveillance of lesbian identity in home environments', in D. Bell and G. Valentine (eds), *Mapping Desires: Geographies of Sexualities*. London: Routledge. pp. 99–113.

Kaplan, Ann (1983) *Women and Film: Both Sides of the Camera*. London: Methuen.

Kaye, Harvey, J. and McClelland, Keith (eds) (1990) *E.P Thompson: Critical Perspectives*. Cambridge: Polity Press.

Kear, Adrian and Steinberg, Deborah Lynn (eds) (1999) *Mourning Diana*. London: Routledge.

Kearney, Hugh (1989) *The British Isles: A History of Four Nations*. Cambridge: Cambridge University Press.

Kimmel, Michael (1996) *Manhood in America*. New York: Free Press.

Kellner, Douglas (1997) 'Overcoming the divide: cultural studies and political economy', in Marjorie Ferguson and Peter Golding (eds), *Cultural Studies in Question*. London: Sage. pp. 102–20.

King, Katie (1987) 'Canons without innocence', Unpublished PhD thesis, University of California, Santa Cruz.

Kristeva, Julia (1984) *Revolution in Poetic Language*. New York: Columbia University Press.

Kristeva, J. (1986) 'Women's time', in T. Moi (ed.) *The Kristeva Reader*. London: Blackwell.

Kuhn, Annette (1984) 'Women's genre', *Screen*, 25 (1): 18–28.

Kuhn, Annette (1994) *Women's Pictures: Feminism and Cinema*, 2nd edn. London: Routledge and Kegan Paul.

Kuhn, Annette (1999) 'A journey through memory', in Susannah Radstone (ed.), *Memory and Methodology*. Oxford: Berg. pp. 179–96.

Kuhn, Thomas (1970) *The Structure of Scientific Revolutions*. Chicago: Chicago University Press.

Laclau, Ernesto and Mouffe, Chantal (1985) *Hegemony and Socialist Strategy: Towards a Radical Democratic Politics*. London: Verso.

Larrain, Jorge (1983) *Marxism and Ideology*. Basingstoke: Macmillan.

Lash, S. and Urry, J. (1994) *Economies of Signs and Space*. London: Sage.

Latour, B. and Woolgar, S. (1979) *Laboratory Life: The Social Construction of Scientific Facts*. Beverley Hills: Sage.

Lefebvre, Henri (1991) *The Production of Space*. D. Nicholson-Smith (tr.). Oxford and Cambridge, Massachusetts: Blackwell.

Legene, S. (1998) 'Nobody's objects: early nineteenth-century ethnographic collectors and the formation of imperial attitudes and feelings', *Ethnfor*, XL (1): 21–39.

Leonard, Diana (2000) 'Transforming doctoral studies: competencies and artistry', *Higher Education in Europe*, XXV (2): 181–92.

Leonard, Diana (2001) *A Women's Guide to Doctoral Studies*. Buckingham: Open University Press.

Levi-Strauss, Claude (1968) *Structural Anthropology*. London: Allen Lane.

Lhamon, W.T. (1989) *Raising Cain: Black Face Performance from Jim Choco to Hip Hop*. Cambridge, MA: Harvard University Press.

Lidchi, H. (1994) 'The poetics and politics of exhibiting other cultures', in Stuart Hall (ed.), *Representation: Cultural Representations and Signifying Practices*. London: Sage.

Longhurst, Derek (1989) 'Sherlock Holmes: adventures of an English gentleman', in Derek Longhurst (ed.), *Gender, Genre and Narrative Pleasure*. London: Unwin Hyman. pp. 51–6.

Ludlam, Steve and Smith, Martin (eds) (2001) *New Labour in Government*. Basingstoke: Macmillan.

Lukacs, Georg (1971) *History and Class Consciousness: Studies in Marxist Dialectics*. Rodney Livingstone (tr.). London: Merlin Press.

Lukes, Stephen (1973) *Emile Durkheim, His Life and Work: A Historical and Critical Study*. Harmondsworth: Penguin.

Lury, Celia (1996) *Consumer Culture*. Cambridge: Polity.

Mac An Ghaill, Mairtin (1994) *The Making of Men: Masculinities, Sexualities and Schooling*. Buckingham: Open University Press.

MacCabe, Colin (1974) 'Realism and the cinema: notes on some Brechtian theses', *Screen*, 15(2): 7–27.

MacKinnon, Catharine (1982) 'Feminism, Marxism, method and the state: an agenda for theory', *Signs*, 7: 515–44.

McGuigan, Jim (1992) *Cultural Populism*. London: Routledge.

McGuigan, Jim (1996) 'Cultural populism revisited', in M. Ferguson and P. Golding (eds), *Cultural Studies in Question*. London: Sage.

McGuigan, Jim (ed.) (1997) *Cultural Methodologies*. London: Sage.
McRobbie, Angela (1981) 'Settling accounts with subcultures: a feminist critique', in Tony Bennett, Graham Martin, Colin Mercer and Janet Woollacott (eds), *Culture, Ideology and Social Process*. London: Open University Press. pp. 112–24.
McRobbie, Angela (1991) *Feminism and Youth Culture: From* Jackie *to* Just Seventeen. Basingstoke: Macmillan.
McRobbie, Angela (1997) 'The Es and the anti-es: new questions for feminism and cultural studies', in Margorie Ferguson, and Peter Golding (eds), *Cultural Studies in Question*. London: Sage.
McRobbie, Angela and Nava, M. (1984) *Gender and Generation*. London: Macmillan.
McRobbie, R. (1978) 'Working-class girls and the culture of femininity', in Centre for Contemporary Cultural Studies, *Women Take Issue*. London: Routledge.
Macherey, Pierre (1978) *A Theory of Literary Production*. London: Routledge and Kegan Paul.
Mandelson, Peter (2002) *The Blair Revolution Revisited*. London: Politico Publishing.
Marcus, George (1986) 'Contemporary problems of ethnography in the modern world system', in James Clifford and George Marcus, *Writing Culture: the Poetics and Politics of Ethnography*. Berkeley, California: University of California Press. pp. 165–93.
Marcus, George E. (1992) *Rereading Cultural Anthropology*. Durham: Duke University Press.
Marcus, George E. (1994) 'What comes (just) after "post"? The case of ethnography', in Norman K. Denzin and Yvonna S. Lincoln (eds), *Handbook of Qualitative Research*. London: Sage.
Marcus, G. (2000) 'The twistings and turnings of geography and anthropology in winds of millenial transition', in I. Cook, S. Naylor, J. Ryan and D. Crouch (eds), *Cultural Turns/Geographical Turns*. Harlow: Pearson.
Marx, Karl (1962) 'Preface to a contribution to a critique of political economy', in Karl Marx and Friedrich Engels, *Selected Works*, vol. 1. Moscow: Foreign Languages Publishing House. pp. 361–5.
Marx, Karl (1973) 'The eighteenth brumaire of Louise Bonaparte', in Karl Marx, *Surveys From Exile*. David Fernbach (ed. and Introduction). Harmondsworth: Penguin.
Marx, K. (1976) *Capital*, vol. 1. Ben Fowkes (tr.). Harmondsworth: Penguin.
Marx, Karl and Engels, Friedrich, (1973) 'Manifesto of the communist party', in David Fernbach (ed.), *The Revolutions of 1848*. Harmondsworth; Penguin.
Marx, Karl and Engels, Friedrich (1977) *The German Ideology*. C.J. Arthur (ed. and Introduction). London: Lawrence and Wishart.
Massey, Doreen (1994) *Space, Place and Gender*. Cambridge: Polity.
Massey, Doreen (1998) 'The spatial construction of youth culture', in Tracey Skelton and Gill Valentine (eds), *Cool Places: Geographies of Youth Cultures*. London: Routledge. pp. 121–9.
Massey, Doreen (1999) 'Imagining globalization: power-geometries of time-space', in A. Brah, M.J. Hickman and M. Mac an Ghaill (eds), *Global Futures: Migration, Environment and Globalization*. Basingstoke: Macmillan. pp. 27–44.
Mercer, Kobena (1994) *Welcome to the Jungle: New Positions in Black Cultural Studies*. London: Routledge.
Mercer, Kobena and Julien, Isaac (1988) 'Race, sexual politics and black masculinity: a dossier', in Rowena Chapman and Jonathan Rutherford (eds), *Male Order: Unwrapping Masculinity*. London: Lawrence and Wishart. pp. 97–164.
Merrifield, A. (2000) 'Henri Lefebvre: A Socialist in space', in M. Crang and N. Thrift (eds) *Thinking Space*. London: Routledge.
Metz, Christian (1974) *Film Language: A Semiotics of the Cinema*. Michael Taylor (tr.). Oxford: Oxford University Press. p. 2.

Miller, Daniel (1987) *Material Culture and Mass Consumption.* Oxford: Blackwell.
Miller, Daniel (2002) 'The unintended political economy', in Paul du Gay and Michael Pryke (eds), *Cultural Economy.* London: Sage. pp. 166–84.
Miller, P. (1998) 'The margins of accountancy', in M. Callon (ed.), *The Laws of the Market.* Oxford and Keele: Blackwell and *Sociological Review.*
Mitchell, Juliet (1974) *Psychoanalysis and Feminism: A Radical Reassessment of Freudian Psychoanalysis.* Harmondsworth: Penguin.
Mitchell, Juliet and Oakley, Ann (eds) (1976) *The Rights and Wrongs of Women.* Harmondsworth Penguin.
Modleski, Tania (1982) *Loving with a Vengeance: Mass-produced Fantasies for Women.* London: Methuen.
Modleski, Tania (1986) 'Introduction', in Tania Modleski (ed.) *Studies in Entertainment: Critical Approaches to Mass Culture.* Bloomington, Indiana: Indiana University Press. pp. ix–xix.
Modleski, Tania (1988) *The Women who Knew Too Much: Hitchcock and Feminist Theory.* London: Methuen.
Moi, Toril (ed.) (1986) *The Kristeva Reader.* Oxford: Basil Blackwell.
Monaco, James (1981) *How to Read a Film: The Art, Technology, Language, History and Theory of Film and Media.* Oxford: Oxford University Press.
Moore, H.L. (1988) *Feminism and Anthropology.* London: Polity.
Morley, David (1980) *The Nationwide Audience.* London: BFI.
Morley, David (1986) *Family Television: Cultural Power and Domestic Leisure.* London: Routledge.
Morley, David (1992) *Television, Audiences and Cultural Studies.* London: Routledge.
Morley, David (1997) 'Theoretical orthodoxies: textualism, constructivism and the "new ethnography"in cultural studies', in Margorie Ferguson and Peter Golding (eds), *Cultural Studies in Question.* London: Sage.
Morley, David and Silverstone, Roger (1990) 'Domestic communications: technologies and meanings', *Media, Culture and Society,* 12 (1): 31–55.
Morley, Dave and Worpole, Ken (eds) (1982) *The Republic of Letters: Working-class Writing and Local Publishing.* London: Comedia.
Morris, Meaghan (1997) 'A question of cultural studies', in Angela McRobbie (ed.), *Back to Reality? Social Experience and Cultural Studies.* Manchester and New York: Manchester University Press. pp. 36–57.
Morrison, Toni (1987) *Beloved.* London: Picador.
Morrow, R.A. (1994) *Critical Theory and Methodology.* London: Sage.
Mulvey, Laura (1975) 'Visual pleasure and narrative cinema', *Screen,* 13 (3): 6–18.
Munt, Sally R. (ed.) (2000) *Cultural Studies and the Working Class.* London: Cassell.
Murdoch, Graham (1997) 'Base notes: the conditions of cultural practice', in Margorie Ferguson and Peter Golding (eds), *Cultural Studies in Question.* London: Sage.
Nava, Mica (1996) 'Modernity's disavowal: women, the city and the department store', in M. Nava and A. O'Shea (eds), *Modern Times: Reflections on a Century of English Modernity.* London: Routledge.
Nayak, Anoop (2003) 'Ivory lives: white ethnicities and economic restructuring in a post-industrial youth community', *European Journal of Cultural Studies,* Special Issue of Peripheral Youth, 6(3): 305–26.
Neale, Stephen (1980) *Genre.* London: BFI.
Nightingale, Virginia (1993) 'What's "ethnographic" about ethnographic audience research', in G. Turner (ed.), *Nation, Culture, Text: Australian Cultural and Media Studies.* London: Routledge. pp. 164–77.

Nora, Pierre (1997) *Realms of Memory: The Construction of the French Past: Conflicts and Divisions*, vol. 1. Lawrence D. Kritzman (ed.) and Arthur Goldhammer (tr.). New York: Columbia University Press.

O'Byrne, D. (1997) 'Working-class culture: local community and global conditions', in J. Eade (ed.), *Living the Global: Globalization as Local Process*. London: Routledge.

Parker, Ian and Bolton Discourse Network (1999) *Critical Textwork: An Introduction to Varieties of Discourse and Analysis*. Buckingham: Open University Press.

Participatory Rural Appraisal (1992) *Utilization Survey Report, Part 1, Rural Development Area, Sindhupalchak*. Actionaid-nepal, Monitoring and Evaluation Unit, July 1992.

Passerini, Luisa (1990a) 'Mythbiography in oral history', in Raphael Samuel and David Thompson (eds), *The Myths We Live By*. London: Routledge. pp. 49–60.

Passerini, L. (1990b) 'Attitudes of oral narrators to their memories: generations, genders, cultures', in D. Wiles (ed.), *Oral History and Social Welfare, Oral History Association of Australia Journal*, 12: 14–19.

Passerini, Luisa, Fridenson, Patrick and Neithammer, Lutz, (1998) 'International reverberations: remembering Raphael', *History Workshop Journal*, 45 (Spring): 246–60.

Philips E.M. and Pugh, D. (1994) *How to Get a PhD: A Handbook for Students and their Supervisors* (2nd edn). Buckingham: Open University Press.

Pilkington, Hilary and Johnson, Richard (eds) (2003) 'Peripheral youth', Special Issue on Youth Cultures, *European Journal of Cultural Studies*, 6(3).

Plummer, K. (1995) *Telling Sexual Stories*. London: Routledge.

Popular Memory Group (1982) 'Popular memory: theory, politics, method', in Centre for Contemporary Cultural Studies, *Making Histories: Studies in History-writing and Politics*. London: Hutchinson. pp. 205–52.

Portelli, Alessandro (1990) 'Uchronic worlds: working-class memory and possible worlds', in Raphael Samuel and David Thompson (eds), *The Myths We Live By*. London: Routledge. pp. 143–60.

Probyn, Elspeth (1993) *Sexing the Self: Gendered Positions in Cultural Studies*. London: Routledge.

Propp, Vladimir (1968) *The Morphology of the Folktale*. Austin: Texas University Press.

Rabinow, Paul (1984) *The Foucault Reader*. New York: Pantheon Books.

Radford, Jean (ed.) (1986) *The Progress of Romance: The Politics of Popular Fiction*. London: Routledge and Kegan Paul.

Radway, Janice, (1984) *Reading the Romance: Women, Patriarchy and Popular Literature*. London: Verso.

Radway, Janice (1997) 'Reading "*Reading the Romance*"', in Ann Gray and Jim McGuigan (eds), *Studying Culture: An Introductory Reader* (2nd edn). London: Arnold. pp. 62–79.

Raghuram, P. (1993) 'Coping strategies of domestic workers: a study of three settlements in the Delhi Metropolitan region, India'. Thesis submitted to the University of Newcastle-upon-Tyne, UK.

Redman, Peter and Mac An Ghaill, Mairtin (1997) 'Educating Peter: the making of a history man', in Deborah Lynn Steinberg, Debbie Epstein and Richard Johnson (eds), *Border Patrols: Policing the Boundaries of Heterosexuality*. London: Cassell. pp. 162–82.

Richards, L. (1990) *Nobody's Home: Dreams and Realities in a New Suburb*. Melbourne: Oxford University Press.

Richards, L. and Richards, T. (1987a) 'Qualitative data analysis: can computers do it?', *Australian and New Zealand Journal of Sociology*, 23: 23–25.

Richards, L. and Richards, T. (1987b) *User Manual for NUDIST: A Text Analysis Program for the Social Sciences* (2nd edn). Melbourne: Replee.

Richards, L. and Richards, T. (1988) 'NUDIST: a system for qualititative data analysis', *ACS Bulletin*, October: 5–9.
Ricoeur, Paul (1984) *Time and Narrative* (vol. 1). Chicago and London: University of Chicago Press.
Ricoeur, Paul (1985) *Time and Narrative* (vol. 2). Chicago and London: University of Chicago Press.
Ricoeur, Paul (1988) *Time and Narrative* (vol. 3). Chicago and London: University of Chicago Press.
Ricoeur, Paul (1991) *Hermeneutics and the Human Sciences*. John B. Thompson (ed. and tr.). Cambridge and Paris: Cambridge University Press and Maison des Sciences de l'Homme.
Ricoeur, Paul (1992) *Oneself as Another*. Chicago: University of Chicago Press.
Ricoeur, Paul (1996) 'Essays', in Richard Kearney (ed.), *Paul Ricoeur: The Hermeneutics of Action*. London: Sage. pp. 3–40.
Riessman, Catherine (1990) *Divorce Talk: Women and Men Make Sense of Personal Relationships*. New Brunswick, New Jersey: Rutgers University Press.
Riessman, Catherine K. (1993) *Narrative Analysis*. Newbury Park, California: Sage.
Riessman, Catherine (2002) 'Doing justice: positioning the interpreter in narrative work', in Wendy Patterson (ed.), *Strategic Narrative: New Perspectives on the Power of Personal and Cultural Studies*. Boston, Massachusetts: Lexington Books. pp. 193–214.
Ritzer, George (1993) *The McDonaldization of Society*. Newbury Park, California: Pine Forge Press.
Robbins, Kevin (2001) 'Changing spaces of global media', in Shoma Munshi (ed.), *Images of the 'Modern Woman' in Asia: Global Media, Local Meanings*. Surrey: Curzon Press. pp.17–33.
Roman, L. (1988) 'Intimacy, labour, and class: ideologies of feminine sexuality in the punk slam dance', in Leslie Roman, Linda Christian-Smith with Elizabeth Ellsworth (eds), *Becoming Feminine: The Politics of Popular Culture*. London, New York and Philadelphia: Falmer Press.
Roman, Leslie, Christian-Smith, Linda and Ellsworth, Elisabeth (eds) (1988) *Becoming Feminine: The Politics of Popular Culture*. London, New York and Philadelphia: Falmer Press.
Rosaldo, R. (1989) *Culture and Truth: The Remaking of Social Analysis*. London: Routledge and Boston, Massachusetts: Boston Press.
Rose, Nikolas (1996) *Governing the Soul* (2nd edn). London: Free Association.
Rose, Nikolas, (1999a) *The Powers of Freedom*. London: Routledge.
Rose, Nikolas (1999b) *Inventing Our Selves: Psychology, Power and Personhood*. Cambridge: Cambridge University Press.
Rose, Nikolas (2000) 'Identity, genealogy, history', in Paul du Gay, Jessica Evans and Peer Redman (eds), *Identity: A Reader*. London: Sage. pp. 311–24.
Rowbotham, Sheila (1973) *Hidden from History: 300 Years of Women's Oppression and the Fight Against It*. London: Pluto Press.
Rudé, George (1959) *The Crowd in History*. Oxford: Oxford University Press.
Said, Edward W. (1978) *Orientalism*. Harmondsworth: Penguin.
Said, Edward (1994) *Culture and Imperialism*. London: Vintage.
Salmon, P. (1992) *Achieving a PhD: Ten Students' Experience*. Stoke-on-Trent: Trentham Books.
Sampson, E.E. (1993) *Celebrating the Other: A Dialogic Account of Human Nature*. Hemel Hempstead: Harvester Wheatsheaf.
Samuel, Raphael (ed.) (1981) *People's History and Socialist Theory*. London: Routledge.
Samuel, Raphael (1989) '"Philosophy teaching by example": past and present in Raymond Williams', *History Workshop Journal*, 27 (Spring): 141–52.

Samuel, Raphael (1994) *Theatres of Memory: Past and Present in Contemporary Culture* (vol. 1). London: Verso.

Samuel, Raphael (1998) *Island Stories: Unravelling Britain: Theatres of Memory* (vol. 2). London: Verso.

Samuel, Raphael and Thompson David (eds) (1990) *The Myths We Live By*. London: Routledge.

Sanjek, R. (ed.) (1990) *Fieldnotes: The Making of Anthropology*. Ithaca, New York: Cornell University Press.

Saukko, P. (1998) 'Poetics of voice and maps of space: two trends within empirical research in cultural studies', *European Journal of Cultural Studies*, 1 (2): 259–74.

Saussure, Ferdinand de (1974) *Course in General Linguistics*. London: Fontana.

Schiller, Herbert (1968) *Mass Communications and American Empire*. New York: A.M. Kelly.

Schutz, A. (1964) 'The stranger: an essay in social psychology', in A. Schutz (ed.), *Collected Papers* (vol. 2). The Hague: Martinus Nijhoff.

Schwarz, Bill (1982) '"The people" in history: the communist party historians' group, 1946–56', in Centre for Contemporary Cultural Studies, *Making Histories: Studies in History-writing and Politics*. London: Hutchinson. pp. 44–95.

Schwarz, Bill (1994) 'Where is cultural studies?', *Cultural Studies* 8 (3): 377–93.

Scott, J.W. (1988) *Gender and the Politics of History*. New York: Columbia University Press.

Seale, Clive (ed.) (1998) *Researching Society and Culture*. London: Sage.

Sedgwick, Eve K. (1990) *Epistemology of the Closet*. Berkeley: University of California Press

Sedgwick, Eve K. (1994.) *Tendencies*. London: Routledge.

Selden, Anthony (ed.) (2001) *The Blair Effect: The Blair Government 1997–2001*. London: Little, Brown and Company.

Sharp, J. Routledge, P. Philo, C. and Paddison, R. (eds) (2000) *Entanglements of Power: Geographies of Domination/Resistance*. London: Routledge.

Sievers, Sharon (1992) 'Expanding the boundaries of women's history: essays on women in the Third World', in Cheryl Johnson-Odim and Margaret Strobel (eds), *Expanding the Boundaries of Women's History: Essays on Women in the Third World*. Bloomington, Indiana: Indiana University Press. pp. 319–30.

Sinfield, Alan (1992) *Faultlines: Cultural Materialism and the Politics of Dissident Reading*. Oxford: Oxford University Press.

Skelton, Tracey and Valentine, Gill (eds) (1998) *Cool Places: Geographies of Youth Cultures*. London: Routledge.

Smith, Anna Marie (1994) *New Right Discourse on Race and Sexuality: Britain 1968–1990*. Cambridge: Cambridge University Press.

Smith, D. (1988) 'Femininity as discourse', in L G. Roman, L.K. Smith with E. Ellsworth (eds), *Becoming Feminine: The Politics of Popular Culture*. London: Falmer Press.

Smith, L.T. (1999) *Decolonizing Methodologies*. London: Zed Books.

Sommer, Doris (1988) 'Not just a personal story: women's testimonios and the plural self', in Bella Brodzki and Celeste Schenck, *Life/Lines: Theorizing Women's Autobiography*. Ithaca, New York: Cornell University Press. pp. 107–30.

Spivak, Gayatri C.(1988) '"Can the subaltern speak?"', in C. Nelson and L. Grossberg (eds), *Marxism and the Interpretation of Culture*. London: Macmillan.

Spivak, Gayatri C. (1990) *The Post-colonial Critic: Interviews, Strategies, Dialogues*. Sarah Harasym (ed.). London and New York: Routledge.

Stacey, Jackie (1987) 'Desperately seeking difference', *Screen*, 28 (1): 48–62.

Stacey, Jackie (1994) *Stargazing: Hollywood Cinema and Female Spectatorship*. London: Routledge.

Stallybrass, Peter and White, Allon (1986) *The Politics and Poetics of Transgression*. London: Methuen.

Stanley, Liz (1993) 'The knowing because experiencing subject: narratives, lives and autobiography', *Women's Studies International Forum*,16 (3): 205–15.

Steedman, Carolyn (1986) *Landscape for a Good Woman: A Story of Two Lives*. London: Virago.

Steedman, Carolyn (1992) 'Culture, cultural studies and the historians', in Laurence Grossberg, Cary Nelson and Paula Treicher (eds), *Cultural Studies*. London: Routledge.

Steinberg, Deborah Lynn; Epstein, Debbie and Johnson, Richard (eds) (1997) *Border Patrols: Policing the Boundaries of Heterosexuality*. London: Cassell.

Sternberg, D (1981) *How to Complete and Survive a Doctoral Dissertation*. New York: St Martin's Press.

Stevenson, N. (1995) *Understanding Media Cultures: Social Theory and Mass Communication*. London: Sage.

Storey, John (1993) *An Introductory Guide to Cultural Theory and Popular Culture*. Hemel Hempstead: Harvester Wheatsheaf.

Storey, John (ed.) (1996) *What Is Cultural Studies? A Reader*. London: Edward Arnold.

Subden, Helen (1998) 'Ethnography, representation and memory: an analysis of four ethnographic exhibitions', (unpublished MA dissertation, Nottingham Trent University.)

Suchting, Wal (1979) 'Marx's theses on Feuerbach: a new translation and notes towards a commentary', in John Mepham and D.H. Ruben (eds), *Issues in Marxist Philosophy* (vol. 2). Brighton: Harvester.

Tasker, Yvonne (1993) *Spectacular Bodies: Gender, Genre and the Action Cinema*. London: Routledge.

Thomas, Sari (1999) 'Dominance and ideology in culture and cultural studies', in Marjorie Ferguson and Peter Golding (eds), *Cultural Studies in Question*. London: Sage. pp. 74–85.

Thompson, Dorothy (1976) 'Women and nineteenth-century radical politics: a lost dimension', in Juliet Mitchell and Ann Oakley, *The Rights and Wrongs of Women*. London: Penguin. pp. 112–38.

Thompson, E.P. (1961) 'The long revolution: Part two', (Review) *New Left Review* 1/10 (July/August) 34–39.

Thompson, E.P. (1963) *The Making of the English Working Class*. New York: Pantheon.

Thompson, E.P. (1972) 'Anthropology and the discipline of historical context', *Midland History*, 3 (Spring): 41–55.

Thompson, E.P. (1978) *Poverty of Theory and Other Essays*. London: Merlin Press.

Thompson, E.P. (1981) 'The politics of theory', in Raphael Samuel, *People's History and Socialist Theory*. London: Routledge and Kegan Paul. pp. 396–408.

Thompson, E.P. (1993) *Customs in Common*. London: Penguin.

Thompson, John B. (1984) *Studies in the Theory of Ideology*. Cambridge: Polity.

Thompson, Jon (1993) *Fiction, Crime and Empire: Clues to Modernity and Postmodernism*. Urbana and Chicago, Illinois: University of Illinois Press.

Thornton, Sarah (1995) *Club Cultures: Music Media and Subcultural Capital*. Cambridge: Polity Press.

Tincknell, Estella (1991) 'Enterprise fictions: women of substance', in Sarah Franklin, Celia Lury and Jackie Stacey (eds), *Off-centre: Feminism and Cultural Studies*. London: Harper Collins Academic. pp. 260–73.

Tincknell, Estella (2003) 'Virtual members? The internal party culture of New Labour', in Richard Johnson and Deborah Lynn Steinberg (eds), *Blairism and the War of Persuasion: Labour's Passive Revolution*. London: Lawrence and Wishart.

Tincknell, E. and Chambers, D. (2002) 'Performing the crisis: fathering, gender and representation in two nineties films'. *Journal of Popular Film and Television*, 29(4) Winter.

Tincknell, E. and Raghuram, P. (2002) '*Big Brother* – reconfiguring the "active" audience in cultural research?', *European Journal of Cultural Studies*, 5 (2): 199–216.

Tincknell, E., Chambers, D., van Loon, J. and Hudson, N. (2003) 'Begging for it: "new femininities", social agency and moral discourse in contemporary teenage and men's magazines', *Feminist Media Studies*, 3 (1): 47–63.

Tomlinson, John (1999) *Globalization and Culture*. Cambridge: Polity Press.

Townsend, J. in collaboration with Ursula Arrevillaga, Jennie Bain, Socorro Cancino, Susan Frenk, Silvana Pacheco and Eelia Pérez (1994) *Voces Femininas de las Selvas*. Mexico City: Colegio de Postgraduados.

Townsend, Janet (1995) in collaboration with Ursula Arrevillaga, Jennie Bain, Socorro Cancino, Susan Frenk, Silvana Pacheco, Elia Pérez, *Women's Voices from the Rainforest*. London: Routledge.

Turnbull, C. (1973) *The Mountain People*. London: Cape.

Turner, Graeme (1988) *Film as Social Practice*. London and New York: Routledge..

Turner, G. (1990) *British Cultural Studies: An Introduction*. London: Unwin Hyman.

van Zoonen, Liesbet (1994) *Feminist Media Studies*. London: Sage.

Veeser, H.A. (1989) *The New Historicism*. New York: Routledge.

Volosinov, V.N. (1973) *Marxism and the Philosophy of Language*. L. Matejka and I.R. Titunik (tr.). New York: Seminar Press.

Walkerdine, Valerie (1990) *Schoolgirl Fictions*. London: Verso.

Walkerdine, Valerie (1997) *Daddy's Girl: Young Girls and Popular Culture*. Basingstoke: Macmillan.

Walkerdine, Valerie and Johnson, Richard (2004) 'Transformations under pressure: New Labour, class, gender and young women', in Richard Johnson and Deborah Lynne Steinberg (eds), *Blairism and the War of Persuasion: Labour's Passive Revolution*. London: Laurence and Wishart.

Ware, Vron (1992) *Beyond the Pale: White Women, Racism and History*. London: Verso.

Weeks, Jeffry (1977) *Coming Out: Homosexual Politics in Britain from the Nineteenth Century to the Present*. London: Quartet Books.

West, Cornel (1988) 'Marxist theory and the specificity of Afro-American Oppression', in C. Nelson and L. Grossberg (eds), *Marxism and the Interpretation of Culture*. London: Macmillan.

Wetherell, M. (2003) 'Paranoia, ambivalence and discursive practice: concepts of position and positioning in psychoanalysis and discursive psychology', in R. Harre and F. Moghaddam (eds), *The Self and Others: Positioning Individuals and Groups in Personal, Political and Cultural Contexts*. New York: Praeger/Greenwood.

White, H. (1973) *Metahistory: The Historical Imagination in Nineteenth Century Europe*. Baltimore: John Hopkin University Press.

Whyte, W.F. (1943) *Street Corner Society: The Social Structure of an Italian Slum*. Chicago: University of Chicago Press.

Williams, Christopher (2000) 'After the classic, the classical and ideology: the differences of realism', in Christine Gledhill and Linda Williams (eds), *Reinventing Film Studies*. London: Arnold and Oxford University Press. pp. 206–20.

Williams, Raymond (1961) *Culture and Society 1780–1950*. Harmondsworth: Penguin.

Williams, Raymond (1965) *The Long Revolution*. Harmondsworth: Penguin.

Williams, Raymond (1973) *The Country and the City*. London: Chatto and Windus.

Williams, Raymond (1973) 'Base and superstructure in Marxist cultural theory', *New Left Review*, 82.

Williams, Raymond (1976) *Keywords: A Vocabulary of Culture and Society*. Glasgow: Fontana.

Williams, Raymond (1977) *Marxism and Literature*. Oxford: Oxford University Press.

Williams, Raymond (1981) *Culture*. London: Fontana.
Williams, Raymond (1990) *People of the Black Mountains 1: The beginnings*. London: Paladin.
Willis, Paul (1977) *Learning to Labour: How Working-class Kids Get Working-class Jobs*. London: Saxon House.
Willis, Paul (1978) *Profane Culture*. London: Routledge and Kegan Paul.
Willis, Paul (2000) *The Ethnographic Imagination*. Cambridge: Polity Press.
Willis, P. with Jones, S., Canaan, J. and Hurd, G. (1990) *Common Culture*. Buckingham: Open University Press.
Winfield, G. (1987) *The Social Science PhD: The ESRC Inquiry on Submission Rates*. London: Economic and Social Research Council.
Winship, Janice (1987) *Inside Women's Magazines*. London: Pandora Press.
Wittel, A. (2001) 'Towards a network sociality', *Theory, Culture, and Society*, 18 (6): 51–76.
Women's Study Group, Centre for Contemporary Cultural Studies (1978) *Women Take Issue*. London: Hutchinson.
Wright, Patrick (1985) *On Living in an Old Country*. London: Verso.
Zukin, Sharon (1996a) *The Culture of Cities*. Oxford: Blackwell.
Zukin, Sharon (1996b) 'Space and symbols in an age of decline', in A.D. King (ed.), *Representing the City*. London: Macmillan.

Speeches and so on Prime Minster Tony Blair (2001)

27 September, 'Prime Minister's meeting with the muslim communities in Britain – press conference', Downing Street available at: www.number-10.gov.uk
2 October, 'Let us reorder this world', speech to 2001 Labour Party Conference, printed verbatim in the *Guardian*, 3 October 2001.

Speeches of President George W. Bush (2001)

Following available at www.whitehouse.gov
16 September, 'Remarks by the President upon arrival', from the South Lawn, White House.
20 September, 'Address to the joint session of Congress and the American people'
17 October, 'President rallies troops at Travis Airforce Base', Travis Airforce Base, California.
23 October, 'President says terrorists won't change American way of life', from Cabinet Room.
24 October, 'Economy an important part of homeland defence', at Dixie Printing Company.
25 October, 'Education partnership with muslim nations launched', from Thurgood Marshal Extended Elementary School.
31 October, 'President calls for economic stimulus', at National Association of Manufacturers.
6 November, 'No nation can be neutral in this conflict', at Warsaw Conference on Combating Terrorism.
7 November, 'President Announces Crackdown on Terrorist Financial Network', at Vienna, Virginia.
8 November, 'President discusses war on terrorism', at World Congress Centre, Atlanta, Georgia.
21 November, 'President shares thanksgiving with troops', at Fort Campbell, Kentucky.
29 November, 'President says US attorneys on front line in war', at US Attorneys' Conference.
4 December, 'President meets with displaced workers in town hall meeting', at Orange County, Orlando, Florida.

Index

Please note that page numbers representing illustrations and other non-textual material will be in *italics*.

abstract objectivism 162
abstraction
  Althusser on 29
  chaotic 100
  levels of 99–100
  meaning 103
  spatiality and 118
  strengths and limits 100–1
  theory as 98–9
academic disciplines, relations to cultural studies 19–20
accountability 59, 216
accounts, abstract 99
action codes 159
actors' meanings, reading for 227–9
Adorno, T.W. 138
agency, popular 15–16
Al-Qa'ida 174, 183, 184, 185
Alasuutari, P. 26
Althusser, L.
  abstraction and 29
  ideological address 194–5
  language (Althusserian) 30
  Marxism 31, 93, 94, 195
  structural readings 158
  theory, limits of 97
Altman, R. 161, 162
Amadiume, I. 241
analysis
  close reading 236–7
  as dialogue 225–6
  listening around 235–6
  recalling 234–5
  representing self and others 237
Ang, I. 101, 206, 207, 251, 252, 266
anti-terrorism
  and Bush presidency 174–5
Appadurai, A. 115–16
appropriation
  and transdisciplinary strategies 24
Archaeology of Knowledge (Michel Foucault) 132
archaeology metaphor 131
Around the World in Eighty Days (Jules Verne) 195
Astaire, F. 161
Atkinson, P. 79
audiences *see* media audiences, studying
Augustine, St 120, 121
Austen, J. 190, 198, 199
authorial power
  multiple authorships 83–4
  referencing 82–3
auto/biographical and ethnographic research 205–24
  see also auto/biography; auto/ethno continuum
  checklists 216–22
    interviews 217–20
    memory work 220–2
  cultural psychology 264–5
  fourth reading 265
  meetings, indispensability of 209–16
    accountabilities 216
    dialogue, as participation 215–16
    ontological reasonings 210–12
    reflexivity, and power 213–14
    social class 212–13
  researcher's role 222
  self-production 265
auto/biography
  description 208–9
auto/ethno continuum
  limits 222–4
  ontological reasonings 210–12
  as process 206–8
  as range of methods 208–9
  social class 212
autobiographical voice
  and writing 81–2

Bakhtin, M. 58, 166, 230
Balibar, E. 93
Barthes, R. 34, 138, 158, 159, 166
Belsey, C. 196
Benjamin, W. 192
Bennett, T. 11, 250
Bernstein, B. 24
Bhabha, H. 111
Big Brother 253–4
biography 209
Birmingham City
  and spatiality 109–10
black self-representation 16, 54, 145

Blair, T.
Bush compared 174
listeners' questions, answers to (1999) 178
on Muslim peoples 143
speeches by 76, 77, 170, 171, 173, 176, 177, 178
strengths and weaknesses 175–6
Blake, W. 226
Bordwell, D. 160
Bourdieu, P. 36, 143, 150
Brannigan, J. 193
British Royal Ordnance Survey
maps produced by 116
Bromley, R. 191, 193
Brunsdon, C. 27, 33, 206, 207, 250, 251
Bush, G. W.
on Americanism 181
anti-terrorism and 174–5, 181
enemy, description of 183
on Muslim peoples 143
speeches by 162, 170–1, 173
Butler, J. 167, 263

Capital (Karl Marx) 100, 246
capitalism 100
capitalist modernity
and culture agenda 14
Castaway 2000 253
Centre for Contemporary Cultural Studies (CCCS), Birmingham University 20, 33
Changing the Subject (Julian Henriques et al.) 258–9
character, and location 161–2
Chene, Mary des 114
circuits, cultural 37–42, *38*, *39*
configuration 39, 40, 96, 247
cultural research as 44–6, *45*, *180*
economic and 148–9
hermeneutics 38, 45, 46
methods and 40, *41*, 42
mimesis 1, 2 and 3 38, 39, 247
poststructuralism 38
prefigurative level 120, 122
refiguration 39, 96
representation, and limits of ideology critique *141*
schematization 39, 40, 120, 247
City of London 150
class consciousness 28
classification, and framing 24
Clifford, J. 79, 239
clock time 121
close reading 226, 236–7, 254
Cohan, S. 167
Cohen, P. 32
cohesion, culture as 11–13
collective biography 209
Collins, P. Hill 54
colonialism, British 55
Common Culture (Paul Willis) 212
concrete
auto/ethno range 210
meaning 99
concrete accounts 99
concretion, meaning 103
Confessions of St Augustine 120, 121
configuration 39, 40, 96, 120, 247
consumption, materiality of 149
contextualization, and operating distance 77–8
conventions
and truthfulness 50–1
truth as convention 51–2
Couldry, N. 27, 44, 213
Country and the City (Raymond Williams) 27, 122, 189
Coward, R. 256, 257
Crang, M. 108
Critical Practice (Catherine Belsey) 196
cultural circuits *see* circuits, cultural
cultural formations, culture as 30–3
cultural hegemony, Gramsci on 21, 30, 91, 144, 150, 183, 191, 193
cultural identity *see* subjectivities, researching
cultural materialism 31, 189–93
cultural populism 143–5
cultural production, and culture agenda 14
cultural reflexivity 55–6
cultural research *see* research, cultural
cultural structures and processes, reading for 229–30
cultural studies
academic disciplines, relations to 19–20
consumption question 149
education, value of 18
method in 3
philosophy and 17–19
and political economy, dialogue failures 136–7
political/cultural question, distinguished 15
populism 16
psychology and 258–9
remaking methods 266–8
social movements and 14–15
Cultural Studies in Question (Marjorie Ferguson and Paul Golding) 136
culture
as cohesion 11–13
critique of 33–7
as cultural formations 30–3
economy as 151–2
'inside' 44–6, 45
as language or understanding 13–14
as policy 11
and power *see* power and culture

culture – *continued*
as standardization 13
as 'value' 10
as 'way of life' for groups/nations 27–30, 182
studying way of life 28–30
culture agendas
historical contexts 14
types 10–14
Culture and Imperialism (Edward Said) 198
Cyperspace 113

Daddy's Girl (Valerie Walkerdine) 244
Dallas 206, 251
de Certeau, M. 111–12, 116
decoding, and encoding 246–7
Deleyto, C. 165
Denzin, N. 228
dialogue
analysis as 225–6
authorial power 83–4
difference 58
dominance 178–9
failures, political economy and cultural studies 136–7
internal nature of 77
interviews 219
listening to other 239
monologue and 238
objectivity 57
as participation 215–16
relational 238
self,
not leaving aside 238
reflexive 238
risking 239
text-reading 172, 179–81
Diana, Princess of Wales 144
see also 'Mourning Diana', essay on
diaries 220
Die Hard 167
Discipline and Punish (Michel Foucault) 131, 197
discursive form 246
Disneyfication 13
dissertation work 65, 68
dominance, and populism 143–5
dominance, reading texts of 170–86
choice of texts 171, 178–9
credibility of readings 184–5
dialogue commencement 172, 179–81
elaboration 172, 182
first and later drafts 173
moral absolutism 183–4
opening of text 172, 179–81
political speeches 76, 77, 162, 173–6
presentation, writing for 173
questions 172
reflecting 172
sample sizes 171–2, 176–8
strengths and limits, text analysis 171
textual approach 173–4
unconscious processes 183–4
validity 172
dreams, Freudian analysis of 195
du Gay, P. 137, 259
du Maurier, D. 191–2
Durkheim, E. 11
Dutton, R. 193
Dyer, R. 166

Eco, U. 161
economic circuits, and cultural 148–9
economic systems, cultural conditions 150
economies
culturally embedded 145–8
as representation and discourse 146–8
economy
and cultural studies, dialogue failures 136–7
as culture 151–2
empirical research
see also research, cultural; research practice; research process; theory, in research practice
concept-led approaches 93–4
difficulties, empiricist 94–6
objections, empirical 94
other, empirical as 96
emplotment 120
encoding, and decoding 246–7
Encoding and Decoding in the TV Discourse (Stuart Hall) 245
Engels, F. 48, 137–8
epistemology 17
Evans, J. 259
Evans, P.W. 165

family album research, Australia 231, 233
Female Desire (Rosalind Coward) 256
feminism
film theory 249–50, 251, 253
second-wave 256
theorizing 130
transdisciplinarity and 21
women's genres 32–3
Ferguson, M. 136
Feuer, J. 159
fiction, reading
and/or history 121, 187–9
Fleming, I. 161
focus groups 209
fore-meanings 17–18, 44, 169
Fortmann, L. 55
Foucault, M.
cultural policy 11

Foucault, M. – *continued*
discourses 34, 107, 197
effective history, defined by 130–1
genealogies 130–2
power 197–8
Ricoeur's review of 132–4
systematic knowledge 91
truth effects 142
framing, and classification 24
Frankfurt School theorists 13, 138, 151, 157
Freud, S. 183, 194, 195, 263
Friedan, B. 256
Friedman, M. 147
Friends 159–60, 162
Full Monty 196, 197

Gadamer, H.-G.
consciousness 54–5
historical 45, 189
contextualization 77
dialogue 57, 58, 238
hermeneutic tradition 17–18, 27–8, 55, 207
prejudices 44
theory 89
writing 268
genealogy 130–2, 259–61
Genette, G. 160
genre
changes in 165
film 159
intertextuality and 162–3
specific nature of 166
women's 33
German Ideology (Karl Marx and Frederich Engels) 144
Gibson, W. 112
Giddens, A. 177
Gilroy, P. 12–13, 133
Glasgow Media Group 139, 141
globalization theory 13, 14
Golding, P. 136
Goodwin, A. 243–4
governmentality 11
Grace, H. 146
Gramsci, A.
common sense/philosophy distinction 39, 91
cultural formations 31
cultural sedimentation 133–4
dialogue 215
fiction 191
hegemony 21, 91, 144, 150, 183, 191, 193
Marxism 184
nations 182
self-knowledge 45, 51
Green, M. 62
Greenblatt, S. 193, 194
Griffin, C. 30
Grossberg, L. 27
Grundrisse (Karl Marx) 37, 148, 246

Hall, S.
cultural formations 30, 31
Marxism 148
media audiences 245–6
structuralism 34
theory and practice 93
Hammersley, M. 79
Haraway, D.
accountability 59
dialogue 58
objectivism 47, 48, 57
partiality 17
standpoint theories 49
Harding, S. 57
Hartsock, N. 48, 57
'haunted geographies' 116
headnotes 234
hegemony, Gramsci on 21, 91, 144, 150, 183, 191, 193
Heidegger, M. 17
heritage 127
hermeneutics
circuit model 38, 45, 46
Gadamer on 17–18, 27–8, 55, 207
philosophy 17–19
understanding the other, and 13
historical perspectives 119–34
archaeology metaphor 131
contemporary histories 132
convergence, and tension 126–7
cultural histories, writing,
history's cultural turn 124–6
radical popular histories 123–4
Foucault, Ricoeur's review 132–4
genealogies 130–2
Gramsci, and cultural sedimentation 133 4
historicizing present 130–4
historicizing theory 129–30
new historicism, historical discourse 193–4
oral history 128
representations of past, and popular memory 127–9
tension, and convergence 126–7
time considerations 120–3
temporality in history 121–3
history
contemporary 132
cultural turn 124–6
cultural, writing 123–6
oral 128
interviews 209
reading and/or 121, 187–9
History of Sexuality (Michel Foucault) 197
Hitchcock, A. 163, 164

Hoggart, R.
  indiscipline of 243–4
  methodological combinations and 29–30
  working-class life, account of 106–7, 114
Horkheimer, M. 138
Household, G. 191
hunches 234
Hunslet, Leeds (working-class study) 106–7

I Love Lucy 167
identity, and locality 106–7
identity work, and integration 265–6
ideology analysis 139–40
  representation, and limits of ideology critique 140–2
'indiscipline' 243–5
international relations
  post-Cold War 12
interpellation 194
intertextuality, and genre 162–3
interviews
  Asian schoolgirls 231–2
  contacts/permissions 218
  control of process 219
  dialogues, conducting 219
  group interaction 219
  life history 209
  meetings, setting up 218
  method selection/combination 218
  note taking 220
  oral history 209
  person research, profiling 217
  piloting 219
  practicalities 218
  public sources 217
  questions 218, 219
  recording 220
  reflection 219
  resources, auto/biographical 217
  sequencing 219
  technique choices 220
  thematic 209

James Bond phenomenon 250
Jenkins, H. 112
Johnston, L. 117
Joyce, J. 248

Kellner, D. 26, 137
keywords, deciding on 68–9, 87
Kimmell, M. 176
King, K. 57
Kingsley, M. 115
Kristeva, J. 162
Kuhn, T. 93

Lacan, J./Lacanian theory 249, 256
Landscape for a Good Woman (Carolyn Steedman) 244, 245
language 13–14, 88
Learning to Labour (Paul Willis) 211, 213, 229
Lefebvre, H. 108–9, 112
Leningrad circle (1920s and 1930s) 162, 230
Leonard, D. 62
Lethal Weapon 167
Levi-Strauss, C. 166
Lhamon, W. T. 133
Lincoln, Y. 228
literature 121, 187–9
locality, and identity 106–7
Locke, J. 146
Longhurst, D. 197
Lukes, S. 11

Mac an Ghaill, M. 231–2, 233
MacCabe, C. 164–5
McDonaldization 13, 136
McGuigan, J. 137, 143
Macherey, P. 194, 195, 196
Making of the English Working Class (E. P. Thompson) 28, 29, 106, 122, 255
Mandelson, P. 177
Mansfield Park (Jane Austen) 198
mapping
  meaning 103
  spatiality, and maps 110, 116
mapping the field 31–2, 68
Marcus, G. 79
Marxism
  see also Grundrisse (Karl Marx)
  Althusser on 31, 93, 94
  capitalism 100
  consumption question 149
  culture as 'way of life' 28, 29
  Gramsci, A. 184
  ideology theories 30, 48
  power, separation from culture 137–8
  surplus labour theory 94
  Williams on 146
Marxism and Literature (Raymond Williams) 27, 30, 122, 189
Marxism and the Philosophy of Language (V. N. Volosinov) 231, 264
Mass Observation archive, Sussex University 74–5
Massey, D. 108, 118
media audiences, studying
  audiences, without texts 251–2
  circuits and 42
  disappointments of research 249
  encoding/decoding 246–7
  integrative possibilities 245–9
  recomposing media research 252–5
  recompositions in media 253–4
  remaking methods 254–5
  Ricoeur, on reading 247–9

media audiences, studying – *continued*
  social audiences/spectatorship 250
  splits/neglects 251, 252–3
  texts, without audiences 249–50
media deregulation (1980s and 1990s) 138
meetings
  cultural research, indispensability in 209–16
    accountabilities 216
    dialogue, as participation 215–16
    ontological reasonings 210–12
    reflexivity, and power 213–14
    social class 212–13
  and readings 153
  setting up 218
  supervisors, with 66–7
memory work
  conducting 221–2
  constituting work group or circle 220–1
  contacting members 220–1
  episode choice 221
  ethnographic 30
  explanation of procedures 221
  ground rules, negotiating 221
  group 209
  group profiles 220
  individual 209
  meeting places 221
  stories, reading/discussing 222
  themes, negotiating 221
  writing rules 221–2
Mercer, K. 239
Merrifield, A. 118
methods
  see also methods, cultural
  accountability, and responsibilities 59
  approach to, research practice 2–3
  combination, logics of 60–1
  conventions 50–1
  cultural circuit, cultural research as 44–6, *45*
    see also circuits, cultural; research, cultural
  in cultural studies 3
  culture, 'inside' 44
  dialogue *see* dialogue
  objectivism, self and other 46–8
  pluralism, methodological or 26–7
  positionalities 46, 49–50
  as procedure 3
  as reading 153–4
    for theory 97–8
  reflexivity *see* reflexivity
  'standpoint' theories 48–9
  transdisciplinarity, implications for 22–3
  truthfulness 50–1
methods, cultural
  see also method; research, cultural
  circuits and 40, *41*, 42
  combined and multiple 42–3
  remaking 243–69
    'indiscipline', and combination 243–5
    media audiences *see* media audiences, studying
    subjectivities *see* subjectivities, researching
  and way of life, studying 28–30
Metz, C. 158
mimesis 1, 2 and 3
  cultural circuits 38, 39, 247
misrepresentation
  popular 15–16
models, research 73
moments 62, 246
  writing as 78–80
Monaco, J. 163
monetary theory 147
moral absolutism
  text reading 183–4
Morrison, T. 16
'Mourning Diana', essay on 68, *69*, *70*
MTV, and popular culture 143
Mulvey, L. 164
Murdoch, R. 138
myth 138, 166
Mythologies (Roland Barthes) 166

narrative 120, 248
narrative structuralism, organizing meaning 158–60
nationalism 14, 28
Nayak, A. 223
Nazism 12
Neale, S. 159
Neuromancer (William Gibson) 112
New Labour 171, 173
New Left theory 28, 30, 145
New Right 192
News of the World 141
Nora, P. 127
Nottingham Trent University 112
NUDIST (Non-numerical Unstructured Data Indexing, Searching and Theorizing) 236

objectivism
  abstract 162
  self and other 46–8
    modest witness 47
objectivity
  and accountability 59
  and dialogue 57
observation 209
O'Byrne, D. 107
oeuvre, authorial 249
Oneself as Another (Paul Ricoeur) 207
ontological reasonings 210–12
  concrete 210
  forms of thinking 211

ontological reasonings – *continued*
  sensuousness 211, 212
  way of life 210–11
  working-classness 211–12

'paired dualities' 161
partiality
  accountability 59
  disciplines 23
  objectivity 57
  philosophy 17, 18
  reflexivity 52
  standpoint theories 49
participant observation/enquiry 209
participation
  dialogue as 215–16
Passerini, L. 124–5
Pearl Harbor 185
peers, working with 67
person research 209–10
PhD research 65, 68, 72, 78, 240–1
philosophy, and cultural studies 17–19
  feminist 19
photograph album research, Australia 231, 233
piloting 219
plot, and story 160
pluralism, methodological 26–7
Policing the Crisis 40
policy, culture as 11
political economy
  and cultural studies, dialogue failures 136–7
  ideology analysis 139–40
  power and culture, separating 137–9
political speeches 76, 77, 162, 173–6
populism 16
  and dominance 143–5
positionality 46, 49–50
  as spatiality 105–6
post-colonialism 36, 198–9, 223
postmodernism
  culture, critique of 33, 37
  subjectivities, researching 257–8, 262–4
poststructuralism 167–8
  accountability 59
  circuit model and 38, 44–5
  cultural research, object/strategies 34
  methodologies 36–7
  subjectivities 257
power
  and culture 10
    agenda expansion 142–3
    separating 137–9
  dominance 143–5
  effects of 91–2
  Foucault's view of 197–8
  populism 143–5
  reflexivity and 213–14
  representation across 239–41
Practice of Everyday Life (Michael de Certeau) 111–12
Praise of Theory (Hans-Georg Gadamer) 89
praxis, theory and practice as 90–3
  embedded theory 90–1
  explicitness, theory as 91–2
preferred reading 247
prefiguration 120, 122
prejudices (fore-meanings) 44
Pride and Prejudice (Jane Austen) 190
Prison Notebooks (Antonio Gramsci) 31, 182
Probyn, E. 266
Propp, V. 147, 158, 161
Pryke, M. 137
Psycho 163
psycho-social relations 261–2
psychoanalytic theory 250
psychology, and cultural studies 258–9
Pulp Fiction 165

queer theory 36, 263
questions
  dominance, reading texts of 172
  interviews 218, 219
  research proposals 71–2
  and sources 74–5
quotations 70

racism 12
Radway, J. 168, 206, 252, 256
reading
  active 70
  actors' meanings, for 227–9
  close 226, 236–7, 254
  conventional forms, individualizing 230–1
  cultural structures and processes, for 229–30
  fiction and/or history 187–9
  meaning 103
  as method 153–4
  secondary texts 70
  structure and content, for 233–4
  texts of dominance *see* dominance, reading texts of
Reading the Romance (Janice Radway) 168, 206, 253
readings
  and meetings 153
  multiple 226–7
  structural *see* structuralist texts
realism
  problematizing 163–5
reality TV 253–4
Rebecca (Daphne du Maurier) 191–2
recalling 234–5
recording 220, 222, 234

Redman, P. 259
referencing 82–3
refiguration, and circuit model 39, 96
reflection 103, 172, 219
reflexive modernization 136
reflexivity 52–6
  and confessional 53
  cultural aspects 55–6
  futures and 122–3
  power and 213–14
  realizing 53–6
  social aspects 53–4
  spatial aspects 55
  temporal aspects 54–5
regulation, disciplinarity as 23
representation
  see also representing others
  auto/biographical, and cultural psychology 264–5
  circuits and 40
  economies as 146–8
  ideology critique, limits 140–2
  power, across 239–41
  self and others 237
representing others
  see also interviews; representation
  actors' meanings, reading for 227–9
  analysis,
    close reading 236–7
    as dialogue 225–6
    listening around 235–6
    recalling 234–5
    representing self and others 237
    review and 235–6
  conventional forms, individualizing 230–1
  cultural structures and processes, reading for 229–30
  dialogic implications 237–9
  interview, Asian schoolgirls 231–2
  multiple readings/theories 226–7
  structure and context, reading for 233–4
research, auto/biographical and ethnographic *see* auto/biographical and ethnographic research
research, cultural
  see also empirical research; methods; methods, cultural; research process; theory, in research practice
    critique of 'culture' 33–7
    as cultural circuit 44–6, *45*, *180*
    cultural formations, culture as 30–3
    'local', redefined/contextualized 32–3
    mapping the field 31–2, 68
    meetings, indispensability of *see* meetings: cultural research, indispensability in
    objectivism, self and other 46–8
    objects and strategies 27–37
    spatial dimensions in *see* spatialities
  way of life, culture as 27–30, 182
    studying, and methods 28–30
research practice
  see also theory, in research practice
  method, approach to 2–3
  praxis, theory and practice as 90–3
  theorizing as practice 102–3
  as theory 92–3
  theory as opposed to 89–90
  theory as practice 92–3
research process
  see also empirical research; methods; methods, cultural; research, cultural; theory, in research practice
  analysis, and textuality 75–7
  contextualization, and operating distance 77–8
  intertextual relationships 76
  keywords, deciding on 68–9
  literature, reviewing 68–70
  mapping the field 31–2, 68
  models 73
  part-time activity, as 65
  proposals, developing 71–2
  searching,
    keywords 68–9
    recording and reviewing 69
  secondary texts, reading 69–70
    see also reading
  sources,
    and questions 74–5
    starting from 74
  starting research 64
  time management 65–6
  topic selection and development 63–4
  working with others 66–7
    peers 67
  writing *see* writing
research proposals
  aim clarification 71
  questions, formulating 71–2
  writing 71
researcher bias 47
researcher's role
  auto/biographical and ethnographic research 222
Resistance Through Rituals (Stuart Hall and Tony Jefferson) 30
Ricoeur, P.
  circuit model 38, 39
  fiction 121
  on Foucault 132–4
  on Gadamer 18
  high forms of culture 28
  media studies 252
  reading 246, 247–9
  self and identity 207
  time issues 119, 120, 122

Riessman, C. 213–14, 239
risk society 13
Rogers, G. 161
Rogue Male (Geoffrey Household) 191
Rose, N. 261

Said, E. 126, 198
Samuel, R. 121–2, 124, 127
Saussure, F. de 34, 158, 162, 165
scales, and spatiality 114–15
scapes, and spatiality 115–16
schematization, and circuit model 39, 40, 120, 247
Sedgwick, E. K. 126
self, and other 46–8
September 11 2001 attacks 170, 175, 180
sequencing 219
Sherlock Holmes stories 188, 196, 197
Sievers, S. 130
Sinfield, A. 193
Singing' in the Rain 167
sitcoms 159
sites, and spatiality 113–14
Smith, A. 195
Smith, D. 241
Smith, L. T. 101, 213
soap opera studies 33
social class 28, 29, 106, 212–13
social dissolution, theme of 11
social movements, and cultural studies 14–15
social reflexivity 53–4
socialism
  see also Marxism
  and cultural studies 14, 15
sociology
  and literary studies 135
Sommer, D. 256
Sony Walkman personal stereo 148–9
spatial reflexivity 55
spatialities
  abstraction and 118
  complex 107–8
  complicated places,
    maps 116
    scales 114–15
    scapes 115–16
    sites 113–14
  identity, and locality 106–7
  positionality as spatiality 105–6
  power metaphor, as 110–12
  technologized places 112–13
  theoretical tools for researching 108–10
  transdisciplinary integrations 117–18
  virtual spaces 112–13
  women's spaces 117
Spectacular Bodies: Gender, Genre and the Action Cinema (Yvonne Tasker) 167
speeches, political 76, 77, 162, 173–6
splitting 251, 252–3
Stacey, J. 74–5
Stalinism 29
standardization, culture as 13
standpoint theories 48–9
Steedman, C. 244, 245
Steel, D. 192
Storey, J. 195
story, and plot 160
street crime, racialization of 12
structuralism 31, 34–5
structuralist texts 157–69
  combination of methods 168
  contextualizing strategies 162–5
  genre and intertextuality 162–3
  organizing meaning,
    character and location 161–2
    narrative 158–60
    plot and story 160
  poststructuralism and 36–7, 167–8
  realism, problematizing 163–5
  social and cultural formations 165–7
  textual strategies 158–62
structure and content, reading for 233–4
subjectivities, researching
  approaching subjectivity 259–64
  cultural studies, and psychology 258–9
  'experience', limits of 255–7
  genealogy, limits of 259–61
  identity work, and integration 265–6
  postmodernism 257–8, 262–4
  poststructuralist interventions 257–9
  psycho-social relations 261–2
  psychology 258–9
    and auto/biographical representation 264–5
supervisors 66–7
surplus labour theory 94
Survivor 253
Sussex University, Mass Observation archive 74–5

Taliban 174, 183
Tasker, Y. 167
Taylor Bradford, B. 192
temporal reflexivity 54–5
texts
  audiences without 251–2
  dominance, of *see* dominance, reading texts of
  explicit/implicit meanings 194–5
  multisighted 240
  recording 220, 222
  secondary 69–70
  silencing, gender and history 196–7
  staging, class and history 194–5
  structuralist *see* structuralist texts
  without audiences 249–50

textuality 75–7, 246
Thatcherism 12, 192
theorizing
  feminist 130
  as practice 102–3
theory, in research practice
  see also method; methods, cultural; research, cultural; research process; theorizing
  as abstraction 98–9
    levels of 99–100
    strengths and limits 100–1
  approaches 97
  embedded theory 90–1
  empirical research and *see* empirical research
  as extending experience 92
  fear and loathing 87–9
  multiple theories 226–7
  as opposed to practice 89–90
  praxis, theory and practice as 90–3
  reading for, as method 97–8
  theorizing, as practice 102–3
  theory as practice 92–3
thesis work 65, 68
Third World, mapping exercises 116
Thompson, E. P.
  epistemologies 94
  history, description of 60
  law, English study of 145–6
  paternalism 30
  social class 28, 29, 106, 122, 255
Thompson, J. 197
Thrift, N. 108
time 120–3
time management
  research process 65–6
Time and Narrative (Paul Ricoeur) 120, 132, 246
Top Hat 161
topic selection and development 63–4
Townsend, J. 83
traditionality 247
transcription 220, 235
transdisciplinarity
  classification/framing distinction 24
  disciplinarity as regulation 23
  explanation 20–2
  implications for method 22 3
  strategies 24
Truth and Method (Hans-Georg Gadamer) 17, 54–5, 189
truthfulness
  and conventions 50–1
    truth as convention 51–2
Twin Towers, attack on 170, 175, 180
Typical Girls (Christine Griffin) 229

Ulysses (James Joyce) 248
understanding
  culture as 13–14
  knowing the other 47
United Kingdom
  black self-representation 16
  digitalized commercial television, failure of (2002) 149
  ideology analysis, television news study 139, 140
  popular histories 123
  scales, and spatiality 114
United States of America
  black self-representation 16, 54, 145
  popular histories 123
Uses of Literacy (Richard Hoggart) 29–30, 106, 243–4

Valentine, G. 117
value, culture as 10
Verne, J. 195
verstehen (understanding) 17
Vertigo 164
video diary
  description 209
Volosinov, V. N. 140–1, 264

Walkerdine, V. 58, 239, 244
Walkowitz 117
way of life
  culture as 27–30
  ontological reasonings 210–11
  reading, research on 182
Weber, M. 13
Williams, C. 165
Williams, R.
  cultural materialism 189–91
  identity, and locality 106
  keywords 68, 87
  literature 189
  Marxism 27, 30, 122, 146, 189
  methods, and cultural studies 27, 30
  policy, culture as 11
  praxis 90
  R. Samuel, review of work by 121–2, 124, 127
  selective tradition 9
Willis, P. 27, 30, 211–12
Wilson, R. 193
Woollacot, J. 250
working with others 66–7
World Trade Center, attack on 170, 175, 180
writing
  authorial power 82–4
  and autobiographical voice 81–2
  cultural histories,
    history's cultural turn 124–6
    radical popular 123–4
  diversity in process 80–1

writing – *continued*
  ethics and politics 82–4
  forms 79
  functions 78–80
  memory work 221
  as a moment 78–80
  and planning 80–1
  research proposals 71
  time management 65
Writing Culture (James Clifford and George Marcus) 79